BABUR

BABUR

The Chessboard King

AABHAS
MALDAHIYAR

VINTAGE
An imprint of Penguin Random House

VINTAGE

USA | Canada | UK | Ireland | Australia
New Zealand | India | South Africa | China | Singapore

Vintage is part of the Penguin Random House group of companies whose addresses can be found at global.penguinrandomhouse.com

Published by Penguin Random House India Pvt. Ltd
4th Floor, Capital Tower 1, MG Road,
Gurugram 122 002, Haryana, India

Penguin
Random House
India

First published in Vintage by Penguin Random House India 2024

10 9 8 7 6 5 4 3 2

ISBN 9780670099542

Typeset in Sabon by Manipal Technologies Limited, Manipal
Printed at Replika Press Pvt. Ltd, India

www.penguin.co.in

Dedicated to my family, standing strong beside me through every ebb and flow

Contents

Part 2: Kābul

Introduction

A generation which ignores history has no past—and no future.
—Robert Anson Heinlein*

This phrase was once recounted to me by my father, a historian. I was just ten years old then and these golden words by Heinlein didn't appear as weighty to me as they do today. My memories are filled with historical anecdotes coated with a syrup of academia. Though my father's library would handsomely showcase the enormous works of stalwarts like S.R. Goel, Sir Jadunath Sarkar and R.C. Majumdar, I never knew that they carried a lot of truth far away from anecdotes I was familiar with. And I never cared to ever ask my father what those books say about our past. My life went on as smoothly as it could, carefree but full of ambition to become something someday so that I could make my parents proud.

As history lessons percolated through me over time, and when I was all set to pursue post-matriculation studies in physics, chemistry and mathematics with the goal of accomplishing just another Bihari dream, that of cracking IIT, it appeared that:

- All invaders except the British were not bad.
- No invaders including the British had any religious zeal.
- Before the arrival of the great invaders, India was the place of all the worst practices like Sati, untouchability, etc.

* Robert A. Heinlein, *Time Enough for Love*, New York: ACE, Penguin Random House, LLC., 1987. p. 250.

Despite that (not so) illustrious stint with history at school, there was something at the D.A.V. Public School which sprinkled a few seeds of pride for the nation through a small booklet called *Dharam Shiksha*. The small book told us the tales of the valour of many warriors, freedom fighters who had no mention in the books that were supposed to tell the thing called *history*.[1]

Yet, how could I do away with the *millennial* complex? The book of 'history' was only supposed to *teach* 'history'.

Metaphorically speaking, I was like an *unbaked* pot. The history lessons in books were like adulterated water and interestingly anything going against them was like sterilized water, whose percolation was strictly prohibited.

One may then ask, what harm does the narration through the academia and NCERT books bring? However brutal it may seem in my opinion, *it is not merely wee-sized harm, but a catastrophe set to dismantle the pride and respect of our land and civilization*. I state it with utmost responsibility and honesty after having gone through abundant *primary* sources about varied historical anecdotes. I'll leave the readers with one such instance of the past. The NCERT books tell us that after looking at the blood the great Ashoka shed in the battle of Kalinga, guilt caught up with him[2] and he chose to be inducted into the faith of compassion, Buddhism.

Interestingly, the primary source that the academic book on Ashoka cites,[*] disagrees with the former.[3] As per the *primary* source (cited), Ashoka was already a Buddhist when he attacked Kalinga.[†]

Of the hundreds of thousands of such historical instances, I have cared to cite just one. Now, keep your hand on your heart and ask, isn't it unethical that which it is being inflicted upon us? What do we call it? *Intellectual dishonesty*?

It is bound to happen. And why not . . .? When the gatekeepers of narratives chose to tell what our latest colonialists (British) and their loyalists wanted to spread around.[4] While Scott was analytical about the effect of the British-tailored education system of India, Macaulay

---

[*] Romila Thapar, *Asoka and the Decline of the Mauryas*, Oxford: Oxford University Press, 1961, pp. 34, 259.

[†] Charles Allen, *Ashoka: The Search for India's Lost Emperor*, s.l.: Hachette UK, 2012.

had emphasized it as a goal in the 'Minute on Indian Education', 1835:*

> We must at present do our best to form a class who may be interpreters between us and the millions whom we govern; a class of persons, Indian in blood and colour, but English in taste, in opinions, in morals, and in intellect. To that class we may leave it to refine the vernacular dialects of the country, to enrich those dialects with terms of science borrowed from the Western nomenclature, and to render them by degrees fit vehicles for conveying knowledge to the great mass of the population.

This circumstantial set of evidence clearly hints at why propagated academic history has been in form as it is. Even I couldn't save myself from becoming a prey to it.

Coming back to my teenage days—after the days of school were over, I stepped into undergraduate studies aspiring to specialize in architecture. This was a phase where I not only made the architectural drawings but also read more and more. The architectural school (that's what I have seen) is that part of the world where the literature on the subject is highly post-modern, and a *rational* mind is quite prone to get drenched in communism and woke-ism.[5] It gave me the sense to grasp the history of the structural model, led mostly by Antonio Francesco Gramsci.†

The ultra-protestant proletarian idea of *secularism*‡ § ¶ that was well embedded in me ensured that the indigenous narratives of history appeared to *disdain* and oppose the academia.[6] But that was not the core problem. It had also assured this belief within me that the thump

* Minute by the Hon'ble T.B. Macaulay, 2 February 1835, http://www.columbia.edu/itc/mealac/pritchett/00generallinks/macaulay/txt_minute_education_1835.html, accessed 18 June 2023.

† Thomas Bates, 'Gramsci and the Theory of Hegemony', 1975, *Journal of the History of Ideas*, Vol. 36, pp. 351–366.

‡ Joseph Blankholm, *The Secular Paradox: On the Religiosity of the Not Religious*, New York: NYU Press, 2022. p. 8.

§ Jack David Eller, *What Is Atheism*; Phil Zuckerman, *Atheism and Secularity: Volume 1: Issues, Concepts, and Definitions* (Praeger Perspectives), Santa Barbara, California: Praeger, 2010, pp. 1–18.

¶ Martin Luther, 'On Secular Authority: How Far Does the Obedience Owed to It Extend?' s.l.: http://www.yorku.ca/comninel/courses/3020pdf/Luther.pdf, 1523.

of every invader's horse added glory for India time and again.[*] [†] [‡] [§] [¶] Just to set the perspective in order, I must quote Karl Marx. He says as below:

> England, it is true, in causing a social revolution in Hindostan, was actuated only by the vilest interests, and was stupid in her manner of enforcing them. But that is not the question. The question is, can mankind fulfil its destiny without a fundamental revolution in the social state of Asia? If not, whatever may have been the crimes of England she was the unconscious tool of history in bringing about that revolution.[**]
>
> England has to fulfill a double mission in India: one destructive, the other regenerating – the annihilation of [the] old Asiatic society, and the laying the material foundations of Western society in Asia . . . When a great social revolution shall have mastered the results of the bourgeois epoch . . . and subjected them to the common control of the most advanced peoples, then only will human progress cease to resemble that hideous, pagan idol, who would not drink the nectar but from the skulls of the slain.[††]

[*] Murali Balaji, *Saving History from Historians*, New Delhi: Open, 2015.

[†] Aabhas Maldahiyar, 'History-Phobia of Audrey Truschke: Denial of Islamic invaders and the hara-kiri of credibility', Firstpost, 2022.

[‡] Aabhas Maldahiyar, 'Whitewashing Genocides: Why KS Lal's Claims of 80 million Hindus Killed by Islamic Barbarism Hold Water', Firstpost, 13 November 2022, https://www.firstpost.com/opinion-news-expert-views-news-analysis-firstpost-viewpoint/whitewashing-genocides-and-history-phobia-why-ks-lals-claims-of-80-mn-hindus-killed-by-islamic-barbarism-hold-water-11618501.html.

[§] Aabhas Maldahiyar, 'Tipu Sultan: When an Islamist Tyrant Is Turned into a Freedom Fighter, Missile Man and Dharma Saviour', FIrstpost, 1 April 2022, https://www.firstpost.com/india/tipu-sultan-when-an-islamist-tyrant-is-turned-into-a-freedom-fighter-missile-man-and-dharma-saviour-10508661.html.

[¶] Aabhas Maldahiyar, 'Why Audrey Truschke Should Stop Inventing History to Suit Her Vicious Agenda', Firstpost, 23 February 2020, https://www.firstpost.com/india/why-audrey-truschke-should-stop-inventing-history-to-suit-her-vicious-agenda-10399601.html.

[**] Karl Marx, 'The British Rule in India', *New York Daily Tribune*, 10 June 1853.

[††] Karl Marx, 'The Future Results of British Rule in India', *New-York Daily Tribune*, 23 June 1853.

So however proletarian[*] the vouch for the character of Marx may be, with respect to India he was very clear that British rule was mandatory to kill the *Asiatic backwardness*.[†]

> I often say that perhaps time only is God and vice versa. It is powerful and is potent to flip the things beyond general expectations.

It took me a good time of almost a decade to realize the vitriol injected in me by the ideas of Marxism. A trip to the unbelievably terrific architectural marvels, Kailasa Mandir and Ajanta Caves[7] came out as an antidote against the *flu*[8] I was infected with. And once this infection was gone, the key thing in the *neo-itinerary* was about unlearning the opinions fed in as history and learning history through the primary contemporary sources.[9]

Perhaps, had I learnt Marx's views on British colonization of India through the primary sources,[10] (refer earlier page where Marx is quoted) this would have been clear that he was certainly not a friend of India. It left me wondering that if such was the view of Marx, then how did the communists fighting against the British keep eulogizing him as a godly figure of ideas for long?

As I began to dabble in the primary sources to understand our past, I got exposed to not only how effective the *Bharatiya* resistance was to the invading forces right from the period of Umayyads but also to the atrocities and crimes committed by them that had long remained hidden under the carpet masquerading as the N.C.E.R.T. books.[11] The façade of being the epitome of greatness built around the deeds of Alexander, Ashoka[‡] and Akbar[12] simply crumbled, exposing the mundane monochromatic brutal character they all owned. Of all, the two very important aspects that touched me deeply were—

---

[*] Karl Marx and Frederick Engels, *The Buying and Selling of Labour-Power*; Samuel Moore and Edward Aveling, *Capital, A Critique of Political Economy, Book One: The Process of Production of Capital*, First English Edition, based on fourth German Edition. Moscow: Progress Publishers, 1887, Vol. 1, 6, pp. 118–24.

[†] Karl Marx, The British Rule in India, *New York Daily Tribune*, 10 June 1853.

[‡] Sanjeev Sanyal, *The Ocean of Churn*, Gurgaon: Penguin, 2017.

'neither freedom made a walk-in without any dragger or shield[13], nor was Tipu Sulṭān the first freedom fighter[*] as told'.

India's recent colonialists'[†] loyalists manhandled our past the most.[14] While taking up the responsibility of writing our history, they not only covered up the deeds of the European colonialists but also veiled past colonialists like Tīmūrids.[15] Interestingly, the latter have been very honest about their deeds and all the *-namas* shrink our hearts with descriptions of the worst kind of atrocities they inflicted upon our ancestors.[16] In their eyes, atrocities upon the *kafirs* (disbelievers/infidels) were virtuous, hence they saw no harm in flaunting it.[17] Not many would know that the records also exist wherein religious leaders in the time of Akbar lament the *Padishah* becoming softer towards the Hindus in the latter phase of his reign.[18]

After Jawaharlal Nehru waved a see-off to them in August of 1947, our stories began to turn more problematic than earlier. A brigade of intellectuals came into being who reinforced the 'culture disparaging projects'[*] by initiating the task of popularizing the fictional narratives of the 'Aryan Invasion', [19] which later matured as 'Aryan Migration'.[†] Narratives were woven stating that Britishers gave us the great language, with which we use in the world and it could tie India together.[20] [‡] The narrative-weavers also said that we were given the boon of 'rail', but none said that it was the infrastructure crafted to boost their economic benefits and neither were we told how this project of railway led to the invitation of the disastrous disease called malaria.[§] We were told that Bhagat Singh was not a revolutionary but a terrorist and so were his comrades in the cause. The family of legend

---

[*] Aabhas Maldahiyar, 'Tipu Sultan: When an Islamist Tyrant Is Turned into a Freedom Fighter, Missile Man and Dharma Saviour', Firstpost, 1 April 2022, https://www.firstpost.com/india/tipu-sultan-when-an-islamist-tyrant-is-turned-into-a-freedom-fighter-missile-man-and-dharma-saviour-10508661.html.

[†] The British.

[*] CIA, *The KGB in Asia: Society of Subversion*, New York: CIA, 1999.

[†] Michael Witzel, *Indocentrism*. (ed.) Edwin Bryant and Laurie Patton, *Indo-Aryan Controversy Evidence and Inference in Indian History*, London, New York: Routledge, 2005, p. 348.

[‡] Akshat Rathi, 'The Lies Brits Tell Themselves about How They Left Behind a Better India', Quartz, 15 August 2017, https://qz.com/india/1053297/independence-day-what-good-did-the-british-do-for-india-during-the-raj.

[§] Sheldon Watts, 'British Development Policies and Malaria in India 1897-c 1929', 1999, *Past & Present*, pp. 141–181.

Hutatma Bhagat Singh had to appeal to the government of the day to disassociate the word 'terrorist' from Bhagat Singh in textbooks.[*]

As Rajiv Malhotra says, the *Grand Narrative* needs to be established and it will be done by numerous intellectuals over several years.[†]

It has taken some decades, but the same band of intellectuals also popularized the narrative that Vinayak Damodar Savarkar wasn't a '*Veer* Patriot' but a 'Petition-Writing Servant of British'. Unfortunately, not many giant attempts were made to vaporize the odour of these tarnishes. But then came one of the most serious projects on Savarkar, accomplished by Vikram Sampath almost seven decades after Independence.

I felt that with this project, Sampath, for once and all, settled the debate around Savarkar and hit the final nail in the coffin of lies around the 'Veer'. But I had wrongly perceived this. Even in the conclusion of this very book, the controversy keeps rising, buttressed in shoddy articles and op-eds. This shows us that irrespective of which way the truth lies, the agenda of politics will always remain in vogue. While in academic opinion, the smoke around Veer Savarkar seems to have settled, a lot many stories of revolutionaries await eagerly to be told. As we talk about revolutionaries and freedom fighters, the narrative would need to go back more than a millennium when Indians had begun to resist the Arabic and Turkic forces.[21]

The tale of the Chandela Rajput King Vidhyadhara and how he halted the advance of *But-Shikan*[‡] Mahmud of Ghazni[§] is not known to the world. We are still to be exposed to elaborate details around warriors like Marthanda Varma, under whose leadership the European powers were crushed by an Asian power for the first time. We are yet to mainstream the detailed story of Lachit Borphukan who single-

[*] PTI, 'DU Book Calls Bhagat Singh a "Revolutionary Terrorist", Courts Controversy', *The Hindu*, 27 April 2016, https://www.thehindu.com/news/national/du-book-calls-bhagat-singh-a-revolutionary-terrorist-courts-controversy/article8528456.ece.

[†] Rajiv Malhotra, 'Weaving India's MAHAKATHA (Grand Narrative) for the 21st Century', Radhakrishnan Memorial Lecture, Indian Institute of Advanced Study, Infinity Foundation, 2018.

[‡] Breaker of Idols.

[§] André Wink, *Al-Hind the Making of the Indo-Islamic World: The Slave Kings and the Islamic Conquest: 11th-13th Centuries*, Leiden, New York, Koln: BRILL, 1991. p. 321. Vol. 2. 9004102361.

handedly led a relatively smaller army to defeat the mighty Tīmūrid Gūrkāniyān horde (of Aurangzeb) in a battle fought in waters—on the Brahmaputra river at Saraighat. We are yet to be narrated the tale of great Bajirao I who never lost a single battle of his life and in my opinion, was one of the greatest army-generals that the world has ever seen. There are many more such tales that must be known to the children of Bharat and beyond.

This is a never-ending tale of tragedy (keeping us away from history that would bring a sense of pride among us) that was unfortunately brought upon us by our people.* It has been more than seventy-five years since Independence, yet we read history passively. These fault lines in academic history are becoming fodder for the Western world to bash us each day through hopeless pieces in print and the web.[22]

One such narrative is about how Tīmūrid Gūrkāniyān (distorted as Moghūls) made India greater than how it stood in the past. The subject has invited debates across spectrums. People who have read stalwarts like Sir Jadunath Sarkar certainly have huge disagreements with the popular school of thought that essentially has roots in the academia of Jawaharlal Nehru University and Aligarh Muslim University. The Tīmūrid Gūrkāniyān has been a matter of extensive discussion among politicians too. We have heard the debates around renaming the places like Allahabad (now Prayagraj). There is another side of this discussion that claims this isn't about simply changing a name, rather it is about renaming a place. On the contrary, the opposing side debates that the issue of name, etc. is merely being brought across to erase the Muslim identity of India. Though the truth is certainly far from the shallow debates which are covered with layers and layers of nuances, it is not just black and white. But the density of apologia being read for the Tīmūrid Gūrkāniyās is thickening with each passing day. Various strands of public figures, ranging from film stars and industrialists to journalists etc. have some way or the other tried to be part of these debates passionately.

As a curious mind, the subject drew an objective interest from my end. I wanted to know about those who called themselves 'Tīmūrid Gūrkāniyān' and got popularized as 'Mūghals'. The journey began with the purpose of knowing more than telling the tale to others. I

* Surajit Dasgupta, *A History of 'Tolerance'*, Bengaluru, Coimbatore: Swarajya, 2015.

was expecting that these much-debated subjects would already have a lot of literary works based on primary contemporary sources. But the truth was stranger than my expectations. It was impossible to get hold of works in detail about history of Babur, the man who founded the empire. People have translated the Persian version of the *Baburnama*, and a few books have been written as biographies of Babur but nothing substantial encompassing complete details has appeared recently, except *Babur: Tīmūrid Prince and Mughal Emperor* by Stephen F. Dale.[*] This is an attempt to showcase the complete life of Babur using primary sources but very briefly. A book which can be considered one of the most substantial works on Babur (except the *Baburnama*) is *Babar* written by Stanley Lane-Poole, published way back in AD 1899, but it was too concise with a count of around 200 pages.[†] Not so long ago (2015) a book appeared centred on the life of Babur, titled *Babur: Conqueror of Hindustan* written by Royina Grewal, but this falls under the genre of historical fiction and is more of a eulogizing project, far from the truth on many accounts.[‡] The concern with the *Baburnama* is that it rightfully focuses entirely on Babur and fails to give relative context from an Indian perspective. While Babur was chronicling his life, he was not entirely aware of the happenings around the world. And today when I superimposed the *Baburnama* with the happenings around the world during that period, an entirely new perspective has appeared.

While most only saw a protagonist or an antagonist in him, I began to see him as a human being. Like any other human being, he too was affected by the circumstances and legacy which were nowhere under his control. There were moments when I felt pain for him, while there were times when I was anguished because of his deeds. He was as good or as bad of a human being as a warlord of the Tīmūrid clan in general would be. Without any exception, he was someone who was certainly not secular—deep religious portrayal was the virtue of his place and his time.

Finally, I decided to write books on history about those whom we wrongly call Moghūls.

---

[*] Stephen Fedric Dale, *Babur: Timurid Prince and Mughal Emperor, 1483–1530*, Cambridge: Cambridge University Press, 2018.

[†] Stanley Lane-Pool, *Babar*, Oxford: Oxford, 1899.

[‡] Royena Grewal, *Babur: Conqueror of Hindustan*, New Delhi: Rupa Publications, 2015.

The job was certainly no cakewalk and sought abundant efforts including the translations of original manuscripts in Persian to verify the translations already available. I had set my intent very clear right from the first day of this exercise that the work must not pass *any verdict* or frame opinions, rather it should only provide facts extracted from the *primary source*. The verdict and opinion-making should be left to the *readers* based on the facts given.

I decided to ensure nothing except *primary sources* are used to tell the tale of the second Tīmūrid wave[23] (Babur onwards). Accordingly, the narrative concerning Babur in this book is entirely based on the Persian manuscript of the *Baburnama*[24] and wherever confusion prevailed, the existing translated version by Annette Susannah Beveridge[25] has been referred to. Elsewhere, the respective sources referred to are mentioned in the bibliography. At the same time, the historical narratives have been supported with appropriate footnotes and endnotes, and appendices have been duly acknowledged with references.

This volume comprises a two-part narrative. While one part primarily focuses on Babur's journey for the first thirteen–fourteen years of his life post the demise of his father thereby setting the premise very right as to why he wanted to invade Hindustan, the second part deals with a brief analysis of sour situations created by the Tīmūrids (especially economy). These will be dealt with in detail in respective volumes dedicated to the biography of various *Padishah*s. Often claims are made that Babur came and he, along with his successors, became Hindustani. Is this true? Although this volume doesn't answer this question, the next volume would set the case in the right perspective by citing Babur's writings.

In my observation, the subject of history has always been a casualty of biases, which come from different ends of extremities. Things about history need to be read in conjunction with context and time. You can only read about 'historical instances' but never learn 'history' if the 'context' goes ignored. The context creates perspectives through the region of the milieu and the witnesses.

In the case of Tīmūrids (distorted as Moghūls) too, we have more opinions and fewer facts on the mainstream table though they exist in abundance. We have seen extreme fantastical vilification by people like James Todd, while there is extreme eulogizing by others. There are many promoting the Tīmūrids (in the name of Moghūls) for good. But if I look at the records of Tīmūrids themselves, it seems that had anyone of them been alive, they would have possibly rejected all these narratives of glorification. And the texts like the *Baburnama* etc. stand apart as the testimony of this matter. In the world of Turco-Mongols, secularism as it is glorified today, was never a virtue of glory back then.

It all begins with the name itself. They have always been addressed as *Moghūls*, but did they ever address themselves as so? While penning the *Baburnama*, Babur ensured a clear distinction between him being a Tīmūrid Prince establishing a *Tīmūrid Gūrkāniyān Sulṭānate* and not the *Moghūl,* which has been a popular claim of late. One may argue that Babur may have not used the term 'Moghūl' at all and hence the different term. But that too is not the reality. Babur has used the term '*Moghūl/ Mūghal/Mūgal*' more than 400 times in the

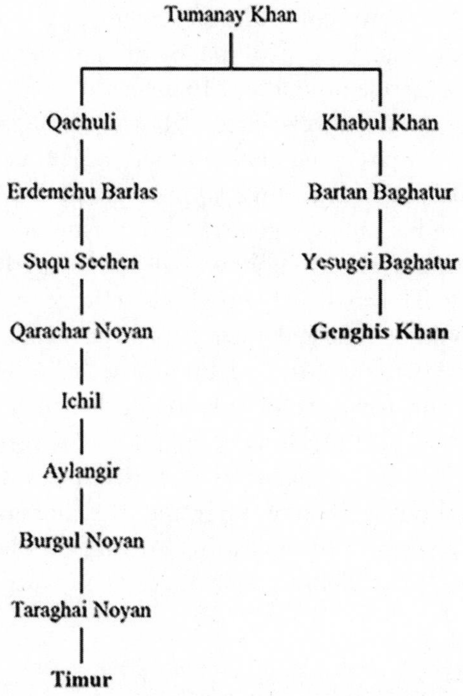

Figure I: Family Tree of Tumanay Khan

Baburnama, drawing a clear distinction. In fact, he has the worst opinion of the '*Moghūl* clan'.

But the question that may arise is, why should we bring in the name of the clan while we are just chronicling their history? The answer lies in the fact that even this name distortion occurred only because there was something to hide. Humbly speaking, the wrong name was used to create a narrative. Or else why suddenly in the nineteenth century, Indologists would begin calling Tīmūrid Gūrkāniyān Mūghals almost after three centuries of their establishment in what they called Hindustan? Abul-Fazl in the *Ain-i-Akbari* does mention them being the empire of 'Hindustan'.[26]

So, coming back to the name, Timur never liked to see himself as *Moghūl* even though both him and Genghis Khān had a common ancestor Tumanay Khān (Figure 1). Timur was in the tenth generation while Ghengis was in the fifth generation.

Babur's ancestors were sharply distinguished from the classical Mongols (Moghūls) insofar as they were oriented towards Persian rather than Turco-Mongol culture. According to John Joseph Saunders, 'Timur was "the product of an *Islamized and Iranized* society", and not steppe nomadic (Mongols).' [*]

If one looks at Timur's character, he was an opportunist. Taking advantage of his Turco-Mongolian heritage, he frequently used either the religion of Islam, *Sharia* law, *fiqh*, or traditions of the Mongol Empire to achieve his military goals and domestic political aims. This exactly was the trait of those whom we call Moghūls from the period of AD 1526 onwards. They had all the barbaric traits of the steppe nomads, but the same would be reflected when Persian strategies failed to core.

Though barbaric, the Mongol Empire was known to be highly secular and tolerant towards all existing faiths. In fact, after having given protection to the Muslims, Genghis Khān earned the title of 'Defender of Religions'.[†] What is very interesting is that the Mongol passion for religious tolerance charmed the European writers of the eighteenth century very broadly. Edward Gibbon, an English historian, writes in a celebrated passage, 'The Catholic inquisitors

---

[*] John Joseph Saunders, *The History of the Mongol Conquests*, Philadelphia: University of Pennsylvania Press, 2001, p. 173.

[†] Amy Chua, *Day of Empire: How Hyperpowers Rise to Global Dominance and Why They Fall*. New York: Double Day, 2007.

of Europe, who defended nonsense by cruelty, might have been confounded by the example of a barbarian, who anticipated the lessons of philosophy and established by his laws a system of pure theism and perfect toleration.' He goes on to add, in a footnote that 'singular conformity may be found between the religious laws of Zingis Khān and Mr. Locke'. [*] Well, for people who don't know about John Locke (29 August 1632–28 October 1704), he was an English philosopher and physician, widely regarded as one of the most influential 'enlightenment thinkers' and commonly known as the 'Father of Liberalism'.[†] He had influenced people like Voltaire.[‡] Perhaps the European idea of *imperialism* had a façade of *liberalism* and *secularism,* which appeared as a cool buttress.

In contrast, Timur had a record of persecution in the name of religion. As explained earlier, Timur had a high Persian influence. Before he could lay the siege of Persia, the condition of Christians was already horrendous with the rise of Islam as the 'state religion' for long.

The history of the church in Asia in the thirteenth and fourteenth centuries was very much tied up with the rise of the Mongol/Moghūl power under Hulegu, Kublai and Timur. The first two were brothers, sons of the Nestorian princes Sorkaktani and were known to be protectors of Christians' while Timur became known for their destruction.[§]

> And in the year fifteen hundred and seventy-six of the Greeks (a.d. 1265), in the days which introduced the Fast [of nineveh], Hulegu, King of Kings, departed from this world. The wisdom of this man, and his greatness of soul, and his wonderful actions are incomparable. And in the days of summer Tokuz Khatun, the believing queen, departed, and great sorrow came to all the Christians throughout the world because of the departure of these two great lights, who made the Christian religion triumphant.[¶]

---

[*] David Morgan, *The Mongols*, Second, Illustrated, New York: Wiley, 2007, p. 272.

[†] Carl L. Becker, *Declaration of Independence: A Study in the History of Political Ideas*, New York: Knopf Doubleday Publishing Group, 1970, p. 27.

[‡] Ibid.

[§] Samuel Hugh Moffett, *A History of Christianity in Asia, Vol. I: Beginnings to 1500*, s.l.: Orbis Books, 2014, p. 276.

[¶] Bar Hebraeus, *The Chronography of Abu'l-Faraj*, Oxford: Oxford University Press, 1932, p. 444.

The Mongol ruler of Persia (IlKhān), Ghazan (AD 1295–1304), converted to Islam and what followed was highly disastrous. The systematic persecution of Christians, Jews and Buddhists had become persistant and their places were destroyed at a huge pace. The initial days of Mongol rule had seen Christians being favoured extensively, but since the Islamic Conversion and after a lapse of seven decades, Islam had yet again risen as the state religion in Persia, changing things from how they were earlier.

Bar Hebraeus in his chronography describes the conditions of the Christians as extremely horrible. He writes:*

> No Christian dared to appear in the streets (or market), but the women went out and came in and bought and sold, because they could not be distinguished from the Arab women, and could not be identified as Christians, though those who were recognized as Christians were disgraced, and slapped, and beaten and mocked.

The persecution of Christians continued unabated under the subsequent *IlKhāns*. With the dawn of the 1340s, the Mongol power began to cease as Timur took control. Timur was clear and sound, knowing exactly what he wanted. He wanted to revive an Islamic Caliphate by hook or by crook with a definitive plan to make Samarkand the capital of Asia. One can say that he was a great conqueror concerning the parameters set in the West and the Middle East, but, in our eyes, his image was the sum of extreme brutalities. Between AD 1380 and AD 1393, Timur captured Central Asia, Persia, Egypt and the northern parts of India. By AD 1383, Baghdad, with the unabridged Mesopotamia, was completely under his control, the route to which was indeed horrific to the indigenous people. As per several accounts, Timur had made twenty towers of skulls, each having a minimum of 1500, in the ruins of Isfahan and Baghdad.† A few historians describe a 'systematic use of terror against towns', as 'Tamerlane's strategic element'. This was also a ploy through precedents by which he would

* The Son of Aaron, the Hebrew physician, commonly known as Bar Hebraeus, being the first part of his political history of the world. Bar Hebraeus, (trans.) Sir Ernest Alfred Wallis Budge, *The Chronography of Gregory Abû'l Faraj*, Oxford: Oxford University Press, 1932. p. 507. Vol. 1.

† P. Jackson, J.A. Boyle, W.B Fisher, *The Cambridge History of Iran*, Vol 5. p. 55.

avoid bloodshed. The widespread fear precluded any resistance as people chose to submit instead. But at the same time, his massacres were highly selective, and he spared the people who in his eyes were experts of art and knowledge.* Undoubtedly, this is the same model that Babur and his successors followed. This was not the Mongol or Moghūl case in general.

In India, he captured and ordered the execution of a hundred thousand prisoners to free his soldiers, thereby concretizing his aspiration of Delhi. Of course, within these misfortunes, both Muslims and non-Muslims suffered despite the intention being to target non-Muslims largely. Unlike the general Mongol traditions of governance, Timur ensured systematic persecution on account of religion.[27]

The control of Delhi was one of the very important victories of Timur. And why not? Delhi was one of the richest cities in the world back then.† Retaliations began after Delhi fell into his hands. Timur led the Turco-Mongol Army and inflicted widespread bloodshed and massacres against all the retaliations within the city walls. After three days of tussling between resisting forces and the Turco-Mongol Army, it is said that the city smelt of the decomposing bodies of its sons with their heads being placed over one another and the bodies left as food for the birds by Timur's soldiers.‡ This destruction of Delhi had opened the doors for long-lasting chaos that would consume India for long. The great city of Delhi founded by Anangpal Tomar§ would not be able to recover from the great loss it suffered for at least centuries.

As stated earlier, Timur was an excellent politician. The precedents that follow would prove this case.

Timur's Turco-Mongolian heritage offered him both prospects and contests. He had all desires to rule the Muslim world, being the head of the Mongol Empire. But the existing Mongol tradition posed outright trouble for his ambition. He was not the direct descendant of

---

* Gerard Chaliand and Arnaud Blin Gérard (eds.), *The History of Terrorism: From Antiquity to Al Qaeda*, California: University of California Press, 2007, p. 87.

† I. Batuta, *Travels in Asia and Africa*: *1325–1354*, Taylor & Francis, pp. 195–203.

‡ Justin Marozzi, *Tamerlane: Sword of Islam, Conqueror of the World*, HarperCollins, 2004, pp. 269–74.

§ Richard J. Cohen, 'An Early Attestation of the Toponym Ḍhillī.', *Journal of the American Oriental Society*, Vol. 109, No. 4, pp. 513–9.

Genghis Khān (refer to Figure 1) and hence he couldn't claim the title of 'the Khān' or rule the 'Mongol Empire'.

Henceforth, the cunning Timur set up a puppet in Chaghatay Khān, Suyurghatmish, as the titular ruler of Balkh by pretending to be a 'protector of the member of a Chinggisid line (Genghis Khān's eldest son, Jochi).'* At the same time, Timur took up the title of 'Amir'. It was as good as not only being the general but also acting in the name of the Chagatai ruler of Transoxiana.†

To underpin this position, Timur further claimed the title 'Guregen' (royal son-in-law) when he married Saray Mulk Khānum, a princess of Chinggisid descent.‡

While Timur aspired to rule both the Muslim and Mongol worlds, he could neither take the title of 'Khān' nor he could become the 'Caliph', as the latter's office was limited to the tribe of the Prophet Muhammad (PBUH). Hence to solve this crisis, Timur did something very different (later his successor Abu'l-Fath Jalal-ud-din Muhammad Akbar would do something similar in the sixteenth century). Timur got a myth formulized and portrayed himself as a 'supernatural personal power' ordained by God (say, Allah).§ Interestingly and radically enough, this myth was propagated that he was a spiritual descendant of Ali, thus linking his lineage to both Genghis Khān and the Quraysh.¶

So, this makes the narrative clear that Timur aspired to become powerful by hook or by crook. He wanted to be known as the head of all humanity without compromising on principles laid by Prophet Muhammad (PBUH).

This sets the precedent very correctly for Babur, who established a 'Tīmūrid Empire' in India to push for not only Islamism but also to retain control over the Mongols. He simply meant business and being a follower of Timur, he would not shy away from inflating and using religion whenever required.

---

* Beatrice Forbes Manz, 'Tamerlane's Career and Its Uses', 2002, *Journal of World History*, Vol. 13, p. 25.

† Ibid.

‡ Beatrice Forbes Manz, *The Rise and Rule of Tamerlane*, Cambridge: Cambridge University Press, 1999. pp. 13–14.

§ Ibid.

¶ Denise Aigle, *The Mongol Empire between Myth and Reality: Studies in Anthropological History*, Leiden: BRILL, 2014, p. 132.

Perhaps intolerance was a part of their conduct and it would be dishonest to expect the progenies of Timur to begin a new chapter of tolerance. If one understands 'Timur', it will not be tough to get into the psyche of the politics of Babur and his successors. Not to forget, the history of Timur had a strong impact on Babur.

Before this project of books on the Tīmūrid Gūrkāniyān, I deep-dived into the lives of Babur, Humayun, Akbar and Aurangzeb. Their religious and economic policies were very clearer to me, but as research progressed, a lot opened even about Jahangir and Shah Jahan. It was quite astonishing for me to discover that Jahangir began his tourney as the king of the Tīmūrid Empire, who was intolerant towards non-Muslims. Earlier the Jahangir's image was known to me as the 'Salim' of *Mughal-e-Azam,* but the historical records didn't agree with my impression of him. The maiden *farmans* of him indicated very strongly that he wanted to make his empire a hardcore *Islamist* one. Although people talk of his drug and alcohol addictions, with fervour to show how distant he was from Islam in his own words, he had asked the *Ulemas* to prepare a set of 'idiosyncratic appeals to Allah' which he could easily remember and repeat without any disturbance on his rosary. His sadistic nature is also well-recorded in his writings. When he went to war against Mewar, he declared it to be a *qital fi sabilillah.*[*] Many mandirs were destroyed in this campaign. Similar emotions reigned high in his Kangra Campaign of AD 1621. His aggression against the Sikh Guru Arjan Dev too is very well recorded. Guru Arjan Dev was killed after being brutally tortured by Jahangir. Jahangir's ill-treatment of Guru Arjan Dev's successor, Guru Hargobind, too is well recorded.[†]

Jahangir went overboard in penalizing anyone who disagreed with him. During his reign, many prominent Muslims had disagreements with him, after which they couldn't escape his wrath however important they were to society. The noteworthy Sufi Sheikh Ahmad Sirhindi once pronounced that 'he once came closer to Allah than the Caliphs in his dreams'. This made Jahangir furious as he saw this as an insult to the Caliphs. Yet another Sufi named Sheikh Nizam Thanesari was expatriated to Mecca on the charge of accompanying Khusrau Mirza

[*] Henry Beveridge, Alexander Rogers, *The Tūzuk-i-Jahāngīrī, Or Memoirs of Jahāngīr*, London: London Royal Asiatic Society, 1909. p. 16.

[†] Ibid, p. 72. Vol. 1.

for some distance.* Jahangir had this trend of rewarding people after testing their knowledge and realizing their economic condition every day. But he ensured that his patronage and support went especially to the Muslims.†

Shah Jahan, son of Jahangir, was way ahead of his father in terms of barbarity. It was merely in the first decade (sixth year) of his regnum year that he passed a farman to raze mandirs, whose foundations had been laid during his father's period and stood unfinished. He was high with the zeal to revive Islam in the best possible way. He intended to reflect Islam as a dominant religion, and hence apart from demolishing mandirs, he commissioned many grand mosques like the Jama Masjid in Delhi.‡

Well, even the Taj has enough baggage of a gory past. There is a school of thought that claims it to be a mandir in reality. I'm not going to address the *truth* of this matter (based on primary sources) here. It will be addressed in the volume which will exclusively talk about Shah Jahan. Here, I would briefly touch on a part of the issue, which when revealed, had shocked me enormously. It is recorded that when the Taj Mahal was built (AD 1631), it cost around 41.8 million silver rupees.§ To set things in perspective, I am providing some mathematics for the readers. On average, the mean income of a farmer's family was 'one *Dam* (copper coin) per day'. One silver rupee was equivalent to forty *Dams*,¶ and a single rupee would get you around 280 kilograms of general-grade rice during Shah Jahan's reign. Now, the question arises as to why this analysis was important and how it brought more shocks in my NCERT-history-educated life.

This was the time when the great Deccan Famine (AD 1630–31 AD) had occurred, and around 7.4 million** had succumbed to

* Henry Beveridge and Alexander Rogers, *The Tūzuk-i-Jahāngīrī, Or Memoirs of Jahāngīr*, London: London Royal Asiatic Society, 1914. pp. 60, 91–92, 161. Vol. 2

† Lisa Balabanlilar, *The Emperor Jahangir: Power and Kingship in Mughal India*, Noida: Bloomsbury Publishing, 2020.

‡ Abdul Hamid Lahori, *Badshahnama*; Henry Miers Elliot, *Shah Jahan*, Lahore: Hafiz Press, 1875, pp. 39, 3–78.

§ Olivier Nogùes, *Wonders of the World*, https://www.wonders-of-the-world.net/Taj-Mahal/Cost-of-the-Taj-Mahal.php.

¶ Shireen Moosvi, *The Economy of the Mughal Empire, C.1595: A Statistical Study*, Oxford: Oxford University Press, 2015. p. 301.

** A famine in Surat in 1631 and Dodos on Mauritius: a long lost manuscript rediscovered. R. Winters, J.P.Hume, M.Leenstra. 1, s.l.: The Society for the History of Natural History, 2017, Archives of Natural History, Vol. 44, pp. 134–50.

the same. It may sound strange, but this famine was created by the Tīmūrid Prince Shah Jahan himself. In AD 1631, the army under Shah Jahan marched to Malwa as one of his commanders stationed there had rebelled and joined hands with *Adilshahis* of Bijapur and *Nizamshahis* of Hyderabad. The army intended to teach the rebel commander a lesson. The records state that Tīmūrids (distorted as Moghūls) extracted an annual revenue of not less than around ten million rupees from the Malwa province in the seventeenth century.[*]

The fertile belt of Malwa was a hen with the golden egg for the Tīmūrids. The rebellion had eclipsed this massive income and the attack on Malwa as well as Deccan had become inevitable. Two years before it, commander Khwaja Abu Hasan had invaded Malwa. These acts briefly led to the massive famine of 1630–32.[†] The destruction of crops in Malwa and Deccan by Shah Jahan's Regal armies has been well recorded by court chroniclers and foreign travellers. For example, Inayat Khān, in *Shah Jahanama,* talks about how Shah Jahan had ordered the imperial army to 'ravage the country from end to end'. The order of Shah Jahan was carried very comprehensively, and Inayat writes, 'There is scarcely a vestige of cultivation left in this country'. Like his ancestors, Shah Jahan didn't leave his wives during the war campaigns. And it was during his campaign of Burhanpur that Mumtaz Mahal died from a post-partum haemorrhage while struggling to give birth to their fourteenth child. She suffered around thirty hours of labour. And it was here that he decided to dedicate the tomb to her corpse which is known to the world as the Taj Mahal.[‡] [§] On the other hand, Shah Jahan's campaigns were of course set to bring results. The scarcity of rain when coupled with devastations brought by the Imperial

---

[*] Edward Thomas, *The Revenue Resources of the Mughal Empire in India, from A.D. 1593 to A.D. 1707: A Supplement to The Chronicles of the Pathàn Kings of Dehli*, Oxford: Trübner, 1871. p. 28.

[†] Abdul Hamid Lahori, *Badshahnama*; Henry Miers Elliot (ed.), John Dowson, *The History of India, as Told by Its Own Historians*, London: Sh. Mubarak Ali, 1867–77, Vol. VII, p. 12.

[‡] (ed.) Wayne Edison Begley Z. A. Desai. (trans.) Abraham Richard Fuller, *The Shah Jahan Nama of 'Inayat Khan: An Abridged History of the Mughal Emperor Shah Jahan, Compiled by His Royal Librarian: The Nineteenth-Century Manuscript Translation*. London: Oxford University Press, 1990. pp. 251-52.

[§] Anant Kumar, 'Monument of Love or Symbol of Maternal Death: The Story Behind the Taj Mahal', June 2014, Case Reports in Women's Health, Vols. 1-2, pp. 4-7.

Tīmūrid Army added to the great famine of 1630–32. The regions affected were Gujarat, Malwa and Deccan.

Just to set a perspective, we read about the devastating Bengal famine of 1943, in which three million people were killed, and for which Winston Churchill was held accountable. Yet, the Deccan famine of 1630–32, which killed more than twice that of the Bengal famine, gets whitewashed at ease. And of course, even if we hear few murmurs of famine, no one asks, 'Why did Shah Jahan kill so many?'

I was shaken after reading the agony of people and surprisingly court chronicler Abdul Hamid Lahori didn't roll a carpet over it:*

> Inhabitants were reduced to the direst extremity. Life was offered for a loaf, but none would buy. Dog's flesh was sold for goat flesh. The pounded bones of the dead were mixed in flour and sold. Men began to devour each other, and the flesh of a son was preferred to his love. The number of deaths caused obstructions in the roads. Those lands which had been famous for fertility and plenty of resources retain no traces of production.

Peter Mundy, the seventeenth-century British traveller and merchant who visited the region during the famine, wrote in his diary:†

> Surat (Gujarat)- Great famine, highways unpassable, infested by thieves looking not for gold but grain; Kirka- Town empty. Half inhabitants fled. Another half dead; Dhaita- Children sold for 6 dams or given for free to any who could take them so they might be kept alive; Nandurbar (Maharashtra)-No space to pitch a tent, dead bodies everywhere. Noisome smell from a neighboring pit where 40 dead bodies were thrown. Survivors searching for grains in the excrement of men and animals. Highway stowed with dead bodies from Surat to Burhanpur.

---

* Abdul Hamid Lahori, *Badshahnama*; Henry Miers Elliot (ed.), John Dowson, *The History of India, as Told by Its Own Historians*, London: Sh. Mubarak Ali, 1867–77, Vol. VII, p. 12.

† Peter Mundy, *The Travels of Peter Mundy in Europe and Asia*, 1608–1667. (ed.) Lt. Col. Sir Richard Carnac Temple. Cambridge: Cambridge University Press, 1907. pp. 40–48. Vol. II.

He gives complete details about how the Tīmūrid lords were treating people. He wrote:

> In Bazar lay people dead and others breathing their last with the food almost near their mouths, yet dying for want of it, they not having wherewith to buy, nor the others so much pity to spare them any without money. There being no course taken in this Country to remedy this great evil, the rich and strong engrossing and taking perforce all to themselves.

There was no food for the general public while it was abundant for the Royal Tīmūrids. When the entire province was on its deathbed, Shah Jahan's war camp was in fair shape. It was spacious and plentifully stored with all provisions. The camp was receiving supplies from all the corners, far and near.[*]

Not only did Shah Jahan ensure that people felt the wrath of the 'famine' but the great Tīmūrid prince collected tax to build the tomb for Mumtaz. Tīmūrid Empire, established by Babur, was known for collecting the highest taxes in the world. The estimates tell us that they used to take a share of more than half of what the peasants produced.[†] In contrast, Hindu kings like that of the Vijayanagar Empire, charged one-sixth of the produce. This was almost four times less than the Tīmūrids.

I even came across Shah Jahan's revenue utilization. He invested a little more than one-third of the revenue in the sixty-eight princes and Amirs. One-fourth of the revenue went to his 587 officers. This implies that almost 62 per cent of the revenue was spent on merely 665 elites of the court.[‡]

After having read around the subject, it didn't take much time to conclude that Shah Jahan brought the famine over Gujarat, Malwa and Deccan by ravaging the cultivation completely. And then, the diverting of revenue to build the Taj Mahal coupled with the scarcity of rain caused

---

[*] Ibid. p. 50.

[†] Shireen Moosvi, *The Economy of the Mughal Empire, C.1595: A Statistical Study*, Oxford: Oxford University Press, 2015, p. 301.

[‡] Irfan Habib, 'Agrarian Relations and Land Revenue', *The Cambridge Economic History of India*, Cambridge: Cambridge University Press, 1982, p. 242.

the famine in which around eight million people died. This number is well attested in a letter written by a Dutch East India Company lawyer.*

I was startled. If Churchill can be held responsible for 'genocide' in Bengal, then Shah Jahan should also be held responsible for the genocide of around eight million people. Hence, the building which everyone has described as the pride of Bharat, was built at the cost of the blood of so many.

So, this was the ghastly, shocking tale of the Taj Mahal which send shivers down my spine. In childhood, a visit to Delhi's vicinity was all about posing for a picture in front of the Taj. I was heartbroken when the insights came in. It was devastating to realize how a lot of facts had been brushed under the carpet, which would end up making Taj, the pride of Indian 'pain'.

A lot needs to be written about this subject and certainly, this is not something which would get over even in a million words. This book is the first in the long series on the Tīmūrids, whom we know as Moghūls, that I wish to write. While taking up this project, I decided to be as honest as possible concerning the primary sources and present the utmost facts that had been recorded in the contemporary period.

When I began writing about Babur, the book ended up with around two lakh words. This would have made the book around one-and-half-times bulkier than how it stands today. Discussing with experts I came up with three ways:

I. Have the first volume published with the same length.
II. Shorten the narration by reducing the details.
III. Pass on a few parts of Babur's life into the next volume along with Humayun.

After giving it much thought, I decided to go with the third way. But doing so, I invited a risk, too. I was of the opinion that the nation is badly polarized today and everyone has choices when it comes to reading history. Babur's life has so many layers and I thought that dividing his life story may lead to a polarized reading of events. It

* A famine in Surat in 1631 and Dodos on Mauritius: A long lost manuscript rediscovered. R. Winters, J.P. Hume, M. LEENSTRA. 44, Edinburg: Edinburgh University Press, 2017, Archives of Natural History, Vol. 1, pp. 134–150.

was important to sort out this dilemma and I discussed the concern with people of diverse opinions. It appeared that I was misjudging the readers. The risk that I was envisioning was hypothetical and readers are more concerned about knowing complete details of the matter.

Hence, I decided to limit Babur's tale in this volume to his second failed attempt to enter Hindustan. In the volumes to follow, a lot about the Hindustan's resistance will be spoken of. It would also cover more about the economic policies that the Tīmūrids had for the Hindustanis.

One more concern that hit me in the middle of writing this book was why should people prefer my work (say volume 1) when today the translated version of the *Baburnama* is readily available for everyone to read.

The short answer lies in a fact—that until any historical instance is read with context and related past, the matter can't grant us a complete analysis of a particular time. As far as the *-namas* of the Tīmūrid emperors are concerned, they can give us the sequence of events, but contextual elaborations (in the form of footnotes, further readings, appendices, citing other sources during narrative) can incline the greys towards black or white. For example, while talking of Babur's raid into the region of Kafiristan, it becomes essential to elaborate on the past of the place. As another example, the clear distinction that Babur made while fighting the Muslims and non-Muslims becomes an essential pointer to dwell into what exactly was happening in terms of the cultural wars of that period.

I hope that this creation of mine will be well received by the people of Bharat and beyond. The next volume will get into details of the following:

1. Understanding roots of Islamic Colonization with Persia as a case study
2. Babur's campaign in Hindustan
3. The truth of Rana Sanga's correspondence with Babur
4. Humayun's life
5. Resistance to Babur and Humayun
6. Economic Model practised by Babur and Humayun
7. Religious policies of Babur and Humayun in India

Part 1

(October of AD 1493 to May of AD 1504)

Ferghana

1

Babur's Home

'I have not written all this to complain I have simply written the truth. I do not intend by what I have written to compliment myself: I have simply set down exactly what happened.'

—Babur

Babur was just twelve during the month of Ramzan of AH 899 (June of AD 1494) when he became the de facto ruler of the country of Ferghana. Perhaps, at such a tender age, he could not even very well understand the pain of losing his father. Nor do I assume that he saw so well the weight of the responsibility to be a fatherly figure to the land of Ferghana. The populace loved his father. And why not, when he had done so much good in his reign?

His father Umar Shaikh Mīrzā II had met with an unfortunate accident while tending to pigeons in the badly constructed dovecote. It toppled into the canyon below the palace, flowing into the river with his pet pigeons. He died and Babur's fate to become king of chessboard got scripted.

By that period Ferghana's habitation was well-settled. On the east existed Kashghar; on the west, Samarkand; on the south, the mountains of the Badakhshan border. In the early ages before Babur, there existed towns such as Almaligh, Almaty and Yangi (Yany). The local folklore mentioned Yangi as Taraz. In that period, those places remained desolate without a settled population. The city had seen massive destruction at the hands of Mongols.[1] It seemed to have attained restoration at the hands of Aūzbegs.

Back then Ferghana was a small country. Fruits and grains grew there in abundance. It was surrounded by mountains in all directions except on the western periphery, towards Khujand and Samarkand. This was the only probable orifice through which enemies could make a passage into the Ferghana. The Syr River[2] entered Babur's land from the north-east. Turning westward, it passed along the northern edge of Khujand, kissing the southern ends of Fanakat.[3] [4] [*] It finally diverted directly north and moved towards Turkistan. It was popularly known as the 'Water of Khujand'. This river was much different than the other rivers in general. It did not end in any sea, rather it sank into the sands, at an extensive distance below Turkistan.

Babur's land (Figure 1), Ferghana, had seven towns. Five of them lay on the south and two to the north of the Fanakat. The capital city of Andijān was one among the five in the south and it was located centrally. Although the capital produced plenty of grains and fruits, it was best known especially for admirable grapes and splendid melons. Also, the Andijān pears were known to be the best in that region. The fort of Andijān happened to be the third largest in *Mawara'u'n-Nahr* (now known as Transoxiana) after that of Samarkand and Kesh. The fort of Andijān had three gates and the citadel lay on the south. Water entered through nine channels, and eccentrically none came out even in a single place. There was a gravelled highway at the edge of the moat. Babur mentions that it was wide enough to divide the suburbs with affluence. Hunting and fowling were the favourite pastimes of the people of Andijān.

Babur mentions that according to the rumours, the pheasants of Andijān grew so fat that even four people could not finish eating it with its stew.

Interestingly all the inhabitants of Andijān were Turks, but generally, not even a single citizen of the town or the bazaar knew the Turki language. The people of Andijān were known for their good looks and artistic traits. Babur talks of great Andijāni musician, Khwaja Yusuf while trying to emphasize the artistic attributes of the place. He also talks of the writings of Mir' Ali-Shir Nava'i.[5]

---

[*] C.E Bosworth, 'BANĀKAT', Encyclopaedia Iranica, 15 December 1988, https://iranicaonline.org/articles/banaka-benaka-in-jovayni-fanakat-the-main-town-of-the-medieval-transoxanian-province-of-sas-or-cac-to-be-dist. 2330-4804.

Figure 1: Regions of Babur's territory

From Babur's perspective, the climate of Andijān was quite miraculous. He observed that the people commonly contracted fever during autumn in that region.

Osh[6] lies to the south-east of Andijān inclining largely towards the eastern edge. The climate in Osh was fabulous with an abundance of running waters. It had the most stunning spring season. Traditional narratives have sung praises about the excellencies of Osh. To its south-east existed the walled town of Qurghan and an interesting mountain, known as the Bara-Kukh.[7] The mountain was symmetric which made it appear gorgeous all the time.

In AD 1496 (902 AH), Sulṭān Mahmud Khān had built two retreats. One atop the hill and the other below with an interesting porch. Babur mentions that although Mahmud Khān's retreat existed higher, his one was better placed, with the whole of the town and the suburbs being at its foot.

The stream that passed through Andijān, reached there only after traversing the green belts of Osh. Either side of the banks was surrounded by orchards. The tulips and roses blossomed in the springs. This made the panorama of orchids appear more pleasing than anything around.

On the periphery of the Bara-Kukh existed a mosque called the Jauza Masjid (Twin Mosque). The great main canal flowing from the hill separated the mosque and the town. A dappled meadow full of clovers existed below the outer court of the mosque. It was the resting place for the travellers. Just a few years before the accidental demise of Babur's father, Umar Shaikh Mīrzā, a peculiar stone was discovered in Bara-Kukh. It had an unusual tint of red and white. People had begun making knife handles, belt clasps, etc. from the stone.

The other important city of Ferghana was Margilan[8] located to the west of Andijān. It was said to be a fine settlement full of good things such as an excellent crop of apricots and pomegranates. The city had a different kind of pomegranate, which they called the Dana-i-Kalan, and its sweetness was akin to the pleasant flavour of the small apricot. It was supposed to be much better than the Semnan[9] pomegranate.

Babur in general didn't have a very pleasant opinion of the people of Margilan for they were bullies in his eyes. He found them noisy and tempestuous. But he goes on to shower praises for the author of *Al-Hidayah,*[10] Burhan al-Din al-Margilali. He was a Margilanian from the village of Rashdan.

Esfara[11] [*] was another township of Ferghana, lying south-west of Margilan. Like other townships, even Esfara had a running stream of water. It had little but beautiful gardens and many orchards, most of which were covered with almonds. The townsfolk spoke Persian mostly, unlike other parts of Ferghana which were already Turkified.

---

[*] Habib Borjian, 'Esfara', Encyclopædia Iranica Foundation, INC., 1998., https://www.iranicaonline.org/articles/esfara.

A piece of rock known as 'mirror stone' existed towards the hills, two miles south of the town. It got such a name for its ability to reflect things like a mirror. It was almost of a man's height but with a bend in the centre. We do not have much idea about this stone except for Babur's sparse descriptions. The Esfara district was one among the four sub-divisions in the hill country. The remaining three were: Varuk, Sukh and Hushyar. Babur stayed in Sukh and the hill country of Hushyar for a year (AD 1503–1504) after Muhammad Shaybāni[12] defeated the sons of Yunus Khān: Sulṯān Mahmud Khān and Ahmad Alaq. This defeat had cost them Tashkent and Shahrukhiya. Babur mentions this as the period of misery till he took over Kābul.

Below is a brief description of the relationship between the house of Yunus and Umar Shaikh:

> Sulṯān Yunus Khān was the Chagatai Mughal Khān of Mughalistan from AD 1462 until he died in 1487. He is identified by many historians with Ḥājjī `Ali of the contemporary Chinese records.[*] He was a direct male descendent of Genghis Khān, through his son Chagatai Khān and was the maternal grandfather of Babur.[†]
>
> He was actively involved in the affairs of the Tīmūrids in his western frontier. He made a marriage alliance with the most prominent Tīmūrid Sulṯāns. He married off his daughters Mihr Nigar Khānum, Qutlugh Nigar Khānum and Sulṯān Nigar Khānum to Sulṯān Ahmad Mīrzā, Umar Shaikh Mīrzā II and Sulṯān Mahmud Mīrzā respectively in AD 1475. Sulṯān Nigar Khānum gave birth to Babur and Shaikh Vais Mīrzā respectively. Yunus maintained convivial terms with Umar Shaikh. Umar relied on him for assistance against Sulṯān Ahmad and in return gave him territory to reside in during the winters. In AD 1484, Yunus Khān captured Tashkent taking advantage of the conflict between Sulṯān Ahmad and Umar Shaikh. He planned to stay in Tashkent, but it did dismay the Mūghals. Ahmad Alaq, lead people to leave Mūghalistan. In AD 1487, Yunus Khān died in Tashkent after suffering from a long illness. He was

[*] Morris Rossabi, *From Yuan to Modern China and Mongolia: The Writings of Morris Rossabi*, Leiden: BRILL, 2015, p. 48.

[†] Babur, Annette Susannah Beveridge. (trans.), 'Interpolated account of Bābur's mother's family', *The Bābur-nāma in English* (Memoirs of Bābur), London: Luzac and Co., 1922, p. 19.

succeeded in Tashkent by his eldest son, Sulṭān Mahmud Khān, while the Mūghals in the east (Uyghurstan) followed Ahmad Alaq.

Sulṭān Mahmud Khān had a task at his hands. He had to defend Tashkent from the Tīmūrids of Samarkand and Ferghana, who begrudged the loss of the city to his father Yunus Khān. He was successful in nullifying their efforts to take Tashkent. During his fight with Sulṭān Ahmad, the Uzbek Muhammad Shaybāni, an Ahmad's man defected. This appeared very pleasing to Mahmud Khān, and he rewarded Muhammad Shaybāni by giving him Turkistan in AD 1488. Perhaps he wasn't aware of the political foolishness that he had committed. This resulted in him losing a long-time ally in the Kazakhs who were traditional enemies of the Uzbeks. The war became inevitable and when Mūghals and Kazakhs went to war, Mahmud Khān stands defeated. His military prestige well known in the region had gone for a toss.

Babur's rebel minister Sulṭān Ahmed Tambol had held Babur's brothers Jahangir Mīrzā II and Nasir Mīrzā as hostages. In AD 1501, Babur had lost Andijān and Ferghana to him. Not only this, but Babur had also lost Samarkand to Muhammad Shaybāni Khān. The situation was devastating. He was without a kingdom, without a home. He had to take his family to Tashkent under the protection of his maternal uncle, Sulṭān Mahmud Khān, the Chagatai Khān of Western Mūghalistan. He served as an officer in Khān's army without holding any authority over any territory. The tide of Uzbeks under Muhammad Shaybāni was rising heavily. Sulṭān Mahmud Khān allying with his brother Ahmad Alaq in Uyghurstan decided to join forces to stem the growth of the Uzbek power in the west from reaching their borders by invading Central Asia. Babur too was looking at the opportunity to be part of this operation as he was looking for a chance to regain his lost territories.

Sulṭān Mahmud Khān left for Andijān, leaving his son Sulṭān Muhammad in Tashkent with a strong army. He left Uratippa in the hands of Mīrzā Muhammad Hussain Dughlat. He always feared that Uzbeks from rear while he would be conducting operations against Sulṭān Ahmed Tambol in Andijān, and hence he left two major armies behind. He was convinced that Muhammad Shaybāni Khān wouldn't cross those armies. Sulṭān Mahmud Khān marched into the former Tīmūrid territory with the remainder of his army of 15,000 men along with Babur.

But the things were not set to happen as Sulṭān Mahmud had thought. Muhammad Shaybāni Khān received intelligence of the Mūghals' movement. Without any delay he hastened with an army of 30,000 men from Samarkand to Ferghana, passing by Uratippa on his road. The reluctant Mīrzā Muhammad Hussain Dughlat was expecting Uzbeks to besiege him; hence he had all preparations done at the fort. Muhammad Shaybāni had bigger and more thoughtful plans. He arrived in the afternoon itself and encamped close to the town. Beyond anyone's expectations, he broke up his camp and marched towards Ferghana with his fleet at the quickest he could. When inquiry was made, he was already miles away. Several messengers were dispatched to notify the Khāns in the concerned locality. But both messengers and the fleet of Shaybāni reached at the same time. Unfortunately, neither the army of Tashkent nor of Uratippa could come to aid the Khāns.

The Khāns were far far away from Andijān. Akhsi (possibly a town; a few miles away from Namangan), the town with the strongest forts in that country, was occupied by Shaikh Bayazid, brother of Tambol. Muhammad Shaybāni Khān came up with 30,000 men. The Khāns had hardly enough time to draw up in line, when, after a short conflict, the Khāns were put to rout by the overpowering numbers of the enemy. Their horses being rendered useless with fatigue, the two Khāns were taken prisoner. As for Babur, he fled to the hills to the south of Ferghana.[13]

Khunjad was another town in Ferghana. It was located almost in the centre of Andijān and Samarkand, ranging west and east respectively. Khujand was one of the most ancient towns of the locality. Shaikh Maslahat and Khwaja Kamal belonged to this place.

This place too was known for its fruits. Babur says that the pomegranates of Khujand were as famous as the apples of Samarkand. Something quite comparable to that of Margilan. This town stood handsomely at a high altitude. The Syr River coursed picturesquely on the northern side of the town. To its north and the Syr, lay the handsome mountain range of Munughul. As per the popular saying, Munughul was full of turquoise and other mines. People feared going to the mountain as it was full of snakes. Like Andijān, the hunting and fowling grounds of Khujand were full of pheasants and rabbits. It has been said that the climate of the place was conducive to malaria which many contracted, and Babur mentioned the mounts of Munghul to be the source of the same.

Khujand had a dependable village named Kand-i-Badam (Village of the Almond) 18 miles to its east. Though it was not a town, its significance lay in being an approach to an important town. As the name suggests, the almonds of this place were excellent and were exported to Hormuz. On to those 18 miles lay a wasteland known as Ha Darwesh, where the speedy wind blew all the time, travelling to Margilan from the east and towards Khujand from the west. This wind was indeed violent and turbulent. As per local sayings, some dervishes[14] had been lost to the turbulent wind. They kept calling, 'Ha Darwesh! Ha Darwesh,' till all of them perished. It was from then that the place came to be known as Ha Darwesh.

In the north of Syr River, lay the township of Akhsi. Babur mentions that the available literature of that period called it Akhsikit.[15] It was the second-largest township of Ferghana after Andijān, lying to its west. It was made into the capital city by Babur's father, Umar Shaikh Mīrzā.

The Syr River flew below its walled town of Qurghan. It overlooked a great ravine that was used instead of the convention of moats. It was believed that no fort was as strong as Akhsi in the whole of Ferghana. The suburbs of Akhsi extended a couple of miles further from the walled town. People considered it as the most ideal in every respect. The melons of Akhsi seemed to be the best among all. A type of melon called Mir Timuri was considered sweeter than any other in the world. Although the melons of Bukhara were way more famous than those of Akhsi, Babur found no comparison in them. Certainly, Mir Timuri was the winner. Like Andijān and Khunjad, hunting and fowling was an apt retreat here too with abundant hare and pheasants all around.

To the north of Akhsi lay another town of Ferghana called Kasan. It was way smaller than the other towns. One could get the Akhsi water from Kasan, the same way as one could get Andijān water from Osh. Kasan was especially known for its little but elegant gardens. People believed that the air blowing in Kasan was the best in the country. The bed of gardens was no less than a torrent. Interestingly people called those beds like the front of a coat. It wasn't an easy job to decide which town, Kasan or Osh, had more scenic beauty and a pleasing climate.

The mountains around Ferghana had amazing summer pastures. Here, a unique tree called *Tabalghy* with red willows grew. Its timber was used to make staves. It was even used to craft birdcages and scrape stacks of arrows. Babur mentions it to be a source of excellent wood whose rarity was spoken for thousands of miles. Few works of literature of that time talk of mandrake (used for inducing sleep and as a pain-killing agent) being found in those mountain ranges, but nothing was heard of it close to Babur's period. But an herb named Aylq Auti with similar qualities was heard about. Turquoise and iron mines were found in abundance in the mountains of Ferghana.

2

His Family and Early Life

'I have reported every good and evil I have seen of father and brother and set down the actuality of every fault and virtue of relative and stranger. May the reader excuse me; may the listener take me not to task.'[*]

—Babur

If you must trust something in history, it must be the primary source. One can surely argue though that how can one be so sure about the primary source giving the exact version of the happenings of a period? The answer is that indeed we can't grant the certificate of honesty to the person attributed to a particular source, but the corroborations with other primary sources on the same subject can certainly bring us closer to the truth. Moreover, in this game of history, you must choose something as the truth and only then can the narrative be weaved into the contemporary period of the incident we are referring to. If a primary source can't be trusted, then nothing else can ever be trusted either.

Whether you like it or not, the Tīmūrids themselves have been the primary source for their history through their writings. It is said that children always see the most ideal man in their father. The same must have been the case with Babur. Remember that being a conqueror was a heroic act back then.

[*] Babur, Wheeler M. Thackston (ed. and trans.), *The Baburnama: Memoirs of Babur, Prince and Emperor*, New York: The Modern Library, 2002. p. XVIII.

Perhaps what he writes about his father, Umar Shaikh Mīrzā, might have been an exaggerated account. But as mentioned earlier, we have no choice but to believe his words. At the same time, largely the folklore of the region, along with mention of historical incidences support Babur's narrative.

In Babur's opinion, his father Mīrzā, being highly striving and a go-getter, always looked for opportunities to conquer. He was a true conqueror. Although he was not victorious in all his missions, his passion to conquer never ended. On his mission to Samarkand, he tasted defeat on several occasions. At various junctures, he had to retire against his will as adverse situations engulfed the battlefields. But he never let those junctures demotivate him.

His father has described his (maternal) grandfather Yunus Khān[1] an aid. His grandfather was the chief of the Mongols (Moghūls). Once, Umar had called his father-in-law into the country.[2] Before coming to Mīrzā's country, Yunus Khān had been residing in the lands of his ancestor, Chaghatai Khān, the second son of Genghis Khān. Each time Mīrzā brought Khān to Ferghana, lands were gifted to him. In the meantime, Yunus Khān kept on shifting between Ferghana and Moghūlistan. The last time Mīrzā invited Yunus Khān, he had taken possession of Tashkent. Babur mentions in the *Baburnama* that local texts referred to Tashkent as Shash and Chach. He gave Tashkent to Khān in AD 1485 and till AD 1503, it along with Shahrukhiya country was owned by the Chaghatai Khāns.

Till AD 1494, the Moghūl Khānship existed in the hands of Yunus Khān's younger son and half-brother of Babur's mother, Sulṭān Mahmud Khān. Umar Shaikh Mīrzā's offending behaviour had been upsetting Mahmud Khān and his elder brother Sulṭān Ahmad Mīrzā, the ruler of Samarkand. Ahmad Mīrzā and Sulṭān Mahmud Khān forged an agreement. The former married his daughter to the latter. Soon they led their army against Umar Shaikh Mīrzā. The first pack of the soldiers advanced along the south of the Khujand-water and the second along its north.

But the universe had planned something different which neither Ahmad nor Mahmud would have thought of.

The fort of Akhsi was situated above a deep and steep gorge, and misfortune was knocking at the doors of Babur.

On 8 June of AD 1494, Umar Shaikh Mīrzā met with an accident in the palace that stood by the steep edge of the gorge while feeding the birds he adored a lot.

Babur writes, 'Umar Shaikh Mīrzā flew, with his pigeons and their house, and became a falcon.'*

The twelve-year-old prince had lost his father who was just thirty-eight years old then.

Umar was born in Samarkand in AD 1456 to Tīmūrid emperor Sulṯān Abu-Sa'id Mīrzā. He was the fourth son after Sulṯān Ahmad Mīrzā, Sulṯān Muhammad Mīrzā and Sulṯān Mahmud Mīrzā. His father, Sulṯān Abu-Sa'id Mīrzā, was born to Sulṯān Muhammad Mīrzā. Muhammad Mīrzā was born to Timur Beg's third son, Miran-Shah Beg. Umar Shaikh Mīrzā I and Jahangir Mīrzā were his elder brothers and Shahrukh Mīrzā was the younger.

Abu-Sa'id Mīrzā had given him Kābul and was allowed to proceed under the guardianship of Baba-I-Kābuli. In AD 1456, he was called back to Samarkand from Tamarisk Valley for the circumcision ritual, followed by a grand feast. After the feast was over, following the tradition of Timur Beg, he gifted Andijān to Umar Shaikh. Similarly, Timur had gifted Ferghana to his son Umar Shaikh Mīrzā (elder) as a gift on the circumcision ceremony. Umar Shaikh Mīrzā went to Ferghana with his assigned guardian Khudai-Birdi Tughchi.

Details of Umar Shaikh

Umar was short and stout. He sported a round beard on a choppy face. His dressing sense was a bit peculiar, and he wore an absurdly tight tunic.

Babur has humorously elaborated on it: 'He (Umar) used to wear his tunic so very tight that to fasten the strings he had to draw his belly in and, if he let himself out after tying them, they often tore away.'†

* Babur, Annette Susannah Beveridge [editor and translated], interpolated account of Bābur's mother's family, *The Bābur-nāma in English* (Memoirs of Bābur), London: Luzac and Co, 1922, p. 13.

† Babur. Abdul Rahim Khan-i-Khanan (translated), *Tuzk-e Babri*, Delhi: Akbar, 1589. p. Folio 7. This manuscript is available in National Museum, New Delhi. The Persian translation was done from the original Turkic manuscript of Babur. This was translated by author from the copy kept at National Museum, New Delhi.

Unlike the regular four-fold (*char-pech*) style, he used to tie his turban in the single fold (*dastar-pech*). When not in court or the temperature around was not so hot, he would wear a simple Moghūl Cap. From a general contemporary point of view, Umar wasn't too fond of good food and dressings.

Umar had got religious traits from his father Abu Sai'd. Abu was a determined Hanafi *Mazhabi* and followed the same as religiously as possible. He never missed his five-time prayers and read the Holy Qur'an very frequently. Even though the Islamic code allowed him to avoid prayers and fasting during wartime, he made no exception. He volunteered to be a disciple of Khwaja Ahrar.[3]

Nassiruddin Ubaidullah Ahrar, popularly known as Khwaja Ahrar was a *Hanafi Maturidi* member of the Golden Chain of the *Naqshbandi* Sufi order in Central Asia.[*] He was born in Samarkand, Uzbekistan in AD 1404 to a religious and devout Muslim family.[†] Khwaja Mehmood Shashi bin Khwaja Shihabuddin was his father. The traditions say that Ahrar's forefathers had migrated from Baghdad and his lineage connected to Abu Bakr Siddique from his paternal side and Umar Farooq from the maternal side.[‡]

Khwaja's father was a farmer and a Hajji following the footsteps of his father Shahabuddin Shahsi. Shahabuddin had good agricultural trade. His maternal grandfather Khwaja Daud was the son of a well-known Sufi Mystic Khwaja Khawand. Khawand was the son of Umar Baghistani, a famous shaikh who was honoured by Bahauddin Naqshband.[§]

As per the local folklore of Tashkent, various miracles occurred in Ahrar's life right from his birth. Ahrar's initial studies happened in Tashkent itself under the guidance of his uncle Ibrahim Shashi.[¶]

---

* Mir Abd al-Avval Nishapuri, Malfuzat Ahrar, *Markaz-i Našr-i Dānišgāhī*, Tehran: Presses universitaires d'Iran, 2002, p. 208.

† Alī ibn Ḥusayn Kāshifī Ṣafī, Muhtar Holland (trans.), *Beads of Dew from the Source of Life*, Oakland Park: Al-Baz Publishing, 2001, p. 245.

‡ Mawlānā Šayḫ, Masatomo Kawamoto, *Maqāmāt-i Ḫwāǧa Aḥrār: taḏkira-i Ḫwāǧa Nāṣir ad-Dīn 'Ubaydallāh Aḥrār*, Tokyo: Mu'assasa-i Muṭāla'āt-i Zabānhā wa Farhanghā-i Āsiyā wa Āfrīqā, 2004, p. 21.

§ Ṣafī, Alī ibn Ḥusayn Kāshifī, Muhtar Holland (trans.), *Beads of Dew from the Source of Life*, Oakland Park: Al-Baz Publishing, 2001, p. 245.

¶ Jürgen Paul, 'Forming a Faction: The Ḥimāyat System of Khwaja Ahrar', Cambridge: Cambridge University Press, 2009, *International Journal of Middle East Studies*, Vol. 23, pp. 533–48.

In AD 1425, when he had turned twenty-one, Ibrahim took him to Samarkand for further studies. Somehow, his constant ill health did not support these excursions. He had to quit and while fighting the illness, he dreamt of Jesus Christ. The tradition says that Jesus told him, 'I'll teach you.'

He gained mystic training and returned home at the age of twenty-nine. Then, he began to farm after having bought a piece of fertile land which soon began to give him a big yield. Not more than a decade later, he ended up getting more fertile lands, establishing businesses, popular Turkish baths and *Khānqahs*. He had also begun to send his trade caravans into China.[*] Many historians claim that he had become one of the richest men in Central Asia in that epoch.[†] It is said that most of his wealth was invested in religious endowments (*Waqf*). It is claimed that he had done abundant charity in this phase. He owned more than 3500 acres of cultivable land at one time.

Khwaja Ahrar had been extremely involved in the socio-economic activities of Transoxiana. Despite being born into a poor family, he became the richest man in the kingdom as he matured to a certain age.[‡] All dervishes of the time held him in high regard. Among the famous disciples, Maulana Abdur Rahman Jami was one of the important ones.[§] He learned most of the things under the counsel of his father. He was well guided by Khwaja Yaqub Charkhi in the later phase.[¶]

As the story goes, Ahrar had very strong characteristics of a *socialist*. He went to the Tīmūrid prince ruling at Samarkand to discuss the troubling conditions of the people. Sulṭān's chief aid showed no interest and disallowed his entry into the court. Agitated Ahrar bragged, 'I have been commanded by God and His messenger

[*] Hamid Algar, Muriel Atkin, Walter Feldman, Dru C. Gladney, Edward J. Lazzerini, Beatrice Forbes Manz, Christopher Murphy, Oliver Roy, Isenbike Togan, Jo-Ann Gross (ed.), *Muslims in Central Asia: Expressions of Identity and Change*, Durham: Duke University Press, 1992.

[†] Jo-Ann Gross, 'The Economic Status of a Timurid Sufi Shaykh: A Matter of Conflict or Perception?' 1998, *Iranian Studies*, Vol. 21, p. 85.

[‡] Jo-Ann Gross, Asom Urunbaev, 'The Letters of Khwaja 'Ubayd Allah Ahrar and his Associates', 2004, *Journal of Islamic Studies*, Vol. 15, pp. 224–226.

[§] Jo-Ann Gross, 'Aḥrār, ʿUbaydallāh', in *Encyclopaedia of Islam*, THREE, edited by Kate Fleet, Gudrun Krämer, Denis Matringe, John Nawas, Devin J. Stewart.

[¶] Alī ibn Ḥusayn Kāshifī Ṣafī, Muhtar Holland (translator), *Beads of Dew from the Source of Life*, Oakland Park: Al-Baz Publishing, 2001, p. 250.

to come here.' Still, Sulṭān's aid showed no concern. Dejected, Ahrar then wrote the name of the Sulṭān on the wall and having erased it with his saliva said, 'God will replace you with a King who is concerned for his people,' and left.

Some days later, another Tīmūrid Sulṭān Abu Sa'id Mīrzā (Babur's grandfather), gathered his forces and attacked Samarkand thereby winning it for himself. This appeared like an opportunity to Khwaja Ahrar. This union of Abu Sa'id Mīrzā and Khwaja Ahrar lasted for decades and proved to be fruitful for the whole kingdom. Khwaja had a strong influence on Abu Sa'id's family. He had given the name to Babur in his infancy as Zahiruddin Muhammad literally means, *Defender of Religion.*

Khwaja Ahrar often visited Abu and considered him to be no different from his son. Abu Sa'id Mīrzā was quite a well-read person and appreciated art from the bottom of his heart. He had read the poems of Amir Khusrau, Nizami Ganjawi and Jalaluddin Rumi and history through the *Shahnameh*[4] of Ferdowsi. Although he had an affinity for poems, he had never shown any desire to compose one. All these characters are reflected deeply even in Babur's father Umar Shaikh.

In Babur's opinion, Umar was a man of justice . . . a characteristic which can be seen in the following instance. Once he heard the news of a caravan returning from Kara Khitai getting overwhelmed by snow in the mountains of Andijān. It was reported to him that only two out of the 1000 had been able to escape safely. He sent out his people to the place of disaster to collect the abandoned goods. Although the legatee of those who succumbed to the disaster lived far away in Khurāsān and Samarkand, and he was seeing economic disasters, Umar arranged to call them all and return their properties in a couple of years. Babur found him to be a truthful and generous leader. He was sociable, eloquent, sweet-spoken, audacious and bold. In Babur's words, his swordsmanship was well-known and stories of it spread far. It is said that he used to lead from the front and never liked to be shielded by his soldiers. He had shown his skills and bravery at the gates of Akhsi and Shahrukhiya.

Though he was a good wielder of the sword, he was a mediocre archer, but of all, he was too strong at using the fist. Babur says that hardly any could bear his blow. The ambitious Umar brought peace through wars.

Although Umar's father Abu followed religion with utmost sincerity and it had quite a good impact on him, he was an alcoholic in his young years. It was due to childhood learnings that he could recite the Qur'an, Sirrah and Hadiths quite eloquently. As he grew, intoxicating confects became an essential part of his life, while alcohol got distanced. Perhaps it had begun to affect him mentally. His sexual desires were high, and he spent enough time quenching them. Though he was not very fond of playing games, he was a skilled hand at the draught board.

Battles have always been part and parcel of Tuks[5] life and it was no different for Umar Shaikh. Of all the battles fought, three were crucial in his life. Interestingly, his first ranged battle was with the Khān of Mongols, Yunus Khān. The Khān married his daughter to Umar in AD 1475. This battle was fought in the region, north of Andijān on the banks of Syr River at a place called the Goat-Leap. The place had got such a name because the foothills narrowed down the flow of water so much that even a goat could leap across.

Yunus Khān had defeated Umar Shaikh in this war. The latter was made a prisoner. But Yunus showed generosity and let him travel back to his place in Andijān safely. The battle took its name after its location and thus has been known as the Battle of the Goat-Leap. Umar Shaikh's second major battle occurred on the banks of Aras River[6] in Turkistan against the Aūzbegs. The latter had attacked while returning from a raid near Samarkand. This battle is worth remembering for many reasons: Umar crossed the river while ice floated upon it. He gave the Aūzbegs a good bashing. Babur praised his father for this battle. He has said that Umar distributed the booty among the owners without keeping even a bit for himself.

Umar was beaten in the third major battle that he fought with Babur's uncle Sulṯān Ahmad Mīrzā at Khwas, a place between Shahrukhiya and Aūrā-tīpā.

As mentioned earlier, Abu Sa'id had given Umar Shaikh the land of Ferghana. Sulṯān Ahmad Mīrzā, Umar's elder brother had granted him Tashkent and Sairam. All three stayed in his possession for quite some time. Umar Shaikh had even taken away Shahrukhiya by a timid trick and had held it for a while. It was not very late when

Tashkent and Shahrukhiya slipped out of his hands. He was only left with Ferghana, parts of Khujand and Aūrā-tīpā. Sulṭān Ahmad Mīrzā lost Tashkent to Moghūls in the battle fought at the banks of Chirciq River in AD 1488.

Sulṭān Mahmud Khān of Moghūlistan and Sulṭān Ahmed Mīrzā, the Tīmūrid ruler of Samarkand and Bukhara were involved in this conflict. The Tīmūrids had to taste the defeat at the hands of Moghūls. One of the prime reasons for this defeat was the defection of 3000 Aūzbegs under the command of Muhammad Shaybāni Khān.*

Sulṭān Mahmud Khān reached the banks of Chirciq River, crossing the suburbs of Tashkent. On the opposite edge stood the Tīmūrid Army of Sulṭān Ahmad Mīrzā. Initially, it appeared as if it was impossible to cross the river Chirciq and both armies camped on the opposite banks for three days. Mīrzā's army had Muhammad Shaybāni Khān, the son of Shah Budagh Oghlan, the son of Abul-Khayr Khān ibn Dawlat Shaykh ibn Ibrahim Khān. Muhammad Shaybāni Khān was unable to hold his own in the steppes, so he betook himself to Transoxiana and became a retainer of one of Sulṭān Ahmed Mīrzā's Amirs named Mir Abdul Ali. Shaybāni Khān was in control of 3000 men. During the halt of three days, devilish thoughts had engulfed Shaybāni's mind. He sent a message to Sulṭān Mahmud Khān, asking if he would meet and confer with him. They met as soon as the darkness kissed the surroundings. An understanding cooked between the two and it was decided that the next day, Mahmud would attack Mir Abdul Ali, the master of Muhammad Shaybāni Khān. The same happened the next day and Abdul Ali, took it upon himself to throw the army into disorder, and then to take flight.†

Drawn up in the battle array, the Moghūl army and infantry passed the river. The Tīmūrids began to act and soon, the Moghūl cavalry too entered the scene. As thought by Sulṭān Mahmud and Shaybāni, the Moghūl Army directed its force against Mir Abdul Ali. This was the moment when Muhammad Shaybāni defected with his 3000 Aūzbegs and he began the plunder the army baggage (portable military equipment). In fact, in a very disordered rabble began to take

* Mirza Muhammad Haida Dughlt, N. Elias and Sir Edward Denison Ross (trans.), *A History of the Moghuls of Central Asia: The Tarikh-i-Rashidi,* New York: Cosimo Inc., 2008, p. 696.

† Ibid.

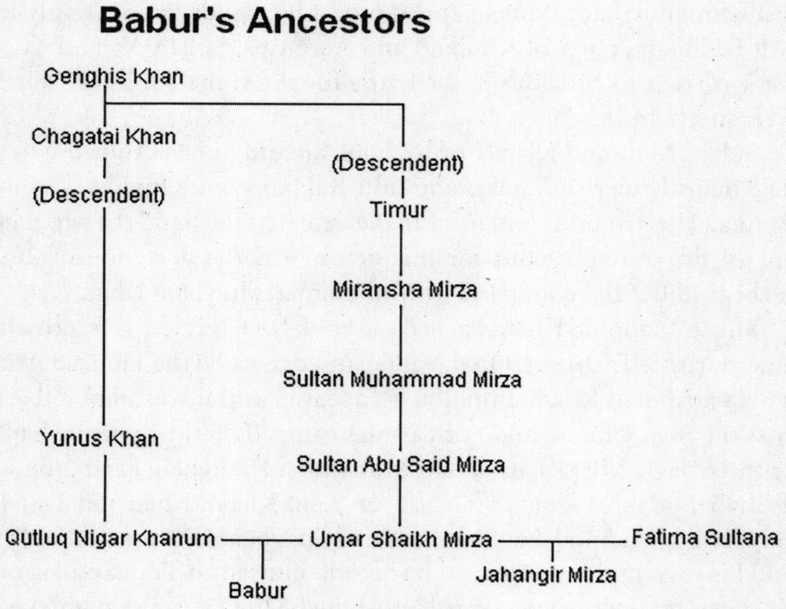

Figure 2: Babur's Ancestry

away the baggage of the Sulṯān Ahmed Mīrzā's army which made them to fly away from the battle. But since the Chirciq River, which the people of Tashkent at that time called Parak, lay ahead of them, most of his soldiers drowned in it. The troops of Sulṯān Ahmed Mīrzā suffered one of the worst defeats. Being discomfited and beaten, he fled to Samarkand. Peace was again brought between the Sulṯān Mahmud Khān and Sulṯān Ahmed Mīrzā.*

The latter handed over Tashkent to his younger brother, Babur's father, Umar Shaikh Mīrzā. From then onwards, Umar retained the Tashkent.

Umar's Children

Babur was the eldest among the three brothers and seven daughters. He was born from Qutluq-Nigar Khānum. Babur in his memoir does mention that only eight grew up, and hence perhaps some died at

* Ibid.

birth. Jahangir Mīrzā was Umar's second son with Fatima Sulṭān Agha. He was born two years after Babur's birth. Fatima Sulṭān was the daughter of one of the begs of Mogul Tumen.[7] [8] Nasir Mīrzā, four years younger than Babur and the third son of Umar Shaikh Mīrzā, was born to Umid Aghacha. She was from Andijān.

Khānzada Begum was the eldest daughter of Umar born to Qutluq-Nigar Khānim. She was Babur's sibling and was five years older than him. Babur has mentioned the agony relating to Khānzada. He had to abandon Samarkand for the second time in AD 1500 after a five-month siege by Aūzbeg lord Shaybāni Khān. He had tried his best to win the war, but no help or reinforcement had come from any beg. The period Babur describes as one of the most despairing and helpless ones although the records find that his worst days were yet to come. Khānzada had only one boy child with Shaybāni Khān. Babur saw him as a pleasant child and he was named Khurram Shah. When Khurram grew a bit, he was given the Balkh. However, he died soon. In that period, Khānzada Begum was in Merv. Shah Ismail had ravished Shaybāni Khān's land in the Battle of Merv and it was a gigantic loss to the Aūzbegs. Shah Ismail showed enough decency to not misbehave with Babur's sister. She was respectfully escorted back to Kunduz.

It was a moment of relief and ecstasy for both Babur and her. Babur met her after ten years and the expressions in his memoir truly reflect the deep emotion they shared. He had gone to meet her with Muhammadi Kukuldash (we don't have many details about this person). Interestingly, Babur writes that neither Khānzada nor people around her could recognize him and it took a bit of time to recall the familiarity.

The other daughters born to Umar were:

- Mihr Banu Begum was the second daughter of Umar Shaikh Mīrzā. She was a sibling to Nasir Mīrzā and two years younger than Babur.
- Shahr Banu Begum was the third daughter and sibling of Nasir Mīrzā. She was eight years younger than Babur.
- Yadgar Sulṭān Begum was the fourth daughter of Umar Shaikh, and she was born to a concubine, Agha Sulṭān. She was eleven years younger than Babur.

- Ruqaiya Sulṯān Begum was the fifth daughter and was born to Makhdum Sulṯān Begum. Makhdum was known for her dark and deep eyes and was accordingly called 'begum with dark eyes'.

The last two were born after Umar's death. Babur has not given any records of their name in the *Baburnama*.

Yadgar Sulṯān Begum was raised by Babur's maternal grandmother Aisan Daulat Begum. Shaybāni Khān had attacked and taken Andijān and Akhshi from Babur. During this struggle, Yadgar fell prey to Sulṯān Abdul Latif's lust and was taken away as a spoil of war. Later during the battle of Ab Darrah Pass in AD 1511, Babur defeated Sulṯān Hamza and other sulṯāns who were his allies. He got his sister back and reclaimed Ḥisār. During Babur's throneless period, Ruqaiya Sulṯān Begum was taken by Sulṯān Jani Beg. She gave birth to two children, but they did not survive. It is said that she lost her life in despair. It was sometime in the period between Babur losing Ferghana to gaining Kābul.

Babur's Mother's Family

Yunus Khān descended from Chagatai Khān, the second son of Genghis Khān. He was fathered by Sulṯān Vais Khān. Following is the family progression:*

1. Genghis Khān
2. Chagatai Khān, Khān of the Chagatai Khānate, AD 1226–1242
3. Mutu Khān
4. Yesünto'a
5. Baraq Khān, Khān of the Chagatai Khānate, AD 1266–1270
6. Du'a, Khān of the Chagatai Khānate, AD 1282–1307
7. Esen Buqa I, Khān of the Chagatai Khānate, AD 1310–1318 (First Khān to convert to Islam)
8. Tughlugh Timur, Khān of Moghūlistan:1347–1363 AD, Khān of the Chagatai Khānate: AD 1360–1363
9. Khizr Khoja, Khān of Moghūlistan, AD 1389–1399
10. Muhammad II, Khān of Moghūlistan, AD 1408–1415

* Ibid.

11. Sher Ali Oghlan
12. Vais Khān, Khān of Moghūlistan, first reign: AD 1418–1421, second reign: AD 1425–1429
13. Yunus Khān, Khān of Eastern Moghūlistan: AD 1462–1487, Khān of Moghūlistan, AD 1469–1487

Yunus Khān and Esen Buqa II were sons of Vais Khān. Yunus' mother was either a daughter or granddaughter of Shaikh Nuru'd-din Beg, a Turkistani *Kipchaq*[9] [10] supported by Timur Beg. Unprecedented things happened after the demise of Vais Khān. The Moghūls were split into two camps. A smaller share remained for Yunus while the larger one went to Esen. Yunus had substantial support from the Biran and Chiras tribes. Airazan, a Barin Tumen Beg and Beg Mirik Turkman, a Chiras Tumen Beg came with Yunus Khān. They took around 4000 Moghūl house heads to Ulugh Beg, who had taken away Yunus' elder sister for his son 'Abd al-'Aziz. Ulugh Beg did not behave soundly with them—they were imprisoned. This phase had an important impact on Moghūl history.

Yunus Khān moved towards Iraq and stayed in Tabriz for a year. After a year, he went to Shiraz in the initial days of AD 1435 or the last days of AD 1434, where lived Shah Rukh,[11] [12] the second son of Sulṭān Ibrahim. It was only five or six months after Yunus' visit that Ibrahim died on AD 3 May of AD 1435, at the young age of forty. Ibrahim's son Abdullah Mīrzā was crowned as the new ruler of Shiraz. Yunus Khān did not miss the opportunity, and he began to mend his relationship with Abdullah Mīrzā. Yunus Khān became his retainer and paid respect as per protocol regularly.

Yunus Khān lived there for around seventeen to eighteen years. It was a period of turbulence between Ulugh Beg and his sons. Esen Buqa saw it as an opportunity and invaded Ferghana. In Babur's own words, Esen Buqa went on plundering the lands as far as Kand-i-Badam. He had not left even the prosperous Andijān and had captured every person in the city.

Sulṭān Abu Sa'id Mīrzā had already seized the throne of Samarkand and led an army beyond Taraz (Yany) to Aspara in Moghūlistan. Esen Buqa, Yunus' brother was beaten badly. Esen had to undo the further disasters and he decided to take Yunus' elder sister as his wife, who was formally the wife of 'Abd al-'Aziz.

He then invited Yunus Khān while the latter was camping in Khorasan and Iraq. He organized a big feast in Yunus's honour and even offered a long-term friendship. Yunus was proclaimed as the Khān of Moghūls. The relationship between Yunus and Esen had started to become better, for the latter was proclaimed as the Khān of the Moghūls. This had annoyed the Sagharichi Tumen Begs. They barged into the Moghūlistan fuming with anger against Esen.

But Yunus again proved his smarts. He went to them and took Aisan Daulat Begum as his wife.[13] She was the daughter of Mir Sher Ali Haji Kunji (Qunchin) Beg, the chief of Sagharichi Tumen Begs. This alliance gave enough benefits to Yunus. They raised him to the Khānship.

Abu Sa'id kept Mihr Nigar Khānum for his eldest son Sulṭān Ahmad Mīrzā. She never bore any child. Babur recalls that in the throneless era (AD 1499), she was taken away by Shaybāni Khān. But soon she was given *talaq* as Shaybāni lusted for Mihr Nigar Khānum's niece, Khānzada Begum, Babur's sister. She left Samarkand for Khorasan with Shah Begum, Yunus Khān's second wife in AD 1501–02. Then in AD 1505, both reached Kābul to meet Babur.

In that period, Shaybāni Khān was fighting Nasir Mīrzā at Kandahar. Babur set out for Lamghan in AD 1507–08. While he was doing so Mihr Nigar Khānum and Shah Begum went to Badakhshan escorted by Mīrzā Wais Khān. Mubarak Shah invited Mīrzā Khān to the Victory Fort on the banks of river Kokcha. The marauders of Mīrzā Abu Bakr Dughlat captured Mīrzā Khān along with Mubarak Shah, his wives and his people along with their families.

Qutlugh Nigar Khānum, Babur's mother was the second daughter of Yunus Khān and the eldest half-sister of Sulṭān Mahmud Khān and Sulṭān Ahmad Khān. She stayed with Babur in most of his guerrilla expeditions and even in his throneless time. She went to Allah's mercy on the day of Muharram of AD 1505, five or six months after Babur captured Kābul.

Khub Nigar Khānum was Yunus Khān's third daughter. She was given to Muhammad Hussain Korkan Dughlat in AD 1493 and bore a son and a daughter. Her daughter Habiba was given to Ubaid Khān. But when Babur captured Bukhara and Samarkand in AD 1511, Habiba stayed back with him. Sulṭān Muhammad Dughlat, her paternal uncle visited Babur being part of Sulṭān Sa'id's envoy. Habiba joined him and went to Kashghar. Her cousin Sulṭān Sa'id Khān was more than delighted to receive her there.

Khub Nigar's boy was named Haidar Mīrzā. He, after growing up, became a good support to Babur. He devoted himself to Babur's service for around four years. However, he was struck by a tragedy in AD 1512. His father was slain by Aūzbegs. Listening to this bad news, he decided to leave for Kashghar to be with Sulṭān Sa'id Khān.

Everything goes back to its source.
Pure gold, or silver or tin.

—Babur*

Haidar started to live a life of a staunch Muslim. Babur has praised Haidar extensively in *Baburnama*. Babur has said that he had mastered calligraphy, painting and arrow making, along with barb and string-grip makings. He had also developed into a mature poet and his writing skills reflected it quite clearly. Even the petitions he wrote to Babur were of a poetic quality.

Shah Begum was the Queen consort of Moghūlistan as the second wife of Yunus Khān. Although Yunus Khān had many women, only Shah Begum and Aisan Daulat Begum became mothers of his children. Shah Begum was one of the six daughters of Shah Sulṭān Muhammad, the Shah of Badakhshan. It is said that he was a descendant of Alexander the Great. Sulṭān Abu Sa'id Mīrzā took one of the other daughters of Sulṭān Muhammad. Her name was Shahzada Begum, and she gave birth to Aba Bikr Mīrzā.

Yunus Khān had two sons and two daughters with Shah Begum. The firstborn son, Sulṭān Mahmud Khān, was younger than all Asian Daulat Begum's daughters. He was initially called Khānika Khān in and around Samarkand. Next to Mahmud was Sulṭān Ahmad Khān who was popularly known as Alacha Khān. As per local traditions, he was called so because he killed many Qalmaqs on various occasions he met them in battles. In Moghūl and Qalmaq tongue, one who kills was called 'Alachi', but with time, his name became 'Alacha'. Both

* Babur, *Tuzk-e Babri*, Delhi: Akbar, 1589. p. Folio 11. This manuscript is available in National Museum, New Delhi. The Persian translation was done from the original Turkic manuscript of Babur. This was translated by the author from the copy kept at National Museum, New Delhi.

Mahmud and Ahmad find quite a significant place in the history of Moghūls.

Sulṭān Nigar Khānim, the youngest daughter of Yunus Khān, was given to Sulṭān Mahmud Mīrzā. She gave birth to one child from Mahmud who was named Wais Mīrzā but was popularly known as Mīrzā Khān. He crafted his place well in the Tīmūrid history. With the death of Sulṭān Mahmud Mīrzā in AD 1495, Nigar took Wais to her brothers who were then located in Tashkent. She ensured that no one got to know about this move of hers. Just a few years after she had joined her brothers in Tashkent, they gave her to Awiq Sulṭān Juji. He came from Juji Khān's lineage, the eldest son of Ghengis Khān and was the chief of the Aūzbeg Qazaqs. Shaybāni Khān had defeated Nigar's brothers and killed them, taking away Tashkent and Shahrukhiya in AD 1502–03. When a helpless Nigar failed to find a way out, she moved to Awiq Sulṭān in Moghūlistan. She was accompanied by a dozen Moghūl servants to guard her en route. Later, she became the mother of two daughters with Awiq. One daughter was given to Abdullah Quchin and the other to Rashid Sulṭān. Rashid Sulṭān was the son of Sulṭān Sa'id Khān.

Soon after, Awiq died and following the Turkic tradition of *yanglik*, Nigar was taken by his brother Qasim Khān. He was Khān of the Qazaq horde. It is said that no one kept the Qazaqs in such an orderly manner as Qasim did. Given his rank, he had quite a large army of 3,00,000 men.

When Qasim died, the Khānship went to Tahir, Khānim's stepson. Records state that Tahir was very close to her. Reflecting her appreciation for Tahir's affection, she said, 'Although you are [as] my child, and I neither think of, nor desire any son but you, yet I wish you to take me to my nephew, Sulṭān Sa'id Khān. For I am grown old, and I have no longer the strength to bear this wandering life in the deserts of Aūzbegistan. Take me where I may enjoy some quiet and repose.'*

She then offered to mediate for him and to obtain the support of the Moghūl Khagans against his foes. Taking into consideration the affection and commitments of his stepmother, he escorted her to the Moghūl Kashghar at the Moghūlistan borders. Impressed by the

* Ibid.

affection and care of Tahir, Sa'id did meet Tahir going against the tradition of the Genghis Family.

Daulat Sulṭān Khānim was the youngest child of Yunus Khān. It was during the Shaybāni Khān's Tashkent campaign of AD 1503 that she was forcefully taken as a concubine of his son, Timur Sulṭān. She became the mother of a daughter with Timur. Babur mentions that Daulat and her daughter got out of Samarkand with him in AD 1512 and took a long stay in Badakhshan. In AD 1520 she made it to her nephew Sa'id Khān in Kashghar.

3

The Amirs of Mīrzās

Return, O Huma, for without the parrot-down of thy lip. The crow will assuredly soon carry off my bones.

—Hasan Yaqub*

Khudai Birdi Tughchi Timur-Tash was an important Amir of Umar Shaikh. He was a descendant of Aq-Bugha Beg, who was the governor of Herat for Timur Beg. The story related to Khudai goes back to AD 1464 when Abu Sa'id Mīrzā had captured Shahrukhiya by defeating Juki Mīrzā. He had awarded Ferghana to Umar, Babur's father and Khudai Birdi Beg was made the head of Mīrzā's Gate. Babur mentions that although Khudai was only twenty-five years of age, his management skills were unparalleled. Just a few years had passed, when Khudai had become an important part of Umar's administration Ibrahim Begchik was on a plundering streak at Osh. But it had not been many years working for Umar, and Khudai thought of teaching a good lesson to Ibrahim. But fortune didn't side with him this time. Khudai was beaten and killed in the face-off with Ibrahim.

Khudai had begun to take all decisions on his own as Sulṭān Ahmad Mīrzā was retiring in the summer pastures of Aq Qacghai, located in Aūrā-tīpā to the east of Samarkand. Sulṭān Abu Sa'id Mīrzā was stationed at Baba Khaki, east of Herat. The news of the disaster was sent to the two Mīrzās through 'Abdu'l-Wahhab Shaghawal. It took four days to carry the message for 500 miles on the road.

* Ibid, Folio 13b.

The Mīrzās were blessed with good Amirs mostly. Hafiz Muhammad Beg Duldai was another one after Khudai. He was the son of Sulṭān Malik Kashghari. After the tragic death of Khudai Beg, he was elevated and sent to control Umar Shaikh Mīrzā's Gate. Unfortunately, he could not build the same rapport with the Andijān Begs, like Khudai. When Sulṭān Abu Sa'id Mīrzā was on the verge of dying, he gave up the job of keeping Umar's Gate and went to Samarkand to serve Sulṭān Ahmad Mīrzā. When Chir was falling, he was stationed in Aūrā-tīpā, which Umar Shaikh passed through on his way to Samarkand, following which he again chose to join Umar.

The generous Umar Mīrzā again gave him the command of Andijān. After serving Umar for quite some time he went on to join Sulṭān Mahmud Khān in Tashkent. He was given the acute responsibility for the guardianship of Wais Mīrzā and taking care of the city of Dizak. Babur mentions that by the time he had taken Kābul in AD 1504, Hafiz had made his way to Mecca, routing it through Hind. From then onwards he dedicated his whole life to the service of Allah and Islam till death touched his fate. He was known to be a simple person without any wicked sense.

Khwaja Husain Beg was another Amir of Umar Shaikh's. He was a well-mannered and a humble person. The records say that during alcohol festivities, he was able to improvise the gatherings with dance and music.

Shaikh Mazid Beg was one of the most important Amirs of Umar Shaikh. He was the first guardian of Babur and was excellent at running the administration. Babur found him to be one of the greatest Begs working for Umar Shaikh. But at the same time, he also mentioned his vicious nature and fondness for catamites. He was known to have served for Abul-Qasim Babur Mīrzā.

Abul-Qasim Babur Mīrzā was a Tīmūrid ruler in Khurāsān who reigned between AD 1449 and AD 1457. He was the great-grandson of Timur and the son of Ghiyath-ud-din Baysunghur ibn Shahrukh Mīrzā. Most of the people connected with studies of Tīmūrid history would be aware of the famous succession struggle that happened in the last years of Shahrukh. Babur* was one of those involved in that struggle. He allied with the great-great-grandson of Timur Khalil

* He is ancestor of Babur (Umar Shaikh's son).

Sulṭān. Together with Khalil, he plundered the army's baggage train and then made his way to Khurāsān. In AD 1488, Ulugh Beg also invaded Khurāsān to defeat Ala al-Dawla Mīrzā, who held Herat. Ulugh Beg defeated him at Tarnab and took Mashhad. In the meantime, his son Abdal-Latif Mīrzā conquered Herat. Ala al-Dawla Mīrzā fled to south-west Afghanistan. But Ulugh Beg considered Transoxiana to be more important and he left Khurāsān and Mashhad. Perhaps he had such a perception because he had ruled Transoxiana for decades. But things were not going to be so rosy for him. While returning, Babur's forces inflicted deep losses on his army. The cunning Babur saw the power vacuum in Khurāsān and quickly seized control. He also took control of Mashhad and Herat in AD 1449. Ala al-Dawla Mīrzā occasionally raided the region but only to a minimal effect. Together with Ulugh Beg and Sulṭān Muhammad (who gained control of central Persia), Babur became one of the three important Tīmūrid rulers.

But misfortune was waiting for him. The beautiful balance of power was soon unsettled by Sulṭān Muhammad as soon as he invaded Khurāsān. Interestingly, the first campaign of AD 1450 started badly for Babur with a defeat at Mashhad. It convinced him to cede parts of his territory. However, the mighty and brave Babur soon recovered. He took Sulṭān Muhammad prisoner and executed him. He then marched to Shiraz to take control of Sulṭān Muhammad's lands.

At this point, Jahan Shah of the Black Sheep Turkmen ended his loyalty to the Tīmūrids quickly putting Qum and Saveh under siege. Babur began to march against him but was forced to return to Herat, due to the overwhelming superiority of the Black Sheep's armies and a plot hatched against him by Ala al-Dawla Mīrzā. Most of Persia was taken from the Tīmūrids by AD 1452, except for Abarquh, which was conquered by the Black Sheep in AD 1453. While Kirman was temporarily conquered sometime later and a few attempts were made to seize Ray, Persia was never retaken by the Tīmūrids.

In AD 1454, Babur invaded Transoxiana, which was then under the control of Abu Sa'id Mīrzā in retaliation for the latter's seizure of Balkh. He quickly laid siege to Samarkand. However, the conflict between the two soon ended with an agreement to declare the Oxus

River as the border. The agreement remained in effect until Babur died in AD 1457. He would be soon succeeded by his son Mahmud.*

Now let's resume the narrative about the Amirs of Umar Shaikh. Hasan Yaq'ub, was another Amir of Umar Shaikh. According to Babur, he was mean but good-tempered, smart, brave and active man, along with being an exceptional archer. He was fond of playing polo and performed well in leapfrog. He controlled Babur's Gate post the unfortunate and tragic demise of Umar Shaikh Mīrzā.

Qasim Beg Quchin was another important Amir in the house of Mīrzās. He came from the ancient army-begs of Andijān. He controlled Babur's Gate after the departure of Hasan Yaqub Beg. Throughout his life as Babur's Amit, his authority kept shining more and more. The stories of his bravery spread for miles. There is a story about him beating Aūzbegs thoroughly. It was in the summers of AD 1499 near Kasan when he overtook the Aūzbegs and butchered them. This happened in front of Umar Shaikh. In AD 1501, he had gone to be with Khusrau Shah in Babur's guerrilla days. That was the period when Babur was on the verge of migrating from the land of Macha Hill to the region of Sulṭān Mahmud Khān. But Qasim Beg Quchin returned to Babur in AD 1504, boosting the former's courage. Babur welcomed him back with abundant affection and respect.

Just a year after Qasim's return, Babur attacked the Turkman Hazara raiders in Dara-i-Khwush. Qasim's presence made a great difference. Babur has mentioned that despite Qasim being in his silver years, he made better advances than many younger men in the fleet. Happy Babur rewarded him with the Bangash district[1] for his acute courage after returning from Kābul. By AD 1522, Babur took hold of Zamindawar.[2] By then, Qasim had devoted himself to the service of Allah completely. Babur describes him as Allah-fearing, a very pious 'Musalman' and, an abstainer from doubtful activities. It is said that he was an excellent judge and counsel, with a facetious attitude. He was illiterate, but his sense of humour was par excellence.

The region Zamindawar had served as the headquarters to the Durrani Pashtun tribe of the Alizai. The region had also turned

* Vasilii Vladimirovitch Barthold, Mir Ali-Shir, 'A History of the Turkman people', *Four Studies on the History of Central Asia*, Volume 3, 1962, p. 21.

into home to Nurzai, Barakzai and Alakozai tribes, besides Durrani and Kuchis tribes. The people of Zamindawar happened to become the strength of Ghazi Mohammad Ayub Khān[3] when he besieged Kandahar. Three centuries later, a Zamindawar contingent of tribesmen almost defeated Sir Donald Stewart's force at the Battle of Ahmed Khel (fought on 19 April 1880).[4] [*] Stewart was the lieutenant general of the British Indian Army during the Second Anglo-Afghan War. On 27 March 1880, Lieutenant General Stewart led a force of 7200 in a march from Kandahar to Kābul to reinforce the forces of General Roberts. General Roberts was the British commander in the Afghan capital of Kābul. It is said that the march ended up being an uphill one as the deserted land of Afghans was continuously shadowed by the local tribesmen.[†] The control of Zamindawar was regarded by the British-Indian forces as the key to the position for safeguarding the route between Herat and Kandahar during the Second Anglo-Afghan War.[‡]

Zamindawar was ruled by Zunbils before Islamization of the area. The title 'Zunbil'[5] can be traced back to the Middle-Persian original *Zūn-dātbar*, 'Zun the Justice-giver'. The geographical name Zamindawar would also reflect this, from Middle-Persian *Zamin-i dātbar* (Land of the Justice-giver).[§] They appear to have an identical faith system as the Hindus, as they primarily worshipped the Sun God.

Author André Wink writes:[¶]

> In southern and eastern Afghanistan, the regions of Zamindawar (Zamin I Datbar or land of the justice giver, the classical Archosia) and Zabulistan or Zabul (Jabala, Kapisha, Kia pi shi) and Kābul, the Arabs were effectively opposed for more than two centuries,

---

[*] 'Battle of Ahmed Khel', https://www.britishbattles.com/second-afghan-war/battle-of-ahmed-khel/

[†] Brian Robson, *The Road to Kābul: The Second Afghan War 1878-1881*, Stroud: Spellmount, pp. 192–197.

[‡] Zamindawar. Encyclopædia Britannica, Vol 28. s.l.: Cambridge University Press, 1911, p. 953.

[§] Bosworth, Clifford Edmund. Zamindawar. The Encyclopaedia of Islam. s.l.: Leiden: Brill, 2002, p. 439.

[¶] Wink, André. Al-Hind: Early medieval India and the expansion of Islam, 7th-11th centuries. s.l.: BRILL, 2002, pp. 112-114.

> from 643 to 870 AD, by the indigenous rulers the Zunbils and the related Kābul-Shahs of the dynasty which became known as the Buddhist-Shahi. With Makran and Baluchistan and much of Sindh this area can be reckoned to belong to the cultural and political frontier zone between India and Persia. It is clear however that in the seventh to the ninth centuries the Zunbils and their kinsmen the Kābulshahs ruled over a predominantly Indian rather than a Persian realm. The Arab geographers, in effect commonly speak of that king of "Al Hind" . . . (who) bore the title of Zunbil.

The south of the Hindu Kush was ruled by the Zunbils, who were the offspring of the southern Hephthalite. The north was controlled by the Kābul Shahis. The Zunbil and Kābul Shahis were strongly connected by culture with the neighbouring Indian subcontinent. The Zunbil kings worshipped a Sun God by the name of Zun from which they derived their name.

André Wink has said that the cult of *Zun* was primarily Hindu, not Buddhist or Zoroastrian.[*]

> In 643 AD the Sun worshiping, Zunbils attempted to defeat Islamized Persia assembling a large army. But the Persians defeated them badly. A decade had passed. 653-4 AD, an Arab general along with his 6,000 Arab Muslim troops penetrated the Zunbil territory and broke into the shrine of Zun (Sun God) in Zamindawar. It was located about three miles south of Musa Qala in today's northern part of Helmand Province of Afghanistan. The General of the Arab army mutilated the idol and plucked out the rubies which were its eyes, to persuade the Marzbān of Sīstān of the god's worthlessness.[†]

Willem Vogelsang makes similar assertions in his book. He states that between the eighth to ninth century AD, the eastern parts of modern Afghanistan were still not Islamized. He talks of their Hunnic or Turkic descent who were deeply connected to the Indian Subcontinent via the *dharmik* culture of Hindus and Buddhists.[‡] At the dawn of the

[*] Ibid, p. 118

[†] Ibid, p. 120

[‡] Sir H.M. Elliot, *The Hindu Kings of Kábul*, London: Packard Humanities Institute, 1867–1877, p. 3.

AD 870, the Saffarids from Zaranj, a city in the south-east of modern Afghanistan, conquered most of what is now Afghanistan. They established Muslim governors throughout the land. This is perhaps the time when the Islamization of land had begun. The situation worsened with the rise of the Ghaznavids in the tenth century.

Though the Zun idol was mutilated, there are texts which talk about it existing till the tenth century. One of the many mentions available is noted below:

> Kábul has a castle celebrated for its strength, accessible only by one road. In it there are Musulmáns, and it has a town, in which are infidels from Hind.—Istahkrí, AD 921[*]

In fact, these people are great evidence to support the theory that Persians were none other than one of the tribes which migrated out of India. They have Persian origin but possessed Central Asian features, and they worshipped Zun from which the Zunbils derived their name.[†]

Politically, and culturally the realms of Zabul and Kābul were considered a part of Al-Hind at the time of initial Muslim conquest. The *Chachnama* for example contains numerous references to Zabul under the corrupt form of *Ramal* or *Ranmal* showing close contacts and marriage relationships between the rulers and subordinate chiefs of Sindh, Kashmir and the king of Zabul in the seventh century. The relationships between these Indian rulers on the north-western frontier appear to have been in constant flux but it seems a safe conclusion that the king of Kashmir had established a claim of suzerainty over Zabul as he had over other Indian Kings.[‡]

So that was a bit of a narrative about the land of Zabuls. Now, we can move ahead, talking about the Umar Shaikh's Amirs.

One of his important Amirs was a descendent of Shaikh Ali Bahadur, one of the Timur's important Begs. Called Baba Quli ('Ali), he was made Babur's guardian after Shaikh Mazid Beg's death. In AD 1493, Sulṭān Ahmad Ali Mīrzā attacked Andijān and Baba Quli

---

[*] Ibid.

[†] André Wink, *Al-Hind: Early Medieval India and the Expansion of Islam, 7th–11th centuries*. s.l.: BRILL, 2002, pp. 112–114.

[‡] Ibid, p. 117.

went on to support him. Pleased by his valour and courage, Sulṭān awarded him Aūrā-tīpā. In AD 1494, Sulṭān Ahmad Mīrzā died, and 'Ali left Samarkand to join Babur. But while he was on the way, Sulṭān Ali Mīrzā, got into a sudden battle over Aūrā-tīpā with him. He was defeated and slain. Records say that his management skills were excellent, and he had a particularly good relationship with men who worked with him. It is also observed that he wasn't a pious Muslim—he neither offered prayers nor kept the Ramzan fasts. He can be considered a heathen. The story tells that when it came to being against the opponents, he was quite a tyrant.

Ali Dost Taghai was another well-known Amir. He was a Sagharichi Tuman Beg. Perhaps, he was a cousin of Babur's maternal grandmother, Aisan-Daulat Begum. Babur favoured him way more than Umar Shaikh Mīrzā had done, although Babur has also been quite critical of him on certain occasions. He goes on to say that no work came from him though people always praised him for being a person of work. He is said to have served Sulṭān Abu Sa'id Mīrzā. He claimed to have the power to bring on rain with the jadestone. Babur frowned and said, 'He was the Falconer, worthless by nature and habit, a stingy, severe, strife-stirring person, false, self-pleasing, rough of tongue and cold-of-face.'

Wais Laghari was another Amir, who came from the lineage of the Samarkand Tughchi people. He served mostly with Umar Shaikh Mīrzā and accompanied Babur on his guerilla excursions. Although he was known for his judgement and counsel skills, he was highly sectarian.

A brother of Ali Dost Taghai's too served as the Amir to the Mīrzās. His name was Mir Ghiyas Taghai and younger brother of Ali. None other than him was as aggressive in front of Sulṭān Abu Sa'id Mīrzā's Gate. He was in charge of the Mīrzā's square seal and was a close confidant. He was also a close friend of Wais Laghari. It was in AD 1494 that Kasan went to the hands of Sulṭān Mahmud Khān and then Mir Ghiyas became his support. He gained high favour from Mahmud Khān. It is said that he was one of the jolliest of all the Amirs and quite sporting when it came to challenges.

Ali-darwesh Khurasani was another important Amir of the family. He had served in the Khurasan cadet corps—one of two special troops of serviceable young men formed by Sulṭān Abu Sa'id

Mīrzā. It occurred in the days when he first began to arrange the government of Khurasan and Samarkand. Naturally, the second troop was called the Samarkand Corps. Ali-Darwesh was a man of valour and courage. Babur was a witness of his character of Bravery at the Gate of Bishkaran in AD 1500 during its conquest. His hands were too good at Nasta'līq. He was quite a flatterer to his masters and very avarice.

Qambar-'Ali Mughul of the Akhtachi was another Amir of a family full of varying characters. He was popularly called 'Skinner'. because when his father came to Ferghana, he worked as a skinner. He was Yunus Khān's water bottle bearer in the initial days, though later became a beg. The records state that till he did not become a beg, he was a smart man but later turned out to be slack. He used to talk a lot but most of it was empty.

4

Umar Shaikh Dies

'My own soul is my most faithful friend. My own heart, my truest confidant.'

—Babur*

Babur has mentioned that he was in the Char-Bagh of Andijān when Umar Shaikh met with his tragic end. Babur was designated as the governor of the place back then. He did not wait much; filled with shock and blanketed by deep grief, he rode home with a train of followers and retainers. He desperately wanted to go inside the fort.

But as Babur and his train reached closer to Umar's Gate, someone took hold of his bridle and moved off towards the Namazgah.

Though he was in just the twelfth year of his life, Babur was quite mature and very thorough with the environment around him. This thought crossed his mind that if a great ruler like Sulṭān Ahmad Mīrzā came to force, the Andijān begs would make over to him and the country. He also thought that if he was taken to Auzkint and the foothills around it, he should go to one of his mother's (half) brothers, Sulṭān Mahmud Khān or Sulṭān Ahmad Khān.

The news of Babur's probable departure spread quickly. When Khwaja Maulana-i-qazi and the begs in the fort heard of the same, they sent Khwaja Muhammad and tailor to the Babur. The tailor was

* Babur, Abdul Rahim Khan-i-Khanim (trans.), *Tuzk-e Babri*, Delhi: Akbar, 1589. This manuscript is available in National Museum, New Delhi. The Persian translation was done from the original Turkic manuscript of Babur. This was translated by author from the copy kept at National Museum, New Delhi.

probably there to craft the new dress for the new king-to-be. Along with this came an old servant of Umar Shaikh accompanied by the foster father to one of his daughters. The arrival of such personnel and conversation allayed some of Babur's fear. Khwaja took Babur to the citadel from the Namazgah. As Babur dismounted the horse, Khwaja Maulana-i-qazi and the begs appeared there at once. They tried to counsel the young Babur, who had just lost his beloved father. Soon the horde was engaged in mending towers and ramparts of the fort which had collapsed leading to the accidental demise of Umar Shaikh.

His death also meant that attacks could be anticipated. Everyone feared for Ferghana and the young Babur. Efforts were being made to keep the fort safe.

Furthermore, not many days had passed when Hasan and Qasim Quchin arrived. Hasan was the son of the great Beg Yaq'ub. They had arrived along with other begs with the assignment to recognize the threats around Margilal and related parts. Some literature does hint that they were called on before the demise of Umar Shaikh which means that they were on task to check the advance of Sulṭān Ahmad Mīrzā.

According to the writings, meeting Babur had given them some kind of energy and they had put their heart and mind in holding the fort strongly.

A turbulent time was about to start for Babur.

By then, Sulṭān Ahmad Mīrzā had already captured Aūrā-tīpā, Khujand and Margilan (all these cities have been spoken about in the chapter on Ferghana). And then he had reached Qaba where he had been reported to have halted. This perhaps is the Kouwa railway station. It was only a few miles away from Andijān and the threat seemed very evident. Ahmad Mīrzā did indeed not have any good intentions.

The traditional narrations tell us that Darwesh Gau, then a notable person of Andijān and once an ally of Umar Shaikh, was sentenced to death for his rebellious stints. The rebellions were rising but the Gau's death brought things to rest.

The duo of Khwaja Qazi and Auzun Hasan was sent to Sulṭān Ahmad Mīrzā to inform him of Babur's ascension after Umar Shaikh. Auzun Hasan was a cousin of Umar Shaikh's father-in-law.

Babur mentions in the *Baburnama* that Sulṭān Ahmad was a mild man, who, for any decision, completely relied on the opinion of his begs. The proposal from Babur's end wasn't very positively replied to.

But Babur believed that Allah was by his side and circumstances prevailed as such that after having begun from Qaba, Sulṭān Ahmad's team had to stop the expedition and return.

The records say that Qaba had a stagnant morass, which one had to pass only through a bridge. Ahmad's horde was a bit too big, and slowly horses and camels started drowning in the muddy pit. They eventually perished. Babur recalls that a similar instance had occurred three years ago at the passage of Chir. It is said that a murrain[1] [2] had appeared among the horses. They massed together and death occurred in bands.

If Babur's words are to be believed, Sulṭān Ahmad Mīrzā also feared the loyalty of his soldiers, who would otherwise lay their lives on one say of their Sulṭān. Hasan, the son of Yaqub was sent to meet Darwesh Muhammad Tarkhān who came from the side of Sulṭān Ahmad. Latter is known to be a distant uncle of Babur's mother and had long been loyal to Ahmad Mīrzā. The meeting occurred in a Namagah, a few miles away from Andijān. The discussions went well, and peace was made, following which Sulṭān Ahmad's forces retired.

But Babur's problems were not going to end soon. Sulṭān Mahmud Khān had begun to march along the north of Khujand and finally laid the siege of Akhsi.

Jahangir Mīrzā controlled Akhsi. He was being assisted by Ali Darwesh Beg, Mīrzā Quli Kukuldash and Muhammad Baqir Beg. His gate was being guarded by Shaikh Abdu'llah. Jahangir also had the company of a few big names like Wais Lagdhari and Mir Ghiyas Taghai. But the fear of Akhsi begs made them retreat. They went back to the Wais' Kasan district.[3] Here, Wais became guardian to Nasir Mīrzā[4] who was already staying there.

But the tide changed again as Sulṭān Mahmud Khān came nearer to Akhsi. The conspiracy to capture the power of Ferghana began to take shape. Mir Ghiyas joined Mahmud's service. Wais Lagdhari cunningly took Nasir Mīrzā to Sulṭān Ahmad Mīrzā, who entrusted him (Nasir) to Muhammad Mazid Tarkhān. Mazid was a close aide of his and the governor of Turkistan.

Finally, Sulṭān Mahmud Khān got a blue nose at the hands of Akhsi begs. They fought their lives out to keep the land safe from him. He had returned to Tashkent.

Babur had another big threat from the neighbourhood—from Mīrzā Abu Bakr Dughlat.

Mīrzā Abu Bakr Dughlat was an Amir of the Dughlat tribe, who ruled in the south-western part of the present Xinjiang Uyghur Autonomous Region of China till his death in AD 1514.[*] In AD 1465, he founded a kingdom in the Western Kashgaria at Yarkand. Yarkand was a fragment of Moghūlistan which included Khotan and Kashgar. He had annexed Kashgar in AD 1480.[†] He was grandson of Amir Sayyid Ali and son of Saniz Mīrzā. Sayyid Ali was the Amir in Kashgar and had regained control of the city by Dughlat dynasty after having expelled the Tīmūrid local ruler in AD 1435.

Abu Bakr's father and grandfather had been loyal to Yunus Khān. But Abu Bakr rebelled against him in AD 1479–80. Yunus Khān's son Ahmad Alaq took away Kashghar from him in AD 1499 but failed to hold it for long. After regaining Kashghar, Abu Bakr took his forces and began campaigning to conquer the entire neighbourhood, which included modern day Ladakh, Balur (around Gilgit), Badakhshan and other fragments of Moghūlistan.[‡]

In AD 1514, Sulṭān Said Khān took Kashgar from him. With age, his control had weakened. He feared losing Yarkand and Khotan next, and hence passed on the government to his eldest son Jahangir Mīrzā. Following the handing over of government, he attempted to flee to Ladakh, but failed.[§] He was just twenty miles north of Xaidulla when he was intercepted and killed by pursuers sent by Sulṭān Said Khān.

Babur mentions in the *Baburnama* that Abu Bakr was the one who never bowed to anyone in his lifetime and now after the demise

[*] Henry Walter Bellew, *History Of Káshgharia*, Foreign Department Press, 1875, p. 62.

[†] Martijn Theodoor Houtsma, *E.J. Brill's First Encyclopaedia of Islam, 1913–1936*, Laiden: BRILL, 1993, Vol. 5, p. 788.

[‡] Dughlát Muhammad Haidar, *The Tarikh-i-rashidi*, N. Elias. (ed.), Sir Edward Denison Ross (trans.), *The Tarikh-i-rashidi: A History of the Moghuls of Central Asia; an English Version*, London: S. Low, Marston and Company, 1895, pp. 253–4.

[§] René Grousset, *The Empire of the Steppes*; Naomi Walford (trans.), *The Empire of the Steppes: A History of Central Asia*, First English Edition, New Brunswick: Rutgers University Press, 1939, p. 497.

of Umar Shaikh Mīrzā, his eyes were all set on Ferghana. With Abu Bakr's desire to capture Babur's rightful land, he came closer and built a fort in the vicinity of Auzkint. He had gradually begun to lay waste to the land. Looking at the ravishing done by him, several begs led by the great Khwaja Qazi were sent to drive him out. The begs proved their worth, and the land was freed from him.

Babur seems to have been very thankful for his begs, whom he has deeply praised in his memoir.

A few days had passed since Babur's father's demise. Several counter-attacks had to be organized to keep the land safe in Babur's hands.

Meantime, Babur's grandmother, Shah Sulṯān Begum, Jahangir Mīrzā and the whole harem along with the Akhsi begs had come to Andijān. As they arrived, the customary mourning was fulfilled, and food and victuals were given to the poor.

As the circumstances threatened to get direr, the focus was laid completely on setting administration rights and organizing the army order.

Following were the major changes made:

1. Hasan was given the responsibility of guarding Babur's Gate and administering the Andijān government.
2. The responsibility of Osh was given to Qasim Quichin.
3. Akhsi and Margilal's responsibility went into the hands of Auzn Hasan and Ali Dost Taghai.
4. The rest of loyal Umar's begs and brave warlords were each assigned district, land, designation in court, or some stipends were committed.

On the other hand, after being kicked out, Sulṯān Ahmad Mīrzā contracted high fever on his route back home. His health began to deteriorate badly. He died in July AD 1494 at the age of forty-four just as he reached Aksu.

Currently, Aksu is a city and the seat of Aksu Prefecture, Xinjiang, China. It lies at the northern edge of the Tarim Basin. The name is derived from Turkic Aksu which literally means 'white water'. This term is used for both the oasis town and the Aksu River. Currently, it is divided into two parts, separated by the Aral city. The northern part hosts the city centre, while the southern part is occupied by the Taklamakan Desert.

According to the primary sources, Aksu was known as Gumo at least from the former Han dynasty (125 BC to AD 23) to the early Tang dynasty (AD 618–907).* During the reign of Hams, the kingdom of Gumo comprised 3500 households with a population of around 24,500. Interestingly around 18.3 per cent of the population bore arms. The three major minerals produced were copper, iron and orpiment.†

The Buddha Dharma had reached the Chinese Land through India. In that period (when Buddha Dharma reached China) Aksu, was known as Bharuka,‡ Bohuan and Baluka§, Bolujia (in Pinyin) and Po-lu-chia (in Wade-Giles). According to the 'Great Tang Records on the Western Regions', Xuan Zang referred to the place as Baluka during his visit in AD 629. As per his records, there were tens of Sarvastivadin Buddhist monasteries with more than a thousand monks in the kingdom. He stated the dimensions of the kingdom being 600 li (Chinese Mile) from east to west, and 300 li from north to south. Its capital was said to be six li in circumference. Xuan Zang reported that the 'native products, climate, temperament of the people, customs, written language and law are the same as in the country of Kuci or modern Kucha', around 200 miles to the east, 'but the spoken language is somewhat different' from the Kuchean language, which is also known as Tocharian B and West Tocharian. He spoke about the export of fine cotton and hemp cloth to the neighbouring country.

The period between the seventh to early ninth centuries saw abundant contest for power. The Chinese Tang Dynasty, the Tibetan Empire and the Uyghur Empire contested to gain control of Aksu. The Tibetan Empire seized Aksu in AD 670, but Tang forces reconquered the region in AD 692. Then we have records that the Tang dynasty

---

* H.W.Bailey. Indo-Scythian Studies: Being Khotanese Texts Volume VII. s.l.: Cambridge University Press, 1985.

† Anthony François Paulus Hulsewé, *China in Central Asia: The Early Stage: 125 BC - AD 23* ; an Annotated Transl. of Chapters 61 and 96 of the *History of the Former Han Dynasty*, s.l.: Brill Archive, 1979, p. 162.

‡ Bernard Samuel Myers, *Encyclopedia of World Art*, New York: McGraw-Hill, 1959, p. 445.

§ Section 20 – *The Kingdom of Suoche* (Yarkand); the Western Regions according to the Hou Hanshu: The Xiyu Juan 'Chapter on the Western Regions' from Hou Hanshu 88. 2003.

in a campaign by Chinese General Tang Jiahui led the Chinese to defeat an Arab-Tibetan attack in the Battle of Aksu (AD 717 AD).*
On 15 August of AD 717, Uch Turfan and Aksu were attacked by the Turgesh, Arab and Tibetan forces. Qarluqs were serving under the Chinese command. Arsila Xian, a Western Turkic Qaghan was serving under the Chinese Assistant Grand Protector General Tang Jiahui. Together, they defeated the Arabs. The Arab commander and his army fled to Tashkent after they were defeated.† ‡

The Tibetan empire regained the Tarim Basin in the third decade of the eighth century. But the Tang dynasty again annexed the region just two decades later. In AD 751, the Battle of Talas took place between the Abbasids backed by the Tibetan Empire and the Tang Dynasty. This led to the gradual withdrawal of Chinese forces completely. Later, it became a land of contest only between the Uyghurs and the Tibetans.

Aksu was always a critical destination for all powers given its strategic position. It existed on the junction of the Northern-Tarim route Silk Road, and the dangerous route north via the Tian Shan's Muzart Pass to the fertile Ili River valley.§

Then came the era of one of the most dominating forces of that period. Between AD 1207–08, they had submitted to Genghis Khān. By AD 1220, Aksu had become the capital of the Kingdom of Mangalai. The region served as a part of the great Mongol Empire but in AD 1286, it slipped out of Kublai's Yuan Dyasty and went to Chagatai Khānate under the House of Ogedei. Yuan Dynasty and Chagatai Khānate had completely declined by the mid- and the end of the fourteenth century, respectively, following which Turkic powers and Mongol warlords took complete control.

Babur's Narrative Resumes

As Sulṭān Ahmad Mīrzā died, his loyal, demotivated begs agreed to invite Sulṭān Mahmud Mīrzā with the intent to offer him succession.

---

* *Insight Guides Silk Road*. s.l.: Apa Publications (UK) Limited, 2017.

† Christopher I. Beckwith, *The Tibetan Empire in Central Asia: A History of the Struggle for Great Power Among Tibetans, Turks, Arabs, and Chinese During the Early Middle Ages*, s.l.: Princeton University Press, 1993, pp. 88–89.

‡ Marvin Whiting, *Imperial Chinese Military History*, s.l.: iUniverse, p. 277.

§ George Frederick Wright, *Asiatic Russia, Volume 1*. s.l.: BiblioBazaar, 2009, pp. 47–48.

They sent a courier by the mountain road to him. On the other hand, Babur's grandfather, Abu Sa'id Mīrzā's eldest brother, Manuchihr Mīrzā's son Malik Muhammad was aspiring to become the ruler. The desperate begs, who were focused on their goals, had drifted away from Sulṭān Ahmad Mīrzā's camp aligning with Samarkand. Few say that Ahmad Mīrzā's control had weakened. He was failing to affect anything. His miscalculated and ineffective steps not only cost him his life but many other loyal patrons of the house.

Without wasting much time, Sulṭān Mahmud Mīrzā accepted the begs' invitation and went off to Samarkand, seating himself on the throne with ease. This made the begs happy. However, many soldiers, lower staff and peasants were disgusted. As one of his first moves, Sulṭān Mahmud Mīrzā exiled his cousin and son-in-law Malik Muhammad, and the three Mīrzās to Kuk-sarai to the prison from where no one ever returned. Later, he killed Malik Muhammad and a Mīrzā.

Except for Malik Muhammad, none aspired to be the ruler but the insecure Mahmud Mīrzā continued being as brutal as he could. The second thing that disgusted people was his tyrannical acts, even though he was excellent in the administration of regulations and revenues. After reaching Samarkand on the invitation of the begs, he began to mend new regulations and implemented a new model of taxation. Both were being forced onto people. His tyranny can very well be imagined from the treatment he was giving to the dependents of Khwaja Ahrar, under whose protection poor people always lived their lives free from dues and imposts. They were being oppressed massively. As a result, the populace was not happy. Babur mentioned that oppressive extractions were made from Khwaja's every child.

His begs, retainers and followers were equally tyrannical and vicious. The Hisaris and, in particular, the followers of Khusrau Shah had turned into habitual womanizers. They picked random women from the vicinity. Once when a beg took away a man's wife, he came to Khusrau Shah seeking justice. But the response of Khusrau could have only brought more anger in the man. He said, 'She has been with you for several years, let her be with him for a few days.'

The young sons of townsmen, shopkeepers, Turks and soldiers too could not venture out from their houses for fear of being taken for catamites. The people of Samarkand after having passed around twenty-five years under the kingship of Sulṭān Ahmad Mīrzā were deeply wounded in heart and soul by this oppression and vice. The rich, destitute—all opened their mouths to curse, all lifted the hands for redress.

Beware the steaming up of inward wounds.
For an inward wound at the last makes head;
Avoid while thou canst, distress to one heart,
For a single sigh will convulse a world.

—Babur*

The infamous tyranny of Sulṭān Mahmud Mīrzā ensured that he could not rule for more than half a year. During his reign, Sulṭān Mahmud Mīrzā had wedded his eldest son Masud Mīrzā with the second daughter of his eldest brother in the family, Sulṭān Ahmad Mīrzā. As a wedding gift, he had received gold, silver, almonds and pistachios. He did care to send a part of the gift to Babur through an envoy led by Abdul Qadus Beg.

Babur postulated that this envoy was sent to initiate a friendly relationship with Hasan, to make him look at Sulṭān Mahmud even for the rule of Andijān. But as an action, Hasan returned the envoy with no deliberations towards the intended proposal. But within half a year from then, he had begun to behave quite unusual and ill with people who cared and stood for Babur. Once it even began to appear that Hasan would dismiss the rulership of Babur and elevate Jahangir Mīrzā instead. Gradually, his intentions appeared very much known to the body of begs and the soldiers.

Looking at the upcoming threat Khwaja-i-qazi and Qasim Quchin accompanied by Ali-Dost Taghai met Babur's grandmother, Aisan Daulat Begum in the presence of other well-wishers. The meeting concluded with the decision to give quietus to Hasan for disloyalty by his deposition.

Babur's grandmother was a strong woman, and, in Babur's eyes, none could have matched her strength of perfect judgement and

* Babur, Abdul Rahim Khan-i-Khanim (trans.), *Tuzk-e Babri*, Delhi: Akbar, 1589. p. Folio 24. This manuscript is available in National Museum, New Delhi. The Persian translation was done from the original Turkic manuscript of Babur. This was translated by author from the copy kept at National Museum, New Delhi.

counsel. She was said to be very wise and far-sighted. Almost all affairs related to Babur were dealt with by her advice.

That day, Aisan's and Babur's mother was in the gatehouse of the stone fort and Hasan was in the citadel. With the intent to materialize the decision, Babur went to the citadel only to realize that Hasan had probably gone out for falconry. But the news reached him on the way, and he headed for Samarkand.

All the Hasan-sympathizer begs were arrested and the control of Babur's Gate was given to Qasim.

Soon the news reached Babur that on his way to Samarkand, Hasan had reached Kand-i-Badam. From there he went near the Khuqan sub-division with ill intentions to capture Akhsi. Without wasting any time, Babur sent out several begs and brave soldiers to counter him. Hasan with his men attacked the party sent by Babur in the night while they rested. But fortune was not ready to stand by Hasan. He was hit by an arrow from one of his men.

If you have done ill, keep not an easy mind,
For retribution is Nature's law.

—Babur*

Now, the tide of time had begun to turn a bit for Babur, but this fortune didn't last too long for the chessboard king.

In January of AD 1495, Sulṯān Mahmud Mīrzā succumbed to a six-day violent illness at the age of forty-three. His Amir, Khusrau Shah unsuccessfully tried to conceal the the death to lay his hand on Mīrzā's deep treasure. It was naïve of him to assume that the news could be concealed. It spread through the town like a wildfire. The people of Samarkand were more than delighted to have received the news. Then came the phase when the populace rose in tumult against Khusrau Shah. But Ahmad Haji Beg and the Tarkhāni begs somehow succeeded in mitigating the uprising, which might have led to Khusrau's lynching. They ensured to get Khusrau a way out to Ḥiṣār safely with an escort.

Sulṯān Mahmud had given Ḥiṣār and Bukhara to Sulṯān Masud Mīrzā and Baysonghor Sulṯān Mīrzā, respectively. But, just before his

* Ibid.

death, he had dismissed both governments and hence, neither of the two were present at the places in that moment.

After having arranged Khusrau's escape to Hisar, the begs mutually agreed to call Baysonghor Sulṭān Mīrzā to Samarkand from Bukhara to have him seated on the throne. He was just eighteen years old when he took the title of Padshah of Samarkand.

The country was going through a deep crisis. Sulṭān Mahmud Khān (Chaghatai) was persuaded by Junaid Barlas and other notable people from Samarkand to capture the town of Kan-Bai. The persuaded Mahmud Khān took his army and marched near the town. Hearing the news, Baysonghor Sulṭān Mīrzā marched out with his warriors to counter Mahmud. A massive fight took place near Kan-Bai. The Moghūl Army was led by Haidar Kukuldash. He and his fabulous soldiers were rained arrows on the opponents. But soon came the warriors of Ḥiṣār and Samarkand. Their ravishing attack brought all the Moghūls under their horses' feet. Haidar was made captive which led to the remaining Moghūl soldiers retreat. Baysonghor was brutal to the survivors. They were beheaded mercilessly in front of his eyes. It is said that his tent had to move three times as the pile of beheaded bodies kept growing.

While the political crisis was on, Ibrahim Saru appeared again. He was once dismissed by Abu Sa'id Mīrzā. He entered the fort of Asfara where Khutbah now read Baysonghor's name, and he was there to stand with him against Babur.

In May, Babur's army marched to crush this rebellion. Qasim, the lord of Babur's Gate, took charge and rammed in with his sharp sword along with Sulṭān Ahmad Tambal and Muhamamd Dost Taghai. Qasim kept marching, killing multiple people on his way to find Babur's uncle (his mother's brother) Mahmud Khān. Babur mentions that Qasim took away the championship, which in the Moghūl context meant that anyone who charged in to lead the campaign would be entitled to maximum benefits during each feast thereon.

Babur's guardian, Khudai-Birdi Beg was hit by a crossbow on the first day of the battle and died. One of Ibrahim Saru's crossbowmen was excellent and Babur acknowledged to have never seen anyone better than him. Instructions were given to construct pits in a couple of places to run mines. Attempts were being made to take the fort as quickly as possible. The siege lasted forty days. After having lost all the resources, he decided to go on in mediation with Khwaja-i-Qazi from Babur's side. In June of AD 1495, he came out with his sword and quiver hanging from his neck. Finally, he surrendered the fort to Babur.

On the other hand, problems were waiting for Babur in Khujand. For quite a long time, it had been dependent on Umar Shaikh Mīrzā's diwan, but after the turbulence caused by his death, they had begun to align towards Sulṭān Ahmad Mīrzā. Babur with the guidance of elders and well-wishers was able to crush this rising rebellion with ease. He sent out a strong party to Khujand which was now being controlled by Mir Moghūl's father, Abdul Wahhab Shaghwal and he didn't hesitate much to surrender. In that period, Sulṭān Mahmud Khān was in Shahrukhiya.

Babur wanted to settle things with Sulṭān Mahmud Khān on a good note. He considered him to be close and thought that only dialogue could settle things. Babur thought that if the bygone resentments were laid aside, it would bring the two close again. Thinking so, Babur went to Shahrukhiya. Sulṭān Mahmud Khān was seated in a tent in the middle of the garden. Babur entered the tent and knelt three times to honour him. In return, Mahmud Khān rose in respect. Both looked into each other's eyes, and the Khān returned to his seat. After the twelve-year-old Babur had again knelt, Mahmud called him to his side in a show of affection and fondness. The initial meeting between the two relatives indeed went well.

Babur spent three days there and set off for Akhsi and Andijān passing by the Kindirlik pass. At Akhsi, Babur circumambulated around his father's tomb. He left the place at the hour of Friday prayer and reached Andijān by the Band-i-Salar road between the evening and night prayers.

In the wilds of Andijān lived a tribe called Jigrak, located in the mountains between Kashghar and Ferghana. The tribe had around 6000 households and kept horses, sheep and yaks. With the ambiguity of borders, they also had the tradition of not paying any tribute. Babur sent out an army led by Qasim Beg to collect the tribute and ordered to have them distributed among the soldiers. Qasim nabbed around 20,000 sheep and 15,000 horses. He shared them with all of his men.

After this campaign against Jigraks, the army set out to Aūrā-tīpā. It was once held by Umar Shaikh Mīrzā, but after his demise, it had slipped into the hands of Sulṭān Ali Mīrzā on behalf of his elder brother Baysonghor Sulṭān Mīrzā. Hearing of Babur's upcoming attack, he ran to Macha hill country leaving land under his guardian, Shaikh Zun-nun Arghun. From halfway between Khujand and Aūrā-tīpā, Khalifa was sent as an envoy to Shaikh Zun-nun. Shaikh behaved wrongly on this occasion and ordered his death, but somehow Khalifa was able to escape and reach Babur in three days. Babur and his troops had almost reached Aūrā-tīpā, but the approaching winter forced them to turn back.

Although Babur's men retired, the new ally Mahmud Khān advanced. His men moved forward and Zun-Nun was unable to defend himself. Thus, he surrendered. Mahmud Khān offered the place to Muhammad Husain Kurkan Dughlat. Aūrā-tīpā remained under his control until AD 1503.

5

Sulṭān Husayn Mīrzā Khusrau Shah and Other Mīrzās

A brief about Sulṭān Husayn Bayqara Mīrzā

Sulṭān Husayn Bayqara Mīrzā was the Tīmūrid ruler of Herat from AD 1469 to AD 1506, barring some interruption in his reign in AD 1470.[*] He was a skilled statesman and had a keen interest in arts. He was renowned as a benefactor and patron of learning in his kingdom.[†] His reign was popularly known as the second Tīmūrid Renaissance.[‡] He has been described as 'the quintessential Tīmūrid ruler of the later period in Transoxiana'. Even Babur found his sophisticated court and generous artistic patronage as a source of inspiration.[§] One can even say that Sulṭān Husayn Bayqara was the last Tīmūrid ruler of consequence in Khurāsān.[¶]

He was born in Herat to great-grandson of Timur, Ghiyas ud-din Mansur Mīrzā and his wife Firuza Sulṭān Begum in July of AD 1438. Firuza was the daughter of Sulṭān Husayn. He came from the powerful

---

[*] Maria Subtelny, *Timurids in Transition: Turko-Persian Politics and Acculturation in Medieval Iran, Volume* 7, s.l.: Brill, 2007, pp. 43–44.

[†] Hans R. Roemer, Encyclopædia Iranica Foundation, 15 December 2004, https://iranicaonline.org/articles/hosayn-bayqara.

[‡] Warwick Ball, Norman Hammond Raymond Allchin, *The Archaeology of Afghanistan: From Earliest Times to the Timurid Period*, s.l.: Edinburgh University Press, 2019, p. 379.

[§] Lisa Balabanlilar, 'The Begims of the Mystic Feast: Turco-Mongol Tradition in the Mughal Harem', February 2010, *The Journal of Asian Studies*, Vol. 69, p. 128.

[¶] Hans R. Roemer. Encyclopædia Iranica Foundation, 15 December 2004, https://iranicaonline.org/articles/hosayn-bayqara.

Tayichiud tribe. He also claimed descent in the ninth generation from Khwaja Abdullah Ansari of Herat, also known as Pir-e-Herat.*

Ghiyas ud-din Mansur Mīrzā died when Sulṭān Husayn was just eight years old. It is worth noting that he was not a very influential one from the Tīmūrid family. Hence Sulṭān Husayn adopted the name Bayqara after his more illustrious grandfather, Bayqara Mīrzā I.† His mother suggested that he join the service of his older cousin Abul-Qasim Babur Mīrzā, who was the ruler of Herat in AD 1452.

However, it is said that Abul-Qasim Babur Mīrzā was a weak ruler who was prone to mismanagement. In an instance of a bad decision, he went into battle against Abu Sa'id Mīrzā.‡—an event which was disliked by Husayn Bayqara. He thought to shake hands with Abu Sa'id Mīrzā. Although Abu Sa'id was inclined to take him into his service, a rebellion on the part of Husayn Bayqara's relative, Sulṭān Awais Mīrzā, son of Muhammad Mīrzā, son of Bayqara Mīrzā, induced Abu Sa'id to arrest Husayn Bayqara and other relatives as a precaution. Eventually, on the plea of his mother, Firuza Begum, he was freed, and he re-joined Abul-Qasim Babur Mīrzā till the latter's death two years later.§

Babur's Narrative Resumes

It was the winter of AD 1495. Sulṭān Husayn Mīrzā led his army out of Khurasan against Ḥiṣār and went opposite of Tirmiz. Sulṭān Masud Mīrzā brought an army from Ḥiṣār to set them in Timriz. Khusrau Shah strengthened himself in Qunduz and sent his younger brother to help Sulṭān Masud Mīrzā.

Both armies kept looking at each other for the whole winter, lying on opposite banks of Timriz. No crossing happened. But the shrewd and experienced Hussain Mīrzā was not going to leave it that plain. He marched up to the river facing Qunduz straight. He sent Abdul Latif Bakshi with around six hundred serviceable men, down the river

* Maria Subtelny, *Timurids in Transition: Turko-Persian Politics and Acculturation in Medieval Iran, Volume* 7, s.l.: Brill, 2007, pp. 43–44.

† Ibid.

‡ Ibid.

§ Ibid.

to the Kilif ferry. Before Sulṭān Masud could get any sign of them, they had already entrenched themselves on the riverbank.

But even when he heard of it, he did not react as aggresively as expected. He did not march against those who had crossed the river. Instead, he broke up his camp and turned back towards Ḥisār. No one knows if this was suggested by Baqi Changhaniani or his half-brother Wali.

And then, Sulṭān Husayn Mīrzā crossed the river ferociously. He sent Badi'-al-Zaman Mīrzā, Ibrahim Hussain Mīrzā accompanied by Muhammad Wali Beg, Zunnun Arghun against Khusrau Shah. And against Khultan, he sent Muzaffar Husain Mīrzā accompanied by Muhammad Baranduq Barlas. Then, he made a move towards Ḥiṣār.

He was not going to take it so easy.

Soon, news of him nearing Ḥisār reached Sulṭān Masud. Masud decided to leave his fort and take refuge in Kam Rud Valley. He travelled through Sara-Taq to his younger brother, Baysonghor Sulṭān Mīrzā put up in Samarkand. On the other hand, Wali was already heading towards Khutlan. Baqi Changhaniani, Mahmud Barlas and Quch Beg's father supporting Sulṭān Ahmad had reinforced the fort of Ḥisār. Hamza Sulṭān and Mandi Sulṭān (Aūzbeg) with all his Aūzbegs left for Qara Tigin. It has to be noted that Mahdi was once an aide of Shaybāni Khān, but later came to join the service of Sulṭān Mahmud Mīrzā. They were supported by Muhammad Dughlat, Sulṭān Hussain Dughlat and other Moghūls in Ḥisār.

Sulṭān Husayn Mīrzā sent Abul Mushin Mīrzā after Sulṭān Masud up in Kam Rud Valley. But Mīrzā Beg's sword was awaiting him.

Now, Sulṭān Husayn Mīrzā sent Ibrahim Tarkhān an Yaqyub-i-Ayub. They fought bravely and overtook the Sulṭāns. The Mīrzā's detachment was defeated badly and most of his begs were unhorsed, though all of them were allowed to go free.

After the exodus, Hamza Sulṭān along with his son Mamaq Sulṭān, and Sulṭān, Muhammad Dughlat along with his brother Sulṭān Hussain Dughlat came to see Babur. They were also accompanied by the Aūzbegs and Moghūls who had been dependent on the Sulṭān and Sulṭān Mahmud Mīrzā's retainers. They waited for Babur the whole month of Ramzan (AD 1496) being put at Andijān.

And then Babur came to see them. He reciprocated the custom of Timuriya Sulṭāns and accordingly sat on a raised seat popularly known as *tushak*. Haza Sulṭān and Mamaq Sulṭān came inside the tent of Babur. The humble Babur rose from his tushak and went down to receive them with honour. They spoke with their eyes for some time. Perhaps, the emotion of old familial ties had sprouted in them. Babur made them sit to his right. Several Moghūls had come too, who were to now remain in service of Babur.

Once Sulṭān Husayn Mīrzā reached Ḥisār, he laid a strong seige. The records say that there was no rest, day nor night, from the labours of mining and attack, of working catapults and mortars. Mines were run in four or five places.

When the first mine set towards the gate went well, the counter-attack came as a surprise to Sulṭān Husayn Mīrzā. The folks from the town showed amazing courage in the face of adversity. They did terrific counter-mining, and the smoke was thrust down on Mīrzā's army by closing the void. The closure to the hole pushed the smoke strongly, and the men on Mīrzā's side appeared to buzz like bees from a disturbed hive. Babur has mentioned that the men in distress hurriedly fled from the maw of death.

The account mentions that the townsmen poured jars and jars of hot water on the besiegers forcing them out of their own mine's mouth.

The records also mention that one of the discharges of catapults and mortars had cracked the fort's tower. But when Mīrzā's men looked at carrying the assault through the cracks, they were instructed not to do so considering it was night.

In another surprise for Mīrzā and his horde, the besieged had rebuilt the whole tower by the next dawn. Interestingly, no assault was ordered for the next day. Almost ten weeks went by without any attacks by Mīrzā's begs. Occasionally, they made blockades by mining, rearing head-strikes and discharging stones.

Husayn Mīrzā had sent his son Badi'-al-Zaman Mīrzā loaded with a strong troop against Khusrau Shah.

A Brief About Badi-'al-Zaman Mīrzā

Badi-'al-Zaman Mīrzā was a Tīmūrid ruler of Herat from AD 1506 to 1507. He was the son of Husayn Bayqarah, who was a great-

great-grandson of Timur Beg.* The records tell us that in the 1490s, he was in conflict with his father. Husayn had transferred Badi from his governorship in Astarabad (present-day Gorgan) to Balkh, and then passed over Badi's son Muhammad Mu'min to replace him in Astarabad. This made Badi highly furious and he launched a rebellion. He was defeated and his son, who had been imprisoned in Herat, was executed. Husayn finally made peace with his son Badi', but tension remained between the two. In AD 1499, Badi' besieged Herat.

Husayn died in AD 1506, and Badi took the throne, but this was not going to be so welcoming. He quickly became embroiled in a conflict with his brother Muzaffar Husain. During this, the Uzbeks under Muhammad Shaybāni were threatening Badi. Babur had begun to march from Kābul to assist Husayn. He arrived in Herat and heard the news of Husayn's death. But he stayed there for a while with the hope of reinforcing things. But he noted his brothers' weakness and left without battling the Uzbeks. The very next year, the Uzbeks captured Herat. This ended Tīmūrid rule there, and the brothers fled. Muzaffar died shortly after. Badi' went to Kandahar to muster forces and marched against the Uzbeks but was defeated. He then came to the court of Ismail I of Persia, where he was given lands surrounding Tabriz and 3650 gold *shorafins* a year. He helped influence Ismail's decision to undertake an expedition against the Uzbeks in AD 1510. Badi stayed at Tabriz for seven years until it was conquered by Ottoman Sulṭān Selim I, at which point he travelled to Istanbul, where he died during the plague in AD 1514.

Babur's Narrative Resumes

He dismounted down the Kunduz River. Khushraw Shah arrayed the men with whatever he had and marched to give a good fight to those who arrived. On the way, he halted for a night with his men before finally getting on to Mīrzā's men. His army consisted of around 4000 to 5000 men.

Badi-'al-Zaman Mīrzā marched out from that camp. He made a halt as soon as he reached the Alghu Mountain located in Taloqan.

---

* Branko Soucek, Saint Soucek, *Dynastic tables: A History of Inner Asia*, s.l.: Cambridge University Press, 2000, p. 324.

Khusrau Shah in Kunduz sent his brother Wali with serviceable men to Ishkamish, and hilly regions around the Taloqan to induce a sense of turbulence in the mind of Mīrzā.

Muhibb-'Ali, Wali's armourer, came down and met with Mīrzā's men. The assault began. He chopped a few heads, unhorsed some and was able to run away. In the meantime, doorkeeper Sayyid Ali, his younger brother, Quli Beg and Bihlul-i-Ayub along with a few reliable men tried to grip the Khurasanis on the skirt of 'Ambar Koh. But many Khurasanis retaliated with force. Sayyid 'Ali, Quli Beg and the group lost it completely then.

As the news reached Sulṭān Husayn Mīrzā, his army was already distressed because of the Ḥisār spring rains. Mīrzā finally decided about the peace. Mahmud Barlas came out from among those in the fort. Everyone—musicians, commanders and so on—had assembled. Sulṭān Husayn Mīrzā took the eldest daughter of Sulṭān Mahmud Mīrzā, Bega begum for Haidar Mīrzā. Husayn Mīrzā then set his eyes on Kunduz.

At Kunduz, Husayn Mīrzā had begun to get trenches made and was all set to besiege the place. But Badi-'al-Zaman Mīrzā intervened, and peace was made. Prisoners were exchanged and the Khurasanis retired. This was the second attack of Husayn Mīrzā on Khusrau Shah. Last, he had done it in AD 1490. He had to retire in both cases as campaigns were unsuccessful. This had given Khusrau Shah enough chance to rise much beyond his province.

When the Mīrzā reached Balkh, he made two important decisions in the interests of Mawara al-Nahr. He gave it to Badi-'al-Zaman Mīrzā. He gave Badi-'al-Zaman's district of Astarabad to his son Muzaffar Husayn Mīrzā. In the same assembly, both Badi-'al-Zaman and Muzaffar were made to kneel to accept Mīrzā's ruling. This had offended Badi-'al-Zaman, following which a long rebellion occurred for a couple of years.

Revolt of the Tarkhānis in Samarkand

In the same year, in the month of Ramzan, the Tarkhānis revolted in Samarkand. Badi-'al-Zaman Mīrzā was not so familiar with the begs and soldiers of Samarkand as he was with those of Ḥisār.

Shaikh Abdullah Barlas was one of his favourite begs. His relationship with Shaikh's sons was intimate and that of the lover and beloved. These things displeased the Tarkhāns and the Samarkand begs. Darwesh Muhammad Tarkhān went from Bukhara to Qarshi and brought Sulṭān Ali Mīrzā to Samarkand. He made enough effort to raise Ali Mīrzā to be supreme.

Once people congregated in the New Garden where Sulṭān Baysonqor Mīrzā was. He was treated like a prisoner and dragged to the citadel, where Both Mīrzās were seated. One was to decide the fate of the other. Ali Mīrzā was determined to send Sulṭān Baysonqor Mīrzā to the Guk Sarai. But Baysonqor Mīrzā pleaded and was finally sent to the palace buildings on the east side of the Bustan Sarai.

By then, the gateway leading out to the back had been bricked up for they broke down the obstacle at once. Mīrzā had got out of the citadel on the Kafshir end through the water conduit. He dropped himself from the waterway and went to Khwajaki Khwaja's house in Khwaja Kafshir.

After waiting for long at the door, Tarkhānis and begs barged in but found him long gone. But the Tarkhānis were not going to keep it easy. The next day they went to the gate of the Khwajaki Khwaja, but Khwaja did not give away Mīrzā.

Khwaja was so dignified that they could not even force things on him.

The atmosphere soon turned hostile. Just a few days later, Khwaja Abu'l-Makaram Ahmad Haji Beg and other begs, great and small, soldiers and townsmen, all rose in a mass. They fetched the Mīrzā away from the Khwaja's house and besieged Sulṭān Ali Mīrzā and the Tarkhāns in the citadel. But they could not hold out for even a day; Muhamad Mazid Tarkhān went off through the Gate of the Four Roads for Bukhara. Sulṭān Ali Mīrzā and Darwesh Muhammad Tarkhān were made prisoners.

Darwesh Muhammad Tarkhān was brought in when Baysonqor Mīrzā was confined to Ahmad Haji Beg's house. Baysonqor Mīrzā posed a few questions but got no good answers. Orders were given to execute Darwesh. It is said that in his helplessness, he grasped a column of the house, desperately pleading for mercy. But nothing and only doom was set to come his way. Pleadings brought no help. Sulṭān

Ali Mīrzā was pushed to Guk Sarai.[1] There, thin sticks of fire were drawn across his eyes.

Interestingly, he suffered no harm when the fire sticks were drawn in his eyes. Mīrzā did not reveal it at all and went to the Khwaja Yahya's house and a few days later, to the Tarkhāns in Bukhara.

These occurrences were changing things faster. Khwaja Ubaidullah's elder son Khwajaki Khwaja became the spiritual guide of the elder prince, his younger son Yahya became the guide to the youngest prince.

In a few days, Khwaja Yahya followed Sulṭān Ali Mīrzā to Bukhara. Baysonqor Mīrzā unleashed his army against Bukhara. As he approached, Sulṭān Ali Mīrzā arrayed his troops to battle Baysonqor Mīrzā. A small battle took place, which saw Baysonqor Mīrzā being defeated against the force of Sulṭān Ali Mīrzā. Big losses came in the way of Baysonqor Mīrzā. Most of the soldiers on his side, including Ahmad Haji Beg were taken, prisoners. Most of the soldiers were put to death.

Khusrau Shah and Other Tīmūrid Mīrzās

In AD 1498, Khusrau Shah led an army from Kunduz to Chaghanian, taking Baysonqor Mīrzā with him. Loaded with wrong and traitorous intentions, he sent the following message to Ḥisār for Sulṭān Masud Mīrzā:*

> *Come, betake yourself to Samarkand. If Samarkand is taken, one Mīrzā may seat himself there, the other in Hisar.*

This was the period when the Mīrzā's begs and households were highly displeased by him as he had excessively favoured his father-in-law, Shaikh Abdullah Barlas who had turned his loyalty to him from Baysonqor Mīrzā. Although Ḥisār was a small district, Masud Mīrzā had allotted Shaikh a grand allowance of thousand *tumens* of *fulus* (sets of ten thousand small copper coins), with a bonus of

* Babur, Abdul Rahim Khan-Khanan, *Tuzk-e Babri*, Delhi: Akbar, 1589. p. Folio 56b. This manuscript is available in the National Museum, New Delhi. The Persian translation was done from the original Turkic manuscript of Babur. This was translated by author from the copy kept at the National Museum, New Delhi.

the whole region of Khutlan which had holdings of many Mīrzā's Begs. Shaikh Abdullah and his sons also had control of Mīrzā's Gate. The displeased one began fleeing to Baysonqor Mīrzā one after another.

Having successfully deceived Masud Mīrzā and Khusrau Shah, Baysonqor Mīrzā moved out of Chaghanian, surrounded Ḥisār and took possession. By then Masud Mīrzā was stuck in Daulat Sarai, which his father had built in the suburbs.

Now unable to enter the fort, he drew towards Khultan with Shaikh Abdullah Barlas. He left his companions halfway, crossed the river at the Aubaj ferry, and made a move to Sulṭān Husayn Bayqara Mīrzā.

Khusrau Shah had already taken Ḥisār and made Baysonqor Mīrzā sit on the throne. He gave Khutlan to his younger brother Wali and then rode to lay the siege of Balkh where he garnered the support of many of his father's begs and Ibrahim Hussain Mīrzā. Then, he sent his chief retainer, Nazar Bahadur on a campaign near Balkh with eight scores of men. He along with Baysonqor Mīrzā followed Nazar's troop, laying the seige.

Khusrau was in a big rush to seize as much as possible. He sent Wali with a large force to besiege Shebarghan. Wali was also instructed to raid and ravage the thereabouts. But Wali was unable to execute the siege. Frustrated and anguished, he sent his men to plunder the clans and hordes of the Zardak Chul. Zardak is a village located in Saral Rural District, of Kurdistan Province in Iran. It is also known as Zartak in current times. He took away more than a lakh of sheep and some 3000 camels. Then he proceeded to plunder San-Chirik, a country on the way back. He raided and captivated the clans all around at last joining Khusrau Shah before Balkh.

The madness of destruction was high on the minds of Khusrau Shah. On one fine day during the siege, Khusrau Shah sent Nazar Bahadur to destroy the water channels of Balkh.

This time, Tingri Birdi Samanchi confronted them with the support of eighty men. He beheaded Nazar Bahadur and carried his head to the fort. Tingri was one the most favoured begs of Sulṭān Husayn Bayqara Mīrzā.

Sulṭān Husayn Bayqara Mīrzā and Badiuz Zaman Mīrzā

The very same year, Sulṭān Husayn Bayqara Mīrzā led his army to Bast. He set his camp there with the intent to defeat Zunnun Arghun and his son, Shah Shuja. They had turned out to become retainers of Badiuz Zaman Mīrzā. Zunnun had given his daughter to Zaman and had taken a hostile position for himself.

Sulṭān Husayn Bayqara Mīrzā's cornering of Bast had cut off its core supply. Hunger had begun to starve them. As hunger reigned, the *darogah* of Bast surrendered. But without taking much and marching ahead, Sulṭān Husayn Bayqara Mīrzā retired to Khurasan. This was the second time that he had to return without taking an inch of either Ḥisār or Qandahar, despite having an upper hand and a great army.

This had vexed his sons and begs. The cloud of revolt came in as spring had just set in.

Sulṭān Husayn sent a large army under Muhammad Wali Beg to put down (his son) Muhammad Husayn Mīrzā while he stayed in Nishin meadow (near Herat).

But things were not set to happen as he would have expected. Badiuz Zaman Mīrzā and Shah Shuja Beg attacked him suddenly. Fortunately, Sulṭān Masud Mīrzā had just joined him that day, and the army, which was sent out to put down Muhammad. Sulṭān Husayn Bayqara Mīrzā remained undefeated.

With all that happened, Sulṭān Husayn had grown a soft corner for Sulṭān Masud Mīrzā and later would end up becoming his son-in-law.

But things were not set to remain that sweet for long. Sulṭān Masud Mīrzā was instigated by Baqi Chaghantanif and the former went on to join hands with Khusrau Shah.

Khusrau Shah had begun to grow stronger with Baysonqor Mīrzā already by his side. Miran Shah Mīrzā, son of Aulugh Beg Mīrzā too had joined hands with Khusrau on the pretext of Hazara's rebellion against his father.

Many were looking to kill these three Tīmūrid Mīrzās. Perhaps, they thought that they would become a thorn in the way of Khusrau although he, himself did not think likewise.

Babur Takes on Samarkand

It was the month of Shawwal in AD 1496. The news of the rebellion reached Babur in Andijān. Babur set his men on the horse to fulfil his desire to get Samarkand. Even Sulṯān Masud Mīrzā shared Babur's desire. The retirement of Sulṯān Husayn had added more vigour to Masud's vision. To reinforce Sulṯān Masud came Khusrau Shah and sent across his younger brother Wali.

As a strategy, Babur along with two other Mīrzā brothers beleaguered the town from three sides. They remained in position for around three to four months. Sulṯān Ali Mīrzā sent Khwaja Yahya to mediate an agreement, forming a common aim. Accordingly, an interview was arranged. Babur moved below the town with his forces from Sughd. On the other side, Sulṯān Ali Mīrzā brought his forces to the other side of the bank. Babur crossed the water of Kohik (known as the Zarafshan River today). Babur and Ali saw five men on each one's side. According to Babur, nothing much happened between the two except inquiring about each other's welfare. Soon they left for their respective ways.

But winter was soon set to march in and Samarkand eventually was devoid of any crisis. Believing that this was not the right time for any action, Babur retired to Andijān and Ali Mīrzā to Bukhara. Babur mentions that Sulṯān Masud Mīrzā was in awe of Shaikh Abdullah Barla's daughter. Perhaps, she was the only reason that had drawn him to Samarkand. He took her and marched back to Ḥisār keeping aside his previous ambition of conquering the world.

Babur's Second Attempt on Samarkand

As the winter came, Baysonqor Mīrzā performed well to consolidate his position. When Abdul Karim Ushrit came forward on the part of Sulṯān Ali Mīrzā near Kufin, Mahdi Sulṯān took the lead on the part of Baysonqor Mīrzā's troops. Mahdi and Abdul got into an unavoidable face-off.

Mahdi Sulṯān proved to be an active warrior very early. He pricked Abdul's horse with his *Chirkas* sword and it came down, neighing loudly. In the next attack, Mahdi's sword hit Abdul's wrist and he lay sniffing the earth. Abdul was captured and his troop was thrashed black and blue. Seeing the change of wind in Samarkand and hoping for the tittering of the gates of Tīmūrid Mīrzās, the cunning Aūzbeg Sulṭāns thought of opening the country for Muhammad Shaybāni Khān.

Now the situation was becoming uglier.

However limited the success of the Samarkandis may have been over Abdul Karim, it had made them highly motivated. Now they drew their army against Sulṭān Ali Mīrzā. Baysonqor Mīrzā went to the Sar-i-Pul (bridgehead) and Sulṭān Ali Mīrzā rushed to Khwaja Karzun. Meantime, Khwaja Abul Makaram, at the insistence of Khwaja Munir of Osh rode to Bukhara along with Wais Laghari, Muhammad Baqir (a leader of Andijāni Begs), Qasim Duldai and some from the house of Mīrzās. But the *Bukhariots* were well prepared for the invaders. The news of their readiness reached Abul Makaram and company. Feeling hopeless, Abdul decided to retire from the scenario.

It had been a year since Babur had met Sulṭān Ali Mīrzā. Things were well settled between the two. As per the agreement, that summer, Sulṭān Ali was supposed to come from Bukhara and Babur from Andijān to seize Samarkand. Keeping his word, Babur left Andijān in May of AD 1497. But as he reached Yar Yilaq, he got to know that the two Mīrzās (Ali and Baysonqor) had already opened fronts against each other. Babur sent Tulun Khwaja Moghūl (the *Baburnama* uses Mughul) ahead with around ten to fifteen scores of warriors.

Babur claims that the advance of his troop headed by Tulun, had caused Baysonqor Mīrzā to panic and he chose to retire from the front. But Babur's men didn't let them go at ease. They attacked them and not only beat Baysonqor's horde but even collected a mass of spoils.

The jubilant men of Babur had reached Shiraz in two days after having defeated the men of Baysonqor.

In that period, Qasim Baig Duldai ruled the land of Shiraz for whom fate was not going to be so fortunate, rather it was fortunate more for Babur. It was the last day of Ramzan in AD 1497. The sub-governor of Qasim surrendered to save his life. Perhaps he did not fight enough as well. Babur handed over the place to Ibrahim Sarus and the very next day, on Eid-ul-Fitr, Babur rode back to Samarkand with his warriors.

Perhaps, this Eid was set to bring only good news for Babur. As he marched further with his trip, he met Qasim Duldai, Wais Laghari, Hasan (Muhammad Sighai's Grandson) and Sulṭān Muhammad Wais along with twenty scores of men. They were here to break a deal of interest with Babur. They offered their services and loyalty to Babur by stating, 'Baysonqor Mīrzā came and ran away leaving us behind and hence we have decided to leave him and offer ourselves for the service of Padshah.' Though Babur clarified this as well in his memoir that they had left Baysonqor on his request to defend Shirza but when they found that Babur's men had already captured the land and nothing much could be done, they chose to join hands with him.

Passing the Qarabolaq, Babur's group had just crossed the river Zarafshan. The enthusiastic men of Babur were able to catch hold of Baysonqor Mīrzā. In the minor battle, a spear struck Sulṭān Ahmad Tambal's neck. He was killed without being unhorsed. Khwajaki Mulla-i-sadr,[2] one of the seven brothers who served Babur was attacked from the rear. The nape of his neck was pierced, and he died on the spot. Babur remembered him in his memoir as an 'excellent soldier'. He was a close aide of Babur's father and cherished the responsibility of being the seal's keeper. Khwajaki was an expert in Islamic theology, a wordsmith with an eloquent style. Babur further romanticizes his mysticism by stating that he could invoke rain by using a jade stone.

The small battle was over. While Babur was still in Yam along with his men, Hubbub, one of his generals, rose with his subordinates and plundered all the traders in the vicinity. This disappointed Babur big time, and he instructed the general to return every plundered penny. The trade of respectful return happened in the first watch of the next day itself. Not a single tag of cotton, not even a broken needle's point remained in the possession of this Tīmūrid army of Babur, and all reached back to the hands of respective owners.

They had begun to march away from Yam. When Samarkand was just six miles away, they decided to take a break and work on preparing themselves for the campaigns ahead. They camped in Timur's old avenue for around seven weeks. This period saw small skirmishes from both sides.

While they stayed there, an afternoon a message was delivered. It read, 'Come you tonight to the *Lovers' Cave* side and we will give you the fort.' This left young Babur highly excited and the capture looked like a kid's job to him. Unaware of what was waiting in the stock, he along with his few men went to the Maghnak bridge that night and then sent a party, including men on horse and foot to the rendezvous. Around half a dozen of household foot soldiers went forward as the nuisance began to fall upon them. One among them was known as Haji and had served Babur from his infancy. None could remain alive in the adventure of aspiration.

Babur addressed it as a message of deceit in the *Baburnama*.

The night ended in sourness for Babur.

A few days passed. The Samarkandis came out and began to assemble around them shaping almost like a town. Suddenly, men from all the forts, except the main one in Samarkand came on to attack Babur and his associates. As expected, Babur's men decided not to let them be at much peace and replied with much more vigour. The untrained attackers had no chance against Babur's brave and trained men. They could not maintain themselves and decided to surrender. Accordingly, Khwaja-i-Qazi was sent as the mediator.

Babur while mentioning the incident, takes immense pride and says, 'Having pardoned their offences against ourselves, we went back to beleaguer Samarkand.'

Now, the real challenge for Babur was set to arrive.

When they dismounted in the Qulba meadow behind the Bagh-i-Maidan, Samarkandis came pouncing in big numbers. The attack was unexpected for Babur's men. Before they could settle even a bit and breathe before brandishing their swords, Ali Quli's son had been unhorsed and dragged into the fort. This skirmish was brisk and did not last for long. Perhaps it was an attempt by the Samarkandis to show Babur his place.

But Babur always lived with the desire to conquer Samarkand. He was not going to give up so easily. He took some time. Stayed at peace for some days and made a move to the top of Qulba at the rear side of Kohik. This move of Babur's made Samarkandis believe that he had given up and it was a retreat. Presuming their success, Samarkandi soldiers as well as the civilians, came out of the grand Turquoise Gate, expressing delight. They came too far, arching and dancing in joy. They crossed the Shaikh Zada's Gate, reached Mīrzā's bridge and attempted to cross the Zarafshan River.

Babur ordered the worst possible assault. His tactic and strategy of disillusioning the men of Samarkand had worked. They were attacked from both ends and the men of Samarkand could never recover. They were beaten badly.

That day (sometime in August–September of AD 1497) was indeed remarkable in Babur's life, for he had conquered it merely at the age of fifteen.

Babur's men committed many atrocities on the enemies. The best begs and bravest Samarkandis were unhorsed and brought in. Of all those captured, one was Muhammad Miskin, son of Hafiz Duldai (he once guarded the Gate of Umar Shaikh Mīrzā) whose index finger had been chopped as punishment for rebellion. Most of the captured soldiers were known to Babur, but they faced his hostility in their respective merits. Many traders, and artisans (tunic weavers, etc.) were brought in and tortured before being finally put to death as a punishment for the killing foot soldiers at the Lover's Cave. They resisted while being taken in, cried aloud but no pleading touched Babur's heart. Perhaps he was hell-bent on exacting revenge for the incident that had been forced upon them by the letter of deceit.

Silence prevailed and no Samarkandi could afford to show any resistance. The slaves (men and women) were taken by Babur. Although Babur still did not seem very sure of taking hold of the town as the complete siege had yet not been established.

The sun appeared to have taken a day off and the chilly wind chapped the noses of the Tīmūrid army. Babur summoned the begs and admitted to the council that they must take refuge in Samarkand as soon as possible as he feared that the cold would affect their progress.

They marched in the vicinity of the fort Khwaja Didar which seemed a safe and appropriate place for a winter quarter. They dismounted in the meadow lying before the fort and put a camp right there. While the camp in the meadows acted as shelter, they indulged in creating huts for a comfortable stay. They stayed in the camp till the winter houses were constructed. For the safer side, few men had ridden to Khwaja Rabadi, Kabud and Shiraj.

On the other hand, Baysonqor Mīrzā had already sent out the message to Shaybāni Khān for help in resisting Babur.

Finally, after exercise of few days, the winter houses were ready. On the very morning when they were erected and secured, Shaybāni Khān stood up front with his men, strong and brave, looking at Babur's camp. He had ridden from Turkistan at the call of Baysonqor Mīrzā. His appearance had sent shivers down the spines of Babur's men. They were in no mood to take up any brawl, battle, or fight. But soon they gathered all the motivation they could and stood in a formation deciding to resist Shaybāni strongly. And something unprecedented occurred. Shaybāni Khān showed no sign of any engagement and drove briskly towards Samarkand reaching right up to the main fort. He was not expecting any formidable resistance from Babur's men as informed by Baysonqor Mīrzā. This had left Baysonqor Mīrzā devastated, and he gave no good reception to Shaybāni. The latter left for Turkistan without causing any trouble or turbulence.

Months passed. Baysonqor Mīrzā sustained this siege-like situation quite well, but now he wanted to do something—though Shaybāni Khān had been of no use. With his remaining ten to fifteen scores of men, he rode to Khusrau Shah in Kunduz as the last retort.

While he was on his way, Governor Sayyid Hussain Akbar's land came hard on Baysonqor near Tirmiz, at the Amu Darya ferry. Hussain Akbar was the confidant and kinsman of Sulṭān Masud Mīrzā. Although Baysonqor Mīrzā could cross the river, one of his important aides, Mirim Tarkhān, was drowned in the ruckus while the rest were captured.

When Baysonqor Mīrzā reached Khusrau Shah, he showed enough compassion.

The news of his departure had reached Babur's ears. Without wasting any time, Babur got on his horse and other men and rode to Samarkand from the Khwaja Didar. As they approached Samarkand's core part, the nobles gave them an honourable reception one by one. Perhaps, the city of Samarkand was ready to open doors to the new Sulṭān.

The climate had gotten intensely cold by the end of November of AD 1497. They entered the citadel and dismounted at the Bu-Stan Sarai. Babur was finally able to take hold of Samarkand completely.

6

Babur's Rule in Samarkand

Babur had always dreamt of capturing Samarkand and the winters of AD 1497 had turned this dream into a reality.

Babur knew very well that he had to rule in a calculated manner and with perfection. Taking a wise diplomatic path, as soon as he sat on the throne, he bestowed equal favour and kindness over all the begs of Samarkand. Apart from that, he also gave ranks to the begs who were already with him based on the circumstances and goodwill. The largest share of his benevolence came to the lot of Sulṭān Ahmad Tambal who was raised to the ranks of one of the greatest begs, for he had always been loyal.

The town had come into Babur's hands after seven months of tough seige led by Sulṭān Ali Mīrzā and him. But the hard challenges were set to march in soon. The land had been subjugated to raids and rapines for quite a few months already. The booty taken by Babur and his men too had come to an end. The town was in eager need of seed corn and money advances. There was nothing that Babur could take any further from the place, and he was not even able to give anything to the town. Babur's men suffered major privation.

A lot of time had passed since they had been home. They had begun to yearn and the expressions on everyone's face reflected the mood. Khān Quli ultimately happened to become the first to fly back. He was followed by Ibrahim Begchik. Soon all Moghūls rode back home. Sulṭān Ahmad Tambal was the last one to leave.

When everyone had left, a disappointed Babur sent Khwaja-i-Qazi to Auzun Hasan in Andijān as the latter was always seen as a faithful friend of the former. The intention was to put a stop to the ongoing desertions by putting sanctions and punishments. Babur wanted all to get back to Samarkand as soon as possible.

But to Babur's surprise, Auzun Hasan took a stand against his will. Babur called Auzun a traitor and alleged him for having stirred up a situation of revolt in Andijān of which each one including Sulṭān Ahmad Tambal had become a part.

All along his campaign to Samarkand, Babur had not taken support of his uncle, Sulṭān Mahmud Khān. But now, in the perturbing situation that had arisen, he sought his support and in return, Mahmud cunningly put his eyes on Andijān.

On the other hand, Auzun Hasan and Sulṭān Ahmad Tambal had begun to scheme to capture Andijān and Akhsi for Babur's brother Jahangir Mīrzā. Somehow Babur was not at all convinced that those two districts be given to his younger brother. He mentions the following two reasons why it should not be given:

a) Although not promised to Sulṭān Mahmud Khān, he had asked for them and, as he persisted in asking, an agreement with him was necessary, if they were to be given to Jahangir Mīrzā.
b) Babur feared that since the deserters had fled from Samarkand to join in Andijān, a revolt was on the plate.

Perhaps Babur's fear of revolt was quite genuine as he was in no position to control it if ever it happened in that period. By then all his Moghūl warriors and close ones had retired to Andijān. He was left with only a thousand men, and he certainly did not trust all of them. And all the most trusted ones, taking advantage of goodwill had run home.

When Auzun Hasan and Sulṭān Ahmad Tambal were denied what they wanted, they indeed invited all the dissenters to join them. Those dissenters against Babur's fear denied any support and hostilities became inevitable.

Dejected, Auzun Hasan and Ahmad Tambal led their army from Akhsi against Andijān.

While the hostilities seemed inevitable, Babur reached his closest aide, Tulun Khwaja. He was a bold, dashing and brave lad from Barin. Babur's father had showered abundant favours on him in the past, and Babur too had continued with same. It was Babur who raised Tulun to the rank of beg. According to Babur, he was one of the most deserving Moghūls of that time. When Babur had just begun to fear the possible revolt from the deserters, Tulun was sent to counsel them to avoid any swaying of their position.

While he was still on the way, Auzun got the hint and sent a skirmishing party that killed Tulun. Auzun and Ahmad took a sigh of relief, and after taking Jahangir Mīrzā with them, proceeded to besiege Andijān.

Andijān Is Lost

Babur had bestowed the responsibilities of Andijān's security in the hands of Auzun Hassan while leaving for Samarkand in May of AD 1497.

During his stay in Samarkand, after the deserters had gone, letters had begun coming from Khwaja and his mother about how Auzun and Ahmad Tambal were leading the siege of Samarkand. Babur's mother wanted him to come as soon as possible. She wrote in one letter, 'Samarkand was taken by the strength of Andijān; if Andijān is in your hands, Allah willing, Samarkand can be had again.' *

Multiple letters kept reaching Babur, who was recovering from illness. The sad and worrying news pouring from letters sent by his mother aggravated his sickness. He was broken mentally and physically. His speech was impeded for four days. Such was his condition that he was being provided water through cotton. Every brave man and beg who was by Babur's side had begun to lose hope. While Babur remained in this condition, a servant of Auzun Hasan brought in a message with a wild proposal. Babur did not speak anything but dismissed the messenger after instructing his servant.

By the next week, Babur's condition had bettered; however, he was still unable to speak anything.

Yet the letters kept coming from his maternal grandmother which was turning him more and more anxious. So were the letters from

* Babur. Tuzk-e Babri. (trans.) Abdul Rahim Khan-Khanan. Delhi: Akbar, 1589. p. Folio 53. This manuscript is available in National Museum, New Delhi. The Persian translation was done from the original Turkic manuscript of Babur. This was translated by author from the copy kept at National Museum, New Delhi.

his mentor and spiritual guide Khwaja-i-Maulana-i-Qazi who too implored for Babur's arrival in Andijān. The words were so horrifying and deep that Babur was deeply moved.

Finally, with partial recovery, and having ruled for around fourteen weeks, Babur and the party made a move to Andijān from Samarkand in the month of Rajab (February–March) of AD 1498. It was a Saturday. They reached Khujand after seven days. This is when a bad piece of news reached Babur. Exactly on the day that they left Samarkand, Ali Dost Taghai surrendered Andijān.

This is how the things transpired:

> Auzun Hasan's servant went back after seeing Babur in his terrible health. The servant narrated the incident in as unimpressive form as possible. He said, 'The *Padishah* cannot speak and they are dropping water into his mouth with cotton.' This broke the morale and motivation of Ali Dost Taghai who was guarding Babur's Khānkan Gate. Not being able to think of any other retort, he invited the opponents inside the fort and signed the treaty surrendering Andijān.*

The truth as asserted by Babur is that there was no lack of warrior men, and surrender came out as an act of cowardice that erupted at the behest of the hopeless message conveyed by the messenger.

Now, the news reached the enemies that Babur had already reached Khujand while on the way back to Andijān. Babur's enemies stripped naked Khwaja-i-Maulana-Qazi and hung him to death at the Gate of Citadel. Babur felt his loss deeply. His lineage could be traced back to Burhan al-Din al-Margilali, a well-known Hanafi Scholar of the twelfth century. The family of Khwaja had come to Ferghana to become religion's guide, pontiff and judge. He was a disciple of Nassiruddin Ubaidullah Ahrar and Babur considered him no less than a saint. Babur, a believer in the miracles of Sufis and their connection with Allah, reinforced his claim of seeing him as a saint by mentioning in the *Baburnama* all those who were behind killing him lost everything including life too soon. In the words of Babur, he was a wonderful and courageous man who feared none except Allah. He

---

* Ibid.

talks about how any other brave man would get anxiety and tremors, but this never occurred to Khwaja. While enemies killed him none connected to him in the closest of proximity were left unaffected. They were plundered en mass.

Now, it was a time of regret. In haste and anxiety that had risen from letters of Khwaja and those of his maternal grandmother, Samarkand was lost and the story of the loss of Andijān had just walked in. According to Babur, it was merely ignorance towards an understanding of the situation that led him to lose both places.

Babur felt helpless. Never in his small stint as a ruler, had he been cut off completely from his retainers and his own country. He had never faced such a level of annoyance and hardship.

Khujand: New Base

Well, life was not going to remain the same for Babur. However, with a desire to make a comeback despite all adversaries, Babur had sent Qasim Beg Quchin to Tashkent seeking help from Sulṭān Mahmud Khān about a move on Andijān.

Qasim had been successful in persuading Khān and he arrived with the massive troop by the way of Ahangaran Dale reaching the foot of Kindirlik pass. Babur too reached there from Khujand and meet his maternal uncle Sulṭān Mahmud Khān. Together they crossed the pass and took a halt at the end of Akhsi.

The news of Babur coming with the support of his uncle Mahmud and troops had reached his enemies in Andijān. They too gathered and reached Akhsi.

And what happened next was beyond Babur's comprehension and expectations. He came to know that some misunderstandings and misleading were created among a pack of the army of Sulṭān Mahmud Khān, because of which the enemy stormed strong at it making it the weakest possible. According to Babur's writings, Sulṭān Mahmud Khān was a weak commander and meritless soldier.

Just when he could have saved Andijān by simply marching towards it (even without any fighting), he fell for the enemies' deceit. Auzun Hasan and Tambal promised heavy bribes and gifts to Khān and his intermediaries. Trapped in the web, Khān decided to retire, leaving Babur on his own.

Families and households of most of the Begs were in Andijān itself. Fearing the consequences, the forty scores of them decided not to march and cause any trouble. Instead, they decided to leave Babur in his condition. the begs who deserted included big names like Ali Darwesh, Ali Mazid Quchin, Muhammad Baqir, Shaikh Abdullah and the lord of the gate, Mirim Laghari.

But some choose to stay loyal to Babur in his time of imminent exile. The number of those loyalists won't be more than three hundred and it included Qasim Quchin Beg, Wais Laghari Beg, Ibrahim Saru, Minghlig Beg, Shirim Taghai, Sayyaidi Qara Beg. Few from Babur's household decided to stay back which included names like Mir Shah Quchin, the Lord of Gate Sayyid Qasim Jalair, Qasim Ajab, Muhamamd Dost, Muhammad Ali Muhashir, Khudai Birḍi Tughchi Moghūl, Yarik Taghai, Baba Quli, Pir Wais, Shaikh Wais, Yar Ali Baldi, Qasim Mir Akhwur Haidar Rikabdar.

The loss of men was a massive loss to the young ruler, Babur. It came very hard on him and he often wept in isolation.

Babur and the remaining party returned to Khujand. As a gesture of compassion, his mother and maternal grandmother were sent to him. The families of some other men in exile were also sent with Babur.

They spent the whole Ramzan of AD 1498 in Khujand. Again, Sulṭān Mahmud Khān agreed to support Babur in his quest for Samarkand. Sulṭān Mahmud Khān sent his son Sulṭān Muhammad Khānika, and a party of 5000 men led by his guardian Ahmad Beg.

Babur mounted to ride towards Samarkand and win it again. Khānika, Ahmad and their troops waited to join Babur at Aūrā-tīpā.

Babur's men took the route of Yar-Yilaq, past the fort of Burka Yilaq. This fort was the headquarter of the darogah of the district. Sulṭān Muhammad and Ahmad Beg on the other hand rode on another road much slower than Babur's horde. By the time they had reached Yar-Yilaq, news of Shaybāni Khān raiding Shiraz came. Hearing so, they decided to turn back.

Babur again felt helpless and deserted. He had to again turn back to Khujand. The desire and ambition to rule kept flaming inside Babur. Perhaps he was anxious once more. The throneless Babur yet again asked for help from his uncle Sulṭān Mahmud Khān. This time for Andijān.

Responding to Babur's call, the Khān appointed Sayyid Muhammad Husain Dughlat, Ayub Begchik, Jan Hasan Barin along with 8000 men in aid. With this big reinforcement, Babur rode, crossing Kand-i-Badam. But somehow this campaign too failed and he had to return to Khujand.

7

Babur Leaves Khujand

Earlier, Babur and his hordes had moved twice from Khujand. Once for Andijān and then for Samarkand. But during both times, Babur returned without any success. The place was very poor, and it was impossible to sustain the living of 300 men for long. Babur had realized that no ambition would be fulfilled by being stuck at Khujand.

Babur and his party wanted to return to Samarkand desperately.

To realize this desire, Babur sent people to confer with Muhammad Husayn Kurkan Dughlat in Aūrā-tīpā, seeking a loan to facilitate the winter stay in *Pashghar* till it became practical to move on to Samarkand. Luckily, Husayn agreed, and Babur rode to Pashaghar from Khujand along with his men.

They were just on the way and had made it only till Zamin when Babur contracted a very high fever. But nothing could have been done, and they had to rush on the mountain road until they reached Rabat-i-Khwaja. It was the headquarter of Shavdar Tuman's darogah. Babur hoped to take refuge in the fort using ladders, keeping the refuge a secret from the darogah. But as they reached the fort by dawn, the darogah's men were highly active. Thus, rendered helpless, Babur and his men had to march directly to Pashaghar.

Fighting high fever, Babur had ridden uninterrupted for around seventy miles and finally, reached his destination.

It had been only a few days at Pashaghar, and they appointed Ibrahim Saru Wais Laghari, Sherim Taghai, and other brave begs to make an expedition to get control of the Yar-Yilaq forts. Babur was back to business.

Yar-Yilaq was owned by Sayyid Yusug Beg. After having remained in Samarkand during the exodus period of Babur, he gained a lot of favour from Sulṭān Ali Mīrzā. The fort was being taken care of by Yusuf's younger brother's son Ahmad-i-Yusuf, the governor of Sialkot.

The winter of AD 1498 was proving to be fortunate for Babur. His begs had got possession of many forts. A few were captured peacefully without dropping a single blood droplet, some were gained by fights while some by ruse and craft.

In the whole district, there was perhaps not a single village without its defences because of the Moghūls and the Aūzbegs.

On the other hand, Sulṭān Ali Mīrzā had turned suspicious of Sayyid Yusuf and his nephew on account of Babur's arrival. He dismissed them both towards Khurasan.

While the tug of war continued between the men of Babur and Ali Mīrzā, winter just passed off. Ali was instructed from Samarkand to take an army near Shiraz and Kabud. Babur had a force of merely 300 soldiers while powerful foes were on all sides. Babur felt heavily trapped. Fortune never sided with Babur historically, and so, he had genuine reasons for fear. His luck neither worked when he looked to re-capture Andijān, nor it was by his side when he looked to seize Samarkand. Babur helplessly had to come to terms with the setbacks and ride back to Pashaghar.

Khujand, an impoverished place, did not have much to take care of Babur's men. Babur mentions that they along with their families had been living for more than six months, and the locals had dedicated to do their best to serve them.

Babur again felt helpless and devastated. He did not know with what face would he return to his people. Neither did he know which home (Samarkand and Andijān) he would go nor was he aware of what he would gain for the stay in Khujand.

Anxious and loaded with uncertainty, Babur and his people went to the summer pastures of Aūrā-tīpā. They spent some days there in amazement given the position they were in, not knowing where to go or stay. Babur mentions that his head was whirling without any certain direction in mind.

Khwaja Abul Makaram came to see Babur on one of those days. He, like Babur and his people, was a wanderer driven from his home (Samarkand). He conveyed the best of courtesy by asking Babur about his and his troops' condition and the way forward. He was compassionate about Babur's state and recited the *Fatiha* for him before taking a leave.

Recovering Margilal

After Makaram left, the same day near the afternoon prayer, a horseman named Yul-Chuq, Ali Dost Taghai's servant appeared at the foot of the valley with a message:*

> Although many great misdeeds have had their rise in me, yet, if you will do me the favor and kindness of coming to me, I hope to purge my offenses and remove my reproach, by giving you Margilal and by my future submission and single-minded service.

The coming of such news during such a time of despair and *whirl-of-mind,* was unexpected for Babur. Without wasting any time, hurriedly, Babur along with his pack twenty people rode straight to Margilal on the very evening. The place was around 145 miles from there. Without stopping and delaying anywhere, they kept riding throughout the night only to reach Tang-ab, a village inKhujand by the mid-day prayer on the next day. They decided to halt there. Horses were given some rest after a stressful journey and fed corn. And again, as night approached, they began to ride. Travelling through such region in night had its own problems such as the attack by beasts. In order to avoid such unwanted adventures, they ensured that the drums were beaten loudly. The next dawn came after the dusk, and the night and the dawn. They were just six miles away from the destination, Margilal.

Wais Beg came to meet Babur and narrated all he could about Ali Dost's evil plans. Babur wouldn't trust him, but having ridden for

* Babur, Abdul Rahim Khan-I-Khanan (trans.), *Tuzk-e Babri*, Delhi: Akbar, 1589. p. Folio 60b. This manuscript is available in National Museum, New Delhi. The Persian translation was done from the original Turkic manuscript of Babur. This was translated by author from the copy kept at National Museum, New Delhi.

three nights and two days, he had no desire whatsoever to return. He relied on Allah's will and thought that if he has been made to ride till here then only good would be waiting for him ahead.

At the time of *Sunnat* prayer, they reached Fort Margilal. Ali Dost Taghai spelled his terms from behind the closed gate and when granted, he opened it. He showered obeisance on Babur between the (two) gates. After seeing him, Babur dismounted at a suitable house in the walled town.

Auzun Hasan and Tambal had been tyrannical and opressed Margilal's people. All the clans of the country had been asking for Babur for long, and they were delighted on seeing him. Having heard them for two–three days, Babur made the next move. He had already called on Qasim Beg along with a hundred men from Pashagharis. They along with the new retainers of Margilal, Ali Dost's followers, and other loyal men of Babur were sent to bring over, by force or fair words, such mountain people of the south of Andijān as the Ashpari, Turuqshar, Chikrak and around. On the other hand, Babur sent Ibrahim Saru, Wais Laghari and Sayyidi Qara to induce people on the other side of Khujand River.

Babur had left no stone unturned to get more and more support and loyalty from every corner possible with the intent to prepare a stronghold. He was indeed an ambitious ruler though history does not go by his will in the larger part of his life.

Seeing Babur's progress, Auzun and Tambal were not going to remain silent for long. They gathered the Moghūl soldiers thereby selecting those who had once served in the armies of Andijān and Akhsi. Soon, they travelled to Sapan, having Jahangir Mīrzā as their companion and they dismounted two miles east from Marginal intending to besiege it.

To materialize the intention, they prepared quite well and advanced in a couple of days reaching the edge of the suburbs.

Babur's strength wasn't anything to boast of during this period. Of his many great commanders, Qasim Beg, Ibrahim Saru and Wais Laghari etc. were some of the few veterans left with him. With whatever was left, Babur made the formation and marched up thereby preventing the group of Auzun and Tambal from making any further advance.

Having stopped their advance, Babur took a sigh of relief and on the other hand, his diplomacy had begun to show colours. He had sent Qasim Beg into the hills of the south of Andijān. After his deliberations, the Ashpari, Turuqshar, Chiraq, and other tribes had come in Babur's support. The commanders, Ibrahim Saru and Wais Laghari had crossed the river reaching the other side of Akhsi. The fort of Pap and many other areas were now in Babur's hands with the enormous support of local clans.

Auzun Hasan's and Tambal's tyranny had woven the thread of great misery among the peasants, resulting in each of the local clans supporting Babur.

While Auzun Hasan and Tambal were running away, Hasan Dikcha, the chief of one of the tribes collected a local mob in Akhsi, who being full of rage, lynched them. Then, they invited the commanders, Ibrahim Saru, Wais Laghari and Sayyidi Qara into the fort. Now, it seemed Babur's good time was about to begin.

Banda Ali, the son of Kukuldash and Haji Ghazi Manghit, was appointed by Sulṭān Mahmud Khān to support Babur in administering the newly amalgamated regions. Haji Ghazi Manghit had just escaped from the captivity of Shaybāni Khān and arrived in time when Babur needed his experience and expertise the most.

On the other hand, Auzun Hasan was feeling helpless after having his men captured in the citadel. Dejected, he decided to send off his most favoured retainers and serviceable braves to help his men in the citadel of Akhsi. They reached the brow of the river at the next dawn. The news of their arrival reached Babur right in time. His commanders and the Tashkent Moghūls decided to send a party of opposition as soon as possible. They crossed the river on the side of Andijān leaving away their horses on the other edge.

The men of Auzun were as nervous as their leader. In haste and hassle, they foolishly forgot to ferry the boat upstream. Consequently, they went right away from the landing place and could not cross the fort. They had to go downstream. To the surprise of Auzun's men, Babur's party began to ride bareback into the water from both the banks.

They could not fight back at all since they were stuck in the boat. But wickedness was an integral part of Azun in this case (as expressed by Babur in the *Baburnama*). One Qarlughach Bakhshi from their side called one of the Moghūl beg's sons to him and chopped him in pieces. Although Babur's men had no intention to wreak extreme havoc on those running on the boat, Bakhshi's act ensured that no mercy was shown to them.

Babur's men seized them all and no one was spared. Yet, Qarlughach Bakhshi and Khalil Diwan could escape while Qazi Ghulam and Sayyid Ali committed themselves to be Babur's slaves. Two of the major confidants of Auzun, Haidar-i-Quili, and Qilka Kashghari escaped. Among the eighty men, only six could get free. The news of this mishap did reach Auzun's and Tambal's ears. They knew that being straddled near Margilal would only bring misfortune for them. In Babur's words, they were badly scarred. In haste, with the remaining sparse men, both began to march towards Andijān. Their troop was highly disordered and disorganized. Just to have someone as a precautionary step, Auzun decided to leave Nasir Beg (the husband of his sister). He was indeed a brave man with abundant experience under his belt. But even his presence could not make much difference. Auzun and Tambal had lost it completely and Andijān seemed to be slipping out of their hands.

Smelling defeat, Auzun Hasan rode back to Akhsi to his wife, while Tambal rode to Osh. Jahangir Mīrzā and many from his household fled, joining Tambal.

Andijān Is Recovered

Babur heard the news of Andijān being recovered and that no opposition existed there. Babur saw a ray of hope and rode out from Margilal at dawn and reached Andijān by mid-day.

One can collect from the writings of Babur that he was on cloud nine, after having received Andijān, his ancestor's land once again.

He saw two sons of Nasir Beg along with Dost Beg and Mirim Beg. He was kind enough to have them in his favour and inducted them as his loyals.

Finally, in June of AD 1498, Andijān got Babur as its ruler.

And on the other hand, Sulṭān Ahmad Tambal was joined by Jahangir Mīrzā on his way to Osh. As they entered Osh, Babur's sympathizers attacked their party there too, and somehow only with very few followers Tambal, Jahangir and others confounding themselves could make it to the Auzkint Fort.

Auzun Hasan had safely reached Akhsi and had taken refuge in the fort there. But Babur was in no mood to let him stay safe for long. He was the root of the rebellion and Babur wanted to crush him in the worst way possible.

The news of Auzun's safe passage had reached Babur five days after taking over Andijān. Furious, Babur marched out to Akhsi to teach Auzun a lesson. The tide had begun to sway on Babur's side. On his arrival, helpless Auzun pleaded to grant the status. A kneeling Auzun melted Babur's heart and he thought of forgiving him and no harm was done.

Babur and his whole party stayed in Akhsi for a week to settle the administration. Babur also wanted to settle the administration of Kasan and the nearby countryside.

Now that the issues of Andijān, Akhsi were settled, Babur relieved the Moghūl mercenaries and they were allowed to return to Tashkent. Babur along with his remaining men returned to Andijān. He took Auzun Hasan, his family and dependents with him. Babur had left behind Qasim-i-Ajab by promoting him to the rank of beg to take care of Akhsi.

8

Moghūls Rebel

Some time had passed since Babur had got back Andijān. Things were normalizing at a fast pace. Babur had come to terms with Auzun Hasan and had allowed him to reach Ḥisār via the Qara-Tigin road without being hurt. Although Auzun's retainers had to choose to follow him, most of them chose to stay back in Andijān.

The irony is that they were the same people who had once plundered the Muslims who were dependent on Babur and Khwaja during Babur's throneless era. But the begs of Babur were not very pleased with them staying back and the following position was arrived at in the court:*

> This very band has been the captors and plunderers of our faithful Musalman dependents; what loyalty have they shown to their own (Moghūl) begs that they should be loyal to us? If we had them seized and stripped bare, where would be wrong? And this especially because they might be going about before our very eyes, riding our horses, wearing our coats, eating our sheep. Who could put up with that? If out of humanity, they are not imprisoned and not plundered, they certainly ought to take it as a favor if they get off with the order to give back to our companions of the hard guerilla times, whatever goods of theirs are known to be here.

* Babur, Abdul Rahim Khan-I-Khanan (trans.), *Tuzk-e Babri*. Delhi: Akbar, 1589, p. Folio 64. This manuscript is available in National Museum, New Delhi. The Persian translation was done from the original Turkic manuscript of Babur. This was translated by author from the copy kept at National Museum, New Delhi.

Babur found it to be a reasonable call. He ordered his men to take whatever they had. However, Babur later claimed that he realized that this order of stripping the Moghūl begs bare was a hasty call of the court and should have been avoided.

Jahangir who had been now sitting beside Babur had fear in his eyes. Of course, he feared meeting nasty consequences as seen by Auzun's men.

Babur asserts in the *Baburnama*:*

> In conquest and government, though many things may have an outside appearance of reason and justice, yet hundreds of thousands of reflections are right and necessary as to the bearings of each one of them. From this single incautious order of ours, what troubles! what rebellions arose! In the end, this same ill-considered order was the cause of our second exile from Andijān.

Hostilities seemed inevitable for Babur after his orders. The Moghūls rose and brought in consternation and fear for Babur's reign ahead. They marched through Rabatik Aurchini, that is, Aiki-su-Arasi, to capture Auzkint. They had sent a man to Tambal for building support.

Babur feared something disastrous could occur as Moghūl hordes formed a large part of his reign. In terms of numbers, Babur's mother had around 2000 Moghūls. Recently, more Moghūls had come from Hisar with Hamza Sulṭān, Mahdi Sulṭān and Muhammad Dughlat Hisari. Babur clearly states in the *Baburnama* that Moghūls were known for bringing mischief and devastation. Till then, Moghūls had revolted five times against Babur.

Babur goes on to mention that Moghūls not only rebelled against him, but it was quite regular and natural for them to take on their Khāns too.

Sulṭān Quli Chilnaq brought the news of the revolt to Babur. Years back, Babur had favoured his father Khudai Birdi Buqaq. He was from the horde of the Moghūls who had rebelled, and leaving them behind along with his family, he brought the news to Babur.

* Babur, Abdul Rahim Khan-I-Khanan (trans.), *Tuzk-e Babri*, Delhi: Akbar, 1589, folio 64b. This manuscript is available in National Museum, New Delhi. The Persian translation was done from the original Turkic manuscript of Babur. This was translated by the author from the copy kept at National Museum, New Delhi.

Babur has mentioned that one of Khudai Birdi Buqaq's shameful acts undid hundreds of his good things. Babur has also said that the shameful act was nothing but the by-product of a Moghūl trait.

As the news of the rebellion reached Babur, the begs gathered for counsel reaching out to him. Babur himself wanted to lead the campaign of crushing the revolt but the council suggested as below:*

> This is a trifling matter; what need for the Padishah to ride out? Let Qasim Beg go with the begs and men assembled here.

Although things happened as suggested by the council, he still feared an error of judgement.

Babur was anxious as Qasim Beg led his force out that same day. Babur was aware that Tambal in the meantime must have joined the rebelling Moghūls.

Babur's men led by Qasim crossed the Kara River early the next morning and stood face-to-face with rebels. A massive fight took place. Qasim Beg chopped Muhammad Arghun's head, but victory was not to kiss their fate. Babur stood vindicated owing to an error in judgement.

Qasim Beg, Ali Dost Taghai, Ibrahim Saru, Wais Laghari, Sayyidi Qara, and three or four more of Babur's begs and household got away but the rest fell into the hands of the rebels. Amongst those caught were Ali Darwesh Beg, Mirim Laghart, Taghai Beg's son Tuqa and Ali dost's son, Muhammad Dost, Mir Shah Quchin, and Mirim Diwan.

Babur has talked about the big fight between two soldiers, Samad, Ibrahim Saru's younger brother on Babur's side and Shah Suwar, a Hisari Moghūl from the rebel's side.

Babur found this defeat against the rebellion Moghūls unusual and unexpected given the fact that he had just regained his country, Ferghana. At this defeat, Babur recalled his great support Qambar Ali, who was a Moghūl too and had gone home after Babur had regained Andijān.

---

* Babur, Abdul Rahim Khan-I-Khanan (trans.), *Tuzk-e Babri*, Delhi: Akbar, 1589, folio 65. This manuscript is available in National Museum, New Delhi. The Persian translation was done from the original Turkic manuscript of Babur. This was translated by the author from the copy kept at National Museum, New Delhi.

Tambal Troubles

Tambal's hopes had renewed with the rising Moghūl rebellions. Tambal got Jahangir Mīrzā with him and dismounted two miles east before Andijān in the meadow lying in front of the hill of Aish. Tambal attempted to pick a battle against Babur twice only to be devastated each time. Frustrated, Tambal killed two of Babur's begs, Mirim Laghari and Tuqa Beg, whom he had captured. He lay around there for around a month and then finally turned towards Osh. Babur had placed Ibrahim Saru, who, he believed, would defend the place well.

9

Beyond the Moghūl Rebels

On 8 July of AD 1499, commissaries were sent galloping off at once—a few to call the troops of horse riders and on foot in the nearby districts, and others to urge Qambar Ali to return, and the important ones who were away at home. The available warriors were told to arrange their weapons—shovels, axes and the best of war materials in the store.

The horse riders and foot soldiers from the nearby districts made their way to Andijān. As they reached, those already in the district and those who barged in were gathered.

On 25 August of that year, Babur, relying on Allah, went to Hafiz Beg's Charbagh and stayed there for four days to ensure perfect equipment arrangements for the battle ahead.

Once that was done, an array of right, left and centre was formed which included the van, horse and foot. On 30 August, the army led by Babur began to march for Osh. He was determined to get Tambal. As the news of Babur approaching with such a might reached Tambal, he rode towards Rabat-i-Sarhang, a sub-district in the north. That very night, Babur along with his troop dismounted in Lat-kint. The next day, when they were passing through Osh, news came that Tambal had gone to Andijān. Babur decided to march on for Auzkint. The men of Tambal reached in Andijān but the moats prevented their ladders from entering the fort from working. Babur's raiders on the other hand retired after having overrun the area around Auzkint laying their hands on anything worth their trouble.

Tambal had stationed his younger brother, Khalil in Madu, with around 300 men. Madu was one of the forts of Osh, renowned for its strength.

Babur and his men decided to turn to Khalil and see this strongest of the forts. The northern face of the Madu fort stood very high above the bed of a torrent. The arrows shot from this bed could barely reach the ramparts. On this very side was a water-thief, crafted like a lane with ramparts on both sides that ran from the fort to the water. On the other side, was the rising ground with its circumference surrounded by a big ditch. The torrent had helped those occupying the fort in carrying stones the size of mortars. As per Babur's knowledge, no fort of such class was ever defended with stones of such large size as those taken into Madu.

A large stone was dropped on Kitta Beg's elder brother, Abdul Qasim Kohbur as he went under the ramparts. He came down rolling, without once getting to his feet, from that great height down to the foot of the glacis. And then a stone flung from a double waterway hit Yar Ali Balal in his head leaving it trepanned. The wrath of falling stones spelled disaster for Babur's men. Many of them perished. However, Babur's men made a great comeback by facing the showering stones. The assault began with the next dawn, and they kept fighting till the evening. They had lost the water-thief and hence could not continue the fight the next morning. They came out and sought to agree on the terms. Babur took around four scores of Khalil's men and sent them to Andijān for safekeeping as some of his begs and household were prisoners in their hands. The Madu affair turned out very well for Babur.

After having finished this campaign successfully, Babur and his men went to Unju Tupa, a village in Osh, and dismounted there.

On the other hand, unsuccessful Tambal retired from Andijān and went to sub-district Rabat-i-Sarhang. He dismounted in the village called Ab-i-Khān. Now, Babur and Tambal were merely five miles away from each other.

But despite such proximity, there was no war or battle for around six weeks.

But peace is not eternal.

The foragers on both sides were at play with each passing day. While the people of Tambal could see Babur's camp, ditches were dug all around as a sign of precaution. Babur also made his soldiers go out in their mail along the ditch. Despite such watchfulness, a night alarm was given every two or three days, and the cry to keep arms up.

But one eventful day, when Sayyidi Beg Taghai had gone out with the foragers, the foe (Tambal's forces) came up suddenly in massive strength taking him a prisoner.

Sulṯān Baysonqor Mīrzā Is Killed

Khusrau Shah had already set his plans to lead an army against Balkh. In the same year, he had invited Sulṯān Baysonqor Mīrzā to go with him and they both rode out from Kunduz to Balkh.

But Khusrau Shah showed his true colours as they reached Aubaj ferry. On 17 August of AD 1499, he along with his confidants showered arrows on Baysonqor Mīrzā and his begs killing him immediately.

One can say that Shah's aspiration to gain sovereignty was the reason for his actions. Babur has said that Khusrau indeed was aware that being a man of no merit, lineage, judgment, magnanimity, justice and no legal mindedness could have ever gained so without laying hands on Baysonqor Mīrzā. One scion of sovereignty was martyred in the name of greed.

Babur mentions that Baysonqor Mīrzā was well-accomplished, sweet-natured, and well-adorned by birth and lineage.

He was born to Pasha Begum and Sulṯān Mahmud Mīrzā as the latter's second son in AD 1477 in the district of Hisar. Sulṯān Masud Mīrzā was his first son born to Khānzada Begum. Other sons of Sulṯān Mahumd, younger than Baysonqor Mīrzā were Sulṯān Ali Mīrzā (son of Zuhra Begi Agha), Husayn Mīrzā (died at the age of thirteen, son of the second Khānzada Begum) and Sulṯān Wais Mīrzā known as Mīrzā Khān (son of Sulṯān Nigar Khānum).

Baysonqor Mīrzā has been elaborately described in the *Baburnama*. According to Babur, Baysonqor Mīrzā was of average height and had the features of a Turkman with large eyes buttoned to his fleshy face. Babur described him as an elegant young person, one of the most accomplished scions of the sovereignty and possessed of a humane and pleasant nature. He was tutored by a Shi'a Sayyid Mahmud, and hence he was often considered a heretic.

Babur mentions in the *Baburnama*,[*] that as the sayings in Samarkand went in those days, he reverted from that evil belief to the pure Faith recently. These hints of Babur's extreme contempt against the Shi'a school of Islam.

Babur has further informed that he was addicted to wine but on his sober days, used to attend the prayers, and that he was moderate in gifting and fairly liberal.

He wrote the *naskh-taliq*[†] characters very well and was a very good painter. He gave himself a pen name, 'Adili' and composed many beautiful verses. Babur has mentioned that he would have made a good Diwan had he lived for longer. Below is one of his couplets:[‡]

> Like a wavering shadow I fall here and there;
> If not propped by a wall, I drop flat on the ground.

Baysonqor Mīrzā was reputed as a poet throughout the land, and they were often found in most houses of Samarkand.

He died too young to have engaged in many battles. However, he did fight two ranged battles. The first one was fought with Sulṭān Mahmud Khān when Baysonqor was first seated on the throne in AD 1495. Mahmud Khān had incited and stirred up Sulṭān Junaid Barlas and others to desire the throne of Samarkand. They had led an army, crossed the Aq Kutal and reached Rabat-i-Soghd and then Kanbai. Baysonqor Mīrzā had ridden out from Samarkand and fought with them near Kanbai. That battle had seen abundant bloodbath and success. Around 4000 Moghūls were slain. He had fought the second battle unsuccessfully against Sulṭān Ali Mira at Bukhara in AD 1496.

Sulṭān Mahmud Mīrzā had gifted him Bukhara after Sulṭān Mahmud Khān had died. All his begs had assembled and agreed to make Baysonqor Mīrzā ruler in Samarkand. Bukhara was included in Samarkand's jurisdiction which went out of his hands after the Tarkhān rebellion in AD 1496. Babur got possession of it in AD 1497

[*] Babur, Abdul Rahim Khan-I-Khanan (trans.), *Tuzk-e Babri*, Delhi: Akbar, 1589. p. Folio 68b. This manuscript is available in National Museum, New Delhi. The Persian translation was done from the original Turkic manuscript of Babur. This was translated by author from the copy kept at National Museum, New Delhi.

[†] Ibid.

[‡] Calligraphy.

when Baysonqor Mīrzā decided to go to Khusrau Shah. Khusrau took hold of Ḥisār and gave it to him.

He was married to the daughter of his paternal uncle Sulṭān Khalil Mīrzā but died without an heir. Babur informs that in all his rule one thing was clear—that he never ruled with authority. Hence, it gave his begs lots of free hand.

Babur's Campaign Against Tambal

After Baysonqor Mīrzā's death, Sulṭān Ahmad Qarawal, Quch Beg's father sent his message of intention to Babur. The message had come together with his brethren, families and dependents from Hisar through Qara Tigin country.

Now, Qambar Ali too had risen from sickness, and he had reached Andijān from Osh. Arriving, as it did, in such a moment, Babur took the preordained help of Sulṭān Ahmad and his party for a happy omen. The very next day, Babur's men formed at dawn and moved directly upon their foe, Tambal. Sulṭān Ahmad made no stand at Ab-i-Khān and marched from his round, leaving many tents, blankets and things from the baggage of Babur's men. Babur's men dismounted at his camp.

On that very evening, Tambal with Jahangir Mīrzā turned to the left of Babur's men and rode to the Kuban village, fifteen miles away from them.

The next day Babur commanded his men to move out against the enemy. They created the formation left, right, centre, and van, horses, foot soldiers, bearing mantelets, flung to the front. To the right of Babur's party was Ali Dost and his dependents, on the left was Ibrahim Saru, Wais Laghari, Sayyidi Qara, Muhammad Ali Mubashir and Khwaja-i-Kalan's elder brother, Kichik Beg, with several of the household. On the left, he also had Sulṭān Ahmad Qarawal and Qiich Beg with their brethren. Babur lay in the centre with Qasim Beg Quchin. In the van were Qambar Ali and some of the households. By the time they reached Saqa, a village two miles east of Khuban, the group of Tambal ventured out, arrayed to fight.

The armies roared and thumped into the fight. The mantelets lay at the rear, and it would have needed abundant labour from the foot soldiers to get them going. But eventually, they never needed it in this aghast situation of war. The enemy was made to bend. Babur ordered the beheading of many but on the advice of his begs, Qasim Beg and especially Ali Dost, they did not push anymore. Hence, not all men of the enemy fell into the hands of Babur, and they were allowed to escape.

Babur and his men dismounted finally in Khuban village.

This battle happened to be Babur's first fully-ranged one. He has thanked Allah for this triumph and accepted the victory as an omen from the Almighty. The very morning of victory, Babur's grandmother Shah Sulṭān Begum arrived from Andijān thinking that he had captured Jahangir Mīrzā.*

Winter Comes

Winter had kissed the land, stripping the countryside of grains and fruits. With the continuous lashing of the freezing wind, it was certainly not desirable to move further against Tambal in Auzkint. They decided to make a move to Andijān.

A few days later, prudent men from Babur's side, decided that staying in town would not be wise. They thought that this might end up strengthening the enemy and it would be easier for them to carry on raids with guerilla warfare. They agreed that the soldiers needed to get enough grains and that some blockade against the enemy could be created. With these thoughts, they next marched out of Andijān, respecting the ongoing winter and settled down near Armiyan and Nushab in the Rabatik Aurchini. Upon reaching those villages, they immediately got to the job of preparing winter quarters. This place was popularly known as the 'land between the two rivers'.

The place happened to be a perfect quarter for Babur and his men with its vicinity being more than perfect for hunting. The jungle near Ailaish River was full of pigs, hares and pheasants. They could also spot foxes and Babur admits that they were much swifter than those he had ever seen.

Staying there, Babur had developed this routine of hunting twice or thrice a week. He was especially fond of pheasants and it became his staple food during this whole winter stay.

---

* We do not have much information in the *Baburnama* about this interaction between Babur and his grandmother.

It was during the stay in winter quarters that Khudai Birdi Tughchi was promoted to the rank of beg. He fell to the enemy within a day of this promotion. Along with him, raiders of Tambal beheaded many more from Babur's camp. Babur acted immediately and sent out his warriors from Osh and Andijān, attacking the enemies riding back on their horses. They were caught and enslaved. If the whole winter had been passed in those quarters, it was highly probable that the enslaved ones, including many heads, would have simply broken without any fight.

This winter quarter was proving to be a place from where Babur had begun to break the enemy big time.

But when the enemy was already growing weaker with every passing day, Qambar Ali again pleaded with Babur for leave to go to his district. Babur felt that Qambar Ali grew stupider as more responsibilities fell on him. With each passing day, he had begun to degenerate into a fickle-minded manikin.

But whatever it may be, Babur gave him leave to visit his district. Earlier, Khujand had been his district but after Babur had already taken Andijān, Asfara and Kand-i-Badam were given to him in addition. Amongst Babur's begs, he was the one with large districts and many followers. None except Babur himself had so much land as he had.

Around seven weeks had passed since Babur and his men had taken refuge in the winter quarters. At Qambar's recommendation, some clans of the army too were given leave and they had retired to home. With the remaining men, Babur rode back to Andijān.

Sulṭān Mahmud Khān Supports Tambal

During Babur's stay at the winter quarters, Tambal's communication had increased massively with the Khān in Tashkent. Although in Babur's eyes, Tambal had weakened a lot, this man was playing his diplomatic ploys to defeat Babur the soon as he could.

Perhaps, Tambal was also using his old connections to set things right for himself. His paternal uncle Ahmad Beg was the guardian of the Khān's son, Sulṭān Muhammad. He always enjoyed high favours from the Khān. His elder brother Beg Tilba, was the lord of Khān's Gate. Both these people played a crucial role in bringing Sulṭān Mahmud

Khān closer to Tambal and he had agreed to bring tremendous reinforcements. Beg Tilba came to join his younger brother Tambal, leaving behind his wife, domestics and family in Tashkent.

Beg Tilba since his birth had been living in Moghūlistan. He had neither entered a cultivated land nor had he served anyone else apart from the Khāns. Tambal heard the news of Babur's army disbanding and thought that with the Khān's assured help and the arrival of his brother, he would certainly easily defeat Babur. With such positive intentions, he rode from Auzkint into 'between-the-two-rivers'. In the meantime, the news had reached Babur from Kasan that the Khān had appointed his son, Sulṭān Muhammad Khānika (Sulṭānim) and Ahmad Beg with around 6000 men, to help Tambal. According to the information, they had crossed by the Archakint road and were laying siege to Kasan.

Hearing the news, Babur without any delay and not thinking much about the absence of important men, tore the fog apart as they rode. He had trust in Allah and was determined to oppose his enemy in the strongest way possible by hook or crook. Determined to win and filled with anguish, Babur stopped nowhere until a new day dawned over Akhsi. He dismounted there. The mighty bitter cold did not show any mercy on all those who came as the companion of their king Babur. Their hands and feet were bitten by frost. The ears had swelled up appearing no less than frozen fruit.

Despite being in pathetic condition because of a severe cold, Babur was determined to stay in Akhsi. They kept approaching Kasan as fast as they could. Ahmad Beg heard of their arrival when they were just two miles off Kasan, after which Sulṭānim hurried off in disorder.

Perhaps, Tambal must have gotten the news of Babur's brisk-paced arrival which made him hurry to help his brother. He reached there around midday only to find his absent brother and Babur's hordes approaching. Tambal stopped short.

Looking at the circumstances, Babur said:*

* Babur, Abdul Rahim Khan-I-Khanan (trans.), *Tuzk-e Babri*, Delhi: Akbar, 1589, p. folio 73. This manuscript is available in National Museum, New Delhi. The Persian translation was done from the original Turkic manuscript of Babur. This was translated by author from the copy kept at National Museum, New Delhi.

> It is Allah who has brought them in this fashion! Here they have come with their horses' necks at full stretch; if we join hands and go out, and if God brings it right, not a man of them will get off.

On the other hand, Wais Laghari said:*

> It is late in the day; even if we do not go out today, where can they go tomorrow? Wherever it is, we will meet them at dawn.

Taking counsel of most of the wise designated men from Babur's hordes, it was decided not to attack Tambal that instant. Babur was not happy with this decision. While describing this situation, he has recalled a Turkish proverb: †

> *Who does not snatch at a chance,*
> *will worry himself about it till old age.*

Babur has also recalled a Persian couplet:‡

> *Work must be snatched at betimes.*
> *Vain is the slacker's mistimed work.*

Seizing the advantage of a respite till the morrow, the enemy slipped away in the night, and without dismounting on the road, went into Fort Archian. When a morrow's move against a foe was made, Babur found none to be present. Feeling the failure, Babur and his men went after him. They were not convinced well to lay a close siege on Archian and hence dismounted two miles off in Ghazna Namangan.

Babur and his men stayed in a camp there for around six weeks while Tambal stayed in Fort Archian. Now and then a very few men from Babur and Tambal's side would meet midway, pick up small fights and return to their respective camps.

But, on one fateful night, Babur's enemy attacked them vehemently. He rained arrows from the sky to destroy Babur's camp.

---

* Ibid.
† Ibid.
‡ Ibid.

However, the rain of arrows could not bring much loss to Babur as his camp was encircled by ditches. That apart, Babur also had set surveillance and was aware of what was set to come and hence had kept his whole camp prepared. Amid these hostilities, Babur had some unprecedented and silly challenges. Qambar Ali was determined to go back to his district. Once he even got to his horse and started in anger. Then Babur had to send several begs after Qambar, who persuaded them to return.

Time was running by and Babur had to do something quickly. Sayyid Yusuf of Macham managed to send the headman of one of the two foothills of Andijān, Macham and Awighur to Tambal. At that time, he had been well known in Babur's gate, although he could never become a beg. In Babur's opinion, he was a hypocrite with no substantial principled understanding of his own. Babur could recall that, from his last capture of Andijān (June of AD 1499) to the time of then (February of AD 1500) he had revolted thrice against Tambal and joined him again and again. He had reciprocated the same with Babur too. But Babur recalled that it was the last change of side that he did. Babur always doubted that he and his other companions in the Moghūl horde would betray by joining Tambal. Loaded with such fear, Babur ensured that he had his trustworthy men riding in the middle of those Moghūls.

They had reached Bishkharan just by halting once at night. Babur had been speculating quite a bit. After doubting that Qambar and his companions were siding with Tambal, now he even feared that Tambal's men would have already barged into the fort.

Thinking for quite some time, Babur sent a party of his begs which included Ali Darwesh Beg and Quch Beg. They went near the gate of Bishkharan where a small skirmish took place with the enemies. The Beg brothers and others did well and no harm was inflicted upon them.

Finally, Babur and his men dismounted two miles off from Bishkharan at an altitude good enough to keep a watch. On the other hand, Tambal along with Jahangir dismounted close by too with a fort behind him.

However, Babur was not keen on trusting begs, going by their historical conduct. He had always doubted Ali Dost and Qambar Ali. And now, with their followers, they began to interpose between the peace talks. Babur and many others in his camp were completely unaware of this peace project which two of his main begs had taken up. Now when Babur heard about this, although dejected, he chose to go ahead with the flow of time. He knew that any disagreement with either of the two wouldn't lead to the right consequences.

The peace pact was inevitable, and it occurred. The districts of Khujand at the end of Akhsi, along with control of water, were passed to Jahangir while the districts on the side of Andijān came to Babur. Auzkint remained in Babur's jurisdiction of Babur. Agreements were made and Babur along with Jahangir further decided to go against Samarkand as an ally. It was decided that when Babur owned Samarkand, Anḍijān would be granted to Jahangir.

Soon after signing the settlement, the next day (the last week of February in AD 1500), Jahangir accompanied by Tambal visited Babur showering his deference. The terms were ratified in the court.

Jahangir was given Akhsi and Babur retained Andijān as per the agreement's terms. All prisoners, including Khalil of Tambal, were released. Babur has mentioned that they were conferred with the robe of honour, hence this perhaps would be the Tīmūrid or Moghūl lineage tradition. Even the captured begs, commanders and households of Babur, were released. Taghai Beg, Muhammad Dost, Mir Shah Quchin, Sayyidi Qara Beg, Qasim-i-Ajab, Mir Wais and Mirim Diwan were the few of whom were released.

Babur Arrives at Andijān

Now that Babur had made his comeback to Andijān after ages, things were supposed to strike a happier note; however, he still was burning with the pain of his father's loss in one of the most unfortunate ways. Though it had been a bit more than half a decade since the unfortunate incident, the pain lingered within Babur.

Meanwhile, the behaviour of one of his closest aides, Ali Dost, had begun to change drastically. He along with many other companions of Babur, who had stood by him during his hardships of the guerrilla days, had turned completely discourteous—the reflection of which began to appear in his administrative actions. As a result, Babur dismissed Khalifa. Next, Ali Dost seized and plundered Ibrahim Sam and Wais Laghari. Not only this, but he also dismissed them and took away their districts. Babur found them to be at no fault and the act of Ali Dost to be an error of judgement. When Babur insisted on understanding his actions, he replied that Khalifa and Ibrahim had a certain sympathy for Khwaja-i-Qazi and they would take revenge against Babur someday. But Ali Dost was decidedly not going to stop easily. He was determined to bring more troubles, which Babur could not understand why. He got into some loose brawl with Qasim Beg and made the latter leave from Babur's proximity.

On the other hand, Ali Dost's son Muhammad Dost reinforced himself into the royal footing. He had Ali's support. He had begun to conduct courts and workshops exactly in the way Sulṭāns did. Babur had received clues that the father and son had absolute backing from Tambal. Babur seemed helpless as now Tambal and Jahangir had turned into an ally. And the Dost father-son duo was just doing every possible mischief that came to their heart without restraint. They were in the continual business of humiliating Babur's men. Perhaps they had not spared even Babur.

10

The First Marriage

In AD 1488, Aisha Sulṭān Begum[1] was engaged to Babur in Samarkand. Babur was just six years old then. She was the daughter of his paternal uncle Sulṭān Ahmad Mīrzā and his mother's sister, Qutaq Begum. Sulṭān Ahmad Mīrzā arrived in Andijān with his daughter Aisha sometime in the first quarter of AD 1500. She was married to Babur in the month of Shaban.

Babur has given an account (in the *Baburnama*) of how he was a shy person. And it is even more interesting is that he has blamed the shyness on the fact that it it was his *first* marriage. His assertion of 'first marriage' makes one believe that he was forseeing more marriages, which was an obvious trait of the society he belonged to.

Because of his shyness and modesty (as Babur has claimed in the *Baburnama*), he visited her only once every two or three weeks. But it was not very late when he stopped with those bimonthly visits too. Babur has written in the *Baburnama* that he had begun to lose inclination and attraction for Aisha Sulṭān Begum. And then Babur's mother Khānum intervened as she was not at all happy with her son's actions. Upon his mother's insistence, Babur resumed his visits to Aisha but only once every seven weeks or so. Babur's writings make us believe that something was wrong in his marriage with Aisha. What was it?

Perhaps, Babur was bisexual and was more inclined towards men than women, at least in that period. Babur does mention that in those leisurely days, he had discovered a strange inclination in himself. He writes:*

> I maddened and afflicted myself for a boy in the camp bazar, his very name, Baburi, fitting in. Up till then, I had had no inclination for anyone, indeed of love and desire, either by hear-say or experience, I had not heard, I had not talked.

Relating to the situation he composed the following verse originally in Persian:†

> *May none be as I, humbled and wretched and love-sick.*
> *No beloved as thou art to me, cruel and careless.*

Perhaps this was composed for his newly found love in the young lad, Baburi.

And in this new tourney of affair and friendship, Baburi had begun to visit Babur often. Yet again, modest, and bashful (as asserted by Babur himself in the *Baburnama*) Babur couldn't look straight into his eyes. He was hesitant to even strike up a conversation with him. And every time, he would return, Babur could never thank him and would wonder how again he would address him. Baburi's presence always filled him with joy but being unable to talk brought agitation too. He always wondered what power he had to command the duty of service to himself.

Babur has narrated a very interesting incident. Once, filled with desire and passion, when he was walking along a lane of town with his companions, he bumped into Baburi. He could not decide what to do next and in a state of confusion, he almost went right off without uttering a single word. Babur found it impossible to even look straight

---

* Babur, Abdul Rahim Khan-I-Khanan (trans.), *Tuzk-e Babri*, Delhi: Akbar, 1589, p. Folio 75b. This manuscript is available in National Museum, New Delhi. The Persian translation was done from the original Turkic manuscript of Babur. This was translated by author from the copy kept at National Museum, New Delhi.

† Ibid.

at him, forget uttering a word. Filled with shyness and shame, Babur recalled a Persian couplet by Muhammad Salih[*] in his mind:[†]

I am abashed with shame when I see my friend;
My companions look at me, I look the other way.

Indeed, that couplet went well with Babur's situation.

In Babur's words, entangled in that frothing desire and passion, under that stress of youthful folly, he used to wander, bare-headed, bare-foot, through streets and lanes, orchards and vineyards. As all this proceeded, he cared to show civility neither to his friend nor the stranger. He was completely carefree, not thinking either of himself or others around him.

In the context of the very situation, Babur composed yet another couplet in Turkic whose translation reads as below:[‡]

Out of myself, desire rushed me, unknowing,
That this is so with the lover of a fairy-face.

Babur asserts that he had turned crazy. He used to wander over hills and plains like a madman. Sometimes, he roamed crazily in gardens, suburbs and lanes one by one. He was not being nomadic by choice, but as he has mentioned, it was the time that was making him do so. Although he wandered extensively, he did not at all know where is he going to be put up.

He composed a Turkic couplet describing the situation he was in:[§]

Nor power to go was mine, nor power to stay;
I was just what you made me, o thief of my heart.

---

[*] Author of *Shaybāninama*.

[†] Babur, Abdul Rahim Khan-I-Khanan (trans.), *Tuzk-e Babri*, Delhi: Akbar, 1589, p. Folio 76. This manuscript is available in National Museum, New Delhi. The Persian translation was done from the original Turkic manuscript of Babur. This was translated by author from the copy kept at National Museum, New Delhi.

[‡] Ibid.

[§] Ibid.

Brawl of Sulṭān Ali Mīrzā with the Tarkhāns

When Babur got married, Sulṭān Ali Mīrzā fell out with Muhammad Mazid Tarkhān for the following reasons:

a) The Tarkhāns had risen to overwhelming predominance and honour.
b) Baqi-Chaghānīānī had gulped away the whole revenue of the Bukhara government without giving a single penny to anyone else.
c) Muhammad Mazid Tarkhān had taken complete control in Samarkand. He kept all its districts for his sons and dependents. Only a small part's control lay in the hands of Ali Mīrzā and hence the revenue.

Babur kept wondering what made such a mature man like Sulṭān Ali Mīrzā not resist the ills of Tarkhānis. But soon Babur was informed that Ali with the support of a few households, was planning to act against Muhammad Mazid Tarkhān. It was not only Babur, but the cunning and smart Tarkhāni too got the notice of this adventure being planned by Ali. Tarkhān decided to teach a good lesson to Ali Mīrzā and began to ride out with trusted companions like Sulṭān Husain Arghun, Pir Ahmad, Auzun Hasan's younger brother, Khwaja Husain, Qara Barlas and Salih Muhammad, etc.

The Khān joined Khān Mīrzā. He appointed many Moghūl begs, including Muhammad Hussain Dughlat and Ahmad Beg to get into action against Samarkand. Around this period, Hafiz Beg Duldai and his son Tahir Beg were guardians to Khān Mīrzā. Building on relationships as a diplomatic bridge, Muhamamd Sighal's grandson, Hasan and Hindu Beg along with many other brave men fled away from Sulṭān Ali to Khān Mīrzā right in the period of crisis. Right then, Muhammad Mazid Tarkhān invited Khān Mīrzā and the Moghūl Army to Shavdar, and once they arrived, he too made a move to the place. He met the Mīrzā and the Moghūl begs in Shavdar but the meeting wasn't fruitful. Rather it almost turned disastrous for Muhammad Mazid Tarkhān as the Moghūls begs even went on to decide to capture him. Sensing that the worst is yet to come, Muhammad Mazid decided to stand separated from the Moguls along with his begs. On the other hand, Sulṭān Ali Mīrzā swiftly rode out of Samarkand along with a few trusted companions and got hold of the Moghūl begs who had dismounted in Yaryilaq.

Babur found Ali's act to be extremly important as he feared bigger disasters at the hands of the Moghūl begs.

Muhammad Mazid Tarkhān had no hopes from both Mīrzās as well as the Mogul begs. Despaired Mazid sent Mir Moghūl, Abdul Wahhab Shaghawal's son to invite Babur to Samarkand. In the past, during the siege of Andijān in AD 1498, Mir Moghūl had proved his loyalty to Babur. He had risked his life in good accord with Khwaja-i-Qazi.

Now, Babur understood the ongoing business was going to hurt him and his diplomacy. Babur had made a truce with Jahangir and hence had to move on to Samarkand. But before Babur could start for Samarkand, Mir Moghūl was sent to initiate engagements with Jahangir Mīrzā. And then Babur rode out with his whole party. The summer winds of June AD 1500 were not so easy to ride. Nevertheless, even winters were not a great time to venture out.

The journey was going to be tough and taunting. It took them two halts to even reach Qaba which was twenty-five miles away from Andijān. They dismounted there. When they were conducting their afternoon prayers, a piece of news came like a storm. Khalil, Tambal's brother had captured Osh. This was extremely shocking for Babur and he was told that this act of Khalil wasn't expected by the men at guard in Osh.

The narrative of Khalil has been captured as below by Babur in *Baburnama*:*

> Khalil and his men were set free when the peace was made. Then, Tambal sent him to get their concubines, wives, and families from Auzkint. And he went into the fort on this pretext. He kept saying often, 'We will go out today,' and 'We will go out tomorrow,' but he did not go at all. And amid all this drama, he could craft the

* Babur, Abdul Rahim Khan-I-Khanan (trans.), *Tuzk-e Bąbri*, Delhi: Akbar, 1589, pp. Folio 77b–78. This manuscript is available in National Museum, New Delhi. The Persian translation was done from the original Turkic manuscript of Babur. This was translated by author from the copy kept at National Museum, New Delhi.

chance of the hollowness of Osh to go by night and bring shockers to all.

Babur understood that for several reasons there was no advantage in entangling themselves with him. And hence, even though Babur was very close by while en route, he chose to keep going straight without encountering Khalil. Babur mentioned that one of the reasons for doing so was that most of his men had been to their homes on account of the truce. Babur had not bothered about any news from them, relying on the assumption that nothing bizarre would happen against the backdrop of the peace. Perhaps, the treachery and falsity weren't expected from Khalil on any ground though the truth had to be something of great contradiction.

The non-reliability on his begs like Ali Dost and Qambar Ali had also made Babur think against any thought of aggression. That apart, the Samarkand begs under Muhammad Mazid Tarkhān had sent Mir Moghūl to invite Babur and hence he found no interest in wasting days for anything as a capital such as Samarkand stood up in his eyes.

And then, Babur moved from Qaba on to Margilan which was around a score of miles from there. Then, Margilan lay in the hands of Quch Beg's father Sulṭān Qardwal as handed over by Babur years ago.

Babur asked Sulṭān Qardwal to join him on the way ahead, but he refused, claiming that the other ties and responsibilities did not permit him to do so. But his son Quch Beg, along with two of his brothers (younger and elder) came with Babur. Taking the road for Asfara, they dismounted in one of its villages, called Mahan. While they were resting in Mahan, of pleasant surprise for Babur appeared Qasim Beg Quchum accompanied by Ali Dost, Sayyid Qasim and various other warrior men.

Babur along with them and his warriors rode from Mahan crossing the Khasban plain, Chapan Bridge reaching Aūrā-tīpā.

Qambar Ali Reprimands Himself

Now, Qambar Ali, who fully trusted Tambal, went to Akhsi from his Khujand district. He had the sole purpose of discussing military matters with Tambal. Seeing this happen as wished, Tambal imprisoned Qambar Ali and marched against his district.

Babur has cited a Turkish proverb to capture the essence of this situation:*

> Distrust your friend! he'll stuff your hide with straw.

But the cheated Qambar Ali ensured he was freed from Tambal's captivity and reached Aūrā-tīpā on foot, after facing thousands of difficulties.[2]

Meanwhile, Babur came to know that Shaybāni Khān had defeated Baqi Tarkhān in Dabusi and had begun to move to Bukhara. With some trouble woven in mind, Babur decided to continue his leap forward. He along with his men marched from Aūrā-tīpā to Sangzar, through Burka Yilaq. There, the sub-governor, witnessing Babur's power, surrendered and then Qambar Ali was given the place. Affected by Tambal's imprisonment, Qambar had even accepted the mistake and pleaded with Babur to be pardoned.

Samarkand and Decline of Ali Dost

The Samarkand begs under Muhammad Mazid Tarkhān visited Babur as he and his men arrived in Khān Yurti and paid their obeisance. Babur conducted a conference with them and discussed the town's takeover. Mazid informed that Khwaja Yahya (currently controlling Samarkand) held Babur in very good faith and considered him the *Padishah*. Mazid explained that if his consent is taken and things move ahead through goodwill, the town can be easily taken without any fighting.

Accordingly, Babur sent his messenger to Khwaja. But despite Mazid's assertion, Khwaja denied any clear acceptance of having Babur take over the town. Nor did he say anything which could leave them in thorough despair. Babur was confused.

Babur took an unthinkable decision—something he could not have fathomed after the conference with Mazid Tarkhān. He left Khān Yurti and moved to the bank of Dar-i-Gham. He gave a thought

* Ibid.

and then sent the librarian Khwaja Muhammad Ali to Khwaja Yahya after preaching to him exactly what to say.

This time, the mission was successful. Khwaja Yahya said, 'Let them come; we will give them the town.'* Accordingly, Babur's party rode from the Dar-i-Gham straight for the town, at nightfall. But the mission failed. Sulṭān Muhammad Duldai's father, Sulṭān Mahmud had fled from Babur's camp. After fleeing he had taken the audience of Sulṭān Ali and informed him of Babur's plan to take over the town. Babur was informed that Sulṭān Ali was on his guard, which was way stronger than Babur's. Hence, Babur stopped the campaign and returned to Dar-i-Gham's bank.

During Babur's stay in Yar Yilaq, one of his favoured begs, Ibrahim Surdu who was looted and driven off by Ali Dost, came to him. He offered Babur due obeisance along with Muhammad Yusuf who had accompanied him. The latter was the son of Sayyid Yusuf (Aughlaqchi). Soon, one by one, many old servants and Babur's begs appeared. All of them had some sort of enmity with Ali Dost. A few were put off by his arrogance, others for having been imprisoned while many were plundered and hence had collective rage against the tyrant Ali. Muhammad Yusuf and others seemed badly afraid and perturbed. It was Tambal's backing that had prompted Ali to persecute several of those who favoured Babur. Babur was infuriated by the tale of Ali Dost's persecutions.

Now that Babur was familiar with his deeds, Ali Dost could not face the Padishah. He decided to take a leave and Babur obliged by giving him so. Perhaps Babur was unclear on how to punish Ali who had been an ally for long.

To make matters more complicated, a panicked Ali Dost along with his son Muhammad Dost went to Babur's enemy Tambal. Over time, they had become very good friends. Their relationship had turned highly intimate which along with enmity against Babur made them utter multiple seditious phrases against the latter.

It was the July of AD 1500. Ali Dost left the world because of a deadly ulcer on his hand. Now that his father had departed the mortal

* Babur, Abdul Rahim Khan-I-Khanan (trans.), *Tuzk-e Babri*, Delhi: Akbar, 1589, p. folio 79. This manuscript is available in National Museum, New Delhi. The Persian translation was done from the original Turkic manuscript of Babur. This was translated by author from the copy kept at National Museum, New Delhi.

world, Muhammad Dost imagined a good life under the Aūzbegs. Babur has mentioned that perhaps treachery ran in his blood, and he knew nothing of what it meant to respect the one whose salt you eat. He fled to the foothills of Andijān. There he began conspiring to revolt against the Aūzbegs after drawing local support. But Aūzbegs were no pussyfooted and they would teach him a lesson harsh enough to stay with him his whole life. They tracked the traitor Muhamad and pierced his eyes, blinding him for a lifetime.

Now that Ali and Muhammad were off the way, Babur began to think again of some actions to bring favour to his realm. He sent Ghuri Barlas toward Bukhara to get news of his old foe Shaybāni Khān. He returned with the news that Shaybāni Khān had taken Bukhara and was on his way to Samarkand. Here-upon, seeing no advantage in staying in that neighbourhood, Babur set out for Kesh where the families of most of the Samarkand begs lived.

While Babur was there for a few weeks, he heard the news that Sulṭān Ali Mīrzā had handed over Samarkand to Shaybāni Khān. Mīrzā's mother, Zuhra Begi Agha (Aūzbeg), in her ignorance and folly, had secretly proposed a deal to Shaybāni Khān through a letter that if he would take her (as wife), her son would give him Samarkand and that when Shaybāni had taken (her son's) country, he should give her son a country to rule.

11

New Rule at Samarkand

In the last week of July in AD 1500, Shaybāni Khān reached Samarkand after trusting the promises made by Zuhra Begi. He dismounted in the garden of the plain at noon. Sulṭān Ali Mīrzā went out to him through the four-roads gate without intimating any of his begs or trusted aides. Just keeping his mother's promise, he cared not to take the counsel of anyone and went ahead accompanied only by the most trusted people. What is very interesting is that even though the conspiracy was perhaps planned by Khwaja Yahya, Mīrzā did not share with him the fact that he was with Shaybāni.

Although Mīrzā expected the things to happen as schemed by his mother, Shaybāni Khān did not come out to receive him and further when he reached inside, he was made to sit on a seat symbolizing a person of lower stature compared to the owner.

Khwaja Yahya came to know about Sulṭān Ali Mīrzā's gullible adventure. Anxious and helpless, he rode out to Khān. The Khān looked at him in anger on his arrival and showering heated words asked him to take a leave. Helpless yet again, Yahya departed.

The news of Shaybāni Khān's arrival and Ali Mīrzā's meeting him had reached various corners. Now, Khwaja Ali Bay's son, Jan Ali came to know about it, and with the expectation to gain larger favour from Khān, he too went ahead to see him.

Babur has mentioned that it was indeed a dreadful act of Zuhra Begi who, in her folly, gave her son's house and other possessions to the winds to get herself a husband, Shaybāni Khān. But the latter didn't care even a bit for her. For him, she was neither equivalent of a mistress nor a concubine.

Ali Mīrzā was confounded by his act, and his penitence was extreme. Some from his close circle suggested he escape without creating much fuss. They even made a fool-proof plan but Mīrzā chose not to listen to any of it. When nothing seemed working, they killed him in the plough meadows.

He died, but by carrying a bad name for himself just because he went ahead to fulfil the promise made by his mother. Babur declared that such doing by any person should never be heard or discussed. Ironically, he ended up talking about its particulars in the *Baburnama* which informed us about what exactly had transpired.

Now that news of Ali's death had reached Shaybāni's ears he thought he could play an even smarter game. He sent Jan Ali to take his place. Jan immediately dismissed Khwaja Yahya and his sons, Muhammad Zakariya and Khwaja Baqi, ordering them to confine themselves somewhere towards Khurasan.

A few Aūzbegs followed them, and near Kardzan they killed Khwaja along with his sons.

Though Shaybāni Khān had made his stand clear, Babur found it hypocritical. According to Babur, he had outrightly denied any role in this killing and had passed on all blame to Qambar Bi and Kupuk Bi. Babur has asserted, 'His excuse is worse than his fault, for if begs, out of their heads, start such deeds, unknown to their Khāns or Padishahs, what becomes of the authority of Khānship and sovereignty?'

Babur Departs from Kesh

Now that Aūzbegs had possessed Samarkand, Babur left Kesh and began to move in the direction of Ḥisār. During this move, he was joined by Muhammad Mazid Tarkhān, the Samarkand begs along with their families and people. But Mazid Tarkhān, Samarkand begs and their people took off to Khusrau Shah, becoming his retainer when Babur's party dismounted in the Chultu meadow of Chaghanian.

Babur was seeing the pain of being away from his own country and town. While traversing the district of Khusrau Shah, his mind was sunk in thinking about where to go and where to stay. Of course, Khusrau had inflicted the worst of miseries on Babur's house. Babur was keen to see his younger 'Khān Dada', Alacha Khān (Babur addressed his maternal uncles as 'dada') while passing through Qara Tigin and Alai but somehow this never materialized.

Next, they began to go up the valley of the Kam torrent and over the Sara Taq Pass. One of the servants of Khusrau Shah appeared with a gift of nine horses and clothes for Babur as they reached Nundak. The number nine was considered a good omen in Turco-Mongol tradition. Babur dismounted with his party once he reached the mouth of Kam Valley.

Then, Sher Ali a close confidant of Babur, deserted to Khusrau Shah's brother. The very next day, Wali and Quch Beg parted from Babur too and rode to Ḥisār. They entered the valley and scaled it. The roads were extremely narrow and steep. Before reaching the Sara Taq pass, they had to make three- or four-night halts. Babur was overwhelmed by the sight of the pass. In his words, he had never come across any pass of such shape and form. He had never traversed such ravines and precipices. They could manage to pass through the dangerous narrow passage which had sudden falls, perilous heights and knife-edge saddles. The range was known as Fann Mountain which had a large lake called Iskanderkul. It ranged to a circumference of two miles and its beauty had left Babur stunned. It had come at the cost of thorough difficulty and suffering, with countless hardships and miseries.

As Babur marvelled at the beauty of the stunning lake, a piece of bad news arrived. Ibrahim Tarkhān had got himself positioned at the Fort Shiraz. Furthermore, Qambar Ali and Abu'l Qasim Kohbur had come to Yar Yilaq. They had strengthened the lower forts and had them occupied. Qasim Kohbur had been unable to stay in Khwaja Didar with the Aūzbegs in Samarkand.

Leaving Fann, Babur moved ahead to Keshtud. The headman of Fann had a reputation for great hospitality, generosity and kindness. He was known to have given tribute of four scores of horses to Sulṭān Masud Mīrzā at the time when the latter had attacked Hisar, and he had been through Fann to see his younger brother Baysonghor Sulṭān Mīrzā in Samarkand. It is said that he had given a similar reception to others as well. However, he did not receive Babur in such a fashion. In Babur's own words, he had sent a worse than ordinary horse to him and he did not wait to receive him.

The man who had always been generous turned out to be a miser, short-hearted person when it came to treating Babur (in the latter's opinion). Babur says that 'the politeness of the polite was forgotten'.

While the thoughts around the leader of Fann were running through Babur's mind, he couldn't help but recall Khusrau Shah. He was also celebrated for liberality and kindness. He had given outstanding services and reception to Badi'-al-zaman Mīrzā, Baqi Tarkhān and many other begs. Many had received his generosity, but Babur never received it although he passed through his country twice (the second time, it would happen in AD 1522–23). Babur has recorded that all his peers and even the lowest of his servants had received better treatment than Babur. Perhaps, things had hurt Babur hard, and hence he penned it down:*

Who, o my heart! has seen goodness from worldlings?
Look not for goodness from him who has none.

Now that Babur was of the impression that the Aūzbegs were in Keshtud, he made sure to visit the land after passing through Fann. Babur was clear that no one was keen to occupy the place. And then he along with his troops dismounted on the banks of the Zarafshan River. From there, Babur sent a few begs under Qasim Quchin to surprise Rabat-i-Khwaja. After having accomplished that, they crossed the river by a bridge opposite Yari. They went through Yari and over the Shunqar-Khāna range into Yar Yilaq. The begs had already reached Rabat-i-Khwaja and had set up ladders to breach the fort. Unfortunately, people inside got to know about it and with not many options left, they had to retire and join Babur through Yari.

* Babur, Abdul Rahim Khan-I-Khanan (trans.), *Tuzk-e Babri*, Delhi: Akbar, 1589, p, Folio 82. This manuscript is available in National Museum, New Delhi. The Persian translation was done from the original Turkic manuscript of Babur. This was translated by author from the copy kept at National Museum, New Delhi.

12

Babur Returns to Samarkand

While Babur was on his route after crossing Yari, Qambar Ali came to see him. He had kept Sangzar in absolute control. Abu'l Qasim Kohbur and Ibrahim Tarkhān proved to be loyal enough, and in good faith sent efficient men for Babur's service. Babur along with his men without, wasting any time, barged into Asfidik, one of the Yar Yilaq villages. At the same time, Shaybāni Khān was lying near Khwaja Didar with around 4000 Aūzbegs and many more soldiers gathered locally. He had passed on the governance of Samarkand at the hands of Jan Wafa Mīrzā. And in that period, he was in the fort with around 600 men. Hamza Sulṭān and Mahdi Sulṭān were lying near the fort as a quail reserve. Babur did not have a group of more than twenty dozen men.

Despite having a lesser number of men, Babur decided to go ahead after having a broad discussion with his begs around this matter. They assumed it to be a right move considering that Shaybāni Khān had taken possession of Samarkand very recently and he hardly had any connection with the people. They were convinced that once they got in through the ladders, leaving Jan Wafa Mīrzā's men surprised, the Samarkandis would come in support.

However, Babur was still clouded by doubt about the loyalty of Samarkandis post his attack. But then Babur was convinced that even if they didn't shower any help, they wouldn't stand by Aūzbegs opposing him either. He wove his thoughts further into the future and said that 'once Samarkand comes in our hands, whatever was Allah's will, would happen'.

And with full confidence and faith in Allah, Babur rode out of Yar Yilaq after the mid-day prayer. They reached Khān Yurti by midnight. The news reached them that the Samarkandis somehow knew of Babur's approach.

Babur felt disturbed. His idea to take them by surprise wasn't going to work now, given the fact Babur had fewer troops in comparison. He decided not to go further. Sleeplessly riding for the whole night, they once again reached Yar Yilaq after crossing the river Zarafshan (known as Kohik River in Babur's time) below Rabat-i-Khwaja. While dawn had arrived his dream to get back to Samarkand was fading away in a distant dusk.

Days had passed since his last attempt to capture Samarkand.

One day in late autumn, Babur along with Dost-i-Nasir, Nyyan Kukuldash, Khān Quli-i-Karim, Shaikh Darvesh, Mirim-i-Nasir and other household parties were sitting in the Fort Asfidik discussing Samarkand.

Babur said, 'Come now! Say when, if Allah brings it right, we shall take Samarkand.'

Someone from among those attending the meeting replied, 'We shall take it in the summers.'

Some said, 'Forty days.' Others said, 'Twenty days' and a few others said, 'A month.'

While each was shouting to claim the most appropriate time to attack Samarkand, Nuyan Kukuldash said, 'We shall take it in fourteen days.' *

Babur claimed that perhaps Allah had shown him the right vision, as they took Samarkand exactly in fourteen days.

Babur has written in the *Baburnama* that it was then that he got trapped in dreams, and he saw His Highness Khwaja Ubaid'l-lah. He has described the dream as follows:†

---

* Abdul Rahim, (trans.), *Khan-i-Khanan*, s.l.: Akbar. p. Folio 83b. This manuscript is available in National Museum, New Delhi. The Persian translation was done from the original Turkic manuscript of Babur. This was translated by author from the copy kept at National Museum, New Delhi.

† Babur, Abdul Rahim Khan-I-Khanan (trans.), *Tuzk-e Babri*, Delhi: Akbar, 1589, p. Folio 79. This manuscript is available in National Museum, New Delhi. The Persian translation was done from the original Turkic manuscript of Babur. This was translated by author from the copy kept at National Museum, New Delhi.

> Babur goes to meet him and seated himself nearby. People were laying a tablecloth before him and something seemed to come into his Highness Khwaja's mind. Mulla Baba (Pashdghari) signaled about the improper laying of Tablecloth and Babur too replied in sign language expressing an apology. The Khwaja understood and accepted the excuse. And when he rose, Babur escorted him out. While they were in antechamber, he took hold of Babur's arms and lifted him till his feet were off the ground and said in Turki, 'Shaikh Maslahat has given Samarkand.'

Though this was merely a dream, Babur indeed took over Samarkand in a few days to come (two weeks).

Babur Barges into Samarkand

In a couple of days, Babur along with his men made a move from Fort Asfidik to Fort Wasmand. Although during the first approach, there were loose ends that had let their plan be known, this time they put their trust in Allah and made another expedition to Samarkand. It was after the mid-day prayer that they rode out of Fort Wasmand, with Khwaja Abu'l-Makaram accompanying them. By midnight, they had reached a deep-fosse bridge in an avenue.

From there, Babur sent forward a detachment of eighty people to set up ladders opposite the Lovers' Cave. They had clear instructions to mount them and get inside, stand up to those in the Turquoise Gate, get possession of it, and send a man to Babur carrying the information. As per the plan, those warriors of Babur went and set their ladders up opposite the Lovers' Cave. They successfully got inside it without drawing anyone's notice and straightway approached the gate. Fazil Tarkhān was at the guard; he was brutally attacked by Babur's men. He was beheaded and none of his retainers were spared. Soon they dismantled the lock using an axe and left the gate wide open.

By then Babur had reached the spot with his remaining men. He barged inside the Turquoise Gate with full force.

Abu'l Qasim Kohbur did not make it to join Babur but had sent his forty retainers under his younger brother Ahmad-i-Qasim. Neither Ibrahim Trakhān had joined Babur. He too had sent his few retainers led by his younger brother Ahmad Tarkhān. By the time Tarkhān's retainers and his younger brother reached, Babur had already made it into the monastery of the town.

Since it was night, almost all of the town were deep asleep unaware of the major political changes that won't await even the dawn. But hearing the slow but evident ruckus, few traders peeped out of their shops. They were surprised and happiness ran deep in their hearts as they recognized Babur easily. They prayed to Allah, perhaps thanking him for having sent him. The news of Babur's arrival begun to spread like fire. People were delighted, and they fearlessly joined Babur's men in slaughtering the Aūzbegs. None of them were left alive. They were killed in every lane and alleys by the outraged public. They used clubs and stones effectively, treating the 400 to 500 Aūzbegs as no more than the mad street dog.

Jan-Wafa, the then governor, was living in Khwaja Yahya's house but realizing the contempt of the public, he decided to run away and take refuge at the feet of Shaybāni Khān.

Babur had taken a post over the arch of the Monastery. A hullabaloo of 'Down! down!' was echoing thereby making the night highly festive for Babur. On hearing the hullabaloo, some of the notable people and traders came forward to see Babur. They not only showered him with blessings but also brought good food. Dawn had kissed the land of Samarkand and so to the fate of Babur.

Babur appeared to be in absolute control but then the news came from the Iron Gate, which was not very pleasing for him. The Aūzbegs were giving a good fight there. The sleep-deprived Babur did not think twice and with a score of warriors rushed towards the Iron Gate. By the time Babur reached there, the mob of townspeople had ransacked every corner of the newly taken town for loot and had driven the Aūzbegs out thoroughly.

Babur stood vindicated.

The news reached Shaybāni Khān soon. With the sun getting higher, he rushed to the Iron Gate with around 140 trustworthy warriors. Babur was in a dilemma. He thought that it was a great chance to get hold of him and negotiate for a bigger cause, while on the other hand, he was worried that the lack of men might push him to backfoot.

But as he arrived, the townsfolk appeared in unison making him run away for his life. Yet, Babur didn't deliberate to even think about any negotiations. He still was scared about the number of fighter men he had although the populace of town had proven to be his great ally.

Having seen him disperse away into the sands of Samarkand, Babur went to the citadel from the Iron Gate and dismounted at the Bustan Palace.

The happy faces, including those of men ranging from varying ranks and consequences to various headmen, came to get an audience with Babur. They blessed this young man of the Tīmūrid dynasty. Babur felt highly satisfied after having gained it once again. Samarkand had been the capital of the Tīmūrid dynasty for almost 140 years then.

Babur pondered joyfully upon his victory saying, 'An alien, and of what stamp! An Aūzbeg foe had taken possession of it! It had slipped from our hands; Allah gave it again! Plundered and ravaged, our own returned to us.' *

While Babur took Samarkand, Sulṭān Husayn Mīrzā took Herat leaving the former surprised. Babur hadn't expected it to occur at all.

Babur observes in the *Baburnama* that there was a vast difference between him and Husayn's way of doing things. He did not see any similarity between the taking Samarkand and Husayn taking Herat. Babur has pronounced the differences as follows:†

Husayn Mīrzā

1. He had ruled many years, passed through many experiences and seen many affairs.
2. He had for the opponent, Yadgar Muhammad Nasir Mīrzā, an inexperienced eighteen-year-old boy.
3. Head-equerry (Yadgar Mīrzā's), Mir Ali, a person well-acquainted with the particulars of the whole position, sent a man out from amongst Sulṭān Husayn Mīrzā's opponents to invite him to surprise them.
4. His opponent was not in the fort but was in the ravens' garden. Moreover, Yadgar Muhammad Nasir Mīrzā and his followers are

* Babur, Abdul Rahim Khan-I-Khanan (trans.), *Tuzk-e Babri*, Delhi: Akbar, 1589, p. Folio 85. This manuscript is available in National Museum, New Delhi. The Persian translation was done from the original Turkic manuscript of Babur. This was translated by author from the copy kept at National Museum, New Delhi.

† Ibid.

said to have been so prostrate with drink that only three men were at the gate.
5. Husayn surprised and captured Herat in the first go itself.

Babur

1. Babur was just a year due to turn twenty when he took over Samarkand (Husayn was thirty-two).
2. Babur had Shaybāni Khān as his opponent, who was of mature age and a witness of multiple warfare.
3. In the beginning, none came out of Samarkand to stand by Babur, though their hearts rested with him. The dread of Shaybāni Khān was the reason for it.
4. Babur's foe was in the fort and was driven off quite eloquently.
5. Babur had tried to get back to Samarkand once already but remained unsuccessful. It was the second time that he came and Allah brought it right! Samarkand was won.

By saying this, Babur certainly placed himself on a much higher pedestal than Husayn although he claims in the *Baburnama* that he had no desire to belittle the force of Husayn Mīrzā but to state the truth as it was.

Many chronograms of Babur's victory were composed by the poets of the day and region, but one piece of prose got deeply registered in his mind. It read, 'Know that its date is the Victory (*Fath*) of Babur Bahadur.' *

Having conquered Samarkand, Babur had begun to bring all nearby forts including, Shavdar, Soghd and the Tumans into an alliance. This was a phase of revolution towards goodness for Babur. Many Aūzbeg commanders had fled from those forts, fearing the worst consequences. Many were shown the way out by the inhabitants. In many forts, they were imprisoned by the people. The tide of the land was in favour of Babur with all might. People had stood with Babur wholeheartedly.

* Babur, Abdul Rahim Khan-I-Khanan (trans.), *Tuzk-e Babri*, Delhi: Akbar, 1589, p. Folio 86. This manuscript is available in National Museum, New Delhi. The Persian translation was done from the original Turkic manuscript of Babur. This was translated by author from the copy kept at National Museum, New Delhi.

One can say that his fortune had begun to shine once again for Babur.

Shaybāni Khān with all his households and family despite arriving from Turkistan, went back skirting the Khwaja Didar and Ali-Abad as he had smelled the environment, which certainly won't have swayed in his favour. He set his way back to Bukhara.

It took around fifteen to sixteen weeks for Babur to get back all the nearby forts in his favour. Over and above this, Baqi Tarkhān helped occupy Qarshi, Khuzar and Qarshi and the Aūzbegs over there were crushed too.

Babur's fate was soaring.

13

Babur Becomes a Father

Since the departure from Andijān last year (AD 1500), Babur's family has seen abundant hardships. Now finally after things had begun to settle for him in Samarkand, his mother and wife reached Aūrā-tīpā. Babur sent a party to receive them and bring them to Samarkand.

He was more than delighted to see them. Just after a few days from their arrival Aisha Sulṭān Begum gave birth to a baby (probably in AD 1501). They named her Fakhr-un-Nissa (Ornament of Women). Babur was nineteen years old then. He was on cloud nine with the child's arrival. But happiness did not stay for long. Fakhr-un-Nissa did not live for more than forty days, leaving Babur devastated.

Despite being in a state of despair, Babur had to move on with affairs and take care of the newly acquired Samarkand. He sent his envoys and summoners to the Khāns, Sulṭāns and Begs, reiterating the requests for aid and reinforcement on every side. But results didn't appear as Babur would have hoped them to be. Many refused the proposal, while others seemed to have ignored it outrightly. Only a few sent aid and reinforcements but highly insufficient in counts.

Ali Sher Beg[1] was alive when Babur took over Samarkand. He and Babur had exchanged letters. Babur replied to him affectionately with a Turki couplet. But before his reply could reach Babur, separations (*tafarqa*) and disturbances (*ghugha*) occurred. When Shaybāni Khān had taken possession of Samarkand, Mulla Binai had dedicated himself to Khān's service. But when Babur took over Samarkand, he came into the town to submit himself to Babur.

Although Babur trusted him to a great measure, Qasim Beg was always suspicious of him. Believing in his distrust, Qasim often dismissed him towards Shahr-i-Sabz, but the cunning one never left any trace of errors. He was able to impress Babur enough, and hence was called back into the town.

He constantly presented ghazals for Babur. One of the quatrains composed by him read as below:*

No grain have I by which I can be fed,
No rhyme of grain wherewith I can be clad;
The man who lacks both food and clothes,
In art or science, where can he compete?

In those days of the pause, Babur was generally in a poetic mood. He went on to answer the quatrain of Mulla Binai through a Turki quatrain which when translated into English reads as below:†

As is the wish of your heart, so shall it be;
For gift and stipend both an order shall be made;
I know the grain and its rhyme you write of;
The garments, you, your house, the corn shall fill.

The sequence of poetic exchange took place for a while. Mulla responded with a quatrain which read as below:‡

Mīrzā-of-mine, the Lord of sea and land shall be;
His art and skill, the world over, the evening tale shall be;
If gifts like these reward one rhyming word;
For words of sense, what guerdon will there be?

The winter continued well for Babur and Shaybāni's fate had begun to wane exponentially except for two things:

---

* Babur, Abdul Rahim Khan-I-Khanan (trans.), *Tuzk-e Babri*, Delhi: Akbar, 1589, p. Folio 87. This manuscript is available in National Museum, New Delhi. The Persian translation was done from the original Turkic manuscript of Babur. This was translated by author from the copy kept at National Museum, New Delhi.

† Ibid.

‡ Ibid.

1. The Merv men who had taken Qara-kul, could not be persuaded to stay there and it went back into the control of the Aūzbegs.
2. Shaybāni Khān besieged Ibrahim Tarkhān's younger brother, Ahmad in Dabusi. He had stormed into the place and massacred the inhabitants before Babur's army could even begin to march becoming a saviour.

Babur was able to take back Samarkand with the help of only twenty dozen of his able men. Babur has mentioned that for five to six months, Allah seemed to favouring his fate completely. And to him, this certainly was no less than a miracle when his men fought the arrayed battle of Sar-i-Pul (below) with a man like Shaybāni Khān. Babur was getting good rounds of help. A few of them have been recorded in the *Baburnama*:

1. Around 5000 Barins along with Ayub Begchik and Qashka Mahmud had come from the Khān.
2. Babur got around 200 men led by Khalil, Tambal's brother from Jahangir Mīrzā.

Babur was also expecting a good amount of help to pour in from Sulṭān Husayn Mīrzā, whom he considered experienced in dealing with enemies like Shaybāni Khān. But nothing turned up from his side—no help came from Badi'-al-Zaman Mīrzā or Khusrau Shah.

Battle of Sar-i-Pul

It was the summer of AD 1501 (month of Shawwal; probably April or May). Babur, high with the desire to give a blue nose to Shaybāni Khān, marched out of Samarkand. Babur stayed in a nearby new garden attempting to gather the best of men and equipment. The camp was well protected with the ditches dug all around. After having stayed there for five days, Babur and his men advanced and they dismounted near Sar-i-Pul. Shaybāni Khān came from the opposite direction and dismounted at the Khwaja Kardzan around five miles away from where Babur's camp.

Having maintained their positions for five days, men from both camps began to take on each other. And then one day, the fight grew intense, but neither of the two parties could end up advantageous. Finally, frustrated with the continued standoff, Shaybāni Khān decided to lead his party and attack Babur's camp at night. He wanted to demolish Babur for a long time, but it wasn't materializing for long.

However, he was taken aback after coming close to the camp. The fire of his desires was vanquished looking at the mammoth ditches. He couldn't do anything but instruct his men to merely shower arrows. But that rain of arrows brought no dent whatsoever to Babur's camp. Finally, he had to retire leaving Babur and his whole camp unharmed.

After this incident, Babur became over-precautious and Qambar Ali took the lead to assist the soldiers with the uphill task ahead. Baqi Tarkhān was lying in Kesh along with a couple of hundred brave soldiers and he was to join Babur in a couple of days. At five miles in Diyul, Sayyid Muhammad Mīrzā Dughal was stationed. He was bringing around a couple of hundred soldiers sent by Babur's maternal grandfather, the great Khān, whom he addressed as Khān Dada. He along with the massive troops was set to join Babur by the next dawn.

In such circumstances, Babur was eager to expedite the fight. Justifying his haste, he quoted the following lines from the Bustan in the *Baburnama*:*

Who lays with haste his hand on the sword?
Shall lift to his teeth to the backhand of regret.[2]

In the *Baburnama*, he has narrated more reasons to justify his haste to fight. On the day of battle (that was to happen), the Great Bear constellation was between the two armies. Babur had particularly decided the day for the battle. This constellation of eight stars would have lain behind Babur's enemy for a couple of weeks if the fight had been deferred.

Perhaps there was a superstition that Babur had woven in his mind based on traditions of astrology that prevailed in his vicinity. He has said, 'I now understand that these considerations are worth nothing and that our haste was without reason.'

---

* Babur, Abdul Rahim Khan-I-Khanan (trans.), *Tuzk-e Babri*, Delhi: Akbar, 1589, p. Folio 89. This manuscript is available in National Museum, New Delhi. The Persian translation was done from the original Turkic manuscript of Babur. This was translated by author from the copy kept at National Museum, New Delhi.

With a high desire to fight, reinforced with omens of stars, Babur marched ahead with his soldiers as the dawn broke. They formed up in an array of right and left, centre and van. The right was led by Ibrahim Saru, Ibrahim Jani, Abu'l-Qasim Kohbur, and other major begs. The left was led by Muhammad Mazid Tarkhān, Ibrahim Tarkhān, other Samarkandi begs, Sulṯān Husain Arghun, Qara (Black) Barlas, Pir Ahmad and Khwaja Husain. Qasim Beg was along with Babur who was leading in the centre. This central band included several of Babur's close circle and household. The van had veterans like Qambar Ali, Banda Ali, Khwaja Ali, Mir Shạh Quchim, Sayyid Qasim, Lord of the Gate—Banda Ali's younger brother Khaldar and Haidar-i-Qasim's son Quch. Together with all the good warriors and the rest of the household thus arrayed, they marched from the camp.

Meanwhile, Shaybāni Khān and his men marched out from his camp. His left band was led by Sulṯān Hamza, Sulṯān Mahdi and other important sulṯāns. The right band was led by Sulṯān Mahmud and other Timur Sulṯāns.

And then the two armies began to approach each other. Shaybāni wheeled his right towards Babur's men's rear side. Babur turned to match the blow. This brought repercussions. Babur's best braves and those inscribed in the Van lied to his right. This uncovered their front of the centre. Nonetheless, Babur's troops fought those attacked from the front, forcing them way back to their centre. Babur asserted that the setback was so harsh to the enemies' camp that one of the old chiefs told Shaybāni Khān, 'We must move off! It is past a stand.' However, Shaybāni did not bother to hear him and continued to give a great fight. Eventually, his right beat Babur's left and then he wheeled (again) to Babur's rear.

As mentioned earlier the front of Babur's centre was bare through the van's being left to the right. Babur's enemy attacked his horde front and rear, left and right, shooting arrows ferociously. Ayub Begchik's Moghūl Army did arrive as a helping aide to Babur, but ultimately it didn't come of use for, they immediately began working against Babur's interest. Against expectation, they began to plunder and unhorse Babur's men.

And to bring dismay to many those who call the dynasty of Babur 'Moghūls', the former has lamented and abused the latter. He has said, 'Not this once only, this is always the way with those ill-omened

Moghūls! If they win, they grab at booty; if they lose, they unhorse and pilfer their own side.'

Babur's men drove away the Aūzbegs who attacked his front with several vigorous assaults, but those who had wheeled to the rear came up and rained arrows. Falling on them in this way, from the front, and the rear, Babur's men were made to hurry off.

Babur has said that this turning movement was one of the great merits of Aūzbeg fighting, and no battle of theirs was ever without it. He talks of another merit of theirs. They all, including the begs and retainers, rode and shouted as they charged in. They never scattered even till the time they rode out in a body.

Time was not right for Babur as he had thought it would be, looking at the astrological omen of eight stars. Around fifteen men were left with Babur. The Zarafshan River was close by. Babur made straight for it in the season when Zarafshan came down with floods. They rode right into it—man, and horse in the mail. The river was just fordable for halfway over, and after that, one had to swim. For more than an arrow's flight Babur's men mount in the mail. They made their horses swim, and that is how they got across. After getting out of the water, they cut off the horse armour. By thus crossing over to the north bank of the river, Babur and his men were temporarily free of the Shaybāni's clutches. Babur had known the Moghūls being wretched, the captors and pillagers of many of his friends so far in the battle. Ibrahim Tarkhān and many other excellent braves were unhorsed and killed by the Moghūls. The Elph. Codex of the *Baburnama* contains an interesting assertion made by Humayun in this context. It reads as below:[3]

> Where the Moghūl race angels, they would be bad;
> Written in gold, the name Moghūl would be bad;
> Pluck not an ear from the Moghūl's corn-land,
> What is sown with Moghūl seed will be bad.

Babur and his troops moved along the north bank of the Zarafshan River. They crossed it near Qulba and entered the town by the Shaikh Zada Gate, reaching the citadel in the middle of the afternoon.

Many of the best begs and the bravest of Babur's men had perished in the battle. Ibrahim Tarkhān, Ibrahim Saru, and Ibrahim Jani were among the dead begs. Others who perished were Haidar-i-Qasim's eldest son, Abu'l Qasim Kohbur, Khudai Birdi Tughchi, and Khalil, Tambal's younger brother. Many of Babur's men had fled in various directions. Muhammad Mazid Tarkhān went towards Qunduz, Khusrau Shah to Hisar, Karim-dad-i-Khudai-birdi Turkman, Janaka Kukulddsh, and Mulla Baba of Pashaghar got away to Aūrā-tīpā. Mulla Baba had been there with Babur not in service but as a guest and had to run away seeking refuge for his life.

14

Babur Is Besieged in Samarkand

The next day after having reached the citadel beyond the river Zarafshan, Babur summoned Khwaja Abul Makaram, Qasim, the other begs and the household. They were admitted in the counsels and after consultation, they decided to go into the citadel considering it was a matter of life and death. Babur took up quarters in the middle of the town, in tents pitched on the roof of Aulugh Beg Mīrzā's college. The other begs and soldiers were assigned quarters in the gates or on the ramparts of the walled town.

But Babur's fear was soon to turn real. Three days later, Shaybāni Khān dismounted at some distance from the fort. Despite the ongoings, the town was indeed quite affectionate about Babur. The town-rabble came out of lanes and wards, to the College Gate. They began to shower good wishes on Babur and went out to fight as a lynch mob. They tried their best to petrify the mighty Shaybāni Khān as much as they could for some days to come by. The mob and rabble cared neither for the sword nor the arrow wounds. They had begun to turn bolder with every passing day. They had begun to sally further and further out. Despite the warning of caution being issued by Babur's officials they continued to do what they had been doing.

And then on one very day, Shaybāni Khān directed his attack towards the Iron Gate. The emboldened mob went out, daringly as usual, but a bit too far. To cover their retreat, Babur sent several braves including foster brethren, and members of his own household such as Nuyan Kukuldash, Qul-Nazar Taghai Beg and Mazid towards the Camel's Neck. A couple of Aūzbegs caught up with them at Qul-Nazar crossing swords. The rest of the Aūzbegs dismounted and put all their strength to counter the rabble. They jostled the rabble off and rammed them in through the Iron Gate. Quch Beg and Mir Shah Quchin were trying to make a stand at the side of Khwaja Khizr's Mosque. While the townsmen were being moved off by those on foot. A party of horse riding Aūzbegs went towards the Khwaja Khizr's Mosque. Quch Beg exchanged blows with them. Babur says that this fight was a treat to watch for the skills shown by Quch. Many on Babur's side had begun absconding and were occupied only with their escape. Perhaps, the time to shoot arrows and make a stand had gone by.

Babur was shooting with a slur bow from above the gate along with some men. This attack had kept the enemy from advancing beyond the mosque, and Shaybāni was successfully made to retire from there.

During this siege, routine rounds of ramparts were made each night which at times were also done by Qasim Beg and Babur himself. The rounds couldn't be completed entirely on horse. One could ride from the Turquoise Gate to the Shaikh-Zada's Gate, but the rest of the way had to be walked. The round was indeed a big one as when some did it entirely on foot, it wouldn't end just before dawn.

But things were not set to remain settled for long.

One very fateful day, Shaybāni Khān attacked from between the Iron Gate and the Shaikh-Zada's Gate. Given the surprising nature of his raid catching the troops unawares, Babur along with a bunch of few went ahead as the reserve. Babur's shots were going well that day through the slur bow. However, Khān's men attacked so vigorously this time that they got close under the ramparts very easily. This happened largely as even though a bunch of men along with Babur were giving a great fight, the remaining troops were not there to counter the intense vigour that Shaybāni's men had brought to the battlefield. Babur and his men were entirely off their guard on the other side of the town. There, the enemy had posted eighty good men in ambush. They had around two dozen ladders which were so wide that two or three could be mounted in a horizontal row on it at a time. Now they captured all of Babur's men near the Iron Gate, following which they quickly set up their ladders between the two gates. This was exactly the spot where a road led from the ramparts to Muhammad Mazid Tarkhān's houses. That post was controlled by Quich Beg and Muhammad Quli Quchin. Having lost their brave subordinates, they had taken refuge in Muhammad Mazid's houses.

Meanwhile, the Needle Maker's Gate was controlled by Qara (Black) Barlas. The Bleaching-Ground Gate was in control of Qutluq Khwaja Kukuldash along with Sherim Taghai and his brethren. While the other side of the town was being attacked, the men attached to these posts weren't on guard. They were at peace at their quarters or off to the bazar for necessary matters of domestic service. Only the begs were at their posts, with a couple of members of the local populace. Quch Beg, Muhammad Quli, Shah Sufi and one other brave did fight well and boldly. Now some Aūzbegs were on the ramparts, and some were coming up. The four of the Babur's men ran the fastest they could to deliver the best blow to the approaches. The quartet forced them all down very strategically and delivered a harsh drubbing.

Babur observes in the *Baburnama* that Quch Beg turned out to be the best one.

On the other hand, Qarā Barlās was left alone at the Needle-Makers' Gate. He too gave a good fight despite being all alone. Qutluq Khwaja and Quinazar Mīrzā were also keeping their stand firm at their posts at the Bleaching-Ground Gate. They held out well too and charged the enemy from the rear.

Once again, Qasim Beg led his braves out through the Needle-Makers' Gate, pursuing the Aūzbegs as far as Khwaja Kafsher. While returning they carried the heads of a few of them, which indicated that many were beheaded.

Babur's men had fought the storm brought by Shaybāni Khān very well despite having disadvantages in some stages. There were times when Babur was even short of sufficient men to fight at his end, but fortune swayed by his side.

Now that Shaybāni's storm was at rest, something else was to bring trouble for Babur. The time of ripening rain had come but none could bring new corn into the town. Babur and the populace along with him were stuck in the unavoidable siege as neither could get in nor get out of the town. And this long siege caused great hardships to the townspeople. It was so heartening that the destitute began to survive on the flesh of dogs and asses. Since there was little grain for the horses, the people began to feed them mulberry and elm leaves.

Some people scraped dry wood and began to give the shavings after being damped to their horses.

For more than fifteen weeks, Shaybāni Khān did not come near the fort at all but had kept doing rounds from post to post.

It was midnight. Babur was lying undressed in his resting chamber and his men were off the guards. Shaybāni's men came near the Turquoise Gate and began beating the drums and shouted their war cries. The drumbeats and war cries had begun to cause great trepidation and anxiety among each, including Babur. This action of drumbeating amplified the fear of war cries, and it happened night after night.

The anxious Babur had begun living in fear each night. He somehow managed to send his envoys and messengers repeatedly to all sides and quarters, who always appeared to be an ally. But Babur could only wait for the help and reinforcement to come. None came.

Dejected Babur has written in the *Baburnama*, 'No one had helped or reinforced me when I was in strength and power and had suffered no sort of defeat or loss; on what score would anyone help me now?' *

Devoid of any hope of help from anyone, Babur could only see it as a recommendation to prolong the siege.

With a philosophical tinge, Babur has described the incident in the *Baburnama* as follows:†

> The old saying was that to hold a fort there must be a head, two hands, and two legs, that is to say, the Commandant is the head; help and reinforcement coming from two quarters are the two arms and the food and water in the fort are the two legs.

It appears from the primary source that Babur was expecting a lot at least from Sulṭān Husayn Mīrzā. However, he did not even send a message of encouragement, forget help. A dismayed Babur sent Kamālu'd-dīn Ḥusain Gāzur-gāhī as an envoy to Shaybāni Khān.

---

* Babur, Abdul Rahim Khan-I-Khanan (trans.), *Tuzk-e Babri*, Delhi: Akbar, 1589, p. Folio 94. This manuscript is available in National Museum, New Delhi. The Persian translation was done from the original Turkic manuscript of Babur. This was translated by author from the copy kept at National Museum, New Delhi.

† Ibid.

15

Samarkand Is Lost to Shaybāni (AD 1501)

Shaybāni Khān's siege had prolonged. This also extended the unavailability of provisions and supplies in all quarters. There was no succour and reinforcement from any side. Both soldiers as well as the common men and peasants had begun to become hopeless. They began to flee one by one, by crossing the walls.

The news of distressed townsfolk reached Shaybāni Khān. This is exactly what he had been waiting for quite some time. Certainly, his besieging of the fort had paid off. He came riding and dismounted near the Lovers' Cave. Full of fear, Babur ran to Malik-Muhammad Mīrzā's house in the low lane.

At the same time appeared the old devil (as Babur has mentioned in the *Baburnama*). Khwaja Husain's brother Aūzūn Hasan came into the town with more than two dozen men. He had been the cause behind Jahāngīr Mīrzā's rebellion that led to Babur's exodus from Samarkand in March of AD 1498 and his appearance seemed no less than a bold and embellished act of treachery to Babur.[1]

Civilians and the soldiers had grown more and more distressed. The men whom Babur had trusted the most had begun to get down the ramparts. Those trusted men included known begs and old family servants such as Pīr Wais, Shaikh Wais and Wais Lāgharī. Babur was in complete despair and saw no ray of hope. Their supplies and provisions were completely wretched and what was there in stock was nearing end.

Then came a ray of hope, which certainly was not the kind Babur would have liked. Shaybāni Khān proposed peace talks. Given that he was besieged for a long time, Babur was left with no other choice but to agree. He has mentioned in the *Baburnama* that he would have given less ear to the truce talks if there had been any hope or food from any side.

The truce had to follow all conditions laid by Shaybāni which would let the things transpire as mentioned below:

At midnight, Babur and his folk departed from the town by the Shaikh-Zada's Gate. Babur took his mother Khānīm out along with two other women folks, namely: Bīshka-i-Khalīfa and Mīnglīk Kūkūldāsh. Babur's whole party included more than 200 people.

According to Babur (as said in the *Baburnama*), this exodus saw his elder sister, Khān-zāda Begum falling into the hands of Shaybāni Khān. But *Humayun Nama* by Gulbadan Begum has given us a different picture. According to her, Shaybāni had asked for a *nikaah* with Khān-zāda as one of the primary conditions of the truce.* She didn't fall in his hands; rather a proper nikkah was solemnized that too with the consent of Babur's mother.[2]

The starch darkness of the midnight made them lose their way. For long they kept wandering around the main irrigation channels of *Soghd*. As the dawn broke, they were able to pass Khwāja Dīdār after encountering multiple difficulties in the night. By the time of Sunnat prayer, they had made it to the rising ground of Qarā-būgh. Following the northern gradient of Qarā-būgh, they quickly hurried past the foot of Judūk village dropping down into Yīlān-aūtī.

As Babur went through these hardships, he thought of indulging in lighter moments in the tourney. Qāsim Beg, Qaṃbar-'alī and he began to race with each other. Babur's horse was leading initially but out of excitement, he looked behind to check how far his two competitors were and ended up twisting himself round. He was thrown head-on to the ground. Perhaps the girth may have slackened, leading to the turning of the saddle and hence the accident. Although Babur soon got up and remounted, his head didn't appear steady till evening. He kept feeling delirious. Soon they dismounted in Yīlān-aūtī. A horse was killed and roasted for food. They could make it to Khalīla village before dawn. Now they were on the way to Dīzak,

* Annette Susannah Beveridge, *Humayun-Nama*: *The History of Humayun*, London: Royal Asiatic Society, 1902, p. 85.

which was controlled by Ḥāfiẓ Muhammad Dūldāī's son, Ṭāhir. They were served with plenty of food which included fleshy meats, loaves of fine flour, sweet melons and abundant juicy grapes. Babur's side felt the repose of seeing the abundance after a long period of deprivation. They all ate like there was no tomorrow. To capture this emotion Babur composed the following prose in the Turkic language:*

> From fear and hunger rest we won;
> A fresh world's newborn life we won.
> From out our minds, death's dread was chased;
> From our men, the hunger-pang kept back.

They had never felt such relief in their lives before. Babur does acknowledge that they had never appreciated security and plentiness so much. Babur writes, 'Joy is best and more delightful when it follows sorrow, ease after toil. I have been transported four or five times from toil to rest and from hardship to ease. This was the first. We were set free from the affliction of such a foe and the pangs of hunger and had reached the repose of security and the relief of abundance.'

They stayed in Dīzak for four days in complete peace, resting the best they could. And then they set out for Aūrā-tīpā. Babur ensured that he visited the recently-occupied Pashāghar, which was at a little detour. There they came across one of Khānīm's old servants and a teacher. They were informed that Khūb-nigār Khānīm, Babur's mother and Khānim's younger sister had already bidden farewell to the transitory world leaving him in grief.

After consulting Muḥammad Ḥusayn Mīrzā, it was decided that Babur's party would settle in a village called Dikh-kat in Aūrā-tīpā for the upcoming winter. thereafter reaching there, Babur immediately got over his impediment and set out to visit Shāh Begum, Khān Dada and other relatives. Babur spent a few days in Tashkent and waited on Shāh Begum and Khān Dada. His mother's elder sister, Mihr-nigār Khānum had come from Samarkand too and was in Tashkent.

---

* Babur, Abdul Rahim Khan-I-Khanan (trans.), *Tuzk-e Babri*, Delhi: Akbar, 1589, pp. Folio 95b–96. This manuscript is available in National Museum, New Delhi. The Persian translation was done from the original Turkic manuscript of Babur. This was translated by author from the copy kept at National Museum, New Delhi.

When they visited there, Babur's mother fell very ill and just survived a large risk.

His Highness Khwājaka Khwāja had somehow managed to get out of Samarkand and settle down in Far-kat. Babur gave a respectful visit to him. He was hoping that his Khān Dada would shower affection and kindness on him. Babur was also expecting at least a district if not a country. Eventually, he did promise to give Aūrā-tīpā to Babur but Muhammad Ḥusain Mīrzā came in the way. After spending a few days with him (in Aūrā-tīpā), Babur again returned to Dikh-kat.

Dikh-kat was a village in Aūrā-tīpā's hill tracts below the range. On the other side of this range existed a country called Macha. It housed Turks, herdsmen and shepherds—all villagers. Babur and his companions dismounted at the houses of village peasants. Babur stayed in the house of a headsman, who appeared to have seen no less than eighty winters. Babur mentions that his mother too was alive, beyond the age of a hundred. He heard the story that a few of her cousins had gone to Hindustan with Tīmūr Beg's army when he had raised the flag of Islam at Delhi in AD 1398. Dikh-kat alone had ninety-six descendants from her. They were her grandchildren, great-grandchildren and grandchildren's grandchildren. She goes on to count those dead, and the number as told by her was no less than a couple of hundred. Now her grandchild's grandson was a strong twenty-five-year-old man. She chuckled talking of his youth mentioning the deep dark beard he had then.

While staying in Dikh-kat, barefooted excursions among the mountains became a routine for Babur. By doing so for long, his feet had turned immune to the piercing sharp stones. During one such wandering, sometime between afternoon and evening prayers, Babur saw a cow going down a narrow, badly defined road. Babur said to Khwāja Asadu'l-lāh, 'I wonder which way that road will be going; keep your eye on that cow; don't lose the cow till you know where the road comes out.' * Khwāja Asadu'l-lāh then cracked a joke. He said, 'If the cow loses her way, what becomes of us?'

* Babur, Abdul Rahim Khan-I-Khanan (trans.), *Tuzk-e Babri*, Delhi: Akbar, 1589, p. Folio 97b. This manuscript is available in National Museum, New Delhi. The Persian translation was done from the original Turkic manuscript of Babur. This was translated by author from the copy kept at National Museum, New Delhi.

Babur chuckled and then they moved ahead ignoring the cow, cracking more of the lighter jokes.

Things had begun to change in Babur's life. After a series of prolonged raids and fights, his life resembled that of a wandering vagrant's. And then in the winters many of Babur's soldiers asked for leave to visit Andijān. Perhaps, they felt sense in their demand for this was the period devoid of wars. While the party had come to seek the leave, Qāsim Beg with much insistence said, 'As these men are going, send something special of your own *wear* by them to Jahāngīr Mīrzā.' Babur cherished this idea so much that he sent his ermine cap as a gesture. Interestingly, Qāsim Beg even urged, 'What harm would there be if you sent something for Taṃbal also?' Hearing this appeal Babur wore a frown for obvious reasons. But for the respect, Babur held for his every advice, very unwillingly he sent Taṃbal a large broadsword which Nuyān Kūkūldāsh had made for himself in Samarkand. In the very next year, this would be the same sword dancing around to vanquish Babur. Now, in a matter of few days his maternal grandmother, Aīsān-daulat Begum arrived in Dikh-kat. She had stayed back in Samarkand with the families and a few households.

16

The Khān's Country Under Threat

No one in their dreams would have thought of messing with the Khān. But perhaps, Shaybāni wasn't just 'anyone'.

In the winter of AD 1501, after having taken Samarkand and showing Babur out, Shaybāni was looking to take more. The Khujand River was frozen and was not very rideable. But Shaybāni Khān did cross the river and undertook a massive plunder near Shahrukhiya and Bish-kint.

The news of Shaybāni's new deed reached Babur. He was already filled with vengeance and fire, awaiting an opportunity to knock down Shaybāni. Forgetting the smallness of his own numbers, Babur along with his men went for the villages below Khujand, opposite Hasht-yak. The weather was bitterly cold, and the wind was raging violently the whole time piercing the skin wherever exposed. Babur heard the news of a few deaths too because of the cold in that region.

Babur approached an irrigation channel with a desire to perform his ablution. Although the edges were completely frozen and were devoid of any flow, the mid-portion was not frozen because of the swift current. Babur dipped in sixteen times and was left badly bitten by the cold.

The next day, Babur and his men crossed the river from opposite Khaslar and went on through the dark to reach Bish-kint. But till then Shaybāni Khān had already gone away after having plundered the neighbourhood of Shahrukhiya.

Nuyān Kūkūldāsh Dies

In that period, Bīsh-kīnt was held by Mullā Ḥaidar's son, 'Abdu' l-minān. Once upon a time, his younger son, Mūmin had visited Babur in Samarkand and had been showered with all kindness. Babur had observed him to be a worthless and dissipated person. Mūmin was a sodomite* too. There had been some sort of quarrel between Nuyān Kūkūldāsh and him which lasted till the end.

On the other hand, when Babur heard of Aūzbegs' retiring, he sent a man to Khān and marched from Bīsh-kīnt with the purpose to spend a couple of days amongst the villages in the Blacksmith's-dale. Mullā Ḥaidar's son, Mūmin invited Nuyān Kūkūldāsh, Aḥmad-i-Qāsim, and some others in the name of returning them the hospitality received in Samarkand. Hence when Babur left for Bīsh-kīnt, they chose to stay back. Mūmin hosted this treat on the edge of a canyon.

The next day, the news about Nuyān reached Babur while he was stationed in Sām-sīrak, a village in the blacksmith's-dale. He had fallen into the ravine in an inebriated state and had succumbed to his injuries. Babur sent a search party headed by his own mother's brother, Ḥaq-naẓar, to find the body from where he had fallen. His body was found at the bottom of the ravine and was buried with the rituals in the earth in Bīsh-kīnt. Many, including Babur, suspected that it was indeed Mūmin, who, blinded by petty rancour, committed the crime against Nuyān. But the truth never came out.

Babur was broken by this incident. He had not felt such grief, except after the unfortunate death of his father. He kept weeping perpetually for ten days.

Now, summer had begun to approach; and with this pleasing moment came a piece of pale news that Shaybāni Khān was coming to Aūrā-tīpā. Thereby without wasting any time, Babur along with his men crossed the Āb-burdan pass into the Macha hill country. Āb-burdan was the last village of Macha. Just below it, a spring sent its water down to the river, Zarafshan. A tomb existed at the springhead.

* A person who engages in anal sexual intercourse.

At the edge of the springhead, Babur inscribed three couplets on a rock after having got it shaped:*

I have heard that Jamshīd, the magnificent,
Inscribed on a rock at a fountain-head
'Many men like us have taken a breath at this fountain,
And have passed away in the twinkling of an eye;
We took the world by courage and might,
But we took it not with us to the tomb.

It was a regular tradition to inscribe verses on the rocks in the country of hills. While they were in Macha, an acclaimed poet Mullā Hijrī came from Ḥiṣār and waited on Babur. During this period, Babur had composed the following opening lines:†

Let your portrait flatter you never so much, than it you are more;
Men call you their Life than Life, without a doubt, you are more.

Meanwhile, Shaybāni Khān retired after having plundered enough in Aūrā-tīpā. While he was up there, Babur disregarded the lack of numbers of men and their scarce arms supply. They left their impedimenta in Macha and crossed the Āb-burdan pass rushing to Dikh-kat. The intention was very clear that they wanted to gather close at hand and had no desire to miss any chance. However, nothing could progress as they desired. Shaybāni had retired straightway and Babur along with his men had nothing more to do than to return to Macha helplessly.

Babur had turned highly dismayed in that period. He has written in the *Baburnama*, 'It passed through my mind that to wander from mountain to mountain, homeless and houseless, without country or abiding-place, had nothing to recommend it.'

And then Babur realized that there was no other way than going to the great Khān himself. 'Go you right off to the Khān.' Words

* Babur, Abdul Rahim Khan-I-Khanan (trans.), *Tuzk-e Babri*, Delhi: Akbar, 1589, p. Folio 99. This manuscript is available in National Museum, New Delhi. The Persian translation was done from the original Turkic manuscript of Babur. This was translated by author from the copy kept at National Museum, New Delhi.

† Ibid.

echoed in his mind and conveyed the same to Qāsim Beg. But he wasn't so impressed and happy with this proposition. Perhaps he was uncomfortable because once he had killed the Moghūls at Qarā-būlāq, setting an absolute example of terror, guilt had trapped him big time. Babur tried his best, but he couldn't convince him. Finally after losing each argument, yet not changing his opinion, Babur along with a few followers crossed the Āb-burdan pass to get Khān's audience in Tashkent. On the other hand, Qāsim Beg moved forward to Ḥiṣār with all his brothers and following.

Babur Arrives to See Khān

A year ago, Taṃbal had drawn his men out and gone into the blacksmith's-dale. It was then that many men at the top of his army conspired to assassinate him. A few such men were Muhammad Dūghlāt (Ḥiṣārī), his younger brother Ḥusain, and Qaṃbar-'alī. When he discovered this weighty matter, they, unable to remain with him, had gone to Khān.

It was the day of 'Īd-i-qurbān on 16 June of AD 1502. Babur had presented a quatrain to Khān. He was not very well-versed with the poetic idioms and hence asserted that the creation was ordinary. He was also quite hesitant to present it to Khān for he too wrote verses, although none extraordinary. By presenting his quatrain, Babur also raised his doubts to Khān but it came to be of not much help. The verse was as under:*

> One hears no man recall another in trouble;
> None speak of a man as glad in his exile;
> My own heart has no joy in this exile;
> Called glad is no exile, man though he be.

A few days passed. Khān came to know that Taṃbal had gone into Aūrā-tīpā with his army riding out from Tashkent. He formed an array of men on the left and right between Bīsh-kīnt and Sām-sīrak

* Babur, Abdul Rahim Khan-I-Khanan (trans.), *Tuzk-e Babri*, Delhi: Akbar, 1589, p. Folio 100. This manuscript is available in National Museum, New Delhi. The Persian translation was done from the original Turkic manuscript of Babur. This was translated by author from the copy kept at National Museum, New Delhi.

and counted his men. Having known this, the standards were raised in Moghūl fashion. Babur describes it as below in the *Baburnama*:*

> The Khān dismounted and nine standards were set up in front of him. A Moghūl tied a long strip of white cloth to the thigh bone of a cow and took the other end in his hand. Three other long strips of white cloth were tied to the staves of three of the (nine) standards, just below the yak-tails, and their other ends were brought for The Khān to stand on one and for me and Sulṭān Muḥammad Khānika to stand each on one of the two others. The Moghūl who had hold of the strip of cloth fastened to the cow's leg, then said something in Moghūl while he looked at the standards and made signs towards them. The Khān and those present sprinkled qumīz in the direction of the standards; hautbois and drums were sounded towards them; the army flung the war-cry out three times towards them, mounted, cried it again and rode at the gallop round them.

One must note that the Moghūls followed and observed the rules precisely as Genghis Khān had laid them down a couple of centuries back. A typical trait of Moghūls, each man had his place determined, as it had been held by the ancestors—right, left, left, or centre. It was practised that the most reliable men would take the extreme left and right positions. The Chīrās and Begchīk clans always demanded to take the point in the right. In that period, the Beg of the Chīrās Tūmān was one the bravest ever known. His name was Qāshka (Mole-marked) Mahmud, and Ayūb Begchīk was the renowned beg of the Begchīk Tūmān. Horrifically enough, both drew swords on one another, disputing who would take the right point. Finally, when elders intervened, it was concluded that both would take the very position respectively in the hunting circle and the battle-array.

The next day they made enough rounds and finally decided to go hunting near Sāmsīrak. Following this, they moved to the Tūrāk Four-Gardens. Babur seemed to have cherished this moment. On that

* Ibid.

day and in that camp, he finished his first ode. The opening couplet reads as follows:*

> Except my soul, no friend worth trust found I;
> Except my heart, no confidant found I.

The ode consisted of six couplets.

Khān had begun to march from Sām-sīrak to the bank of the Khujand River along with Babur. One very fine day, they crossed the water of Khujand like an excursion. There, they cooked food making merry with the soldiers. Babur has recalled that day as an eventful one, marked by an unfaithful occurrence—someone stole the gold clasp of his girdle.

And the next day, after the festivities, something obnoxious occurred which many had suspected from quite long. Bayān-qulī's son Khān-qulī and Sulṭān Muḥammad Wais fled to Taṃbal. At the same time, Aḥmad-i-qāsim Kohbur asked for a leave and went to Aūrā-tīpā, never to return as he too went to Taṃbal.

* Babur, Abdul Rahim Khan-I-Khanan (trans.), *Tuzk-e Babri*, Delhi: Akbar, 1589, p. Folio 100. This manuscript is available in National Museum, New Delhi. The Persian translation was done from the original Turkic manuscript of Babur. This was translated by author from the copy kept at National Museum, New Delhi.

17

Babur in Tashkent (July of AD 1502–June AD of 1503)

His Poverty

The great Khān's new move was useless and unprofitable in Babur's opinion. He was not on a quest to take up a fort or beat any enemy. He was simply entering and leaving the regions. Babur's stay did not seem like a good experience for him either. During his stay in Tashkent, Babur was not only impoverished but also humiliation had become a part of his daily life. The Tīmūrid prince did not own or control any country and it seemed as if despair was there to stay. Most of his retainers had dispersed and those left in small numbers were unable to move about with Babur because of their own insolvency.

The desperation of Babur to get country, lordship and the house was very much evident. When he went to Khān Dada's Gate, only a man or two accompanied him. He would often walk into Shāh Begum's house, bareheaded and barefoot as if it was his own.

This uncertainty and want of house had sent him into a state of loathing. He has written in the *Baburnama*, 'It would be better to take my head and go off than live in such misery; better to go as far as my feet can carry me than be seen of men in such poverty and humiliation.'

Then, Babur decided to move to China. It had always been his wish, perhaps since he was a child, to visit China. But, the royal duties and attachments had always kept this dream at bay. Now that sovereignty itself was gone and his mother seemed settled with her stepmother and younger brother, Babur thought it was an apt time to visit China. Babur sent out Khwāja Abū'l-makāram as his representative to Shāh Begum and the Khān. He conveyed that 'now such a foe as Shaybāni Khān had made his appearance, Moghūl and Turk alike must guard against him; that thought about him must be taken while he had not well-mastered the (Aūzbeg) horde or grown very strong'. In the message, he had sent out a verse:*

To-day, while thou canst, quench the fire,
Once ablaze it will burn up the world;
Let thy foe not fix string to his bow,
While an arrow of thine can pierce him;

And having set this premise, Babur proposed to get out of his circumstances laced with humiliation and pain. Babur was already dreaming that once he reached Moghūlistān and Turfān, his reins would be in his control. He was assuming that the phase of anxiety would vanish. Babur did not put anyone in possession of his over-ambitious plan.

The Khwāja laid out Babur's plan thoroughly before Shāh Begum and the Khān. Initially, they refused to consent. Perhaps they were tied with guilt that Babur was seeking leave for not having received much kindness. But finally, Babur was granted the leave, although delayed.

The Younger Khān Arrives in Tashkent

Babur had planned his visit to China and taken leave by creating a strong, confident image of the younger Khān (Ahmad Alacha) in the minds of the Khān and Shāh Begum. Just then, an emissary informed that the younger Khān was already on his way. Babur knew that his arrival would lead to the cancellation of his journey to China. He could mince the minds of the Shāh Begum and the Khān, but not Babur's.

* Babur, Abdul Rahim Khan-I-Khanan (trans.), *Tuzk-e Babri*, Delhi: Akbar, 1589, p. Folio 101 b. This manuscript is available in National Museum, New Delhi. The Persian translation was done from the original Turkic manuscript of Babur. This was translated by author from the copy kept at National Museum, New Delhi.

The nearing of the younger Khān was then announced by a second emissary. Babur along with others went out to give him an honourable welcome along with Shāh Begum, his younger sisters, Sulṭān-nigār Khānum, Daulat Sulṭān Khānum, Sulṭān Muḥammad Khānika and Khān Mīrzā (Wais).

According to Babur, they went to the tombs of prophets Abraham and Issacs. He mentioned in the *Baburnama* that they were in a village called Yagha somewhere in between Tashkent and Sairām.

The younger Khān arrived. His eyes met Babur's. Though he didn't dismount immediately, Babur bowed out of respect. With Khān were Sulṭān Sa'īd Khān, Bābā Khān Sulṭān, and his two sons who did not bother to dismount. Agitated by the two teens, Khān told them to dismount and bend the knee to (bīla) Babur to confer due respect. Getting over with a courteous welcome they all proceeded to see the most respectable Shāh Begum. The younger Khān, after having bestowed respect on her and seen his sisters, went on to banter almost the whole of the night. Indeed, they had a lot to share for whatever transpired in their lives while he was away.

Despite a long night of conversations, he woke up quite early. The morning's audience between Babur and him was quite intimate. The younger Khān bequeathed Babur his arms and gifted him one of his very special horses. He also presented Babur with a Moghūl head-to-foot dress which included a Moghūl cap, a long coat of Chinese satin with a work of embroidery and Chinese armour. It was much older in fashion wherein on the left side a sack and an outer bag were hung. It also had a few things which women, in general, hung on their collars such as perfume-holders and various receptacles. Similarly, the right side of the armour was loaded with three or four things.

Then, they resumed the travel to Tashkent. Babur's elder Khān Dada too had come out to welcome the younger one. He sat on the temporary awning, waiting at fifteen miles from the Tashkent. The younger Khān went up directly to him with a broad smile. He made around left to right around his elder brother and then finally dismounted in front of him. After advancing to the place of interview (kūrūshūr yīr), he bent the knee nine times. Then he saw his brother from close. The elder Khān, who smiled compassionately, rose and both looked into each other's eyes, and then stood in a close embrace for long. The younger Khān again bent the knee nine times before retiring and offered gifts that he had got for him.

He had arrived with a party of not less than 200 men. All his men had bejewelled themselves in Moghūl fashion, sported the Moghūl caps, long coats of Chinese satin embroidered with stitchery, Moghūl quivers and saddles of green shagreen leather. Their Moghūl horses too were decorated uniquely. In Babur's opinion, he was a man of remarkable mannerisms and a mighty brave master of the sword. The sword was indeed his most trusted arm. He often used to say that 'of arms there are, the *shash-par* (six-flanged mace), the *piyāzī* (rugged mace), the *kīstin*, the *tabar-zīn* (saddle-hatchet) and the *bāltū* (battle-axe), all if they strike, work only with what of them first touches, but the sword, if it touches, works from point to hilt'.

In fact, he never parted from his keen-edged sword. It always lay hanging to his waist or settled in his hands. It was claimed that he was a man with rustic and rough speech owing to having grown up in an out-of-the-way place.

The Khāns Go Against Taṃbal

Soon after the younger Khān returned to Tashkent, they led out an army for Andijān directing an attack straight against Sulṭān Aḥmad Taṃbal on the fifteenth (21 July) day of Muharram in AD 1502. He chose to march on the road over the Kīndīrlīk-pass. He had instructed the younger Khān and Babur to leave from the blacksmith's-dale well in advance. After the Kīndīrlīk-pass had been crossed, they all met near Zarqān of Karnān. They counted their men and came to be no lesser than 30,000.

They heard the news that Taṃbal had also begun to collate his men and was heading to Akhsī. Hearing the news, the Khāns consulted together and decided to send a few men with Babur. He was supposed to cross the Khujand water, march by the way of Aūsh and Aūzkīnt, and bring havoc of attack on Taṃbal's rear side. Babur was assigned Ayūb Begchīk with his Tūmān, Jān-ḥasan Bārīn (var. Nārīn) with his Bārīns, Muḥammad Ḥiṣārī Dūghlāt, Sulṭān Ḥusain Dūghlāt, and Sulṭān Aḥmad Mīrzā Dūghlāt to campaign a rear attack. Their force was being commanded by Sārīgh-bāsh Mīrza Itārchī.

Seeing off the Khāns in Karnān, the men under Babur crossed the river on rafts near Sakan. They traversed the Khūqān sub-district, crushing Qabā and by way of the Alāī sub-districts, finally descending on Osh with complete vigour. Babur had made it to the place at dawn and the foe was taken by surprise. They had no option but to surrender. The people of the country had always been by their side but the remoteness of the Khāns and Babur himself buttressed by the dread of Taṃbal kept them off any action. After Babur barged into Osh, the tribesmen of highland and lowland, southern and eastern Andijān joined hands with him. The people of Aūzkīnt too came in support of Babur.

The Marghīnānīs had also come to join Babur. They beat and chased their commandant black and blue. Every fort to the south of Khujand, except Andijān, had come forward to join hands with Babur. The truth was that Taṃbal was badly broken with the return of many forts and rising revolts. Yet, Taṃbal didn't appear to bend even a bit. He sat down with an army of horsemen and foot soldiers, fortified with ditch and branch, to face the Khāns, between Karnān and Akhsī. Small skirmishes and fights became a regular feature, yet there was no clear sign of success yet.

Now, even all the tribes, hordes, forts and districts of Andijān country had joined hands with Babur. Andijānīs indeed always wished good for Babur although they could never find the right means to express their allegiance. Babur thought that if they went close to the town at night and sent a man in to discuss with the Khwāja and notables, they might perhaps have let them in somewhere. With this belief in mind, Babur rode out from Osh. They were merely a couple of miles away from Andijān around midnight. From there they sent Qaṃbar-'alī Beg forward with some other begs as per the plan to deliberate a discussion with the Khwāja. Babur was quite certain that post that discussion he would be able to get his men into the fort.

After they went, Babur, while being seated on his horse, kept waiting for their return anxiously. Few had patiently humped up, while others had descended into slumber. But soon, at about the third watch, there rose the sound of drums and yells of war cries. Unaware of the enemies' strength, sleepy and startled, Babur's men jumped into the battle without having looked at each other. There was no time for Babur to get at them and he went straight for the enemy. Mīr Shāh Qūchīn, Bābā Sher-zād, Nāṣir's Dost and Babur sprang forward, leading the fight. While Babur was steadily marching forward, the enemy rode rapidly, gave out the war cry and showered arrows like the heaviest of rain. One of the men from the foe's side came too close to Babur, whom Babur shot without wasting a moment and sending him beyond the world briskly. The enemy was turning fiercer with every passing moment and Babur's camp's momentary unpreparedness was also adding fuel to it.

The three others who were leading with Babur said, 'In this darkness, it is not certain whether they are many or few; all our men have gone off; what harm could we four do them? Fighting must be when we have overtaken our runaways and rallied them.'

They were indeed worried. Yet they had to give a fight—they were trying their best. They hurried, got up with their men, beat and horse-whipped some of the enemies but whatever they would do, they stood nowhere close to the strength and pace of the enemy. Babur and the other three leaders kept on showering arrows tirelessly at the enemy. As it was apparent that Babur's strength in numbers had almost zeroed, the enemy retaliated with even more force and fire. They began to unhorse the remaining men.

Babur thrice or more attempted to rally his men, but all in vain. Defeat seemed imminent now. However, the four, including Babur, kept wreaking havoc on enemies relentlessly without any results. Now the enemies had got behind Babur and the rest. They chased them for around six miles, as far as the rising ground opposite Kharābūk and Pashāmūn. Babur and his men could save their lives by a whisker.

Reaching there Babur met Muḥammad 'Alī Mubashir and said, 'They are only a few; let us stop and put our horses at them.' Muḥammad 'Alī Mubashir seemed convinced by what Babur proposed and they did the same. And when they stood up to the enemy, they became still. Babur's scattered men gathered in from the side, but several very serviceable men, scattering in this attack, went right to Osh.

Babur explains this affair in the *Baburnama* as below:*

> Some of Ayūb Begchīk's Moghūls had slipped away from Aūsh to raid near Andijān and, hearing the noise of our troop, came somewhat

* Babur, Abdul Rahim Khan-I-Khanan (trans.), *Tuzk-e Babri*, Delhi: Akbar, 1589, p. Folio 105b. This manuscript is available in National Museum, New Delhi. The Persian translation was done from the original Turkic manuscript of Babur. This was translated by author from the copy kept at National Museum, New Delhi.

stealthily towards us; then there seems to have been confusion about the password.[1] The passwords settled on for use during this movement of ours were Tashkent and Sairām. If Tashkent were said, Sairām would be answered; if Sairām, Tashkent. In this muddled affair, Khwāja Muḥammad 'Ali seems to have been somewhat in advance of our party and to have got bewildered, —he was a Sārt person, —when the Moghūls came up saying, 'Tashkent, Tashkent,' for he gave them 'Tashkent, Tashkent,' as the countersign. Through this, they took him for an enemy, raised their war-cry, beat their saddle drums, and poured arrows on us. It was through this we gave way, and through this false alarm were scattered! We went back to Aūsh.

Bābur Again Attempts to Take Andijān

Apart from the aforementioned incident, the returning efforts of clans from the highland and lowland to the other side made Taṃbal lose heart big time however wicked he may have been. Within a week, his military and people started deserting him. They were fleeing to retired places and the open country. To add to Babur's delight, one from the household of Babur came and conveyed to him, 'His affairs are nearly ruined; he will break up in three or four days, utterly ruined.'

Hearing this, the over-excited Babur decided to ride to Andijān again.

Then the younger of Taṃbal's cadet brothers, Sulṯān Muḥammad Galpuk, was in Andijān. Babur along with his party took the mulberry road. By the time of midday prayer, they had reached Khākān (canal), south of the town. A foraging party was sent. Babur followed it along Khākān to the skirt of 'Aīsh-hill. The scouts brought the message for Babur. According to them, Sulṯān Muḥammad Galpuk had ventured out with whatever number of men he had, beyond the suburbs to the skirt of 'Aīsh. Babur didn't want to miss the chance. He hurried to meet him, although the foragers were still scattered. Galpuk perhaps had more than 500 men, and despite having more men in totality most of them on Babur's side were scattered as foragers.

When the two came face to face, it appeared that both sides had a similar number of men. Without showing much care about the order or array of the formation, they galloped on horses, losing rein. As they got near, Galpuk's men could not stand the fight. The swords were crossed but for no glory to the enemies of Babur. Babur's men chased them almost till the Khākān Gate, unhorsing one after another. By the evening prayer, Babur's men had out-mastered the Galpuk's troops, reaching Khwāja Kitta, on the outskirts of the suburbs.

Babur was very clear with his ideas. He wanted to go quickly right up to the gate but Qaṃbar-'alī Beg and Dost Beg's father, Nāṣir Beg, with their experience, said, 'It is almost night; it would be ill-judged to go in a body into the fort in the dark; let us withdraw a little and dismount. What can they do tomorrow but surrender the place?'

Babur, respecting the advice of the two experienced begs decided to retire to the outskirts of the suburbs. However, he regretted paying heed to their advice. In the *Baburnama* he has written, 'If we had gone to the Gate, undoubtedly, Andijān would have come into our hands.'

Taṃbal Shocks Babur

By the time Babur and his men crossed the Khākān canal, the sun had disappeared completely. They dismounted around nighttime prayers near the village of Rabāṭ-i-Zauraq. Babur knew that Taṃbal had broken from his camp and was on the way to Andijān. In this context, Babur has called out the opinion of his two experienced begs as negligent and inexperienced. Babur has said that by further showing inexperience, they dismounted on level ground close to the village, instead of where the defensive canal would have protected them much more. There they laid down carelessly, without scouts or any rearward troops.

The morning had just begun when Qaṃbar-'alī Beg's shouts echoed hard. He was shouting, 'Up with you! The enemy is here!'

Babur's fear and judgement from last evening had proven to be true.

He asked the men to take positions as soon as possible. Unlike his habit of lying down to think even in times of emergencies, Babur was up in his tunic instantly. He put on the sword and quiver and mounted on the horse briskly. The standard-bearer could not adjust the standards in this time of rush. He just mounted with it in his hand. Babur had around fifteen men with him when he started riding towards the enemy. After riding like an arrow, Babur came across enemies' scouts, numbering around ten. Going briskly as they could, enemies showered arrows on Babur as he overtook them. Babur overmastered his foremost men and hurried them off. Babur along with his men followed them at great speed and came up with his centre where Sulṭān Aḥmad Taṃbal stood firm. He was accompanied by around 100 men. He stood in front of his array like a gatekeeper, strong and brave. He yelled, 'Strike, strike!'

But something unusual happened. Most of his men were sidling. They appeared to be in a state of fix, questioning themselves, 'Shall we run away? Shall we not?'

Of the fifteen accompanying Babur, only three were left namely, Nāṣir Dost, Mīrzā Qulī Kūkūldāsh and Khudāī-bīrdī Turkmān Karīm-dād.

Babur shot off an arrow on his thumb, aimed at Taṃbal's helm. Doing so, when Babur put his hand into his quiver, there came out a new *gosha-gīr*[2] that was given to him by his younger Khān dada. Babur felt that it indeed would have been annoying to throw it away, however, the situation required him to shoot a couple of arrows. Then once again, he placed an arrow on the string and went forward, while his three men held back the stand. Taṃbal moved forward as well. The high road lay between both. Babur from his side and he from his climbed upon the high road finally facing each other. His right hand was towards Babur and vice versa. Except for the mail of his horse, he was fully accoutred. On the other hand, Babur was completely unprotected, devoid of any armour.

Babur shot off the arrow. His foe, Taṃbal adjusted the attachment of his shield conveniently to counter what was coming. They shot at Babur's right leg. Taṃbal came shouting and attacked Babur on the head. The blow created a large wound on Babur's head (thought not a thread of his cap was affected), whacking him out of his senses for long. He had yet not uncovered his sword, and it was lying unused in the scabbard. He never got a chance to draw it. Babur was in a vulnerable position, surrounded by many enemies. He couldn't stand still. And then upon him came Tambal's sword again, this time on his arrows. By then his three remaining companions came in to stand for their king. After having weakened Babur completely with his sword, Taṃbal attacked Nāṣir Dost too. Things had begun to turn extremely disastrous for Babur. With no option left, Babur and his companions began to retreat. But enemies chased Babur and the other three for quite a distance.

The Khākān canal used to be a great main channel. It flowed in a deep cutting that could not be crossed everywhere. But in this instance, Babur thanked Allah, as they came exactly opposite a low place where there existed an overpass. They crossed it directly. In the process, Nāṣir Dost's horse fell, turning weak to the force. They stopped and remounted Dost and drew off for Osh, over the rising ground between Ferghana and Khirābūk. As they reached the elevated spot, Mazīd Ṯaghāī came up to join them. His right leg was injured after being pierced by an arrow and could make it to Osh only after extreme difficulty. In this skirmish, Babur lost many soldiers, including Nāṣir Beg, Muḥammad 'Alī Mubashir, Khwāja Muḥammad 'Alī, Khusrau Kūkūldāsh and Na'man the page along with many unmailed warriors.

The Khāns Make a Move from Kāsān to Andijān

The Khāns had been closely following Taṃbal's trail. Hence, they dismounted near Andijān at the side of the reserve in the garden, known as Birds' Mill (Qūsh-tīgīrmān). It belonged to Babur's maternal grandmother, Aīsān-daulat Begum. Two days had passed since the Khāns had dismounted near Andijān and Babur had travelled from Osh to see the elder Khān in Birds'Mill.

That meeting had been a bit sour for Babur. The elder Khān simply gave away all the forts and places won by Babur to the younger Khān. According to Babur, he did spell out the reasons for doing so. In his opinion, it was done for an advantage. Babur was also told by the elder Khān that Shaybāni Khān had already taken Samarkand, and the younger Khān had no lands of his own and hence the lands under Andijān, on the south of the Khujand-water, must be given to him for encampment. The elder Khān promised to grant Babur the country under Akhsī, on the north of the Khujand-water. He also confirmed that after establishing a firm grip on Ferghana, they would also move to take Samarkand, and it would be given to Babur. The whole of the Ferghana country would then be controlled by the younger Khān.

Babur felt that these words were said to deceive him. Having seen their acts so far it was tough for Babur to believe how much they would stick to their words after having attained the objective. But at the same time, Babur had to agree for he had no other option.

After the interview with the elder Khān, Babur went ahead to meet the younger Khān. Qaṃbar-'alī joined Babur on the way. He said, 'Do you see? They have taken the whole of the country just become yours. There is no opening for you through them. You have in your hands, Osh, Marghīnān, Aūzkīnt, the cultivated land, the tribes, and the hordes. You go to Osh; make that fort fast; send a man to Taṃbal, make peace with him, then strike at the Moghūl and drive him out. After that, divide the districts into an elder and a younger brother's share.'

Babur responded, 'Would that be right? The Khāns are my blood relations; better serve them than rule for Taṃbal.'*

Seeing that his words could not leave an impression on Babur, Qaṃbar-'alī turned away, disheartened by his own words. Babur then went on to see his younger Khān Dada.

At this very first audience, Babur had appeared unannounced and even the Khān had no time to dismount, hence it turned out to be rather unceremonious. This time, Babur got even nearer perhaps, but the Khān ran out as far as the end of the tent-ropes. Babur was finding it quite difficult to walk because of the wound in the leg. Finally, they met, and Babur greeted him as per the protocol. And then Khān said, 'You have talked about as a hero, my young brother!'

He took Babur's arm leading him into his tent. In general, the tents around had very small pitches but the one in which he lived had long pitches at an unusual place. His tent, like that of raiders, was full of melons, grapes, saddlery and every sort of thing. After meeting him, Babur returned to his own camp where he was sent a Moghūl surgeon by the younger Khān to examine the leg wound. In the Moghūl language, a surgeon was also called a *bakhshī*. The one who visited Babur was called Ātākā Bakhshī.

* Babur, Abdul Rahim Khan-I-Khanan (trans.), *Tuzk-e Babri*, Delhi: Akbar, 1589, p. Folio 108b. This manuscript is available in National Museum, New Delhi. The Persian translation was done from the original Turkic manuscript of Babur. This was translated by author from the copy kept at National Museum, New Delhi.

Babur showers abundant praises to this surgeon who according to him, was very skilful. He has written, 'If a man's brains had come out, he would cure it, and any sort of wound in an artery he easily healed.' The surgeon in general used to recommend a form of plaster for wounds along with some medicines.

But for Babur, he ordered a bandage (made from the skin of a fox leg) to be tied on the wound without any seton. He also made Babur consume some sort of a fibrous root. He told Babur, 'A certain man had his leg broken in the slender part and the bone was shattered for the breadth of the hand. I cut the flesh open and took the bits of bone out. Where they had been, I put a remedy in powder form. That remedy simply became bone where there had been bone before.'*

He kept narrating many strange stories to Babur while treating him.

Four days passed. Babur was still recovering, and Qaṃbar-'alī had not shown his face to him so far. Perhaps, he was perplexed about the last conversation he had with Babur. Babur feared that he might have fled to Taṃbal in Andijān.

Babur recovered over the next few days. The Khāns attached Ayūb Begchīk with his tūmān, Jān-ḥasan Bārīn with the Bārīn tūmān, Sārīgh-bāsh Mīrzā as the army-beg and 2000 men with Babur, instructing them to make a move to Akhsī.

Babur Moves to Akhsī

Then, Akhsī was in control of Taṃbal's younger brother, Shaikh Bāyazīd and Shahbāz Qārlūq controlled Kāsān. Shahbāz was lying before Nū-kīnt fort. He was due to cross the Khujand-water opposite Bīkhrātā. Babur and his men hurried to accost him right there. It was just a little before dawn, when Babur was almost near the place when his begs informed that Shaikh Bāyazīd perhaps knew about the plan of attack. The begs advised to not go on in a broken array. Hence Babur ensured that his men kept moving at a slower speed thereby maintaining the array. The information passed on by the begs was perhaps not very true. Babur could sense that Shahbāz was unaware of them until they drew closer. And

* Babur, Abdul Rahim Khan-I-Khanan (trans.), *Tuzk-e Babri*, Delhi: Akbar, 1589. p. Folio 109. This manuscript is available in National Museum, New Delhi. The Persian translation was done from the original Turkic manuscript of Babur. This was translated by author from the copy kept at National Museum, New Delhi.

when he came to know this, he fled into the fort. Babur has recounted this experience in the *Baburnama* as follows:*

> It often happens so! Once having said, 'The enemy is on guard!' it is easily fancied true, and the chance of action is lost. In short, the experience of such things is that no effort or exertion must be omitted once the chance for action comes. After-repentance is useless.

There was a little fighting around the fort at the dawn and no serious attacks took place.

For the sake of foraging, Babur and his men moved from Nū-kīnt towards the hills in the direction of Bīshkhārān. Shahbāz Qārlūq saw this as an opportunity, and he abandoned Nū-kīnt, making a return to Kāsān. Babur occupied Nū-kīnt effortlessly.

Then began Babur's campaigns. Following that flightless victory, Babur's army overran almost all the sides and quarters, the villages of Akhsī and Kāsān. Finally, Shahbāz and Long Ḥasan's adopted son, Mīrīm came out of Kāsān to give a fight only to see a humiliating defeat with the latter's death.

The Businesses of Pāp

Akhsī had a strong fort named Pāp, whose people harboured some plans. They immediately sent out a representative to Babur who conveyed people's desire to join his side. Accordingly, in return, Babur sent Sayyid Qāsim with a few brave men to occupy the fort. Sayyid Qāsim was a noble and administrator in Babur's court. He is particularly known for serving as the wazir (chief minister) and most trusted advisor under Babur's son, Humayun. He would be instrumental in helping Humayun consolidate his rule and administer the empire during the most challenging phase.

They crossed the river, reaching the opposite side of the upper villages of Akhsī and barged directly into Pāp. Soon afterwards, Sayyid Qāsim did an astonishing thing.

---

* Babur, Abdul Rahim Khan-I-Khanan (trans.), *Tuzk-e Babri*, Delhi: Akbar, 1589, p. Folio 101 b. This manuscript is available in National Museum, New Delhi. The Persian translation was done from the original Turkic manuscript of Babur. This was translated by author from the copy kept at National Museum, New Delhi.

There came a time when Shaikh Bāyazīd in Akhsī, Ibrāhīm Chāpūk Ṭaghāī, Aḥmad-of-qāsim Kohbur, and Qāsim Khitika Arghūn were attached with around 200 serviceable warriors and instructed to surprise Pāp on a fateful night. Sayyid Qāsim was in deep sleep without keeping a watch. They reached the fort, set ladders up, and got up on the gate, let the drawbridge down and, when around eighty good men in the mail were inside, the drowsy Sayyid Qāsim got the news of what was happening. Without wasting a moment, dozy with sleep, he got into his *kūnglāk* and then went out,with half a dozen of his men. Surprisingly, he delivered several blows and successfully drove the enemy out. He sent out the heads of beheaded troops to Babur as a present.

Despite setting a bad precedent after being carried away by sleep, his chasing away of troops with just half a dozen support indeed was an act of bravery (as narrated by Babur).

At the same time, the Khāns were occupied with the siege of Andijān, and they were kept on their toes by the garrison, who did not let them get nearer. The fight was on.

Babur Is Bidden into Akhsī

Things, which Babur had never imagined, were about to unfold. Shaikh Bāyazīd had begun to send people to Babur from Akhsī. Those people not only were well-wishing but also pressingly invited him to Akhsī. Perhaps, his intentions were clear. He wanted to separate Babur from the Khāns. Babur's removal from the list of their support would have suddenly brought a big dent. And certainly, if that was the truth, Taṃbal's brain must have been behind it. Babur sent out the hint of the occurrences to the Khāns.

And they said, 'Go! and by whatever means, lay hands on Shaikh Bāyazīd.'

Babur has asserted in the *Baburnama*, 'It was not my habit to cheat and play false; here above all places, when promises would have been made, how was I to break them?'*

* Babur, Abdul Rahim Khan-I-Khanan (trans.), *Tuzk-e Babri*, Delhi: Akbar, 1589. p. Folio 110b. This manuscript is available in National Museum, New Delhi. The Persian translation was done from the original Turkic manuscript of Babur. This was translated by author from the copy kept at National Museum, New Delhi.

And then a thought occurred to Babur that if they could get into Akhsī, they could detach brothers Shaikh Bāyazīd and Taṃbal by making the former take up Babur's side. In fact, Babur wanted to play the same ploy on the brother-duo that they wanted to play on him to separate him from the Khāns. With his aspirations set in the right order, Babur sent out a man to him. Good discussions took place and in return, he invited Babur into Akhsī. Finally, Babur went to meet him. Shaikh Bāyazīd, accompanied by Babur's younger brother, Nāṣir Mīrzā, came to see him. Babur's men were given to camp in the ground amid the town while Babur himself was given his father's houses in the outer fort.

Taṃbal Reaches Out to Shaybāni Khān

Taṃbal delegated his elder brother Beg Tīlba to meet Shaybāni Khān. The intent was to offer service, thereby inviting him to enter Ferghana. To not render Taṃbal hopeless, he replied, 'I will come.'

This news was not going to bode well for Khāns and Babur. It left them perturbed as well as upset. They could no longer afford the comfort of the Andijān. The younger Khān cherished his reputation for delivering justice and respecting traditions. But Moghūls under him, stationed in Osh, Marghīnān, etc. places conquered by Babur, had begun to adopt bullying tactics, against the expectations of the people of the town. They had turned highly oppressive. And then when the Khāns broke up from before Andijān, the Oshis and Marghīnānīs erupted in uproar. An uproar seemed buried under some soft soil.

They seized the Moghūls in their forts. They were plundered and beaten in the worst manner possible. And finally shown the way out from there.

The Khāns were careful not to cross the Khujand-water (for the Kīndīrlīk-pass), rather they left the country via Marghīnān and Kand-i-badām, crossing it at Khujand. Taṃbal chased them as far as Marghīnān. Not only Babur and his men but the Khāns too seemed to be devoid of confidence. Babur was uncertain about his next stand. But he was certainly in no mood to go away, without clear reason, and leave them. He was worried about his reputation, too.

Bābur Fights to Defend Akhsī

The circumstances were not very conducive then. It was one very early morning. Babur was lying in his hot bath when Jahāngīr Mīrzā escaped from Taṃbal and arrived at Akhsī after fleeing from Marghīnān. A meeting took place between the two. Shaikh Bāyazīd was present there as well. Shaikh appeared agitated and afraid to see Mīrzā arriving. The Mīrzā and Ibrāhīm Beg were very clear about what needs to be done to Shaikh Bāyazīd. Mīrzā said, 'Shaikh Bāyazīd must be made prisoner and we must get the citadel into our hands.'

Babur found Mīrzā's proposal very sound and wise. Babur replied, 'Promise has been made; how can we break it?' Then, Shaikh Bāyazīd went into the citadel. Ideally, Babur should have posted men on the bridge, but none were deployed.

Babur goes on to call them big blunders which certainly occurred for his lack of experience. The result was indeed not going to be very promising for Babur. The very next morning, came the vicious Taṃbal with 3000 men in the mail, crossing the bridge and bashing into the citadel without any obstacle.

Babur was left with very few men whom he could deploy on the way to the citadel and once inside it. He had sent the bulk of his men to other forts, and some had been made commandants and summoners all around. The count of men left in Akhsī was not more than a hundred. Shaikh Bāyazīd, Qaṃbar-'alī, and Muhammad-dost came galloping from Taṃbal, proposing a truce. Babur didn't find it in the right taste and instructed his hundred men to approach the horses and prepare for a war.

Babur invited Jahāngīr Mīrzā to join him too and he rode to his father's tomb to address his men before the war. Qaṃbar-'alī and Shaikh Bāyazīd stood with Babur, but Muhammad-dost rode back to Taṃbal. Babur and his men were assembled on the south porch of the tomb discussing the way forward with the Mīrzā. Babur had assumed that he must have settled beforehand with Ibrāhīm Chāpūk to attack the other two. He whispered in Babur's ear, 'They must be made prisoner.' Babur replied, 'Don't hurry! Matters are past making prisoners. See here! with terms made, the affair might be coaxed into something. For why? Not only are they many and we few, but they with their strength are in the citadel, we with our weakness, in the outer fort.'*

With both Shaikh Bāyazīd and Qaṃbar-'alī being present, Jahāngīr Mīrzā looked at Ibrāhīm Beg and signalled him from refraining from making arrests. But perhaps he misunderstood the signal or pretended so. He suddenly seized Shaikh Bāyazīd. Although this was well settled and adjusted, an instance like that shouldn't have occurred in the first place, according to Babur.

They assigned the charge of one side of the town to Jahāngīr Mīrzā. Babur even assigned a few of his men to him as he was short in number. Babur himself went to his side and posted the men and then went to other parts of the town to put the fighters in place.

Babur had posted a party of braves in a rare, less contoured open space in the middle of Akhsī. When Babur left, a large contingent of the enemy arrived. They were full in strength, mounted on the horse and foot. They chased the men from the post and were bound to be shoved into a narrow lane. Hearing about the problem, Babur came up the lane and galloped his horse at the enemies. Babur's force was apt and massive, and he forced them to flee. But while Babur was ferociously at work, one from the enemies' camp shot his horse in the leg. It stumbled and threw Babur amid the herd of the enemy. He hurried to get up as soon as possible and began to shoot arrows again. Babur's squire Kahil came forward to help. He stepped down from his weak pony and offered Babur to mount it. Babur took the pony and cruised to the next lane to behead more enemies.

Perhaps Babur had gained abundant love from his people. Seeing him mount a weak pony, Sulṭān Muhammad Wais offered his horse. As Babur mounted the horse, Qāsim Beg's son Qaṃbar-'alī came yelling but ended up being shattered completely. He was badly wounded. They informed him that Jahāngīr Mīrzā had been attacked some time ago. He had ridden away in a state of panic along with his men.

Babur has said that they were 'thunderstruck' at that moment.

---

* Babur, Abdul Rahim Khan-I-Khanan (trans.), *Tuzk-e Babri*, Delhi: Akbar, 1589, p. Folio 112b. This manuscript is available in National Museum, New Delhi. The Persian translation was done from the original Turkic manuscript of Babur. This was translated by author from the copy kept at National Museum, New Delhi.

When all these ruckuses were demotivating Babur, Sayyid Qāsim, the commandant of Pāp, arrived. He was badly wounded and could neither tell the reason for his arrival, nor he could tell what wrong had happened to him. This was completely unexpected for Babur. In such a period of crisis, it was highly unwise to let the strong fort of Pāp go unattended. Babur called Ibrāhīm Beg and whispered, 'What's to be done now?' Beg's reply hasn't been documented.

Now, Babur began to germinate an idea that he would get across the bridge, destroy it, and get straight to Andijān. Babur was morally boosted by all his compatriots. Bābā Sher-zād said, 'We will storm out at the gate and get away at once.' And many others spelt the words of motivation.

They set off for the gate that very instant. Khwāja Mīr Mīrān also motivated the folks as they marched outwards.

Now, they had reached the opposite end of the gate. There appeared Shaikh Bāyazīd, dressed in his pull-over shirt above the vest, accompanied by a quadrat of horsemen. In the morning, he had been arrested by Jahāngīr's men against Babur's will but needed to be released once the latter chanced upon him at the gate. Though Babur kept wondering what made them keep him alive.

Babur drew and shot off the arrow on his thumb. It grazed Shaikh's neck. He ran down in a lane. Babur and his men followed him instantly. Mīrzā Qulī Kūkūldāsh did not seem to be forgiving. His rugged mace got hold of an enemy. He went on with his attack. One of the men took a shot at Ibrāhīm Beg but it hit Babur in the armpit instead from as near as a man on guard at a gate. Two plates of Babur's Qālmāq mail were cut. The man was coming heavy on Babur. But within a few moments, Babur was able to shoot him down. Next, Babur shot at a man running away along the ramparts, adjusting his cap against the battlements. He left his cap nailed on the wall and went off, gathering his turban-sash together in his hand. Then another man took up the fight with Babur down the lane in which Shaikh Bāyazīd had fled. Babur stabbed the rear of his head with his sword mercilessly. He bent over from his horse and then leaned against the wall of the lane. But he didn't let himself off the seat and fought Babur well.

Slowly and steadily, Babur had driven away his enemy from the gate. And then he along with his men took the gate's possession.

But the challenge was still uphill for him as there were around three thousand men in the citadel against 200 on Babur's side in the outer fort. Moreover, Babur's enemy had chased off Jahāngīr Mīrzā, 'as quickly as it takes milk to boil' (proverb used by Babur). It was a substantial loss for him and with him had gone half of his men. Nevertheless, Babur sent a man, from the gate to Jahāngīr Mīrzā. The messenger was supposed to convey the message as below:*

> If you are near at hand, come, let us attack again.

But perhaps the matter wasn't that simple. They kept waiting at the gate for the men sent to Jahāngīr Mīrzā to come back. They returned with some distressing news— Jahāngīr had gone off long before they reached, and they couldn't trace him. Babur felt that it was a wrong decision to wait for so long. He was just left with around thirty men. Finally, as they propelled out of the gate after waiting for long and had just reached the town side of the drawbridge, several armed men came right down upon them. Banda-'alī, the father of Qāsim Beg's wife, called out to Ibrāhīm Beg and said, 'You are always boasting of your zeal. Let's take to our swords!' Standing beside Babur Ibrāhīm Beg replied fearlessly, 'What hinders? Come along!'

Babur seemed perturbed. He has written in the *Baburnama*, 'The senseless fellows were for displaying their zeal at a time of such disaster! Ill-timed zeal! That was no time to make a stand or delay!'

Babur called to bring a halt to such stupidity as the enemy was following and unhorsing their men somewhere continually.

Babur Falls Short in Front of Taṃbal's Men

Two miles before Akhsī when they were passing Meadow-dome, Ibrāhīm Beg called out to Babur. Babur turned back to find some members of Shaikh Bāyazīd's flock striking at him. Filled with anguish he turned his bridle, but Bayān-qulī's Khān-qulī suggested against the very step and said, 'This is a bad time for going back.'

* Babur, Abdul Rahim Khan-I-Khanan (trans.), *Tuzk-e Babri*, Delhi: Akbar, 1589, p. Folio 11. This manuscript is available in National Museum, New Delhi. The Persian translation was done from the original Turkic manuscript of Babur. This was translated by author from the copy kept at National Museum, New Delhi.

Babur gazed helplessly, seized his rein, and pushed ahead. Many of Babur's men had been unhorsed till they reached Sang, four miles away from Akhsī. Reaching there, they found no pursuers. Seeing the hopeless scenario, they passed it by and turned straight up its water. Babur had seven other men at his service—Nāṣir Dost, Qāsim Beg's son Qaṃbar-'alī, Bayān-qulī's son Khān-qulī, Mīrzā Qulī Kūkūldāsh, Nāṣir's Shāham, Sayyidī Qarā's 'Abdu'l-qadūs and Khwāja Ḥusainī.

The broad valley was at the turning of the stream. There they found a good little road, far from the beaten track. They made straight up the valley, leaving the stream on the right, reached its waterless part, and around the afternoon prayer time, got out of it to reach the level land.

They looked across the plain—darkness reigned till far away. Babur made his party take cover. Then he went to look out from the higher ground when several men came at a gallop, up the hill behind them. Babur wasn't interested in waiting to find out whether their number was larger. He immediately got his men to mount and ride off.

In reality, they were around a couple of dozen in number compared to Babur's strength of eight. Babur has written, 'If we had known their number at first, we should have made a good stand against them, but we thought they would not be pursuing us unless they had good support behind. A fleeing foe, even if he be many, cannot face a few pursuers, for as the saying is, "Hāī is enough for the beaten ranks".'

Khān-qulī put forth his opinion and said, 'This will never do! They will take us all. From amongst the horses, there are, you take two good ones and go quickly on with Mīrzā Qulī Kūkūldāsh, each with a led horse. Maybe you will get away.'*

Babur said, 'He did not speak ill; as there was no fighting to hand, there was a chance of safety in doing as he said, but it really would not have looked well to leave any man alone, without a horse, amongst his foes.'

In the end, they all dropped off, one by one. Babur's horse was a little tired too. Seeing this, Khān-qulī offered his horse to Babur and

* Babur, Abdul Rahim Khan-I-Khanan (trans.), *Tuzk-e Babri*, Delhi: Akbar, 1589, pp. Folio 114b-115. This manuscript is available in National Museum, New Delhi. The Persian translation was done from the original Turkic manuscript of Babur. This was translated by author from the copy kept at National Museum, New Delhi.

took his in return. The foe unhorsed Sayyidī Qarā's 'Abdu'l-qadūs and Nāṣir's Shāham, who had fallen behind. Khān-qulī also was left away. Babur was running out of time, and he was in no position to offer any help or defence. Their horses had begun to flag. Babur's horse had started to get tired while Dost Beg's failed and stopped. At that moment, Qaṃbar-'alī got off and exchanged his horse with Babur. Soon he got left behind too. Now, Babur was left only with Mīrzā Qulī Kūkūldāsh. Their horses no longer galloped but only trotted. When Mīrzā Qulī Kūkūldāsh's horse began to flag, Babur said, 'What will become of me, if you fall behind? Come along! let's live or die together.' Babur hopefully looked at him multiple times. After long he said, 'My horse is done! It can't go on. Never mind me! You go on, perhaps you will get away.'

About this situation, Babur has said, 'It was a miserable position for me; he remained behind, I was alone.'

They could sight two men, Bābā of Sairām and Banda-'alī, of the enemies' camp. Babur's borrowed horse was also almost done, and the mountains were still a couple of miles off. His path was full of a pile of rocks. Babur thought, 'My horse is worn out and the hills are still somewhat far away; which way should I go? In my quiver are at least twenty arrows; should I dismount and shoot them off from this pile of rock?' Then a second thought came to Babur's mind. He thought that he might reach the hills and once there, stick a few arrows in his belt and scramble up. Babur had somehow gained a lot of confidence. His feet seemed to be charged, and so, he went on. His horse was failing to gallop but the two men were within arrow's reach now. But Babur chose not to shoot for the lack of arrows. At the same time, those two men didn't come nearer either. As the dusk came, Babur had almost reached the hills. Suddenly, he could hear the voice of the two men. They said, 'Where are you going in this way? Jahāngīr Mīrzā has been brought in a prisoner; Nāṣir Mīrzā also is in our hands.' Babur chose to not respond and ignoring them went towards the hill. They spoke again, but this time, with more respect dismounting from the horse. But despite so, Babur gave no ear to them and went on up a dale till the bedtime prayer, when he reached near a rock as big as a house. He went behind it and found that his horse could go no further. He would need to skip and jump for the way forward. Those two men followed Babur and dismounted again.

They spoke like servants. They said, 'Where are you going in this manner, without a road, and in the dark? Sulṭān Aḥmad Taṃbal will make you Padishah.' They swore upon this statement.

Babur replied, 'My mind is not easy as to that. I cannot go to him. If you think to do me timely service, years may pass before you have such another chance. Guide me to a road by which I can go to the Khān's presence. If you do this, I will show you favour and kindness greater than your heart's desire. If you will not do it, go back the way you came; that also will serve me well.'

They replied, 'Had it not been for Allah, we had never come! But since we are here, after following you in the way we have done, how can we go back from you? If you will not go with us, we are at your service, wherever you go.'

Babur asked, 'Swear that you speak the truth.' They nodded and made a solemn oath upon the Qur'an.

Then, Babur at once confided in them, saying, 'People have shown me a road through a broad valley, somewhere near this glen; take me to it.'*

Babur didn't trust them despite the oath they had taken on the Qur'an, but he decided that nothing could be better than following them in this moment of despair. Having travelled around four miles, Babur and the two men had reached the bed of a torrent. Babur said, 'This will not be the road for the broad valley.' They replied, 'That road is a long way ahead.' Babur thought in mind that, in reality, this must have been the one we were on, and they were perhaps concealing the fact, to deceive me. About halfway through the night, the three of them reached another stream.

Then they said, 'We have been negligent; it now seems to us that the road through the broad valley is behind.'

Babur appeared dejected and said, 'What is to be done?'

They replied, 'The Ghawā road is certainly in front; by it, people cross for Far-kat.' They guided Babur further for that and together they went on till in the third watch of the night reaching the Karnān gully which comes down from Ghawā. Then Bābā Sairāmī said, 'Stay

* Babur, Abdul Rahim Khan-I-Khanan (trans.), *Tuzk-e Babri*, Delhi: Akbar, 1589. p. Folio 116. This manuscript is available in National Museum, New Delhi. The Persian translation was done from the original Turkic manuscript of Babur. This was translated by author from the copy kept at National Museum, New Delhi.

here a little while, [till] I look along the Ghawā road.' Babur waited along with another person. Soon he returned and said, 'Some men have gone along that road, led by one wearing a Moghūl cap; there is no going that way.'

Babur was alarmed upon hearing these words. Dawn had broken, yet Babur lay in the middle of the cultivated land, far from the road which he wanted to take. Babur said to Bābā Sairāmī, 'Guide me to where I can hide today, and tonight when you will have laid hands on something for the horses, lead me to cross the Khujand-water and along its further bank.' The reply came as, 'Over there, on the upland, there might be hiding.'

'There is no doing without food for ourselves or our horses,' Banda-'alī said, 'Let me go into Karnān and bring what I can find.' He was the commandant of Karnān.

They stopped a couple of miles before Karnān. Here, Banda-'alī went off.

He had gone for long. The next dawn was nearing and there was no sign of him. Time crossed further. The bright day had broken and there he appeared, bringing three loaves of bread but no corn for the horses. Babur smiled looking at him and then they all put a loaf each into the breast of their tunic. They quickly went up the rise, tethering their horses in the open valley. They went to higher ground to keep watch.

Babur assumed that by midday, Aḥmad the Falconer would have gone along the Ghawā road for Akhsī. Babur thought of calling to him and saying, with promise and fair-minded word, 'You take those horses,' for they had had a day and a night's strain and struggle, without corn, and were utterly done. But then again, Babur was a little uneasy as he didn't trust him entirely. Babur conjectured that the two men whom Bābā Sairāmī had seen on the road, would be in Karnān that night. Babur decided that he would fetch one of the horses of Banda-'alī and Bābā Sairāmī. And then each one would go his own way. Around mid-day, something glinting was seen on a horse, as far away as the eye would reach. Babur wasn't sure what it was. Perhaps it was Muḥammad Bāqir Beg himself who had been with Babur in Akhsī. He was also with Babur when he along with his men had got out and scattered during the battle. Perhaps, he had come this way and had been moving to hide here and there.

Banda-'alī and Bābā Sairāmī said, 'The horses have had no corn for two days and two nights; let us go down into the dale and put them there to graze.' Accordingly, they rode down and put them near the green grass. It was around afternoon prayer, that a horseman passed along the rising ground where they had been. He was Qādīr-bīrdī, the headman of Ghawā. Babur instructed Banda-'alī and Bābā Sairāmī to 'call him'.*

He came running after hearing the call. Babur interrogated him for some time, showered enough favours and showed kindness. Babur made promises and spoke fair words. And then Babur sent him to bring rope, a grass hook, an axe, corn for the horses, food, more horses, and material for crossing water (reeds for the raft).

Around the time of evening prayer, a horseman passed from the direction of Karnān for Ghawā. Babur inquired about his identity. Perhaps he was Muḥammad Bāqir Beg himself, on his way from where he was seen earlier by Babur going at nightfall to some other hiding place. But while replying he changed his voice and Babur couldn't recognize him although he had been with him for several years. Babur has mentioned in the *Baburnama* that 'It would have been well if I had recognized him, and he had joined me. His passing caused much anxiety and alarm; tryst could not be kept with Qādīr-bīrdī of Ghawā.' Banda-'alī said, 'There are retired gardens in the suburbs of Karnān where no one will suspect us of being; let us go there and send to Qādīr-bīrdī and have him brought there.' To implement this idea, Babur and the rest went to the Karnān suburbs.

It was a very chilly winter day. On the way, Banda-'alī and Bābā Sairāmī found a used, coarse sheepskin coat, which they brought to Babur. He put it on without thinking twice as winter was biting his skin deep. They also brought Babur a bowl of millet porridge which he ate as a treat for refreshment. 'Have you sent off the man to Qādīr-bīrdī?' Babur asked Banda-'alī. He replied by nodding his head, 'I have sent.' However, they may not have done so in reality, instead,

* Babur, Abdul Rahim Khan-I-Khanan (trans.), *Tuzk-e Babri*, Delhi: Akbar, 1589, p. Folio 117b. This manuscript is available in National Museum, New Delhi. The Persian translation was done from the original Turkic manuscript of Babur. This was translated by author from the copy kept at National Museum, New Delhi.

they had agreed together to send the man to Taṃbal in Akhsī. Babur has made this observation in the *Baburnama*.

Then, they entered an abandoned and unused house that they saw on the way. Babur slept there for some time. Banda-'alī and Bābā Sairāmī said to Babur, 'You must not bestir yourself to leave Karnān till there is news of Qādīr-bīrdī but this house is right among the suburbs; on the outskirts the orchards are empty; no-one will suspect if we go there.'

Accordingly, they mounted at midnight and went to a distant orchard. In the meantime, Bābā Sairāmī kept a watch from the roof of a house. He came downstairs after almost half a day and said, 'Commandant Yūsuf is coming.'

Babur's eyes rolled with fear. 'Find out,' Babur said, adding, 'Whether he comes because he knows about me.'

Bābā Sairāmī spoke to Yūsuf subsequently. He returned and said, 'He says he met a foot soldier at the Gate of Akhsī who said to him, "The Padishah is in such a place," and that he told no one.'

Babur replied without thinking much and said, 'How does it strike you?'

Then he replied, 'They are all your servants, you must go. What else can you do? They will make you, their ruler.'

Babur replied, 'After such rebellion and fighting with what confidence could I go?'

While they were already in discussion, Yūsuf appeared at once. He knelt before Babur and said, 'Why should it be hidden? Sulṭān Aḥmad Taṃbal has no news of you, but Shaikh Bāyazīd has, and he sent me here.'

Babur became miserable on hearing this. With this circumstance in mind, he has written, 'For well is it understood that nothing in the world is worse than fear for one's life.'

'Tell the truth!' Babur said softly, 'If the affair is likely to get worse, I will make ablution.'

Although Yūsuf had taken an oath to not attack, Babur wasn't ready to trust him entirely. But Babur was aware of his own helplessness. He went to a corner of the garden, muttering, 'If a man lives a hundred years or a thousand years, at the last nothing . . .'

Notes from Annette Beveridge's translation of the *Baburnama*:*

Friends are likely to have rescued Bābur from his dangerous isolation. His presence in Karnān was known both in Ghawā and in Akhsī; Muḥ. Bāqir Beg was at hand (f. 117); some of those he had dropped in his flight would follow him when their horses had had rest; Jahāngīr was somewhere north of the river with the half of Bābur's former force (f. 112); The Khāns, with their long-extended line of march, may have been on the main road through or near Karnān. If Yūsuf took Bābur as a prisoner along the Akhsī road, there were these various chances of his meeting friends. (. . .)

* Annette Susannah Beveridge (ed. and trans.), *The Bābur-nāma in English (Memoirs of Bābur), Translated from the original Turki text of Ẓahiru'd-dīn Muḥammad Bābur Pādshāh Ghāzī*, London: Luzac and Co, 1922. pp. 182-185.

Part 2

(14 June of AD 1504 to 23 December of AD 1519)

Kābul

18

First Year of Kābul

Babur Departs from Ferghana

It was the month of Muḥarram in AD 1504. Babur had already left Ferghana and was headed towards Khurāsān. While on the way, he dismounted at Aīlāk-yīlāq, one of the summer pastures of Ḥiṣār. Babur turned twenty-three while staying in this camp. He has mentioned about applying a razor for the first time on his face.[1] Babur was accompanied by 300 people, who saw a ray of hope in him. These people were of varying ages, and each was ready to be in exile with Babur. Almost all of them were on foot and had walking staves in their hands, brogues on their feet, and long coats on their shoulders.

But poverty was the very nature of the whole camp including that of Babur. So insolvent they were that they had only two tents (*chādar*) in all. Babur's tent was used for his mother. They set an *ālāchūq*[2] at each stage for Babur to sit in.

Although they had started for Khurāsān, given the circumstances, they hoped for some respite from the land of Ḥiṣār through the Khusrau Shāh's retainers. Each day someone from the country, a tribe or the Moghūl horde would talk about hope from Babur. Around that period, Mullā Bābā of Pashāghar returned, who had been Babur's envoy to Khusrau Shāh. But he didn't bring anything from Khusrau Shāh that could please Babur and his men. However, he did bring enough pleasing things from the tribes and the horde.

After three or four marches beyond Aīlāk, they halted at a place near Ḥiṣār and called Khwāja 'Imād. However, Muḥibb-'alī the

Armourer appeared instead. He came to Babur from Khusrau Shāh. Perhaps, Babur had felt very bad while passing through the territory of Khusrau Shāh. Reflecting upon the same, he has written in the *Baburnama*, 'Through Khusrau Shāh's territories, I twice happened to pass, renowned though he was for kindness and liberality, he neither time showed me the humanity he had shown to the meanest of men.'

Babur was expecting and hoping to gain something very handsome from the country and the tribes. Accordingly, he kept delaying the journey at each stage. In this critical juncture of Babur's life, Sherīm Ṯaghāī* decided to leave him as he wasn't keen to go to Khurāsān. For Babur, Sherīm Ṯaghāī's importance was unparalleled. He had sent all his family off and stayed unfettered. Yet, it must be remembered that Sherīm Ṯaghāī showed some cowardliness after the defeat at Sar-i-pul (AD 1500) when Babur went back to defend Samarḳand. The acts of cowardice were repeated several times over.

Khusrau Shāh's Kinsman Joins Babur

Babur and his 300 men reached Qabādīān. Bāqī Chaghānīānī, a younger brother of Khusrau Shāh who was more Chaghānīān, Shahr-i-ṣafā, and Tīrmīẕ, sent the khatib of Qarshī to Babur. He certainly wanted to express their good wishes desiring an alliance. Bāqī Chaghānīānī had come himself to wait on Babur when they had crossed the Amū at the Aūbāj-ferry. As requested by Bāqī Chaghānīānī, Babur and his men moved down the river, opposite Tīrmīẕ. There stood fearlessly, the families, when intended to join Babur, laden with their goods. Once this was done, Babur and his men set out for Kāhmard and Bamyan. These places were held by Aḥmad-i-qāsim, the son of Khusrau Shāh's sister. The plan was clear. They wanted to leave the households safe in Fort Ajar of the Kāhmard-valley, and act to reinforce power wherever needed. When they reached Aībak, Yār-'alī Balāl joined Babur along with his men. He had fled from Khusrau Shāh. Before that, he had been with Babur. Babur has asserted in the *Baburnama* that he had been along with him during various battles. He had turned distant

* Sherīm Ṯaghāī was a milatary commander of Babur and came from the influential Barlas tribe. He played a prominent role in Babur's early days.

from Babur in his throneless* period and had gone to join Khusrau Shāh. He told Babur that the Moghūls in Khusrau Shāh's service had great conviction and faith in Babur. When Babur reached Zindān-valley, Qaṃbar-'alī Beg too came to him.

Kāhmard

They reached Kāhmard after four marches and stayed in Ajar for a while. During this stay, Jahāngīr Mīrzā married Aī Begum, the daughter of Sulṭān Maḥmūd Mīrzā and Khān-zāda Begum. This arrangement was made between respective fathers in AD 1490. In the meantime, Bāqī Beg kept on telling Babur repeatedly that the two rulers in one country or two chiefs in one army are always a source of disorder. According to him, it crafted a foundation of discord leading to ruin.

In this context, the *Baburnama* has stated:†

> For they have said, 'Ten darwīshes can sleep under one blanket, but two kings cannot find room in one clime.'
>
> If a man of God eat half a loaf,
> *He gives the other to a darwīsh;*
> *Let a king grip the rule of a clime,*
> *He dreams of another to grip.*

Bāqī Beg explained to Babur that Khusrau Shāh's retainers and followers would come in a couple of days to take service with the Padishah (Babur). Many among them like sons of Ayūb Begchīk had been seditious and the rabble-rousers causing disloyalty amongst their Mīrzās. Bāqī Beg suggested dismissing Jahāngīr Mīrzā on friendly terms, for Khurāsān. According to him, the dismissal would kill the chance of any repentance in days to come.

Babur has written in the *Baburnama*, 'Urge it as he would, however, I did not accept his suggestion, because it is against my nature to do

* Babur's loss of rule in Ferghana and Samarkand.

† Babur, Abdul Rahim Khan-I-Khanan (trans.), *Tuzk-e Babri*, Delhi: Akbar, 1589. p. Folio 121. This manuscript is available in National Museum, New Delhi. The Persian translation was done from the original Turkic manuscript of Babur. This was translated by author from the copy kept at National Museum, New Delhi.

an injury to my brethren, older or younger, or any kinsman soever, even when something untoward has happened.' Though the truth was that earlier there were resentments and recriminations between the two on the grounds of ruling and retainers, Babur was reluctant to see any ill for him. Babur could see the change in the behaviour of Jahāngīr. From the time he had come out of Ferghana with Babur, he had showered abundant loyalty and had ensured to appear no different than a blood relation.

But unlike what Babur wished and desired, Bāqī Beg's predictions ended up becoming true. Babur has written, 'Those tempters to disloyalty, that is to say, Ayūb's Yūsuf and Ayūb's Bihlūl, left me for Jahāngīr Mīrzā, took up a hostile and mutinous position, parted him from me, and conveyed him into Khurāsān.'

Ayūb's Yūsuf was a close companion and advisor to Babur. He was of Turkish origin and held an important position in Babur's court. Ayūb's Bihlūl was another key figure in Babur's court who was known for his wit, humour, and quick thinking. He often served as a jester or humorist in the court, providing entertainment to Babur and the nobles. His witty and satirical remarks were not only entertaining but also served to provide a refreshing perspective in the court.

Helpless Sulṭān Husayn

All of a sudden, out of nowhere, Babur received letters from Sulṭān Husayn Mīrzā spelling out wrong and far-fetched intentions. He wrote similar letters to Badī'u'z-Zamān Mīrzā, Khusrau Shāh and Ẕū'n-nūn Beg. His purpose was very clear. According to Babur, the contents were as follows:*

> When the three brothers, Sulṭān Maḥmūd Mīrzā, Sulṭān Aḥmad Mīrzā, and Aūlūgh Beg Mīrzā, joined together and advanced against me, I defended the bank of the Murgh-āb in such a way that they retired without being able to affect anything. Now if the Aūzbegs advance, I might myself guard the bank of the Murgh-āb again;

* Babur, Abdul Rahim Khan-I-Khanan (trans.), *Tuzk-e Babri*, Delhi: Akbar, 1589, p. Folio 122. This manuscript is available in National Museum, New Delhi. The Persian translation was done from the original Turkic manuscript of Babur. This was translated by author from the copy kept at National Museum, New Delhi.

> let Badī'u'z-zamān Mīrzā leave men to defend the forts of Balkh, Shibarghān, and Andikhūd while he himself guards Girzawān, the Zang-valley, and the hill-country thereabouts.

Having heard of Babur living in that vicinity, he wrote:*

> Do you make fast Kāhmard, Ajar and that hill-tract; let Khusrau Shāh place trusty men in Ḥiṣār and Qūndūz; let his younger brother Walī make fast Badakhshān and the Khutlān hills; then the Aūzbeg will retire, able to do nothing.

The letters of Sulṭān Husayn left Babur in despair. He could never think in his dreams of the helplessness of Husayn. Babur expressed his thoughts on the situation:†

> There was in Tīmūr Beg's territory (yūrt) no ruler so great as Sulṭān Ḥusain Mīrzā, whether by his years, armed strength, or dominions; it was to be expected, therefore, that envoys would go, treading on each other's heels, with clear and sharp orders, such as, 'Arrange for so many boats at the Tīrmīz, Kilīf, and Kīrkī ferries,' 'Get any quantity of bridge material together,' and 'Well watch the ferries above Tūqūz-aūlūm,' so that men whose spirit years of Aūzbeg oppression had broken, might be cheered to hope again. But how could hope live in tribe or horde when a great ruler like Sulṭān Ḥusayn Mīrzā, sitting in the place of Tīmūr Beg, spoke, not of marching forth to meet the enemy, but only of defense against his attack?

Babur moved out of Ajar with all his men.

Babur's Strength Begins to Grow

Babur's fortune had started to shine. Various Moghūls of Khusrau Shāh kept coming to Babur, increasing his hope and strength with each passing day. They said, 'We of the Moghūl horde, desiring the

* Ibid.

† Ibid.

royal welfare, have drawn off from Ṯāīkhān towards Ishkīmīsh and Fūlūl. Let the Padishah advance as fast as possible, for the greater part of Khusrau Shāh's force has broken up and is ready to take service with him.'

Bad news arrived just when Moghūls were submitting themselves to Babur's service. After taking Andijān, Shaybāni Khān was heading to conquer Ḥiṣār and Qūndūz once again. Upon hearing this, the perturbed Khusrau Shāh marched out of Qūndūz and took the road for Kābul with all the men he had. Interestingly, no sooner had he left than his old able and trusted servant Mullā Muḥammad Turkistānī made Qūndūz fast for Shaybāni Khān. The terror of Shaybāni Khān was known to all and hence it was certainly important to secure the place beforehand.

Around 4000 heads of houses in the Moghūl horde, earlier dependents of Khusrau Shāh, brought their families and joined Babur while he and his men were going through Sham-tū near the Qīzīl-sū.

Qaṃbar-'alī Dismissed

Babur has been observing Qaṃbar-'alī's behaviour for a while. The latter had often critiqued and even humiliated the former. Babur has mentioned Qaṃbar-'alī talking foolish things quite often. Qaṃbar had begun to disrespect and displease Bāqī Beg, which Babur found to be unpardonable. Babur dismissed him without thinking twice. Perhaps it was more to gratify Bāqī Beg. Thereafter his son, 'Abdu'l-shukūr, was put in Jahāngīr Mīrzā's service.

On the other hand, Khusrau Shāh was quite dismayed to know that his Moghūl horde had joined Babur. Seeing no better way out, he sent his son-in-law, Ayūb Yaq'ūb to Babur, intending to crack a deal in return for his services. Babur didn't deny his offer after the node of Bāqī Chaghānīānī. Babur considered Bāqī Chaghānīānī an important man, and despite being loyal to him, he did not overlook his brother's side this time. A deal was made that Khusrau Shāh would be given whatever amount of goods he asked for and he would always be safe in Babur's hands. After the deal with Yaq'ūb, they marched down the Qīzīl-sū and didn't dismount till they touched the water of Andar-āb.

August of AD 1504 was about to end. The time of Babur's nomadic life was passing by quickly.

They rested at the bank of Andar-āb. The next day, they crossed the Andar-āb water and arrived close to Dūshī. There, Babur took a seat under a large plane tree, where Khusrau Shāh met him. He displayed acute splendour, and he had brought a great company of men. He followed the tradition and protocol of dismounting at a certain distance from Babur and made his way to him. He knelt three times on arrival and repeated the gesture when seeking leave. He also knelt while enquiring about Babur's welfare and then again when he offered the tribute. He repeated the same with Jahāngīr Mīrzā and Wais Mīrzā Khān.

Babur has described the incident as follows:*

> That sluggish old manikin who through so many years had just pleased himself, lacking sovereignty one thing only, namely, to read the Khuṭba in his name, now knelt twenty-five or twenty-six times in succession, and came and went till he was so wearied out that he tottered forward. His many years of begship and authority vanished from his view.

After the formalities and accepting gifts from Khusrau Shāh, Babur got him seated suitably. They stayed in that place for a couple of *garīs,*† recounting some tales and talking about wellbeing. According to Babur, Khusrau Shāh's conversations were insipid and empty. Babur felt that the reason behind this was Khusrau Shāh's cowardice and the fact that he was false to his salt. However, Khusrau Shāh was noticeably disturbed, perhaps because all his trusted retainers had gone under Babur's service. Such was the agony of Khusrau Shāh's affairs that he, the sovereign-aping manikin, had to come, willy-nilly, abased and without any honour, to a sort of interview he would have never wished for.

In a display of high moral ground, Babur consoled Khusrau Shāh. The latter replied, 'Those very servants have four times left me and returned.'

---

* Babur, Abdul Rahim Khan-I-Khanan (trans.), *Tuzk-e Babri*, Delhi: Akbar, 1589, pp. Folio 12B-124. This manuscript is available in National Museum, New Delhi. The Persian translation was done from the original Turkic manuscript of Babur. This was translated by author from the copy kept at National Museum, New Delhi.

† A garī is twenty-four minutes.

Babur asked Khusrau Shāh at what point his brother Walī would cross the Amū and when exactly he would arrive. Khusraw replied, 'If he finds a ford, he will soon be here, but when waters rise, fords change; the (Persian) proverb has it, "The waters have carried down the fords".'

About this response, *Baburnama* mentioned, 'These words Allah brought to his tongue in that hour of the flowing away of his own authority and following.'

After being seated there for almost an hour, Babur rode back to his camp and Khusrau Shāh returned to his. The latter's bad time had begun, and Babur's stars had begun to shine. After Khusrau Shāh returned, his begs with their servants and several tribes began to desert him. They had begun to come and join Babur along with their families. By the afternoon, of the day he returned, not a man remained in his service.

For this instance, Babur has cited the Qur'an:*

> Say, —O God! who possessest the kingdom! Thou givest it to whom Thou wilt and Thou takest it from whom Thou wilt! In Thy hand is good, for Thou art almighty.[3]

Babur has hailed Allah for his power, for having seen the turning of fate. Khusrau Shāh was once a master of around 30,000 retainers. Once upon a time he owned, Sulṭān Maḥmūd's dominions from Qaḥlūgha (also known as the Iron Gate) to the range of Hindū Kush. Babur tells an interesting anecdote regarding this.

Once his old manikin, a tax-gatherer named Ḥasan Barlās, had made Babur march and halt from Aīlāk to Aūbāj. Against Babur's will, he had used all the tax-gatherer's roughness. But now he stood abased and stripped of power with no blow struck, no command over servants, goods or life, and left with merely 300 men. Today he appeared as defeated and destitute as Babur once was.

And on the same very evening of the day when Khusrau Shāh had returned to the camp, Mīrzā Khān came to seek audience with Babur.

* Babur, Adbul Rahim Khan-I-Khanan (trans.), Tuzk-e Babri, Delhi: Akbar, 1589, pp. Folio 12B–124. This manuscript is available in National Museum, New Delhi. The Persian translation was done from the original Turkic manuscript of Babur. This was translated by author from the copy kept at National Museum, New Delhi.

Full of aggression and anguish, he demanded vengeance on Khusrau Shāh for the blood of his brothers. Baysonghor Sulṭān Mīrzā was shot by an arrow while Sulṭān Mas'ūd Mīrzā was blinded. Although Babur along with his men firmly believed that Mīrzā Khān's demand was right by law and common justice, and a man like him needed to be treated by an iron fist, Khusrau Shāh was let go scot-free. Of course, he had to be given the deal that Babur was in with him. An order was passed that Khusrau Shāh should be allowed to take whatever of his goods he could convey. Accordingly, he loaded up, on four strings of scuffs and camels. He carried all jewels, gold, silver and other precious things he had. Sherīm Ṭaghāī was told to escort him. After setting Khusrau Shāh on his road for Khurāsān, Babur was to go to Kāhmard by the way of Ghūrī, Dahānah and bring the families to Kābul.

Babur Heads Out for Kābul

After setting Khusrau Shāh out, Babur and his party began to march towards Kābul. En route, they halted at Khwāja Zaid. On the same day, Ḥamza Bī Mangfīt was overrunning at the head of Aūzbeg raiders around Dūshī. Babur sent the lords of the gate, Sayyid Qāsim and Aḥmad-i-qāsim Kohbur, with several warriors to counter Ḥamza Bī Mangfīt. They ferociously attacked the Aūzbegs. As a celebratory note, they brought back the heads of some they had beheaded.

Babur got complete control of Khusrau Shāh's armoury. There were around 800 coats-of-mail and horse accoutrements. Babur also got his hands on a few marvellous works of porcelain. These were the only good things salvaged from the leftovers.

In five sets of marches, Babur and his men reached Ghūr-bund. They dismounted in the locality of Ushtur-Shahr. Babur heard the news that Muqīm's chief beg, Sherak Arghūn, was lying along the Bārān and he had led an army out to deter 'Abdu'r-razzāq Mīrzā from passing along the Panjhīr-road after he had fled from Kābul. He had been lying along with Tarkalānī Afghāns towards Lamghān. Without any delay, Babur marched forward in the afternoon. He pressed on through the dark till the dawn. And then, they surmounted the Hūpīān-pass.

Babur came out of the pass and above stood a star too bright in lustre. Looking at it inquisitively, Babur said, 'May, not that be Suhail?' [4] Bāqī Chaghānīānī replied, 'It is Suhail,' and read the couplet mentioned in the preface of *Anwār-i-suhailī:*[*] [†]

How far dost thou shine, O Suhail, and where dost thou rise?
A sign of good luck is thine eye to the man on whom it may light.

Babur had never seen Suhail.

By the time they reached Sanjid Valley, the sun had already reached dusk and had just set in. They dismounted there. The scouts sent by Babur to Sherak, Muqīm's chief beg, below the Qarā-bāgh, had caught up with him near Aīkarī-yār. After a little fight with Sherak and his people, Babur's men got the upper hand. They hurried their adversaries off unhorsing at least eighty soldiers and imprisoning them.

Babur forgave him and chose not to kill him despite popular opinion being otherwise. Finally, Sherak took service with Babur.

Walī, Brother of Khusrau Shāh Dies and Kābul Is Gained

There were various tribes and clans and half a dozen bodies[5] of the Moghūl horde, which Khusrau Shāh had left in Qūndūz. He was reluctant to even think about their condition and it would bring him many troubles in the future. One such was Rūstā-hazāra from Badakhshān. He traversed the Panjhīr-pass to this camp with Sayyidīm 'Alī darbān. He showered Babur with obeisance and committed to serve him.

One person under Ayūb Yūsuf and Ayūb Bihlūl submitted to Babur. Soon came another one from Khutlān, under Khusrau Shāh's younger brother, Walī. The next one consisted of the Moghūl tribesmen, Aīmāq who had been in parts of Yīlānchaq, Nikdiri and the Qūndūz. At the Sar-i-āb the tribesmen were ahead and Walī was behind. They blocked his route and thrashed him. Walī, with the hope

[*] Ḥusain Wā'iẓ Kāšifī, *Anwār-i Suhailī*, s.l.: Asiatic Lithographic Company, 1834.

[†] Babur, Abdul Rahim Khan-I-Khanan (trans.), *Tuzk-e Babri*, Delhi: Akbar, 1589. p. Folio 125. This manuscript is available in National Museum, New Delhi. The Persian translation was done from the original Turkic manuscript of Babur. This was translated by author from the copy kept at National Museum, New Delhi.

of a rescue and to stay safe, fled to the Aūzbegs. But unfortunately, Shaybāni Khān got hold of him and had him beheaded at a square in Samarkand. His followers were beaten and plundered as well. They followed the tribesmen and took service with Babur.

And then from the camp, Babur with his strengthened party marched through the Āq-sarāī meadow of the Qarā-bāgh. Khusrau Shāh's people were well known for violent oppression. They domineered over one after another quite frequently, but things had to stop someday. Babur got one of the braves of Sayyidīm 'Alī beaten black and blue when he forcefully tried to take a jar of oil. The blows imparted were so severe that he died immediately on the spot. In Babur's opinion, this cold-blooded murder set an example for the rest so that such a mistake is never replicated.

Babur called for a counsel in that camp to deliberate whether it was the right choice to go to Kābul. Babur received mixed opinions. Sayyid Yūsuf and a few others suggested that the first move should be into Lamghān as winter was near and Babur could act from there utilizing the advantage offered by the weather. Bāqī Beg and many others said it would be good to move to Kābul at once. After enough brainstorming, Babur went with the latter plan. They resumed the journey. Their next halt was at Ābā-qūrūq.

Babur's mother and the rest of the family members who were left behind in Kāhmard rejoined Babur at Ābā-qūrūq. But they had to face a lot of danger and tough times before they met Babur. Sherīm Ṭaghāī was to fetch Babur's families from Kāhmard after having set Khusrau Shāh on his way to Khurāsān. After reaching Dahānah, he found he was not his own master, as Khusrau Shāh accompanied him to Kāhmard, where the latter's sister's son, Aḥmad-i-qāsim was waiting for him. Sherīm Ṭaghāī had secretly arranged for several Bāqī beg's Moghūls, who were with Babur's families to lay hands on Khusrau Shāh and Aḥmad-i-qāsim. But the news of this strategy reached the two and they fled along the Kāhmard valley (on the side of Ajar) finally making it to Khurāsān. Perhaps this is what Sherīm Ṭaghāī and the Moghūls wanted. Now those in charge of Babur's families were away from the fear of Khusrau Shāh. They guided the families out of Ajar, but some troubling surprises awaited at Kāhmard. The Sāqānchī tribe, like an enemy, blocked the road and plundered the families. Qul-i-bāyazīd's little son, Tīzak was made prisoner and he would reach Kābul four years later. The plundered and ill-fated families crossed by the Qībchāq pass, and rejoined Babur finally in Ābā-qūrūq.

Babur and his company left that camp and went to the Chālāk meadow, with one night's halt. They had already decided to lay siege to Kābul, and they marched forward the very next morning. Moving ahead for the next stopover, people at the centre dismounted somewhere between Ḥaidar Tāqī's garden and the Qul-i-bāyazīd's tomb. The people on the right led by Taster (bakāwal) and Jahāngīr Mīrzā, dismounted Babur's great Chār-bāgh. Nāṣir Mīrzā was leading the left wing and he chose to stopover in the meadow of Qūtlūq-qadam's tomb.

In the meantime, Babur's men repeatedly kept deliberating with Muqīm. But, while returning, they only carried excuses though at times there were words of agreement too. Perhaps his plan of bringing confusion was because he was expecting a dispatch of a courier to his father and elder brother in Qandahār post-Sherak's defeat. And perhaps he was delaying concrete actions in the hope of that dispatch.

On one very fine day, Babur ordered the party in the left, right and centre to reach close to the town by putting on their own as well as horses' mail. The order was very clear from Babur. They were supposed to display armoury to strike terror in those within. The right party under Jahāngīr Mīrzā went straight forward by the Kūcha bāgh. The centre party under Babur went along the side of Qūtlūq Qadam's tomb to a mound facing the rising ground.

As the men of Babur careered close to the Curriers' Gate showing off all the force and power they had, a bunch of fighters who had come out through it, fled away looking at the Babur's display of power. Curious Kābulīs, who had come merely to observe the happenings, could only rush away from the glacis of the citadel (*Bālā-ḥiṣār*). While they ran away, the dust rose to the heights as far as one could see. Several pits had been dug in the rise between the bridge and the gate. They were meticulously hidden and covered by plants and sticks. Sulṭān Qulī Chūnāq and several others fell prey to it easily. Soon, a few brave Kābulīs came forward, jumping from the lanes and gardens to attack with swords, but they had to face the strongest possible defence of Babur's men. Perhaps, there was no clear order of engagement and hence they soon retired without causing much damage.

When the force of Babur seemed undefendable, the perturbed Muqīm thought of sending out the offer of surrendering the town through the begs. And hence came his mediator, Bāqī Beg. He waited on Babur with fear in each breath he took. But as Babur mentioned, his fears were driven away by kindness and favour showered on him. A settlement and truce was made. As per the decisions, Muqīm was to march out with his retainers and followers handing over the town to Babur.

Bearing in mind the indisciplined acts of Khusrau Shāh's retainers, Babur appointed Jahāngīr Mīrzā and Nāṣir Mīrzā with some of the household begs, to escort Muqīm's family out of Kābul. Babur ensured that a good camping ground was assigned to him at Tipa, a place nine miles north of Kābul on the road to Āq-sarāī. But the journey wasn't going to be so easy for Muqīm and his family. A mob of common people had gathered at the gate by dawn and hullabaloo was turning more and more intense. One of the men conveyed the message and said, 'Unless Babur comes himself, there will be no holding these people in.' Hearing the news, Babur reached to control the situation. Perhaps deliberations of talk would have sorted the situation, but Babur chose a harsher path. He got more than a couple of people shot and some others chopped into pieces. Commoners were rattled with fear. They let Muqīm and his family get out safe and sound.

To conclude, it was sometime in October of AD 1504 that it happened. Babur has mentioned it in the *Baburnama*:

> It was in the last ten days of the Second Rabī' that without a fight, without an effort, by Almighty God's bounty and mercy, I obtained and made subject to me Kābul and Ghaznī and their dependent districts.

Kābul in Babur's Eyes[6]

The country (as addressed by Babur in the *Baburnama*) of Kābul was situated in the Fourth climate (Babur calls places of colder climate by this term) amid the cultivated lands. Lamghānāt, Parashāwar (Peshāwar), Hash(t)-Nagar and some of the countries of Hindustan lied to the east of Kābul. The mountain region in west had Karnūd and Ghūr, which Babur mentions to be the refuge and dwelling-places of the Hazāra and Nikdīrī tribes. The ranges of Hindū-kush on the north separated the countries of Qūndūz and Andar-āb. On the south to Kābul lay Afghānistān, Bannū, Farmūl and Naghr.

a. Town and environs of Kābul

The district of Kābul has small extent with greatest length from east to west and is wrapped around by mountains. The walled towns of Kābul is connected by those Mountains and one at the lower heights is known as Shāh-of-Kābul as once upon a time, a (Hindū) Shāh of Kābul had built a abode on its summit. Shāh-of-Kābul starts and ends at the Dūrrīn narrows and Dih-i-yaq'ūb respectively. It has a perimeter of around 4 miles and its foothills are covered with gardens fed from a canal which was brought along it by Wais Atāka, Aūlūgh Beg Mīrzā's (Babur's paternal uncle) guardian. The canal ends in corner quarter known as Kul-kīna. It was said in Babur's time that the place had seen a lots of debauchery. Babur mentions in the *Baburnama* that sometimes people defined this place using a jesting parody of Khwāja Ḥāfiẓ,—"Ah! the happy, thoughtless time when, with our names in ill-repute, we lived days of days at Kul-kīna!"

A large pool of a perimeter of around 2 miles lied to the east of Shāh-of-Kabūl and south of the walled-town. Three small springs, Kul-kīna; near Khwāja Shamū's tomb; second one near Khwāja Khiẓr's Qadam-gāh, and the third was at a place known as Khwāja Raushānāī, over against Khwāja 'Abdu'ṣ-ṣamad.

The citadel of Kābul stood on 'Uqābain, a detached rock of a spur of Shāh-of-Kābul with great walled-town lying at its north end. At the high altitude where citadel lied, fresh air blew at high speed. It overlooked the large pool (mentioned above) and three meadows, namely, Siyāh-sang (Black-rock), Sūng-qūrghān (Fort-back), and Chālāk (Highwayman). It appeared very heavenly when the meadows were green. In the months of summer, the gushing north winds, known by locals as Parwān-wind helped in making thermal comfort delightful in the windowed houses which lied on the northern part of the citadel. Praising the citadel of Kābul, Mullā Muḥammad Ṭālib Mu'ammāī (the Riddler) often recited a couplet, composed on Badī'u'z-zamān Mīrzā's name:—

Drink wine in the castle of Kābul and send the cup round without pause;

For Kābul is mountain, is river, is city, is lowland in one.

b. Kābul as a trading-town.
Babur mentions in the *Baburnama* that, 'Just as 'Arabs call every place outside 'Arab (Arabia), 'Ajam, so Hindustanīs call every place outside Hindustan, Khurāsān.'

On the land-route between Hindustan and Khurāsān there were two trade-marts. Kābul was one of them and Qandahār was other. While the caravans to Kābul came from Kāshghar, Ferghana, Turkistān, Samarkand, Bukhārā, Balkh, Ḥiṣār and Badakhshān, those to Qandahār came only from Khurāsān. Kābul was known as an excellent trading center as it was well known facts among merchants that if they went to Khīta or Rūm, they would make very small profits. Each year around 10,000 horses and caravans of 10–20,000 heads-of-houses came to Kābul for trade. They would bring slaves, white cloth, sugar-candy, refined and common sugars, and aromatic roots.

Babur mentions in the *Baburnama* that most of the traders were not content with a profit of around 20–30 per cent.

Babur mentions an interesting thing in the *Baburnama*. He says, 'In Kābul can be had the products of Khurāsān, Rūm, 'Irāq and Chīn (China); while it is Hindustan's own market.'*

c. Products and climate of Kābul
The districts of hot and cold climate in the country of Kābul were close to each other.

In a single day, a person could journey from the city of Kābul to a place where snow was a rare sight, or they could reach a location where freezing temperatures persisted for two sidereal hours, unless the weather was exceptionally hot and prevented snow from accumulating.

The areas surrounding the town offered a variety of fruits suited to both hot and cold climates. In the colder regions, within the town itself, one could find grapes, pomegranates, apricots, apples, quinces, pears, peaches, plums, sinjids, almonds, and

* It very much means that even at the time when Babur lived, the stretch till Kābul were seen as part of Bharat.

walnuts. Babur had brought the cuttings of the ālū-bālū there and had them planted which he observed to have grown and done well. People transported various fruits suited for hot climates into the town. These fruits included oranges, citrons, amlūk (diospyros lotus), and sugarcane, the latter of which Babur personally had brought and cultivated there. Additionally, from Nijr-au (Nijr-water), they brought jīl-ghūza, and, from the hill-tracts they bring a lots of honey. Beehives are actively employed, with the exception being Ghaznī, which does not supply any honey. The rhubarb from the Kābul district was of high quality, and its quinces and plums were exceptionally good. The badrang from this region was also noteworthy. It produced an excellent grape known as the water-grape. The wines from Kābul were robust and flavorful, particularly those from the Khwāja Khāwand Sa'īd hill area, which were renowned for their potency. Babur reiterates the commendations of others regarding these wines as below in the *Baburnama*:—

The flavor of the wine a drinker knows;
What chance have sober men to know it?

Kābul's soil was not highly productive when it came to grain; a four or five-fold yield was considered good in that region. The melons from Kābul were not top-tier, but they could be of decent quality when cultivated from Khurāsān seed.

The climate was exceptionally pleasant, and if there was another place in the world equally pleasant, it remained unknown. Even during hot weather, sleeping at night without a fur coat was unthinkable. Although the snow lay deep in most places in winter, the cold was not excessive in Kābul. In contrast, both Samarkand and Tabrīz, like Kābul, were noted for their pleasant climates, but they experienced extreme cold.

d. Meadows of Kābul

There were good meadows surrounding Kābul in all four directions. An excellent one, Sūng-qūrghān, was located approximately 4 miles (2 kuroh) to the northeast. It had lush grass suitable for horses and was relatively mosquito-free. To the northwest, there was the

Chālāk meadow, about 2 miles (1 shar'ī) away. Although it was spacious, it was plagued by mosquitoes that bothered the horses.

On the west, there were the Dūrrīn meadows, actually two of them: Tīpa and Qūsh-nādir (or nāwar), and if one counted both, there would be five meadows in total. Each of these meadows was about 2 miles away from the town. They were relatively small, had good grass for horses, and were free from mosquitoes. Kābul had no other meadows as favorable as these.

On the eastern side, there was the Siyāh-sang meadow, with Qūtlūq-qadam's tomb situated between it and the Currier's Gate. However, this meadow was not highly regarded because during the hot season, it was infested with mosquitoes. Adjacent to it was the Kamarī meadow. Including this one, the meadows around Kābul could be counted as six, but they were typically referred to as four.

e. Mountain-passes into Kābul

The country of Kābul was a formidable fortress, making it challenging for foreign invaders to penetrate. It was surrounded by the imposing Hindū-kush mountains, which acted as a natural barrier separating Kābul from Balkh, Qūndūz, and Badakhshān. These mountains had seven passable roads. Three of these roads extended from Panjhīr (Panj-sher): Khawāk, the highest; Ṭūl, the next lower; and Bāzārak. The Ṭūl road had the best pass, but it was the longest, hence its name. Bāzārak, while more direct, also led into Sar-i-āb, and the main pass through Pārandī was referred to as the Pārandī pass.

Another road led through Parwān, with seven minor passes known as Haft-bacha (Seven-younglings) between Parwān and its primary pass (Bāj-gāh). Two roads from Andar-āb joined it at its main pass, which led to Parwān. This road was quite challenging.

From Ghūr-bund, three roads led over the mountains. The one closest to Parwān was called the Yāngī-yūl pass (New-road), leading to Khinjan. Above it was the Qīpchāq road, crossing where the waters of Andar-āb met the Sūrkh-āb (Qīzīl-sū), offering an excellent route. The third road passed over the Shibr-tū pass. Those crossing it in the warmer months continued through Bamyan and Saighān, while winter travelers took the path through Āb-dara (Water-valley). Shibr-tū was the exception, as it remained open year-round.

With the exception of Shibr-tū, all the Hindū-kush roads were closed for three or four months in winter due to impassable valley-bottoms when waters ran high. Attempting to traverse the Hindū-kush by going over the mountains during this period proved exceptionally challenging. The optimal time for crossing was during the three or four months of autumn when snow was less, and water levels were lower. Highwaymen, including Kāfir, were a constant concern whether traveling on the mountains or in the valley-bottoms.

The road from Kābul to Khurāsān passed through Qandahār, offering a level route without any mountain passes. Four roads led into Kābul from the Hindustan side. One passed through a relatively low Khyber mountain pass, another through Bangash, and another through Naghr (or Naghz), all with low passes. These roads were accessible from three ferries over the Sind. Those who took the Nīl-āb ferry continued through the Lamghānāt. In winter, some forded the Sind-water (at Hāru) above its confluence with the Kābul-water and crossed by foot. Most of Babur's journeys into Hindustan involved using these fords, except during his last expedition in AD 1525, when he defeated Sultan Ibrāhīm and had crossed the Nīl-āb by boat. The Sind-water was generally passable by boat, except at the mentioned location. Those who crossed at Dīn-kot continued through Bangash, while those crossing at Chaupāra, taking the Farmūl road, continued to Ghaznī or, if following the Dasht route, proceeded to Qandahār.

f. Inhabitants of Kābul

The Kābul country was home to numerous diverse tribes. In its valleys and plains, one could find Turks and clansmen, along with Arabs. The town and many villages were inhabited by Sārts, while the districts and other villages were populated by the Pashāī, Parājī, Tājīk, Bīrkī, and Afghān tribes.

In the western mountains, you would find the Hazāra and Nikdīrī tribes, some of whom spoke the Moghūlī tongue. In the northeastern mountains, there were the territories of the Kāfirs, like Kitūr (or Gawār?) and Gibrik. To the south, you'd come across the lands of the Afghān tribes.

g. Kābul was a place where eleven or twelve languages were spoken: Arabī, Persian, Turkī, Moghūlī, Hindī, Afghānī, Pashāī, Parājī, Gibrī, Bīrkī, and Lamghānī. If there was another region with such a wide array of tribes and languages, it remained unknown.

Sub-divisions of the Kābul country

The country of Kābul was divided into fourteen tūmāns. Bajaur, Sawād, and Hash-Nagar may have been linked to Kābul at one point, but they no longer resembled cultivated regions. Some lay desolate due to the Afghāns, while others were now under their rule.

In the eastern part of the Kābul country, you would find the Lamghānāt, consisting of 5 tūmāns and 2 bulūks of cultivated lands. The largest of these was Nangarhār, sometimes written Nagarahār in historical accounts. The dārogha's residence was in Adīnapūr, about 13 yīghāch east of Kābul. The road to Adīnapūr was challenging, passing through small hill-passes and narrows, but it became safer after being populated at Qarā-tū, below Qūrūq-sāī. On this route, the Bādām-chashma pass marked the boundary between the hot and cold climates. Snow fell on the Kābul side of the pass but not in Qūrūq-sāī. After descending the pass, a distinct landscape emerged, with different trees, plants, animals, and customs.

Nangarhār had nine torrents (tūqūz-rūd) and yielded good rice and corn crops. It was famous for its abundant oranges, citrons, and pomegranates. In AD 1508–09, the Four-gardens, known as the Bāgh-i-wafā (Garden-of-fidelity), were established, producing plentiful oranges, citrons, and pomegranates. The year Babur defeated Pahār Khān and took Lāhore and Dipālpūr he had brought and cultivated plantains (bananas) and sugarcane successfully. Sugarcane was brought a year before banana and some of it were sent to Bukhārā and Badakhshān by Babur.

The garden had a favorable location with running water and a mild winter climate.

The Safed-koh mountains ran along the southern border of Nangarhār, dividing it from Bangash. No riding-road crossed these mountains. Nine torrents (*tūqūz-rūd*) originated from the Safed-koh, which retained its snow year-round and hence it got its name. Many places along the Safed-koh had an excellent climate, and its cold waters did not require ice.

The Sūrkh-rūd river flowed to the south of Adīnapūr, where the fort stood on a height with a straight drop of about 130 feet to the river. This isolated fort was well-situated and very strong.

The mountain between Nangarhār and Lamghān was known for its snowfall, serving as a signal for Lamghānīs to know when Kābul had received snow. Traveling from Kābul into the Lamghānāt was achieved through different routes, depending on the starting point. One of the roads led through the Dīrī-pass, crossing the Bārān-water at Būlān, while another went through Qarā-tū, below Qūrūq-sāī, crossing the Bārān-water at Aūlūgh-nūr and proceeding into Lamghān through the pass of Bād-i-pīch. Those coming from Nijr-aū passed through Badr-aū (Tag-aū) and Qarā-nakariq before taking the pass of Bād-i-pīch to enter Lamghān.

Although Nangarhār was one of the five tūmāns of the Lamghān tūmān, the term "Lamghānāt" strictly referred to three specific areas, as mentioned below:

> One of the three is the 'Alī-shang tūmān, to the north of which are fastness-mountains, connecting with Hindū-kush and inhabited by Kāfirs only. What of Kāfiristān lies nearest to 'Alī-shang, is Mīl out of which its torrent issues. The tomb of Lord Lām, father of his Reverence the prophet Nuḥ (Noah), is in this tūmān. In some histories, he is called Lamak and Lamakān. Some people are observed often to change kāf for ghain (k for gh); it would seem to be on this account that the country is called Lamghān.
>
> The second is Alangār. The part of Kāfiristān nearest to it is Gawār (Kawār), out of which its torrent issues (the Gau or Kau). This torrent joins that of 'Alī-shang and flows with it into the Bārān-water, below Mandrāwar, which is the third tūmān of the Lamghānāt.

One of the two bulūks in Lamghān was the Nūr-valley. This unique place had no equivalent, with its fort perched on a rocky promontory at the valley's entrance, flanked by torrents on both sides. Rice was cultivated on steep terraces, and there was only one road through it. The Nūr-valley was abundant in hot climate fruits, including oranges, citrons, and even a few dates. Along the banks of the torrents below the fort, there were many amlūk trees, a variety of fruit that some Turks called qarā-yīmīsh. These trees were numerous here but not found elsewhere. Grapes were also grown in the valley, trained on trees. The wines produced in the Nūr-valley had a good reputation, with two types of grapes cultivated: arah-tāshī and sūhān-tāshī. The former was yellowish, while the latter was a vibrant red. The arah-tāshī grape made a more uplifting wine, although it should be noted that neither wine lived up to its reputation for cheerfulness. Apes (*maimūn*) could be found high up in one of the glens, but none were seen below. The Nūrīs, the people of the Nūr-valley, used to raise swine but had abandoned this practice in recent times.

Another tūmān in Lamghān was Kūnār-with-Nūr-gal. It was somewhat remote, located away from the Lamghānāt, and its borders encroached into Kāfir lands. Due to these factors, the people of Kūnār-with-Nūr-gal paid relatively little tribute. The Chaghān-sarāī water entered this tūmān from the northeast, flowed on into the Kāma bulūk, joined the Bārān-water, and continued eastward.

Babur talks about Mīr Sayyid 'Alī Hamadānī,* and showers praises on him. He had come to Kābul during his journey and had died 2 miles above Kūnār. His disciples carried his body to Khutlān, and a shrine was erected at the revered site of his passing. Babur made the circumambulation of this shrine when he came and conquered Chaghān-sarāī in AD 1514.

In this tūmān, oranges, citrons, and coriander were abundant. Strong wines were brought down from Kāfiristān into this region.

A curious tale is told in this region, one that seems impossible but had been recounted to Babur repeatedly. Babur mentions that, throughout the hill-country above Multa-kundī, including

* He was one of the most important men behind the islamization of Kashmir.

Kūnār, Nūr-gal, Bajaur, Sawād, and the surrounding areas, it was commonly said that when a woman dies and is laid on a bier, she, if she has not been a wrongdoer, imparts such a shake to the bearers when they lift the bier at its four corners that, despite their reluctance and efforts, her body falls to the ground. However, if she has committed wrongdoing, no movement occurs.

Babur recalls, this tale was not only heard from the people of Kūnār but also repeatedly from those in Bajaur, Sawād, and the entire hill-tract. Ḥaidar-'alī Bajaurī, a sulṭān who governed Bajaur effectively, responded uniquely when his mother passed away. He did not weep, engage in lamentation, or wear black attire. Instead, he said, 'Go! Place her on the bier! If she does not move, I will have her cremated.' They laid her on the bier, and the anticipated movement occurred. Upon learning of this, he donned black clothing and began lamenting.

(Annette Susannah Beveridge's note to Multa-kundī.): As Multa-kundī is known the lower part of the tūmān of Kūnār-with-Nūr-gal; what is below (i.e., on the river) belongs to the valley of Nūr and Atar.

Another bulūk was Chaghān-sarāī, a single village with limited land, located at the mouth of Kāfiristān. Although its inhabitants were Muṣalmān, they mingled with the Kāfirs and, as a result, adopted their customs. A significant torrent, the Kūnār, flowed down to Chaghān-sarāī from the northeast, originating from behind Bajaur. Additionally, a smaller torrent called Pīch descended from Kāfiristān. Chaghān-sarāī was known for its strong yellowish wines, although these were quite different from those found in the Nūr-valley. The village itself had no grapes or vineyards; instead, its wines were all imported from the Kāfiristān-water and Pīch-i-kāfiristānī.

The Pīch Kāfirs came to the villagers' aid when Babur took control of the area. Wine was so commonly consumed that every Kāfir carried a leather wine-bag (khīg) around their neck and preferred wine over water.

Kāma, although not considered an independent district and rather dependent on Nangarhār, was also referred to as a bulūk.

Nijr-aū was another tūmān. It lay north of Kābul, in the Kohistān, with mountains behind it that were inhabited solely by Kāfirs, making it a rather secluded place. The region was abundant in grapes and fruits. Its people produced a substantial amount of wine, but they chose to boil it. They raised many fowls during the winter, were enthusiasts of wine, did not observe prayers, had no moral qualms, and displayed Kāfir-like characteristics.[7]

In the Nijr-aū mountains, there was an abundance of archa, jīlghūza, bīlūt, and Khānjak. The first-named three, archa, jīlghūza, and bīlūt, did not grow above Nigr-aū, but they flourished at lower elevations, resembling the trees of Hindustan. Jīlghūza wood served as the primary source of light for the people; it burned like a candle and had remarkable qualities. The flying-squirre was found in these mountains, an animal larger than a bat and having a curtain (*parda*), like a bat's wing, between its arms and legs. People often brought one in; it was said to fly downward from one tree to another, as far as a giz flew; but Babur himself had never seen one fly.

Once Babur and his men had put one to a tree. It clambered up directly and got away, but, when people went after it, it spread its wings and came down, without harm, as if it had flown.

Another of the curiosities of the Nijr-aū mountains was the lūkha (var. lūja) bird, also called bū-qalamūn (chameleon) because, between its head and tail, it had four or five changing colors, resplendent like a pigeon's throat. It was about as large as the kabg-i-darī and seemed to be the kabg-i-darī of Hindustan.

Babur notes an interesting saying of people. He notes in Baburnama, 'When the birds, at the onset of winter, descend to the hill-skirts if they come over a vineyard, they can fly no further and are taken.'

Babur talks about a kind of rat in Nijr-aū, known as the muskrat, which smelled of musk; Babur never saw it. Panjhīr (Panj-sher) was another tūmān; it lay close to Kāfiristān, along the Panjhīr road, and served as the thoroughfare of Kāfir highwaymen who, due to their proximity, also levied a tax on it. They had gone through it, causing a great loss of lives and committing many wicked deeds (in Babur's eyes), since Babur came that last time and conquered Hindustan (AD 1526).

Another was the tūmān of Ghūr-bund. In those countries, a *kūtal* was referred to as a bund, and they journey towards Ghūr through this pass. Apparently, this is why they named the tūmān Ghūr-bund. The Hazāra inhabited the heads of its valleys. It had few villages, and little revenue could be collected from it. There were said to be mines of silver and lapis lazuli in its mountains.

Additionally, there were the villages located on the skirts of the Hindū-kush mountains, with Mīta-kacha and Parwān at their head, and Dūr-nāma at their foot, totalling 12 or 13 in all. These were fruit-bearing villages that produced delightful wines, with those from Khwāja Khāwand Sa'īd being renowned for their strength in the vicinity. The villages all lay on the foothills, and while some paid taxes, not all were taxable because of their remote location in the mountains.

Between the foothills and the Bārān-water, there were two detached stretches of level land, one known as Kurrat-tāziyān, and the other as Dasht-i-shaikh (Shaikh's plain). Because the green grass of the millet grew well there, they served as the gathering places for Turks and Moghūl clans (aīmāq).

Babur once observed that many-colored tulips adorned those foothills. He undertook a count and found that there were thirty-two or thirty-three different varieties. Among them, they (Babur and his men) gave a name to one: the Rose-scented tulip because its fragrance resembled that of the red rose. It grew exclusively on Shaikh's plain, found nowhere else. Another unique variety was the Hundred-leaved tulip, growing by itself at the outlet of the Ghūr-bund narrows, on the hill-skirt below Parwān. A low hill, known as Khwāja Reg-i-rawān (Khwāja-of-the-running-sand), separated the two mentioned pieces of level land. This hill had a strip of sand from top to bottom, and people claimed that the sound of nagarets and tambours could be heard from it during the hot seasons.

Babur came across more villages which depended on Kābul itself. To the southwest of the town, there were great snow-covered mountains[8] where snow fell upon snow, and it was rare for a year to pass without fresh snow accumulating on the previous year's layer. This snow was brought, perhaps 12 miles distant, from these mountains to cool drinking water when the ice-houses in

Kābul were empty. Similar to the Bāmiān mountains, these were formidable fortresses. They were the source of the Harmand (Halmand), Sind, Dūghāba of Qūndūz, and Balkh-āb rivers so that in a single day, a person could drink water from each of these four rivers.

Most of the villages that depended on Kābul were situated on the slopes of one of these ranges, known as Pamghān. Masses of grapes ripened in their vineyards, and they grew every sort of fruit in abundance. None of them equalled Istālīf or Astarghach; these must have been the two places that Aūlūgh Beg Mīrzā used to call his Khurāsān and Samarkand. Pamghān was another of the best, not matching those two in terms of fruit and grapes but surpassing them in terms of climate. The Pamghān mountains formed a snowy range.

There were few villages that could compare with Istālīf, with vineyards and fine orchards on both sides of its large torrent, boasting waters that needed no ice, were cold, and mostly pure. Aūlūgh Beg Mīrzā had forcibly taken possession of its Great Garden, but Babur took it over, after paying its price to the owners. There was a delightful resting place just outside it, under tall plane trees that were green, shady, and beautiful.

A one-mile stream, flanked by trees on both banks, flowed continuously through the middle of the garden. Originally, its course was zigzag and irregular, but Babur had it straightened and organized, making the place even more beautiful. Between the village and the valley bottom, 4 to 6 miles down the slope, was a spring known as Khwāja Sih-yārān (Three-friends), where three different varieties of trees grew. A group of plane trees provided pleasant shade above it, holm-oak (Quercus bīlūt) grew abundantly on the slope at its sides (except for these two Oaklands, no holm-oak grew in the mountains of western Kābul), and the Judas-tree (arghwān) was extensively cultivated in front of it, toward the level ground—cultivated there and nowhere else. People said that the three different types of trees were a gift from three saints, which explained its name. Babur ordered that the spring be enclosed in mortared stonework, measuring 10 by 10, and that a symmetrical, right-angled platform be constructed on each of its sides, providing an overview of the entire field of Judas trees. If there was a place in the world that matched this when the arghwāns were in full bloom, Babur did not know of it. The yellow arghwān grew abundantly there, with both the red and yellow varieties flowering simultaneously. A group of plane trees provided pleasant shade above it; holm-oak (Quercus bīlūt) grew in abundance on the slope at its sides. With the exception of these two Oaklands (bīlūtistān), no holm-oak grew in the mountains of western Kābul. The Judas-tree (arghwān) was extensively cultivated in front of it, facing the level ground—cultivated there and nowhere else. People said the three different types of trees were a gift made by three saints, hence its name.

Babur ordered that the spring be enclosed in mortared stonework, measuring 10 by 10, and that a symmetrical, right-angled platform be constructed on each of its sides, providing an overview of the entire field of Judas-trees. If there was a place in the world to match this when the arghwāns were in full bloom, Babur did not know of it. The yellow arghwān also grew abundantly there, with both the red and yellow varieties flowering simultaneously.

To bring water to a large round seat which Babur had constructed on the hillside and planted with willows, a channel was dug across the slope from a half-mill stream that flowed constantly in a valley to the southwest of Sih-yārān. The date of cutting this channel was noted as jūī-khūsh (kindly channel).

Another of the tūmāns of Kābul was Luhūgur (modern Logar). Its primary village was Chīrkh, and notable individuals from this tūman included Maulānā Ya'qūb and Mullā-zāda 'Uṣmān. Khwāja Aḥmad and Khwāja Yūnas hailed from Sajāwand, another village in this region. Chīrkh boasted numerous gardens, while other villages in Luhūgur lacked such greenery. The people of Luhūgur were referred to as Aūghān-shāl, a term commonly used in Kābul, seemingly derived from a mispronunciation of Aūghān-sha'ār.

Again, there was the wilāyat, or, as some said, the tūmān of Ghaznī, which was believed to be the capital of Sabuk-tīgīn, Sultan Maḥmūd, and their descendants. Some people wrote it as Ghaznīn. It was also believed to have been the governmental center of Shihābu'd-dīn Ghūrī, known as Mu'izzu'd-dīn in the Ṭabaqāt-i-nāṣirī and other historical accounts of Hind.

Ghaznī was also known as Zābulistān and belonged to the Third climate. Some held the view that Qandahār was a part of it. It was situated 14 yīghāch (south-) west of Kābul, and those departing from it at dawn could reach Kābul between the Two Prayers, in the afternoon. In contrast, the 13 yīghāch between Adīnapūr and Kābul could never be covered in one day due to the difficulties of the road.Ghaznī had relatively little cultivated land. A stream, perhaps a four-mill or five-mill one, made the town habitable and irrigated four or five villages, while three or four others relied on underground water-courses (kārez) for cultivation. Grapes in Ghaznī were superior to those in Kābul; melons were more abundant; excellent apples were grown and exported to Hindustan. Agriculture was demanding in Ghaznī because the soil needed fresh top-dressing each year. However, it yielded better returns than Kābul. Ghaznī was known for growing madder, and the entire crop was sent to Hindustan, providing substantial profits for the growers.

The open countryside of Ghaznī was inhabited by Hazāra and Afghāns. It was generally a more affordable place compared to Kābul. The people of Ghaznī adhered to the Ḥanafī faith, were devout and orthodox Muṣalmāns. Many observed a three-month fast, and their wives and children lived in modest seclusion.

Ghaznī was home to notable individuals like Mullā 'Abdu'r-raḥmān, a learned man who was constantly engaged in learning (dars). He was highly orthodox, pious, and virtuous. He passed away in the same year as Nāṣir Mīrzā (AD 1515). In the suburb known as Rauẓa, where the finest grapes grew, you could find Sultan Maḥmūd's tomb. This area also housed the tombs of his descendants, including Sultan Mas'ūd and Sultan Ibrāhīm. Ghaznī boasted many sacred tombs.In the year[9] that Babur took Kābul and Ghaznī, overran Kohāt, the plain of Bannū, and the lands of the Afghāns, and proceeded to Ghaznī via Dūkī (Dūgī) and Āb-istāda, people informed him about a tomb in a Ghaznī village that appeared to move when a benediction on the Prophet was pronounced over it. Babur's party went to see it. Eventually, Babur discovered that the apparent movement was a trick, most likely orchestrated by the tomb's attendants. They had placed a platform above it that could be moved when pushed, creating the illusion of the tomb shifting, much like the way the shoreline seems to move for those in a passing boat. Babur ordered the scaffold to be dismantled and a dome to be built over the tomb. He also sternly warned the attendants not to attempt such a deception again. Ghaznī was a very humble place; it was indeed strange that rulers in whose hands were Hindustan and Khurāsānāt[10] had not chosen it for their capital. In the Sulṭān's (Maḥmūd's) time there may have been three or four dams in the country; one he made, some three yīghāch (18 m) up the Ghaznī-water to the north; it was about 40-50 qārī (yards) high and some 300 long; through it, the stored waters were let out as required. It was destroyed by 'Alāu'u'd-dīn Jahān-soz Ghūrī when he conquered the country (AD 1152), burned and ruined the tombs of several descendants of Sulṭān Maḥmūd sacked and burned the town, in short, left undone no title of murder and rapine. Since that time, the Sulṭān's dam has lain in ruins, but, through God's favor, there is hope that it may become of use again, by means of the money which was sent, in Khwāja Kalān's hand, in the year Hindustan was conquered (AD 1526). The Sakhāndam is another, 2 or 3 yīghāch (12-18 m.), may-be, on the east of the town; it has long been in ruins, indeed is past repair. There is a dam in working order at Sar-i-dih (Village-head).Babur says in the *Baburnama*, 'in books, it is written that there is in Ghaznī a spring such that, if dirt and the foul matter be thrown into it, a tempest gets up instantly, with a blizzard of rain and wind. It has been seen said also in one of the histories that Sabuk-tīgīn, when besieged by the Rāī (Jāī-pāl) of Hind, ordered dirt and foulness to be thrown into the spring, by this aroused, in an instant, a tempest with the blizzard of rain and snow, and, by this device, drove off his foe. Though we made many inquiries, no intimation of the spring's existence was given us.'

In these countries, Ghaznī and Khwārizm were noted for cold, in the same way, that Sulṭānīā and Tabrīz were in the two 'Irāqs and Az̲arbāījān. Zurmut was another tūmān, some 12–13 yīghāch south of Kābul and 7–8 south-east of Ghaznī. Its dārogha's headquarters were in Gīrdīz; there, most houses were three or four storeys high. It did not want for strength and gave Nāṣir Mīrzā trouble when it went into hostility to him. Its people were Aūghān-shāl; they grew corn but had neither vineyards nor orchards. The tomb of Shaikh Muḥammad Muṣalmān was at a spring, high on the skirt of a mountain, known as Barakistān, in the south of the tūmān.

Farmūl used to be another tūmān, a humble place that grew not bad apples, which were then transported into Hindustan. The Shaikh-zādas, descendants of Shaikh Muḥammad Muṣalmān, who were highly regarded during the Afghān period in Hindustan, hailed from Farmūl.

Bangash was once another tūmān, encircled by Afghān highwaymen, which included groups like the Khūgīānī, Khirilchī, Tūrī, and Landar. Due to its secluded location, its inhabitants were not particularly willing to pay taxes. Babur saw a sign of responsibility there an mentions in Baburnama, 'there has been no time to bring it to obedience; greater tasks have fallen to me,— the conquests of Qandahār, Balkh, Badakhshān, and Hindustan! But, Allah willing! when I get the chance, I most assuredly will take order with those Bangash thieves.'

One of the bulūks of Kābul was Ālā-sāī, located 4 to 6 miles (2-3 shar'ī) east of Nijr-aū. The direct road into it from Nijr-aū led, at a place called Kūra, through a relatively small pass that separated the hot and cold climates in that region. During the changing of seasons, many birds migrated through this pass. At those times, the people of Pīchghān, one of the dependencies of Nijr-aū, employed a unique method to catch these birds. They had set up hiding places for the bird-catchers at various points near the mouth of the pass. These bird-catchers had attached one corner of a net a few yards away and secured the lower side with stones to weigh it down. Along one side of the net, for about half its width, they had attached a stick that was about 3 to 4 yards long. The hidden bird-catcher had held this stick and, when the birds had approached, had lifted the net to its full height using the stick. The birds had then entered the net on their own. Sometimes, so many birds were caught using this contraption that there had been hardly enough time to cut there throats.

While the pomegranates of Ālā-sāī were not of the highest quality, they held a local reputation as the best in the vicinity and were frequently transported to Hindustan. Grapes also did well, and the wines produced in Ālā-sāī were known for being of superior quality and higher alcohol content compared to those of Nijr-aū.

Badr-aū (Tag-aū), an adjacent bulūk to Ālā-sāī, did not cultivate fruit but served as a region for grain cultivation, primarily by Kāfir people.

h. Tribesmen of Kābul

Just as Turks and Moghūl clans (aīmāq) had inhabited the open country of Khurāsān and Samarkand, the Hazāra and Afghāns lived in Kābul. Among the Hazāra, the Sulṭān-mas'ūdi Hazāra had been widely scattered, and among the Afghāns, the Mohmand had been prominent. Revenue of Kābul

The revenues of Kābul, together from the cultivated lands, from tolls (tamghā) and from dwellers in the open country, amounted to 8 lakhs of shāhrukhīs.

i. The mountain-tracts of Kābul

In the mountains of Andar-āb, Khwāst, and the Badakh-shānāt, where conifers (archa) flourished, many springs and gentle slopes could be found. However, in the eastern regions of Kābul, the landscape was covered in grass, resembling a beautiful carpet that blanketed the hills, slopes, and valleys. This was mostly būta-kāh grass, which was highly suitable for horses. In the Andijān region, they also spoke of būta-kāh, though the exact reason for this term was unknown to me. In Kābul, it was said that the grass was named so because it grew in tufts (būta, būta). The alps in these mountains were similar to those in Ḥiṣār, Khutlān, Ferghana, Samarkand, and Moghūlistān, all sharing the same mountainous and alpine characteristics. However, the alps in Ferghana and Moghūlistān were unparalleled among the others. In contrast, the mountains of Nijr-aū, Lamghānāt, and Sawād were distinguished by the presence of cypresses, holm-oak, olive, and mastic (Khānjak) and their unique grass.This grass was dense, tall, and not suitable for either horses or sheep. Although these mountains may have appeared less tall than those previously described, they were indeed formidable, with what seemed like gentle slopes proving to be hard rocks, making them impassable for riding. Many animals and birds from Hindustan could be found here, including the parrot, mīna, peacock, lūja (lūkha), ape, nīl-gāu, and hog-deer (kūta-pāī), with some species not even found in Hindustan.

The mountains to the west of Kābul, including Zindān-valley, Ṣūf-valley, Garzawān, and Gharjistān (Gharchastān), were all quite similar. Their meadows were mostly located in the valleys, and they lacked the extensive grassy slopes and tree masses seen in some of the previously described mountains. However, they did have grass suitable for horses. On their flat tops, where crops were grown, there was enough space for horses to gallop. They featured abundant kīyik. The valleys were predominantly strongholds, often steep and inaccessible from above. It was notable that, while other mountains had their fortifications high up, these mountains had theirs below.

Once again, the mountains of Ghūr, Karnūd (var. Kuzūd), and Hazāra were quite similar. Their meadows were in the valleys, and they had few trees, including the absence of conifers. The grass in these regions was suitable for both horses and the numerous sheep they kept. What set them apart from the previously mentioned mountains was that their strongholds were not located below.

The mountains to the southeast of Kābul, such as those of Khwāja Ismā'īl, Dasht, Dūgī (Dūkī), and Afghānistān, were all much alike.

They were low, lacked vegetation, had limited water sources, and were devoid of trees. These regions were unattractive and unproductive. Their inhabitants reflected the nature of their surroundings, as the saying went, 'As the place, so the people.' It was quite possible that there were few mountains in the world as unproductive and repugnant as these.

j. Firewood of Kābul

With heavy snowfall in Kābul, it was fortunate that excellent firewood was readily available nearby. In just one day's effort, one could obtain wood from the Khānjak (mastic), bīlūt (holm-oak), bādāmcha (small-almond), and qarqand trees. Among these, Khānjak wood had been the best choice. It burned with a bright flame, produced plenty of hot ashes, and had a pleasant aroma. It had also performed well even if it was somewhat sappy. Holm-oak had also been considered top-notch firewood, although it had a slightly lower flame than mastic. Similar to mastic, it had generated a fire with ample hot ashes and a pleasant scent. Holm-oak had the unique feature that when its leafy branches were ignited, they had crackled and blazed from the bottom to the top, providing an enjoyable experience during burning.

The wood from the small almond tree had been the most abundant and widely used, although it hadn't sustained a fire for an extended period. Qarqand had been a low, thorny shrub suitable for burning whether it was sappy or dry, and it had been the preferred fuel for the people of Ghaznī.

k. Fauna of Kābul

The cultivated lands of Kābul were situated between mountains that served as natural barriers, resembling large dams, surrounding the flat valley-bottoms where most villages and settlements were located. On these mountains, kīyik and āhū were rarely found. Across these mountains, connecting their summer and winter habitats, the dun sheep, known as arqārghalcha, followed a regular migratory route. Brave hunters ventured out with dogs and birds to capture them. Towards Khūrd-kābul and the Sūrkh-rūd region, wild asses were present, but there were no white kīyik at all. Ghaznī, on the other hand, had both species, and few other places could boast of white kīyik found in such good condition.

During the hot seasons, the hunting grounds of Kābul were bustling with activity. The birds typically followed the path of the Bārān-water. This was because the river was flanked by mountains to the east and west, and it aligned with a significant Hindū-kush pass. Birds had no other convenient crossing route. They couldn't migrate during the north wind or when even a small cloud obscured Hindū-kush. During these times, they would land on the flat lands surrounding the Bārān-water and were captured in large numbers by the local residents.

Towards the end of winter, large flocks of mallards (aūrdūq) arrived at the banks of the Bārān in excellent condition. Following them were the cranes and herons, which were large birds present in vast numbers and flocks.

l. Bird-catching

Along the Bārān, people had used a unique method to capture large numbers of cranes (tūrna), aūqār, qarqara, and qūṭān birds. They had employed a special bird-catching technique by twisting a cord as long as an arrow's flight, attaching an arrow at one end and a bīldūrga at the other, and winding it up from the arrow-end onto a piece of wood, which was about a span in length and as thick as a wrist. Afterward, they had removed the piece of wood, leaving behind only the hole it was in. By holding the bīldūrga firmly in their hand, they had shot the arrow towards incoming flocks of birds. If the cord had looped around a bird's neck or wing, it had brought the bird down. This method of bird-catching had been practiced by everyone along the Bārān, although it had been challenging and had required rainy nights. Birds had typically avoided landing on such nights and had continuously flown low along the river until dawn, fearing predatory beasts. During the night, they had used the flowing river as their path, with its moving water visible in the dark. This had been the perfect time to launch the cord and catch the birds.

Another group of bird-catchers in the area had consisted of slave-fowlers, totaling two or three hundred households. They had been originally brought to the Bārān by a descendant of Tīmūr Beg, who had had them migrate from near Multān. Bird-catching had been their trade, and they had employed various methods, such as digging tanks, placing decoy-birds on them, and using nets to capture birds of all kinds. Bird-catching had not been limited to fowlers alone, as every resident of the Bārān, whether through cord shooting, setting snares, or other techniques, had participated in capturing birds.

m. Fishing

In the same seasons as the birds, the fish of the Bārān migrated. During these times, many fish were captured using nets and wattles (chīgh) placed in the water. In autumn, when the plant known as wild-ass-tail had matured, flowered, and produced seeds, people would take 10–20 loads of the seeds and 20–30 of green branches (gūk-shībāk) to a water source. They would break these into small pieces and scatter them into the water. Then, they entered the water and easily collected the drugged fish. At a convenient spot downstream, near a waterfall, they had prepared in advance a wattle made of finger-thick willow-withes, securing it by piling stones on its sides. The rushing water flowed through the wattle but left behind any fish that had floated down. This method of catching fish was practiced in Gul-bahār, Parwān, and Istālīf.

In the Lamghānāt, a curious device was used to catch fish in the winter. People dug a pit in the stream's bed below a waterfall, similar in depth to a house. They lined it with stones, resembling a cooking area, and built-up stones around it above, leaving only one opening underwater. Except for this single opening, there was no other way in or out for the fish, but the water flowed through the stones. This created a sort of fish-pond from which, in the winter, fish could be taken, typically 30–40 at a time. The sides of the fish-pond, apart from the convenient opening, were sealed with rice straw held in place by stones. A piece of wickerwork was drawn into the opening by its edges and gathered together, and a second piece (a tube) was inserted, fitting at the mouth but reaching only halfway into it. The fish went through the smaller piece into the larger one, from which they couldn't escape. The second piece narrowed toward its inner mouth, with the pointed ends drawn so close that once a fish entered, it couldn't turn around and had to move one by one into the larger piece. They couldn't return because of the pointed ends of the inner, narrow mouth. With the wickerwork in place and the rice straw sealing the pond, the fish inside could be easily retrieved. Even fish that had tried to escape into the wickerwork were captured because they had no way out. This unique method of catching fish was not observed in other locations.

19

Hindustan Project Fails for the Second Time

The Departure of Muqīm and Allotment of Lands

Now that Kābul was in Babur's grip, Muqīm asked for leave to go to Qandahār. He left town on some terms and conditions laid—he was allowed to go to his father (Ẕu'n-nūn) and elder brother (Shāh Beg), along with various household followers, and his valuable assets.

The land of Kābul after Muqīm's departure was being shared between Mīrzās and the guest begs.[1] Ghaznī with its dependencies was given to Jahāngīr Mīrzā. Nāṣir Mīrzā was given the Nangarhār tūmān, Mandrāwar, Nūr valley, Kūnār, Nūr-gal and Chīghān-sarāī. Babur awarded some of the begs, who had been with him in his guerrilla times, villages and fief.

Babur has mentioned in the *Baburnama*: '*Wilāyat khūd hech bīrīlmādī . . .*' This makes it clear that he kept the mainland of Kābul to himself.

Babur wanted to bestow more favours on the guest begs, who were still strangers compared to old servants and Andijānīs. But he made an interesting observation in the *Baburnama*: 'This I have always done whenever Allah has shown me his favour; yet it is remarkable that despite this, people have blamed me constantly as though I had favoured none but old servants and Andijānīs.'

He then cites two proverbs (Turkī and Persian, respectively):*

* Babur, Abdul Rahim Khan-I-Khanan (trans.), *Tuzk-e Babri*, Delhi: Akbar, 1589, p. Folio 144b. This manuscript is available in National Museum, New Delhi. The Persian translation was done from the original Turkic manuscript of Babur. This was translated by author from the copy kept at National Museum, New Delhi.

1. What will a foe not say? what enters not into dream?'
2. A town-gate can be shut, a foe's mouth never.

Grain is Levied

Kābul was now full of clans and hordes that had come from Samarkand, Ḥiṣār and Qūndūz.

Babur has mentioned, 'Kābul is a small country; it is also of the sword, not of the pen, to take in money from it for all these tribesmen was impossible. It, therefore, seemed advisable to take in grain, provision for the families of these clans so that their men could ride on forays with the army.' This gives us a hint that perhaps tax was taken by force and not paid on a written assessment.

Accordingly, Babur decided to levy 30,000 donkey-loads of grain on Kābul, Ghaznī without having any clue about the magnitude of the harvests. What is interesting is that Babur himself acknowledges that this tax impost was unwarranted and eventually caused the Kābulis to suffer.

One thing that must not be missed is that it was during this period that Babur devised his own *Bāburī* script.* †

Babur Raids Hazāra

Sulṯān Mas'ūdī Hazāras was designated to pay a large tribute in form of horses and sheep. But when Babur sent his men to collect them, instead of tributes, the news arrived that the Hazāras were obstinate and in no mood to pay up. They had taken up the Ghaznī and Gīrdīz roads against Babur's sanctions. They denied recognizing Babur as the legitimate sovereign.

Babur decided to march along with his strong horsemen to crush this rebellion. He thought the attack would be a surprise as they would not be expecting it, and he would end up being successful in gaining the tributes. Riding by the Maidān road, Babur and his men crossed the Nirkh pass[2] in the night. They finally caught the rebelling

---

* K̲h̲wājah Niẓāmuddīn Aḥmad, *The Ṭabaqāt-i-Akbarī: A History of India from the Early Musalmān Invasions to the Thirty-sixth Year of the Reign of Akbar*, s.l.: Low Price Publications, 1992.

† Abd al-Qādir ibn Mulūk Shāh Badā'ūnī, *Muntakhabu't-tawārīkh Vol-3*, p. 273.

Hazaras near Jāl-tū around the time of morning prayers. Though the Hazaras fought well, Babur came on them heavily. They had to bend and agree to what Babur wanted them to pay.

After defeating them, Babur returned through Sang-i-sūrākh and Jahāngīr Mīrzā took leave for Ghaznī. As Babur reached Kābul, Yār-i-ḥusain, son of Daryā Khān, came in from Bhīra, waiting on him.

The First Campaign for Hindustan

Some days had passed since they returned to Kābul after having crushed the Hazaras.

> *Author's Opinion: Babur wasn't feeling gratified with having attained what was there so far. Perhaps he always had this dream of re-establishing the legacy of Timur in Bharat. And Timur always desired to establish the rule of Islam in Bharat by hook or crook.**

Babur had readied the army once again. He was up to something really big. The people who were acquainted with the length and breadths of Kābul were summoned. They were tasked with sharing every detail of each side and quarter of the city. Babur was also trying to gather idea about which part he needed to march further to fulfil his imperialistic desires.

He got several suggestions. Few advised marching to Dasht, while some advised for Bangash. A party insisted on Hindustan. Babur chose the third option given his inclination for reconquering the Hindustan like Timur had desired.

It was the month of Sha'bān in AH 910 (January of AD 1505). Babur has mentioned that the sun was in Aquarius when he rode out of Kābul for Hindustan.

Babur along with his men took the road by Bādām-chashma (current Surobi district of Kābul) and Jagdālīk. He reached Adīnapūr (current Jalalabad) in six marches. The high temperature shocked Babur. He had neither witnessed such a hot climate nor the land

* Yazdī, Sharaf al-Dīn 'Alī, *The History of Timur-Bec, Known by the Name of Tamerlain the Great, Emperor of the Moguls and Tartars: Being an Historical Journal of His Conquests in Asia and Europe.* (trans.) John Darby, London: John Darby, 1723. Vol. 2.

bordering Hindustan till before then. It was a new world to him when he reached Nangarhār. The grasses, trees, animals and birds—everything was different. In Babur's own words, 'We were amazed, and truly there was ground for amazement.'

Babur met his half-brother Nāṣir Mīrzā there. He was waiting for Babur after his tourney to another district. Babur's campaign was delayed in Adīnapūr as he waited for the other men to join. He also waited for the contingent of a clan that had joined him from Kābul and had been wintering in the Lamghānāt.

The marching resumed after everybody joined. They dismounted next at Qūsh-guṃbaz below Jūī-shāhī. After having reached there, Nāṣir Mīrzā requested to leave to stay behind. He committed that he would follow in a few days after providing for his dependents and followers.

They eventually resumed the march. From Qūsh-guṃbaz, they dismounted at a hot spring (*garm-chashma*). Then a headman of the Gāgīānī was brought in with his caravan to guide on the way forward, which he did without any hesitation. They were able to cross Khyber in a couple of marches and dismounted at Jām-rūd (Jām torrent).

The headman recounted several tales while travelling with Babur, who has mentioned:*

> Gūr-khattrī was said to be a holy place of the Jogīs and Hindūs who come from long distances to shave their heads and beards there.

Babur had never come across Hindus before, and it looked an exciting sight to him at once.

Babur rode out from Jām to Bīgrām. He saw its great tree and all the country round, but, much as he enquired about Gūr-khattrī, his guide, Malik Bū-sa'īd Kamarī couldn't tell anything about it. Disappointed and disgusted when Babur along with his men returned to camp, he communicated to Khwāja Muḥammad-amīn that Gūr-khattrī was in Bīgrām and he didn't say anything about it because of its narrow passages and confined cells. The Khwāja lost his cool

---

* Babur, Abdul Rahim Khan-I-Khanan (trans.), *Tuzk-e Babri*, Delhi: Akbar, 1589, p. Folio 146. This manuscript is available in National Museum, New Delhi. The Persian translation was done from the original Turkic manuscript of Babur. This was translated by author from the copy kept at National Museum, New Delhi.

and abused him in the worst possible way. He came to Babur and narrated the whole episode, but despite having known about it, Babur decided not to go there as the remaining road was long and they had already spent enough days so far.

Expedition of Kohāt

Babur's next big hurdle was the mighty river Sindh. They were unsure whether to cross Sindh or follow another route. Bāqī Chaghānīānī suggested not crossing the river, and with a night's halt, they would be able to make it to a place called Kohāt. According to him, this place was full of rich tribesmen. The Kābulīs were brought forward for a second opinion and to substantiate what he said. They seconded Bāqī Chaghānīānī's words. Neither Babur nor his men had heard of this place. But Babur chose to go ahead with Bāqī Chaghānīānī's opinion of heading for Kohāt because he was a man of authority and words. Thus, the plan of crossing the Sindh-water into Hindustan was dropped completely. They marched from Jām, forded the Bāra-water and dismounted not far from the pass (*dābān*) through the Muhammad mountain.

At that time Gāgīānī Afghāns were in Peshawar. The 'Gāgīānī Afghāns' refers to a specific group of Afghans who are a Pashtun tribe primarily located in the Ghaznī and Paktika provinces of Afghanistan, but they are also found in some other regions of the country.

They were in trepidation because of Babur's army and drew off to the skirt hills. One of their headmen came to Babur's camp, and paid obeisance and respect good enough to impress him. Babur decided to take him in as the *fajjī* (guide). He thought that they might point out the paths in a much more organized way. Finally, Babur and his men left that camp at midnight, crossed Muḥammad-hajj (pass) at dawn, and by breakfast, they descended on Kohāt. They were able to get hold of abundant cattle and buffalo. They also captured those Afghān owners of cattle who had opposed them. But Babur set them free and kept the cattle. Babur's men found Kohāt houses, filled with humongous quantities of corn.

On the other hand, Babur's foragers raided as far as the Sindh River and then rejoined him after nightfall. Meanwhile, Babur did not get what Bāqī Chaghānīānī had promised, and he was badly ashamed of it.

When Babur's foragers returned and after spending two nights in Kohāt, Babur organized a council to deliberate on the next move. They decided to overrun the Afghāns of Bangash and the Bannū neighbourhood following which they were to go back to Kābul, either through Naghr or by the Farmūl road.

In Kohāt appeared Daryā Khān's son, Yār-i-ḥusain, who had waited on Babur in Kābul earlier. He made a petition to Babur, saying, 'If royal orders were given me for the Dilazāk the Yūsuf-zāī, and the Gāgīānī, these would not go far from my orders if I called up the Padishah's swords on the other side of the water of Sind.' Hearing his petition, Babur was more than delighted, and accordingly, he was allowed to go from Kohāt.

March to Thāl

Babur's party finally began to march out of Kohāt. They took the Hangū road for Bangash. The very road that connected Kohāt and Hangū through a valley was shut from either side by the mountains. Afghāns of Kohāt and its vicinity were waiting for them to gather at the foothill. When they entered this valley, they raised their war cry with great clamour. Babur's guide for the expedition, Malik Bū-sa'īd Kamarī, was well-acquainted with the Afghān locations. He informed that further that there was a detached hill on the right, and if the Afghāns came down to it from the foothills, Babur along with his men could surround the Afghāns and take them on effectively. It went as good as it could for Babur. The Afghāns, on reaching the place, did come down. As suggested by Malik Bū-sa'īd Kamarī Babur ordered a party to seize the neck of land between the hill and the mountains, and asked others to move along its sides, so that if attacks were made from all sides, the Afghāns would be doomed. As planned, they could not stand the might of Babur's trained men. They were butchered mercilessly and a few (around 200) were brought captive along with and a mass of beheaded heads.

Babur talks about a local narrative of what he heard about the Afghāns.

He writes, 'We had been told that when Afghāns are powerless to resist, they go before their foe with grass between their teeth, this being as much as to say, "I am your cow."' And this is exactly what

Figure 3: The Apotheosis of War, 1871. Anti-war painting depicting a pyramid of skulls made by the fourteenth-century ruler Timur. From the Tretyakov Gallery, Moscow. (Vereshchagin, 1871).

happened on the ground. When Afghāns failed to resist, they came to Babur with grass between their teeth. But Babur chose not to show mercy. They were brought in as prisoners and beheaded one by one. The heads were piled up in a tower.

This custom is a Tīmūrid practice. Timur was known to make towers of skulls. In AD 1402, at Smyrna, all civilians were beheaded by him, and two massive towers of heads were erected. Back in AD 1388, as retaliation to inhabitants' rebellion against the tax collectors, he compiled thirty such towers and each is reported to have contained around fifteen hundred heads.*

They camped right there, and on the next day, began to march forward, finally dismounting at Hangū. The local Afghāns had made a *sanger* on a hill. Babur has penned his thoughts about sanger:

> I first heard the word sanger after coming to Kābul where people describe fortifying themselves on a hill as making a sanger.

---

* Marina Belozerskaya, *Medusa's Gaze: The Extraordinary Journey of the Tazza Farnese*, Oxford: Oxford University Press, 2012, p. 88.

The Tīmūrids slaughtered again. Babur's men went straight up, broke into the sanger, and chopped off around 200 'insolent' Afghān heads. Just like Timur, Babur made a tower of heads.

They began to march from Hangū to Thāl. They were able to reach Thāl below Bangash with a night's halt. There too Babur's men made a tower of heads from each one who couldn't escape.

Barging into Bannū and 'Īsa-khail

Leaving from Thāl, they went without a road, right down a steep descent, through narrow strips laid on the road. They halted for a night by the side and very next day came down into Bannū. Each man, horse and camel were all worn out with fatigue. A load of booty was making things miserable on the irregular road, which did not seem fit for riding. The regular road was still a few miles away on the right. The irregular route was known as Gosfandliyār (sheep road; *liyār* is Afghānī for a road). These narrow streets were used by the shepherds and herdsmen to take their flocks and herds. Most of the people in Babur's camp had begun to say that this idea of the left-hand road was a bad idea from Malik Bū-sa'īd Kamarī.

The Bannū lands had very low elevation. They lay immediately outside the Bangash and Naghr hills to the north. The Bangash torrent of the Kūrām River comes down into Bannū making it highly fertile. Sindh River existed to the south-east. To the east lay Dīn-kot and the west existed plain lands known as Bāzār and Tāq. The land of Bannū was cultivated by the Afghān tribesmen like Kurānī, Kīwī, Sūr, 'Īsa-khail and Nīā-zāī, etc.

After dismounting in Bannū, they heard that the tribesmen (Kīwī) in the plain were going to launch a resistance and with that intent, they had begun entrenching themselves on a hill to the north. Babur sent a force headed by Jahāngīr Mīrzā against them in their sanger. He slaughtered them mercilessly, creating yet another tower of heads. After the sanger had been taken, the Kīwī headman, Shādī Khān, came to Babur, with grass between his teeth. He paid obeisance to Babur. Interestingly, Babur took a different stance, atypical of the Tīmūrid practice—he not only pardoned Shādī Khān, but all the prisoners.

As per the decision of counsel post-takeover of Kohāt, they were to return to Kābul after overrunning Bangash and Bannū through

Naghr or Farmūl. But when Bannū had been overrun, people familiar with the locality suggested that the plains were close by, with good roads and abundant wealth. Hence the decision was reviewed, and it was settled to take over the plain and then return to Kābul via Farmūl.

Marching the next day, they dismounted at a spot in 'Īsa-khail village by the bank of river Kūrām. The villagers had gone into the Chaupāra Hills after hearing of Babur's arrival. Babur left the spot where he had dismounted and rose towards the skirt of Chaupāra. Babur sent out his foragers into the hills and destroyed the 'Īsa-khail sanger. In return, they carried booty in the form of sheep, herds, and clothes.

But things were not going to remain so easy for Babur. That very night, the people of 'Īsa-khail attacked him, however, unsuccessfully. Babur's men had kept a good watch and their brisk reaction was almost natural. So cautious were Babur's men that, their right, left and centre van had been aptly stationed where the tribesmen had dismounted. Each man of Babur was in accord with his generic place in battle. Each was prepared for his post—with men on foot all around the camp, at an arrow's distance from the tents. Each night Babur ensured that his army was organized. Three or four households patrolled in turn with torches. Babur too made such rounds once each night. He ensured hefty punishments for those who didn't fulfil their duty of being at their assigned posts holistically. He got their noses slit and then were taken through the army.

Jahāngīr Mīrzā was given the responsibility of taking care of the right wing, with the supervision of Bāqī Chaghānīānī, Sherīm Ṭaghāī, Sayyid Ḥusain Akbar, and a few other begs. The left wing's responsibility was given to Mīrzā Khān with the supervision of 'Abdu'r-razzāq Mīrzā, Qāsīm Beg and a few other begs. The centre was occupied by not many great begs but typical household begs. Lord of the Gate Sayyid Qāsim was the van with Bābā Aūghūlī, Allāh-bīrdī and some other begs. The army had six divisions and each one had its unique day and night on guard.

Marching from that foothills they faced west. They dismounted somewhere between Bannū and the plain. The place lacked water. The soldiers had to fetch water for themselves and their herds by digging deep for a couple of yards into the dried watercourse. Babur has taken this opportunity to talk about the peculiarity of the rivers of Hindustan. He has said, 'Not here only did this happen, for all the rivers of Hindustan have the peculiarity that water is safe to be found by digging down from one to one-and-a-half yards in their beds. It is a wonderful provision of Allah that where, except for the great rivers, there are no running waters, water should be so placed within reach in dry watercourses.'*

Babur and his men left the dry channel the next morning. Some of his men, riding light, reached villages of the plain in the afternoon. They raided a few of them and brought back flocks, cloth and horses bred for trade. The pack animals, camels and the warriors accompanying them, who were outdistanced due to their ultra-slow pace, kept coming into camp all through that night, till that morrow's noon.

During the stay, Babur sent out the foragers who brought herds of sheep and cattle, from villages in the plain. They brought white cloths, aromatic roots, sugars, *tīpūchāqs*, and horses bred for trade from the Afghān traders they met on the roads.

Mindī Moghūl (Babur's military general) unhorsed Khwāja Khiẓr Lūhānī, a well-known and respected Afghān merchant. He beheaded him and brought his head to Babur. But it was not all rosy on the side of Babur's camp. Sherīm Ṭaghāī faced an Afghān while following the foragers on the road and later chopped his index finger.

Return to Kābul

Babur had heard of two roads leading to Farmūl. One was Tunnel-rock (*Sang-i-sūrākh*) road, passing Birk (*Barak*) and the other was along Gūmāl but without touching Birk (Barak).

It rained relentlessly during their stay in the plain, and the river Gūmāl had swollen way beyond its natural width. It would have been very difficult to cross at the ford, where they had reached. Several people well-acquainted with the roads had appraised Babur that while going by the Gūmāl road, he would need to cross this torrent several times—a task that was seemingly impossible when the waters rose. Babur was unable to decide which road to choose. Babur instructed

* It means that none of the artificial runlets were familiar where Babur had lived before getting to know Hindustan.

people to rest, hoping the water level would go down the next day. The drum of departure was loud enough to wake Babur and his men wake up from their slumber. Yet, things did not seem as good as they should have to Babur.

It was the 'Īd-al-fitr, the seventh day of the March in AD 1505. While Babur was engaged in the ablutions to break the fast, Jahāngīr Mīrzā and the begs discussed which road was to be taken. Someone suggested that if they were to turn at the last spur of the Mehtar Sulaimān range, they would get a level road though it might take a few more marches. Babur, when informed, chose to stick with this plan. A lot could have been finished before Babur's ablutions for Īd—his army had already taken the road and most of them had crossed Gūmāl. No one from Babur's side had ever seen that road. Certainly, no one was aware of the exact length of the road. Babur began his journey on this road without giving any second thought—he had decided to trust the hearsay about the route.

They read the 'Id prayer on the bank of river Gūmāl. That Persian New Year's Day, *Nūroz*, occurred close to the 'Id-al-fitr. And when only a few days were left for it to come, Babur composed the following (Turkī) sonnet:*

> Glad is the Bairām-moon for him who sees both the face of the Moon and the Moon-face of his friend;
> Sad is the Bairām-moon for me, far away from thy face and from thee.
> O Bābur! dream of your luck when your Feast is the meeting, your New-year the face;
> For better than that could not be with a hundred New-years and Bairāms.

After crossing the Gūmāl torrent, Babur and his men took the route along the skirt of the hills, while they faced south. After having ridden for a couple of miles, Babur found some bloodthirsty Afghāns on the lower edge of the hill slope. Babur along with a few of his men went after them. Most of them fled, but some began to make silly gestures

* Babur, Abdul Rahim Khan-I-Khanan (trans.), *Tuzk-e Babri*, Delhi: Akbar, 1589, p. Folio 150. This manuscript is available in National Museum, New Delhi. The Persian translation was done from the original Turkic manuscript of Babur. This was translated by author from the copy kept at National Museum, New Delhi.

on the rocky piles of the foothills. One of them took post on a single rock, seeming to have a cliff on the further side of it—he had no way to escape.

Sulṭān Qulī Chūnāq came forward and slashed his head with ease. Having seen it happen in front of his eyes, Babur showered Sulṭān Qulī with favours and promotions. At another pile of rock, Qūtlūq-qadam exchanged blows with an Afghān and chopped off his head.

Kūpūk Beg got hand-on-collar with an Afghān at another hill. They both rolled to the bottom of the hill while fighting. Finally, the Afghān was arrested and presented to Babur. He took quite a few prisoners. However, they were freed instead of being beheaded.

They had begun to march further south through the plain, closely skirting Mehtar Sulaimān. They reached a small township called Bīlah after three nights. It lay on the banks of river Sindh and depended on Multān. Babur saw that some villagers crossed the river on boats, others got into the water to cross it, and some stood on an island in front of Bīlah. Most of Babur's men, and horses in the mail, leapt in the river and crossed to the island. Some, unfortunately, drowned, including a thin slave, Qul-i-arūk, the head tent-pitcher, one Jahāngīr Mīrzā's servant and Qāītmās Turkmān.

Meanwhile, the villagers had already crossed the river and looking at the fiery Sindh water, some of them began to wave swords, trying to scare away Babur's men. Soon, Qul-i-bāyazīd, one of Babur's men had crossed to the island. With intent to dive into the river, he stripped himself and his horse right in front of them. Soon he dived into the river. The water on the other side of the island was perhaps thrice as wide compared to what it was at Babur's end. Qul-i-bāyazīd made his horse swim towards them till they reached a shallow patch where his weight would be up-borne, with the water being as high as the saddle flap. He couldn't stay there for long. No one could come to support him . . . rather there was no chance that anyone could support him. They shot a few arrows at him, but none hurt. They gave up and ran away. It was indeed audacious of him to swim in the mighty Sindh all alone with no one behind, on a bare-backed horse, and to chase off a foe and thereby occupy his ground. Babur calls this, 'a mightily bold deed!'

Now look at the irony, after he drove the enemies away from the island, other soldiers followed and returned with booty—clothes and droves of various sorts. Babur had raised Qul-i-bāyazīd from the position of cook to that of a royal taster in the past—his courage and kindness were always rewarded. This time Babur gave him a position full of bounty, favour and promotions. Babur says, 'In truth, he was worthy of honour and advancement*.'

Babur and two of his men marched down the water of Sindh. Babur's men had now knocked their horses away perpetually for galloping off on raids. They usually took cattle. In the plain, they exclusively took a lot of sheep and clothes as bounty. However, once they left the plains, they had nothing but cattle.

The raids along the Sindh River were rather barbaric. Even merely a servant would bring in around 400 chopped heads. Many of these would rot on the roads.

The Westward March

They had already made three more marches along the Sindh River. They stopped moving forward when they came opposite the Pīr Kānū's tomb. Babur decided to pay his obeisance. When some of his badly injured soldiers tried to pay their tributes, it disgusted Babur to such an extent that he ordered immediately them to have them chopped off into pieces.[3] Babur observed that this tomb lay on the skirt of one of the Mehtar Sulaimān mountains and was accorded great honour in Hindustan.

They began to march from Pīr Kānū and dismounted at the Pawat pass, lying in the bed of a torrent in Dūkī (sub-district of Qandahār). After they left this camp, around thirty followers of Fāẓil Kūkūldāsh, the *dārogha* of Sīwī and the retainer of Shāh Beg were brought in. They were sent to perhaps look at Babur's activities. But after having familiarised with the whole matter, Babur decided to let them go with their horses and arms as he was on good terms with Shāh Beg. After one night's halt, they reached a village named Chūtīālī.

Babur's men had constantly galloped off to raid, before reaching the Sindh water and all along its bank. They did not leave horses

---

* Babur, Abdul Rahim Khan-I-Khanan (trans.), *Tuzk-e Babri*, Delhi: Akbar, 1589, p. Folio 151b. This manuscript is available in National Museum, New Delhi. The Persian translation was done from the original Turkic manuscript of Babur. This was translated by author from the copy kept at National Museum, New Delhi.

behind as there was plenty of green food and corn for them. However, after they left the river and set out for Pīr Kānū, there was no trace of green food. They would find only a little land under green crops every two or three marches, but no corn for the horses was to be found anywhere. So, they began to leave their horses beyond that camp.

Babur has said, 'After passing Chūtīālī, my own felt-tent had to be left from want of baggage-beasts.'*

In that period, one night it poured very heavily. There was knee-deep water inside his tent. All Babur could do was wait the night out, uncomfortably sitting on a pile of blankets.

Bāqī Chaghānīānī's Betrayal

They marched further after the rain stopped. Within a few moments, Mīrzā came and said to Babur, 'have some information that must be delivered privately.' Accordingly, they both moved to a private space. He said, 'Bāqī Chaghānīānī came and said to me, "You make the Padishah cross the water of Sindh with seven to ten persons, then make yourself Padishah."'

Hearing this, Babur said with a smile, 'What others are heard of as consulting with him?'

Jahāngīr Mīrzā replied, 'It was but a moment ago Bāqī Beg spoke to me; I know no more.'

Babur said, 'Find out who the others are; likely enough Sayyid Ḥusain Akbar and Sulṭān 'Alī the page is in it, as well as Khusrau Shāh's begs and braves.'†

Babur was very pleased with Jahāngīr Mīrzā. He writes praise as below:‡

* Babur, Abdul Rahim Khan-I-Khanan (trans.), *Tuzk-e Babri*, Delhi: Akbar, 1589, p. Folio 12. This manuscript is available in National Museum, New Delhi. The Persian translation was done from the original Turkic manuscript of Babur. This was translated by author from the copy kept at National Museum, New Delhi.

† Babur, Abdul Rahim Khan-I-Khanan (trans.), *Tuzk-e Babri*, Delhi: Akbar, 1589, p. Folio 152b. This manuscript is available in National Museum, New Delhi. The Persian translation was done from the original Turkic manuscript of Babur. This was translated by author from the copy kept at National Museum, New Delhi.

‡ Ibid.

> Here the Mīrzā really behaved very well and like a blood-relation; what he now did was the counterpart of what I had done in Kāhmard, in this same ill-fated mannikin's other scheme of treachery.

Impressed by his loyalty, Babur made Jahāngīr lead a body of strong men to raid the Afghāns in the neighbourhood.

Since Babur's men had been leaving horses behind at each camping ground, they only had 300 horses left. The men of the first rank were completely on foot. One such household-brave was Sayyid Maḥmūd Aūghlāqchī. He left his horses behind and began to walk for the rest of the path. In this state, as to horses, we went all the rest of the way to Ghaznī.

By the time they finished four more marches, Jahāngīr Mīrzā had plundered some Afghāns and brought in a few sheep as war booty.

The Āb-i-istāda

In a few marches, they reached Āb-i-istāda—a delightfully large water body picturesque to view.

Babur has sumptuously described the scene:*

> The level lands on its further side could not be seen at all; its water seemed to join the sky; the higher land and the mountains of that further side looked to hang between Heaven and Earth, as in a mirage.

The water was said to have come from the spring-rain floods of the Kattawāz-plain, the Zurmut Valley, and the Qarā-bāgh meadow of the Ghaznī-torrent, floods of the spring-rains, and the over-plus of the summer-rise of streams.

When they were two miles from the Āb-i-istāda, they saw an interesting thing. They kept on seeing rose-like figures rising and vanishing at the horizon above water repeatedly. When they reached closer, they saw large flocks of flamingos—thousands of them. When

* Babur, Abdul Rahim Khan-I-Khanan (trans.), *Tuzk-e Babri*, Delhi: Akbar, 1589, p. Folio 152b, p. Folio 153b. This manuscript is available in National Museum, New Delhi. The Persian translation was done from the original Turkic manuscript of Babur. This was translated by author from the copy kept at National Museum, New Delhi.

the birds flapped their wings in flight, sometimes red feathers appeared and sometimes not. They saw many eggs on the shore.

Two Afghāns came to collect the eggs. They saw Babur's troop. They swam away half a mile out of fear. They wanted to go unnoticed, but they couldn't escape Babur's eyes. He brought them back.

Following these events, Babur dismounted at the inundation coming down to the Āb-i-istāda from the plain of Kattawāz. Each time Babur had gone by it in the past, the channel had been dry, but this time it was full of water. Perhaps no ford could be found due to the spring rains. The channel was deep but not very broad. They couldn't manage to go beyond without crossing it. The horses and camels were made to swim in it and the baggage was towed over with ropes. After getting across, they went on through Old Nānī and Sar-i-dih to Ghaznī. For a few days, Jahāngīr Mīrzā hosted them, offered food and offered the due tribute.

Return to Kābul

Unfortunately, the floods had been massive in AD 1505. They could not find any crossing over the water of Logar. Hence, they had to go straight on to Kamarī, through the Sajāwand-pass. At Kamarī, Babur managed to get a boat. It was one fashioned in a pool and brought and set on the Logar water, in front of Kamarī in which Babur put all his people.

They reached Kābul in the month of Ẕū'l-ḥijja (May) of AD 1505. Babur's four-month-long expedition, full of losses, had just got over. Just a few days ago, Sayyid Yūsuf Aūghlāqchī had succumbed to colic pains.

Nāṣīr Mīrzā's Misconduct

Earlier I had mentioned the incident of Qūsh-guṃbaz, in which Nāṣir Mīrzā had asked Babur for a leave to stay behind on the condition that he would join back in a few days after taking something from his district for his retainers and followers. However, he betrayed, rather misconducted, by going against his desires.

Having left Babur and co, he sent a force against the people of Nūr valley, on the ground of them being rebellious. As mentioned before, it was difficult to move in that valley owing to the strong position of its fort and the rice cultivation of its lands. Faẓlī, the Mīrzā's commander, proved to be highly impracticable on the ground and in that one-road tract, instead of safeguarding his men, sent them for foraging and barged out the farmers of valley. They drove the foragers off and turned the circumstances such that it became impossible for the rest to keep their ground. They even killed a few and captured some with their horses. About this situation, Babur has written, 'Precisely what would happen to any army chancing to be under such a person as Faẓlī? Whether because of this affair, or whether from want of heart, the Mīrzā did not follow us at all; he stayed behind.'

Babur has further written, 'Ayūb's sons, Yūsuf and Bahlūl, more seditious, silly and arrogant persons than whom there may not exist, —to whom I had given, to Yūsuf Alangār, to Bahlūl 'Alī-Shang, they like Nāṣir Mīrzā, were to have taken something from their districts and to have come on with him, but he not coming, neither did they.'[*]

They were the champions of his cups and social pleasures throughout the last winter. They did overrun the Tarkalānī Afghāns in it. During the approaching summer, the Mīrzā made the families of clans, outside tribes and hordes march, driving hard as if they were flocks of sheep (as described by Babur). They marched no different than a herd of sheep carrying all their goods till they reached Bārān water. They were the ones who were lazily enough wintered in Nangarhār and Lamghānāt.

Matters of Badakhshān

Nāṣir Mīrzā was still in the camp on the Bārān-water when he heard the news that the Badakhshīs had united against the Aūzbegs and had killed some of them. The event is explained by Babur:[†]

---

[*] Babur, Abdul Rahim Khan-I-Khanan (trans.), *Tuzk-e Babri*, Delhi: Akbar, 1589, p. Folio 154b. This manuscript is available in National Museum, New Delhi. The Persian translation was done from the original Turkic manuscript of Babur. This was translated by author from the copy kept at National Museum, New Delhi.

[†] Babur, Abdul Rahim Khan-I-Khanan (trans.), *Tuzk-e Babri*, Delhi: Akbar, 1589, p. Folio 155. This manuscript is available in National Museum, New Delhi. The Persian translation was done from the original Turkic manuscript of Babur. This was translated by author from the copy kept at National Museum, New Delhi.

> When Shaybāni Khān had given Qūndūz to Qaṃbar Bī and gone himself to Khwārizm; Qaṃbar Bī, to conciliate the Badakhshīs, sent them a son of Muḥammad-i-makhdūmī, Maḥmūd by name, but Mubārak Shāh,—whose ancestors are heard of as begs of the Badakhshān Shāhs,—having uplifted his own head, and cut off Maḥmūd's and those of some Aūzbegs, made himself fast in the fort once known as Shāf-tiwār but re-named by him Qila'-i-ẕafar. Moreover, in Rustāq Muḥammad qūrchī, an armorer of Khusrau Shāh, then occupying Khamalangān, slew Shaibāq Khān's ṣadr and some Aūzbegs and made that place fast. Zubair of Rāgh, again, whose forefathers also will have been begs of the Badakhshān Shāhs, uprose in Rāgh. Jahāngīr Turkmān, again, a servant of Khusrau Shāh's Walī, collected some of the fugitive soldiers and tribesmen Walī had left behind, and with them withdrew into a fastness.

Nāṣir Mīrzā heard of these details and also got provoked by a few puerile, short-sighted persons. Intending to covet Badakhshān, he marched along the Shibr-tū and Āb-dara road. Babur drove the families of the men who had come into Kābul from the other side of the Amū like sheep.[4]

Khusrau Shāh's Death

When Khusrau Shāh and Aḥmad-i-qāsim were fleeing from Ājar for Khurāsāny,[5] they met Badī'u'z-zamān Mīrzā and Ẕū'n-nūn Beg, together in the presence of Sulṭān Ḥusayn Mīrzā in Herī. All had long been foes of Ḥusayn Mīrzā. They had caused him some discomfort. Perhaps, Ḥusayn Mīrzā too didn't harbour any soft corner for them either.

Despite this, they chose to discuss their distress with him. Babur came to know about the circumstances as all communication went through him. He had a feeling that they would have not gone to see him if he hadn't rendered Khusrau Shāh helpless. Not to forget, Babur had stripped him of his followers and had taken Kābul from Ẕū'n'nūn's son, Muqīm. Badī'u'z-zamān Mīrzā himself was like currency in the hands of the rest, who could do nothing beyond their words.

As their luck would have it, Sulṭān Ḥussayn Mīrzā displayed a courteous attitude towards each one of them. He even gave them good gifts.

Soon after they had arrived, Khusrau Shāh said, 'If I go, I shall get it all into my hands.' And he requested a leave. They finessed a little about his leave, perhaps because he had reached Herī without any equipment and resources. He had turned an absolute importunate. Muḥammad Barandūq retorted, 'When you had thirty thousand men behind you and the whole country in your hands, what did you effect against the Aūzbeg? What will you do now with your five hundred men and the Aūzbegs in possession?'

Babur has written, 'He added a little good advice in a few sensible words, but all was in vain because the fated hour of Khusrau Shāh's death was near.'

At last, he was granted leave for his importunity. Khusrau Shāh with his 400-odd followers went straight into the borders of Dahānah. Praise to the play of stars, Nāṣir Mīrzā and he had to meet. Latter had just gone across—as told in chapter 18.

Now, the Badakhshī chiefs had invited only the Nāṣir Mīrzā and not Khusrau Shāh. Mīrzā tried his best to persuade Khusrau Shāh to go into the hill country (perhaps Ḥiṣār). The latter was quite hesitant to act on Mīrzā's suggestion. He believed that if he marched under the Mīrzā, he would get the country into his own hands. At last, both didn't agree with each other. Finally, he arrayed Mīrzā and his following near Ishkīmīsh, put on mail, drawing out to fight and departed. Nāṣir Mīrzā went on for Badakhshān. After collecting a muddled horde surmounting to around a thousand, good as well as bad, Khusrau Shāh went, intending to lay siege to Qūndūz and Khwāja Chār-tāq.

Shaybāni Khān, after incapacitating Sulṭān Aḥmad Taṃbal and Andijān, made a move on Ḥiṣār. Khusrau Shāh[6] ran away from his own country, Qūndūz, and Ḥiṣār without being struck by a single blow. He was dedicated to saving himself from even a scratch. Subsequently, Shaybāni Khān went to Ḥiṣār along with Sherīm and many other warriors. Ḥiṣār wasn't surrendered, though as their honourable beg had run away from his own country it was an easy job to make Ḥiṣār secure. Having entrusted the siege of Ḥiṣār to Ḥamza Sulṭān and Mahdī Sulṭān, Shaybāni went to Qūndūz. He gave Qūndūz to his younger brother, Maḥmūd Sulṭān and he relocated to Khwārizm against Chīn Ṣūfī without any delay.

While he was already on the way to Khwārizm, somewhere near Samarkand he heard about the demise of his brother Maḥmūd Sulṭān way back in Qūndūz. We have no records of how he reacted to the incident, but we are told that he gave his place to Qaṃbar Bī of Marv.

Khusrau Shāh was furious upon hearing this and wanted to bring in some action. He sent off gallopers to summon Ḥamza Sulṭān and each one whom Shaybāni Khān had left behind. It was not very late when Ḥamza Sulṭān began to march out. He reached as far as the sarāī on the bank of river Amū. He assigned his sons and begs in command of a force there which went on to direct attack against Khusrau Shāh.

Babur has written about the incident in *Baburnama*: 'There was neither fight nor flight for that fat, little man; Ḥamza Sulṭān's men unhorsed him, killed his sister's son, Aḥmad-i-qāsim, Sherīm the page and several good braves. Him they took into Qūndūz, there struck his head off and from there sent it to Shaybāni Khān in Khwārizm.'

Like Khusrau Shāh had predicted, his former retainers and followers, no sooner than he marched against Qūndūz, changed in their conduct towards Babur.[7] Almost all of them marched near to Khwāja-i-riwāj. The men in Babur's service had grown exponentially. Interestingly, the Moghūls in general began to behave well with Babur taking up a position of adherence to Babur unconditionally. But the news of Khusrau Shāh's death was like simply breaking the tip of the iceberg. All his men began to push themselves out of Babur's command.

Qūtlūq-nigār Khānum Dies and Progression to Qandahār

It was the month of Muharram in AD 1505. Almost a decade had passed when Babur had lost his father, Umar, and his mother had contracted a high fever. She was being treated by a Khurāsānī doctor, Sayyid Ṭabīb. Following the Khurāsānī tradition, he gave her watermelon. But fate had nothing good to offer for Babur. She died on Saturday, 10 June 1505.

The next day, she was buried in the New Year's Garden in Kābul. Qāsim Kūkūldāsh accompanied Babur for the final rituals. There also lay Ulugh Beg Mīrzā, Babur's uncle who had built his house long ago at this place. But the streak of mourning wasn't going to stop here. He got to hear the news of the death of his younger Khān dada Alacha Khān (Ahmad Alaq), and grandmother Aīsān-daulat Begum. The news about Ahmad reached around a year later. It was the fortieth day of her mourning when Shāh Begum, the mother of the Khāns, and Mihr-nigār Khānum, Babur's maternal aunt (previously of Sulṯān Aḥmad Mīrzā's ḥaram) arrived with the sad news. It caused another wave of lament for Babur, who was broken to the core once again. He describes the partings to be '*extremely bitter*' in the *Baburnama*. The mourning rites were observed with utmost care. The Qur'an was recited, prayers were offered for the departed souls and victuals were offered to the poor. But time demanded Babur to be stable again, leaving behind all the mourning.

Babur set an army on horses to march towards Qandahār, which Bāqī Chaghānīānī had been insisting for long. The tourney began through Qūsh-nādir. The day Babur dismounted there, he contracted a fever. It lasted for around a week and he couldn't even afford to open his eyes even for a while. Babur calls it a strange sort of illness.

On 5 July AD 1505, a massive earthquake hit the northern belt, which affected Kābul and Agra.[*] The ramparts of forts and the walls of gardens toppled. The houses of towns got levelled to the ground and people got trampled beneath. Babur has said that the village of Paghmān was affected the worst—where each house fell down and around eighty house heads died because of wall collapses. Babur has described the wrath as follows:[†]

> *Between Pagh-mān and Beg-tūt a piece of ground, a good stone-throw wide may-be, slid down as far as an arrow's-flight; where it had slid springs appeared. On the road between Istarghach and Maidān the ground was so broken up for 6 to 8 yīghāch (36-48 miles) that in some places it rose as high as an elephant, in others sank as deep; here and there people were sucked in. When the Earth quaked, dust rose from the tops of the mountains. Nūru'l-lāh the*

[*] Bengal, Asiatic Society of. Journal of the Asiatic Society of Bengal, Part 2. Calcutta: Bishop's College Press, 1843. Vol. 12. p. 1040

[†] Babur, Abdul Rahim Khan-I-Khanan (trans.), *Tuzk-e Babri*, Delhi: Akbar, 1589, p. Folio 157b. This manuscript is available in National Museum, New Delhi. The Persian translation was done from the original Turkic manuscript of Babur. This was translated by author from the copy kept at National Museum, New Delhi.

tambourchī had been playing before me; he had two instruments with him and at the moment of the quake had both in his hands; so out of his own control was he that the two knocked against each other. Jahāngīr Mīrzā was in the porch of an upper-room at a house built by Aūlūgh Beg Mīrzā in Tīpa; when the Earth quaked, he let himself down and was not hurt, but the roof fell on some-one with him in that upper-room, presumably one of his own circle; that this person was not hurt in the least must have been solely through God's mercy. In Tīpa most of the houses were levelled to the ground. The Earth quaked 33 times on the first day, and for a month afterwards used to quake two or three times in the 24 hours. The begs and soldiers having been ordered to repair the breaches made in the towers and ramparts of the fort (Kābul), everything was made good again in 20 days or a month by their industry and energy.

Babur's illness and the earthquake were bound to affect the campaign to Qandahār. Soon Babur recovered from his illness and the fort was repaired. The campaign was taken up again although the intent was not very clear in Babur's mind. Babur along with his party dismounted at Shniz. Still, he was unable to decide if he should choose to go to Qandahār or to overrun the hills and plains. Jahāngīr Mīrzā and the begs were invited in assembly. Babur took the counsel, and with the insistence of Jahāngīr Mīrzā and Bāqī Chaghānīānī, it was decided to make a move to Qalāt. On the way, Babur came to know that Sher-i-'alī along with Kīchīk Bāqī Diwāna and his supporters were planning to desert him. Babur got Sher-i-'alī killed instantly, and the rest arrested as Babur himself had been observing his disloyalty for long. After a while, Babur let go of the arrested, although he retained their horses and arms.

Upon reaching Qalāt, Babur and his men launched their best attack. Kīchīk Khwāja, the elder brother of Khwāja Kalān fought ferociously and bravely. He was great with his sword, but a spear pierced his eye while he climbed the south-west tower of Qalāt. He couldn't survive the wound and succumbed to it in a couple of days. In the same battle, Kīchīk Bāqī Dīwāna (one who had been arrested for disloyalty) got killed by falling on the rocks below the ramparts. Babur has mentioned that it was his expiation of sordidness. Babur lost a couple of other brave men too. The battle went on till the afternoon prayer, till the men of the fort surrendered asking for a truce.

Ẕū'n-nūn Arghūn had offered Qalāt to Muqīm years ago but was now in control of the latter's retainers Farrukh Arghūn and Qarā Bīlūt (Afghān). Finally, when all were killed, the retainers came out with swords and quivers hanging around their necks. Babur decided not to do anything to them. He has mentioned that he saw no merit in bringing annihilation to this family which he considered a high born.[8] Babur has expressed his view about his situation:*

> *It was not my wish to reduce this high family to great straits; for why? Because if we did so when such a foe as the Aūzbeg was at our side, what would be said by those of far and near, who saw and heard?*

Babur had decided to make a move to Qalāt only at the insistence of Bāqī Chaghānīānī and Jahāngīr Mīrzā. Now, Babur made a move to give the whole charge in the hands of Jahāngīr Mīrzā but he rejected the offer. Babur then asked Bāqī Chaghānīānī to take up the responsibility, but he too denied it. This was the moment when Babur found the capture of Qalāt completely useless. The person who had insisted Babur take that step had now denied taking up any responsibility. A disappointed Babur decided to return to Kābul which lied south of Qalāt. On the way, he overran the Afghans of Ālā-tāgh. The night Babur dismounted in Kābul, he anxiously visited the fort, his tent and the stable located in Chārbāgh. In the stable, he came to know that a Khirilchī thief had run away with Babur's mule and one bay horse with its accoutrements.

Bāqī Chaghānīānī Dies

Right from the moment when Babur met Bāqī on the banks of Amu Darya, he had not trusted anyone else more than him.[9] His actual name was Muḥammad Bāqir. Babur has asserted on several occasions

* Babur, Abdul Rahim Khan-I-Khanan (trans.), *Tuzk-e Babri*, Delhi: Akbar, 1589, p. Folio 158b, This manuscript is available in National Museum, New Delhi. The Persian translation was done from the original Turkic manuscript of Babur. This was translated by author from the copy kept at National Museum, New Delhi.

that he was a man of command and absolute authority, and Babur followed his calls blindly. Babur didn't shy away from mentioning in the *Baburnama* that all actions that happened were the Bāqī's words. But at the same time, Babur mentions his incivility. In contrast to his earlier opinions, Babur had a complete outburst:*

> Quite the contrary, he had done things bad and unmannerly. Mean he was, miserly and malicious, ill-tongued, envious, and cross-natured. So miserly was he that although when he left Tīrmīẕ, with his family and possessions, he may have owned thirty to forty thousand sheep, and although those masses of sheep used to pass in front of us at every camping-ground, he did not give a single one to our bare braves, tortured as they were by the pangs of hunger; at last, in Kāh-mard, he gave fifty.

Although he acknowledged Babur as his Padishah, he had ensured that the nagarets were beaten at his own gate. Babur has said, 'He was sincere to none, had regard for none.' Bāqī completely controlled the revenues. He took the Tamgha from Kābul, along with the *dāroghaship* in Kābul, Panjhīr, Gadai, Hazāra, and kūshlūk.[10] He was the only one in control of the gate. He was not gratified despite no favours showered on him. He did enough mischief, but all went unnoticed and unaccounted by Babur. Babur has complained in *Baburnama* that he was always asking for leave though with a little hesitation. Babur was sick of his conduct and character but never said anything at any time. Leave was granted to him but instead he atoned and began to agitate against his own request after it was acknowledged. He wrote as below to Babur:†

> *His Highness made compact not to call me to account till nine misdeeds had issued from me.*[11]

* Babur, Abdul Rahim Khan-I-Khanan (trans.), *Tuzk-e Babri*, Delhi: Akbar, 1589, p. Folio 159. This manuscript is available in National Museum, New Delhi. The Persian translation was done from the original Turkic manuscript of Babur. This was translated by author from the copy kept at National Museum, New Delhi.

† Ibid.

It was then that Babur finally reminded him of his wrongdoings, breaking the silence as an answer. He reminded Bāqī of eleven recent faults in a message sent through Mullā Bābā of Pashāghar. Bāqī had no choice and chose to submit to Babur. Accordingly, he was permitted to make a move towards Hindustan with family and possessions. Few of his retainers returned after escorting him through the Khyber. He crossed the pass at Nilab after having joined the caravan of Bāqī.

A brief about Khyber

The Khyber Pass is a mountainous route in the Khyber Pakhtunkhwa province of Pakistan, on the border with Nangarhar Province of Afghanistan. The summit of the pass is around three miles inside Pakistan, following the Asian Highway 1. It descends 460 metres into the valley of Peshawar at Jamrud, which is around 30 kilometres from the Afghan border by traversing a section of Spin Ghar Mountains.

History tells us that the Greater Bharat always saw invasions predominantly through the Khyber Pass. A few prominent examples are Cyrus, Darius I, Genghis Khan, Duwa Khan, Qutlugh Khwaja and Kebek. Before Kushan led their feet through the pass, it wasn't widely used as a trade route.[*] The Khyber Pass had turned into an important part of the Silk Road (the major trade route that connected Eastern Asia with Europe).[†] One might be able to understand the giantess of this from the fact that once the Parthian Empire fought to control these passes to draw massive profits from the trade in jade, silk and other luxuries that moved to Western Asia and Europe. Once it was the phase when through the Khyber Pass, Gandhara had become a regional node of trade connecting Bagram in Afghanistan to Taxila (now in Pakistan). It catered to Indian luxury goods like pepper, ivory and textiles as a contribution to the Silk Road commerce.[‡]

Islamic invaders such as Mahmud Ghaznavi, Afghan Muhammad Ghori, and the Turkic-Mongols also entered through this pass. It was in AD 1834 that Maharaja Ranjit Singh took complete control of

---

[*] Tarn, William Woodthorpe. The Greeks in Bactria and India. s.l.: Cambridge University Press, 2010, p. 139

[†] Arnold, Guy, *World Strategic Highways*. Routledge, 2014.

[‡] Paddy Docherty, *The Khyber Pass: A History of Empire and Invasion*, Union Square Press, 2008.

Khyber Pass, erasing the Islamic influence. The Khalsa general, Hari Singh Nalwa, who saw through the Khyber Pass for many years had become a household name in Afghanistan.*

It was the period when India was geographically best defined as being 'Khyber to Kanyakumari'.† In the north of Khyber Pass lay the country of Mullagori, which housed the Shalmani tribes. Down the south, lay Afridi Tirah and the pass was full of the people from the Afridi clan. Since the Islamic invasion, the centuries-old Pashtun clans, especially the Afghan Shinwaris and Afridis have regarded the Khyber as their own preserve and interestingly have levied heavy a toll on travellers in the name of safe conduct. They have thoroughly relied upon it as their main source of income, and hence there is resistance to the challenges to the Shinwari Authority.‡ During the First World War, the British built a railway line through the pass for strategic reasons. The Khyber Pass railway from Jamrud, near Peshawar, to the Afghan border near Landi Kotal was opened in AD 1925. In the Second World War, dragon teeth made of concrete were built on the valley floor as the British feared the German (NSDAP) tank invasion.§ The famous 'hippie trail' (1950s to 1970s) saw the Japanese and the Westerners travel across the pass on bus or car right from Kābul to the borders of Afghanistan. At the Pakistani frontier post, the advisory was given to the travellers to not adventure away from the road as the location was in control of the Federally Administered Tribal Area. Following the customs formalities, a brisk daytime drive in the pass was made. One could see the structures built by the British Army units along with hillside forts from the highway of the pass.

The reports tell us that the region of Khyber Pass has been infected by the counterfeit arms industry known to be making various weapons known broadly as Khyber Pass copies. The make of all those weapons including guns is made using local steel and blacksmiths' forges.

---

* Vanit Nalwa, Hari Singh Nalwa, *Champion of the Khalsaji* (1791-1837), New Delhi: Manohar, 2009. p. 319

† Al-Beruni, *Alberuni's India: An Account of the Religion, Philosophy, Literature, Geography, Chronology, Astronomy, Customs, Laws and Astrology of India: Volume I*, Reprint ed., London: Routledge, 2000, pp. 197-200.

‡ Leadership of Tribe.

§ Lonely Planet, https://web.archive.org/web/20110607080116/http://www.lonelyplanet.com/pakistan/north-west-frontier-province/the-khyber-pass.

In Babur's period, Daryā Khān's son, Yār-i-ḥusain was in Kacha-kot located near a place called Hasan Abdal. Hasan Abdal currently lies in the strategic region of northern Punjab (Pakistan).

This is exactly the place from where Tīmūrid (distorted as Moghūl) war expeditions were directed to the north-western frontier.[*] Currently, it lies at the intersection of the M1 Motorway and Karakoram Highway. According to the proposal for the multi-billion-dollar China-Pakistan Economic Corridor (CPEC), the Hasan Abdal area shall serve as the terminus for its Western Alignment, and the Hakla–Dera Ismail Khan Motorway shall commence here as well.[†]

The place has a significant history. Chinese traveller Hiuen Tsang was in this place around twelve centuries ago. He talks of the sacred spring of Elapatra about thirty-five kilometres to the northwest of Taxila. This spring has been identified as the one at the Gurudwara Panja Sahib.[‡] It was built on the spot where Guru Nanak had stayed during his visit to Hasan Abdal. The spring contains a sacred rock which is believed to contain the handprint of Guru Nanak from which the term 'Panja' derives. According to Ain-i-Akbari, Shams al-Din had built himself a vault wherein remained buried Hakim Abu'l Fath. The same document also talks of Abu'l-Fath Jalal-ud-din Muhammad Akbar's visit to the town on his way back from Kashmir. William Flinch, an English merchant in the service of the East India Company had travelled through India amid AD 1608 and AD 1611. He described Hasan Abdal as, 'a pleasant town with a small river and many fair tanks in which are many fishes with golden rings in their noses (. . .); the water so clear that you may see a penny in the bottom'.[§] The Tīmūrid emperor Jehangir (grandson of Abu'l-Fath Jalal-ud-din Muhammad Akbar) also talks about this city in Tuzk-e-Jahangiri and credits it to in the name of Baba Hasan Abdal who stayed for three days. He goes on

[*] Farzana Moon, *The Moghul Saint of Insanity*, Cambridge Scholars Publishing, 2015, pp. 58, 66.

[†] Daily Times, https://dailytimes.com.pk/82850/china-to-finance-90-of-sukkur-multan-motorway/.

[‡] Ram Chandra Prasad, *Early English Travellers in India: A Study in the Travel Literature of the Elizabethan and Jacobean Periods with Particular Reference to India*, Motilal Banarsidass, 1980, p. 244

[§] Ibid, p. 224.

to describe his town as follows: 'The celebrated place at this station is a spring which flows from the foot of a little hill, exceedingly clear, sweet, and nice(. . .).'[*]

A Wah Garden in the vicinity was built by Raja Man Singh. It was a terraced garden divided into four parts.[†] While traversing to Kābul, Shah Jahan stayed in this garden on his visit to Kābul. Even Aurangzeb stayed here for quite some time in the beginning of AD 1674[‡] with the intent to water down the 'Afridi Revolt'. Aurangzeb had succeeded in convincing the local Pashtun tribes to give away the rebellion intent and join his forces.[§]

Babur's Narrative Continues

Babur had issued a farman in Kohat which drew the service of a few Afghāns of the Dilazāk and Yūsuf-zāī, Jats and Gujūrs of the region. Accordingly, with their support, he beat the roads, taking a toll with might and main. As soon as he heard about the approach of Bāqī, he blocked the road without making any delay right on time. He made the whole party prisoner and murdered Bāqī and took away his wife. Babur has written in the *Baburnama*, 'We ourselves had let Bāqī go without injuring him, but his own misdeeds rose up against him; his own acts defeated him.'

Babur composed a couplet as below in the context:[¶]

Leave thou to Fate the man who does thee wrong;
For Fate is an avenging servitor.

---

[*] Ibid.

[†] Catherine Blanshard Asher, Catherine Ella Blanshard Asher, Catherine B. Asher, *Architecture of Mughal India, Volume 4*, Part-1. (ed.) Gordon Johnson. Cambridge: Cambridge University Press, 1992. pp. 81, 103. Vol. 4.

[‡] Surjit Singh Gandhi, *History of Sikh Gurus Retold: 1606-1708 C.E, Vol-2*, Atlantic Publishers & Dist, 2007.

[§] Farzana Moon, *The Moghul Saint of Insanity*, Cambridge Scholars Publishing, 2015, pp. 58-66

[¶] Babur, Abdul Rahim Khan-I-Khanan (trans.), *Tuzk-e Babri*, Delhi: Akbar, 1589, p. Folio 160. This manuscript is available in National Museum, New Delhi. The Persian translation was done from the original Turkic manuscript of Babur. This was translated by author from the copy kept at National Museum, New Delhi.

Babur Attacks the Turkmān Hazāras

That very winter, Babur remained stationed in the Chār-bāgh till it snowed twice at the place. Babur had been facing abundant troubles at the hands of Turkmān Hazāras since the time he had arrived in Kābul. And those insolent acts of them included road robbery as well. Finally, Babur decided to teach them a lesson. He along with his party rode to the house of Aūlūgh Beg Mīrzā' located at the Būstān-sarāī in February of AD 1506.

And then Babur raided a few Hazāras at the mouth of the Dara-i-khūsh (Happy valley). A few of them were hiding near the mouth of the valley in a cave. Shaikh Darwīsh Kūkūldāsh rushed to the cave without any caution. And to his misfortune, he was shot in the chest by a Hazāra. He succumbed to the shot—there was no way he could have been protected. Then Babur, with all force, marched inside the Dara-i-khūsh, with clear intent to crush them all.

The valley was shut down by a half-a-kilometre gully, which stretched inwards from its orifice. A road encircled the mountain with a straight depreciation of around fifty metre and a cliff above. Horsemen were bound to go around it in a single file. Babur and his party crossed the gully and went on going till around three, post noon without encountering any humans. As the night approached, they found a healthy camel, perhaps belonging to the Hazāras. They killed it to quench their appetites, half part in the form of kebab and remaining roasted like mutton. Babur has said in *Baburnama* that, 'such good camel-flesh had never been tasted; some could not tell it [apart] from mutton'.

The next day, Babur headed with his party to hunt for the Hazāras in their winter camp. Around nine in the morning, a man came running and informed me that the Hazāras had blocked a crossing with branches of trees. The winter was acute, and the snow lay deep. One couldn't move anywhere else except a bit on roads. No one could spot the meadows, which in general used to be swampy. There were no streams either. The only way to cross the streams was through the culverts and the bridge of the road. The Hazāras had chopped and laid the branches at the bridge over frozen water. As Babur reached there along with his men, the array of arrows began to shower from both sides. And then in the madness to prove his loyalty and bravery,

Muḥammad 'Alī Mubashshir Beg jumped and barged into the blocked road without his mail. He was shot in the belly, and he succumbed to the injury immediately. Babur had recently promoted him to the rank of Beg and he considered him deserving of all favours showered upon him.

Babur and his party had rushed behind the Hazāras in haste. Most of them didn't wear the mail. As arrows came in, Babur's men began to fall one by one. Yet, Babur was confident to get through. Anxious and worried Yūsuf Aḥmad said, 'Bare like this you go into it! I have seen two arrows go close to your head!'

Babur replied wearing a smile, 'Don't fear! Many as good arrows as these have flown past my head!'

And then while words were being exchanged, Qāsim Beg leading his men, was able to cruise through and cross the stream. Now, the Hazāras were butchered in the worst possible way. They didn't stand much of a chance in front of Babur's well-trained men. They began to fly away looking at the force that was arriving in retaliation after the crossing. Almost all of them were unhorsed and put to death.

Babur was pleased with Qāsim Beg's feat and as a reward, he offered him Bangash. Two other people who had pleased Babur in this fight were Ḥātim the armourer and Bābā Qulī's Kīpik. They were bestowed Shaikh Darwīsh's office of qūr-begī and the office of Muhammad 'Alī Mubashshir, respectively.

While this victory was accomplished, Sulṭān Qulī Chūnāq had begun to chase the Hazāras. Alas! The time went by but there was no coming back of him.

Babur decided to go ahead with whoever he had around. Many sheep and herds of horses were found in the vicinity of the Hazāra winter camp. Babur collected around 500 sheep and twenty-five horses. Babur was leading the campaign to collect the war booty for the second time. He had last done so while coming from Khurāsān (in AD 1506) and then too, the victims were the same—Turkmān Hazāras. The scroungers of Babur brought abundant sheep and horses. The wives and children of Hazāras had climbed up the snowy slope to keep themselves safe. Seeing their dwellings empty, Babur along with his men dismounted there as it had already begun to turn dark. It was next to impossible to ride at night given the thickness of snow this winter. Babur has described the peril:*

> Deep indeed was the snow that winter! Off the road it was up to a horse's qāptāl, so deep that the night-watch was in the saddle all through till shoot of dawn.

The next day, Babur left out of the valley, yet the intense snow couldn't let them go beyond its mouth where they would spend the whole night. They began to march the next day only to dismount after reaching Janglīk. Babur instructed Yārak Ṭaghāī to go with his band and kill the remaining Hazāras, who seemed to be hiding in a cave. Babur has mentioned in the *Baburnama* that around eighty of them were slain by the sword.

Having finished this Hazāra expedition successfully, Babur went to Āī-tūghdī which was a neighbourhood below Bārān.[12] He had come here to collect the revenue of Nijr-aū. It was there that Jahāngīr Mīrzā waited on Babur after having arrived from his mission of Ghaznī.

On 7 February of AD 1506, on the thirteenth day of Ramzan, sciatic pain hit Babur and it was so troublesome that someone had to always help him turn from one side to the other for about six weeks. Finally, people made some arrangements to carry Babur and they traversed along the bank of river Bārān, cruising into the Būstān-sarāī. They stayed there comfortably for a couple of days, and Babur was able to recover from the pain. But as the pain got over, a boil appeared on his left cheek. It was pierced and the infection was purged out through some medication.

Jahāngīr Mīrzā had to further wait on Babur. It was during that period that the sons of Ayūb, Yūsuf and Buhlūl had spit enough seditious venom against Babur. It had changed the attitude of Jahāngīr completely. Just in a few days, loaded with rebellious temperament, he marched out of Tīpa, hurrying back to Ghaznī decorated as a warrior clad in mail. He captured Nānī upon reaching there. In the

* Babur, Abdul Rahim Khan-I-Khanan (trans.), *Tuzk-e Babri*, Delhi: Akbar, 1589, p. Folio 161b. This manuscript is available in National Museum, New Delhi. The Persian translation was done from the original Turkic manuscript of Babur. This was translated by author from the copy kept at National Museum, New Delhi.

process, he killed a few and left the whole vicinity plundered. Soon, he marched ahead through the Hazāras,[13] heading for Bamiyan.

In the *Baburnama,* he states:*

> Allah knows that nothing had been done by me or my dependents to give him ground for anger or reproach. What was heard of later on as perhaps explaining his going off in the way he did, was this; —When Qāsim Beg went with other begs, to give him honoring meeting as he came up from Ghaznī, the Mīrzā threw a falcon off at a quail. Just as the falcon, getting close, put out its pounce to seize the quail, the quail dropped to the ground. Hereupon shouts and cries, "Taken! is it taken?" Said Qāsim Beg, "Who loses the foe in his grip?" Their misunderstanding of this was their sole reason for going off, but they backed themselves on one or two other worse and weaker old cronish matters. After doing in Ghaznī what has been mentioned, they drew off through the Hazāras to the Moghūl clans.These clans at that time had left Nāṣir Mīrzā but had not joined the Aūzbeg, and were in Yāī, Astar-āb and the summer-pastures thereabouts.

Sulṯān Ḥusayn Mīrzā Asks for Help against Shaybāni Khān

With the resolve to repel Shaybāni completely, Sulṯān Husayn had summoned all his sons. He had also sent Sayyid Afẓal, son of Sayyid 'Alī Khwāb-bīn to call Babur, too. Babur was all in right faith to think it to be a perfect time to head for Khurāsān on the call of the ruler who sat on Tīmūr's throne. Babur considered it to be an important call:†

> (. . .) if there were some who went on foot it was for us to go if on our heads! if some took the bludgeon, we would take the stone!

---

* Babur, Abdul Rahim Khan-I-Khanan (trans.), *Tuzk-e Babri*, Delhi: Akbar, 1589, p. Folio 162b. This manuscript is available in National Museum, New Delhi. The Persian translation was done from the original Turkic manuscript of Babur. This was translated by author from the copy kept at National Museum, New Delhi.

† Babur, Abdul Rahim Khan-I-Khanan (trans.), *Tuzk-e Babri*, Delhi: Akbar, 1589, p. Folio 163. This manuscript is available in National Museum, New Delhi. The Persian translation was done from the original Turkic manuscript of Babur. This was translated by author from the copy kept at National Museum, New Delhi.

Early that year, Shaybāni Khān had besieged Chīn Sūfī in Khwārizm for ten months. The brave people of Khwārizm had given a good fight to Shaybāni during the seize and they left no stones unturned to throw him out. They showered arrows furiously which pierced not only the shields, but also one or two cuirasses.

After having sustained the siege for around ten months, they had begun to lose the heart. The suffering was so long and acute that a few of them came forward to initiate the talk with Shaybāni. While those, whose heart had sunk, were in the process to let Shaybāni enter the fort, Chīn Ṣūfī got the news and ran to the spot fighting with the Aūzbegs. But an arrow stuck him from behind which had discharged from his own page and Allah's mercy fell on him. He died immediately and then his entire page collapsed as well.

Although Babur has mentioned in the *Baburnama* of Allah's mercy falling on Chīn Ṣūfī, who never for one moment ceased to stake his life for his chief[14] the page's fatal arrow finds no mention either in the *Shaybānīnāma* or *Tārīkh-i-rashīdī*. Khwārizm was entrusted to Kūpuk Bī by Shaybāni Khān and he marched back to Samarkand.

It was on 5 May of AD 1506 that Sulṯān Husayn Mīrzā died at Bābā Ilāhī having led the army against Shaybāni Khān.[15]

Muharram of AD 1506 was running by. Babur had set out to fight against Aūzbegs through the way of Ghūr-bund and Shibr-tū. Babur still remembered the displeasure of Jahāngīr Mīrzā and he feared that he would side with the enemy. He has gone on to say:*

> 'There might come much mischief and trouble if he drew the clans (aīmāq) to himself;' and 'What trouble might come of it!' and, 'First let's get the clans in hand!'

Having that worm of suspicion still in mind, Babur along with his party hurried forward. He rode light, leaving away all the baggage at Ushtur-shahr. They reached the Ẓaḥāq fort and crossed the pass of Guṃbazak-kūtal. They cruised through Sāīghān, going over the Dandān-shikan pass and finally dismounted in the meadow of

---

* Babur, Abdul Rahim Khan-I-Khanan (trans.), *Tuzk-e Babri*, Delhi: Akbar, 1589, p. Folio 183b. This manuscript is available in National Museum, New Delhi. The Persian translation was done from the original Turkic manuscript of Babur. This was translated by author from the copy kept at National Museum, New Delhi.

Kāhmard. There, Babur sent a letter to Sulṭān Ḥusayn Mīrzā through Sayyid Afẓal and Sulṭān Muḥammad Dūldāī conveying the details of his start from Kābul.[16] Jahāngīr Mīrzā had got delayed and when he reached opposite Bamiyan with his thirty men, he saw the tents of Babur's party where they had left the baggage. Fearing the presence of the party they hurried back to their camp.

Shaybāni Khān's Further Action

During the siege of Balkh, Shaybāni Khān had sent three Sulṭāns with around 4000 men to overrun Badakhshān. In that period, Mubārak Shāh and Zubair rejoined hands with Nāṣir Mīrzā. This happened despite the fact that Mubārak Shāh had a temperament of anguish and bickering. They lay at Shakdān, to the east of the Kishm River.

The Aūzbegs were moving through the night. One party of Aūzbegs crossed the river around the dawn and advanced on to the Mīrzā. But he overcame them quite well. In that period, the river Kishm was also swelling furiously into a flood. Many got drowned while others were shot down by arrows or pierced by swords. The remaining were made prisoners. Another party of Aūzbegs was sent to fight against both Zubair and Mubārak Shāh. As soon as Mīrzā heard of it, he moved to them after treating his own assailants well enough. Not only he, but the Kohistān begs too gathered with horses, and foot higher up the river.

Finally, Aūzbegs fled after failing to defend against this all-around attack. Not less than 1500 died because of the rain of arrows, the slaughter of swords and the flood. In Babur's opinion, it was a great success for Nāṣir Mīrzā, of which he had heard while in the valley of Kāhmard.

Babur's Move to Khurāsān

Babur and his men were living in Kāhmard by fetching corn from Ghūrī and Dahāna. This is where the letter arrived from Sayyid Afẓal and Sulṭān Muḥammad Dūldāī, whom Babur had sent into Khurāsān. The letter was disheartening as it spoke of Sulṭān Husayn Mīrzā's death. Hearing this sad news, Babur immediately instructed to move forward for Khurāsān.

This incident speaks aloud of Babur's faith in the reputation of the Tīmūrid Dynasty:*

> (. . .) though there were other grounds for doing this, what decided us was anxious thought for the reputation of this (Tīmūrid) dynasty.

Babur went ahead, raising the channel of the Ājar valley over Tūp and Mandaghān. He went on to cross the Balkh River and came out on the hill of Ṣāf. Babur came to know there that the Aūzbegs were overrunning Sān and Chār-yak hence, he soon sent a force led by Qāsim Beg to counter them. Qāsim did very well by chopping off many Aūzbeg heads and beating them completely. He returned victorious.

Babur and his party stayed in the meadows of Ṣāf hill for few days, waiting for some news of Jahāngīr Mīrzā and the clans. He had sent representatives to them. In the meadows, they hunted wild sheep and goats which were available in abundance. Finally, the clans did arrive and waited on Babur for a few days. They had come only to see Babur and had no sympathy whatsoever for Jahāngīr Mīrzā. Although Jahāngīr often sent men of various influences to persuade them and finally he sent 'Imādu'd-dīn Mas'ūd but he too couldn't do what the former wanted. And when nothing worked, Jahāngīr Mīrzā came to Babur himself. He met Babur at the foot of the valley when he had come down to initiate his voyage further to Khurāsān. And in the haste to get on with his mission soon, Babur could neither pay any attention to Jahāngīr nor he could see all the clans that had gathered. He went riding into Bām Valley through Gurzwān, Almār, Qaiṣār, Chīchīk-tū, and Fakhru'd-dīn's death. Bām Valley was one of the dependencies of Bādghīs.

A Brief About Bādghīs

Of the thirty-four provinces in Afghanistan, Bādghīs lies in the north-western part, sharing the border with Herat, Ghor and

* Babur, Abdul Rahim Khan-I-Khanan (trans.), *Tuzk-e Babri*, Delhi: Akbar, 1589, p. Folio 184b. This manuscript is available in National Museum, New Delhi. The Persian translation was done from the original Turkic manuscript of Babur. This was translated by author from the copy kept at National Museum, New Delhi.

Faryab provinces and Turkmenistan. Currently, it is one of the most underdeveloped parts of the country with the highest rate of poverty.* Qala-i-Naw is the capital of the land and Bala Murghab is known to be the land of the highest population. This populous city also happens to be the place near to ruins of the medieval city of Marw al-Rudh, the historical capital of the medieval region of Gharjistan.

The total area of the province is 20,591 square kilometres and the Murghab River forms the base for irrigation. It has a few mountains, but characteristically it is dominated by the rolling hills divided by ravines. The current name of the province comes from its very trait of being very windy. The name 'Badhgis' is the corruption of the Persian compound '*bâd-khiz*' which means 'wind source'. It perhaps refers to the steppe winds that blow into the province from the north and north-western edge. The northern border kisses the edge of the Karakum desert and is known as the Sarakhs desert.

Till the marauding invaders from Arab land didn't plunder this land, it was the centre of the Kingdom of Badghis. The king of Badghis Trakhan Tirek had very bravely resisted the Umayyad Invasion of AD 709. Post the Arab conquest for almost two-and-a-half centuries of years, this land became a place of religious dissent by the locals. It was the summer pastures for the Tīmūrids in the fifteenth century (the era that this book addresses) for its great characteristic of being grasslands. But down the four centuries, the place was completely devastated by the Turkmen raids.†

Babur's Narrative Continues

Now, Babur had laid custom duty on the Turks and other clans of the region. By doing so, he had earned not less than 300 tūmāns of kipkī. Just a few days before Babur had arrived at the valley of Bām, Aūzbeg raiders had received a heavy beating from Ẕū'n-nūn Beg's men and the light troops of Khurāsān at places namely, Pand-dih and Marūchāq. A huge mass of Aūzbegs were killed in this scuffle.

* 'National Measures: New Afghan Multidimensional Poverty Report', Multidimensional Poverty Peer Network, 31 March 2019, https://mppn.org/new-afghan-multidimensional-poverty-report/.

† Jürgen Paul, *Bādghīs*; Marc Gaborieau, et al. *The Encyclopaedia of Islam Three*, Leiden: BRILL, 2010, p. 200.

Sons of Sulṯān Husayn, Badī'u'z-zamān Mīrzā and Muẕaffar-i-ḥusayn Mīrzā were still up with the motive to dismantle Shaybāni Khān. They collaborated with Muhammad Barandūq Barlās, Ẕū'n-nūn Arghūn and his son Shāh Beg, determined to overrun Shaybāni Khān and then besiege Sulṯān Qul-i-nachāq in Balkh. Accordingly, they summoned all their brothers, sons of Sulṯān Ḥusayn Mīrzā, and cruised out of Herī to finish the determined purpose.

When they reached Chihil-dukhtarān, other sons of Sulṯān Husayn had begun to join in. Abū'l-muḥsin joined them from Marv and Ibn-i-ḥusayn followed, coming up from Tūn. Qāīn Kūpuk was then in Mashhad. Many words were sent to him, and he approached but gave back nothing but senseless opinions. Babur has talked of a sense of jealousy between Muẕaffar Mīrzā and Qāīn Kūpuk, given that former was made a joint ruler. He said, 'How should I go to his presence?' directly hinting of jealousy being because of his absence.

And when all other brothers of Qāīn had come together to resolute against the enemy Shaybāni Khān, Qāīn Kūpuk did not reflect any emotion whatsoever with regards to the clan of Timur. Everyone saw this as an act of cowardice.

The *Baburnama* has a description of the situation:*

> One word! In this world acts such as his outlive the man; if a man have any share of intelligence, why try to be ill-spoken of after death? if he be ambitious, why not try so to act that, he gone, men will praise him? In the honorable mention of their names, wise men find a second life!

The envoys of Mīrzās along with Muhammad Barandūq Barlās came to Babur too. Babur was all set for this adventure as he indeed had travelled around 600 miles only for it. Babur began to ride with Muhammad Barandūq Beg for Murgh-āb[17] where all Mīrzās had assembled.

* Babur, Abdul Rahim Khan-I-Khanan (trans.), *Tuzk-e Babri*, Delhi: Akbar, 1589, p. Folio 185b. This manuscript is available in National Museum, New Delhi. The Persian translation was done from the original Turkic manuscript of Babur. This was translated by author from the copy kept at National Museum, New Delhi.

Babur Sees the Mīrzās

On 26 October of AD 1506, Babur met the Mīrzās, the people from his clan. One of them, Abū'l-muḥsin Mīrzā came riding around a mile to welcome Babur. Both dismounted and approached each other with a smile. Sharing a courtesy greeting with a hug, both mounted back beginning to ride towards the camp. As they reached closer to the camp, Muẕaffar Mīrzā and Ibn-i-Husayn Mīrzā came to meet them. Since both were younger than Abū'l-muḥsin, Babur expected them to have come further than him for welcome, but they could not think much about the influence of the alcohol. Babur offered his courtesy greetings without dismounting from the horse.

They rode together and greetings and a sense of welcome were continually showered by the crowd till they dismounted at the Badī'u'z-zamān Mīrzā's Gate. The crowd's emotions surged while welcoming Babur. A few jumped off the ground to get a glimpse of Babur marching in. The situation speaks of his heroic image in people's eyes.

Babur along with the other three reached Badī'u'z-zamān Mīrzā's audience tent. It was mutually agreed that Babur on entering would bend the knee for once and the Mīrzā would rise walking to the edge of the estrade. And then both would see each other.

Accordingly, Babur went inside and bent his knee. Then, he went forward swiftly but Mīrzā advanced slowly and languidly. Qāsim Beg, being Babur's well-wisher, intervened and gave a jerk to his girdle. Babur understood and slowed his pace of approach. They met at the pre-arranged spot.

The tent was decorated lavishly. Four divans were placed and one of the sides of the tent appeared like a gateway[18] on whose edge Mīrzā sat. This time, Badī'u'z-zamān Mīrzā and Muẕaffar Mīrzā sat together on a divan located on the edge of the gateway. Babur and Abū'l-muḥsin Mīrzā sat on a divan placed at the right-hand place of honour. On the third divan to the left of Badī'u'z-zamān Mīrzā sat Ibn-i-ḥusain Mīrzā and Qāsim Sulṯān Aūzbeg. The latter was a son-in-law of the late Husayn Mīrzā and father of Qāsim-i-ḥusain Sulṯān. To Babur's right and on the fourth divan, sat Jahāngīr Mīrzā and 'Abdu'r-razzāq Mīrzā. To the left of Qāsim Suktan and Ibn-i-ḥusain

Mīrzā, sat Muḥammad Barandūq Beg, Ẕū'n-nūn Beg and Qāsim Beg at a lower seating than divan.

As the meeting began, viands were brought. Following it came the sherbet set with the food. The crockery and cutlery made of silver and gold were placed by the side.

While mentioning this incident, Babur speaks of Genghis *Tura* (rule):*

> *Our forefathers through a long space of time, had respected the Genghis-tūrā (ordinance), doing nothing opposed to it, whether in assembly or Court, in sittings-down or risings-up. Though it has not Divine authority so that a man obeys it of necessity, still good rules of conduct must be obeyed by whom-soever they are left; just in the same way that, if a forefather have done ill, his ill must be changed for good.*

After spending some time bantering over the lavish meal, Babur rode to the place where he was supposed to dismount and rest.

The next time Babur visited Badī'u'z-zamān Mīrzā, he observed the lessened respect shown by the latter. He conveyed his disgrace to Muḥammad Barandūq Beg and to Ẕū'n-nūn Beg:†

> (. . .) small though my age was, my place of honour was large; that I had seated myself twice on the throne of our forefathers in Samarkand by blow straight dealt; and that to be laggard in shewing me respect was unreasonable, since it was for this (Tīmūrid) dynasty's sake I had thus fought and striven with that alien foe.

After Babur expressed his displeasure, they admitted to having committed the mistake of not honouring Babur enough and began to

* Babur, Abdul Rahim Khan-I-Khanan (trans.), *Tuzk-e Babri*, Delhi: Akbar, 1589, p. Folio 186b. This manuscript is available in National Museum, New Delhi. The Persian translation was done from the original Turkic manuscript of Babur. This was translated by author from the copy kept at National Museum, New Delhi.

† Babur. Tuzk-e Babri. (trans.) Abdul Rahim Khan-I-Khanan. illuminated. Delhi: Akbar, 1589. p. Folio 187. This manuscript is available in National Museum, New Delhi. The Persian translation was done from the original Turkic manuscript of Babur. This was translated by author from the copy kept at National Museum, New Delhi.

shower all the due respect at once. After a couple of days, when Babur visited Badī'u'z-zamān Mīrzā after the mid-day prayer, an elegant wine feast was in progress. Along with multiple variants of wine, brochettes of goose and fowl, and all kinds of viands were set on perfect table linen. Mīrzā's wine parties and entertainment activities were very known. Babur chose not to drink even a drop of wine at this event. He has mentioned in the *Baburnama* that no one pressured him to drink—it could simply mean that, in general, people would insist on non-drinkers consuming alcohol.

Finally, after three months, the Mīrzās agreed mutually to set out of Herī with troops and reach Murghāb. It was heard that Sulṭān Qul-i-nachāq had crossed the extremes of being passive. He had surrendered Balkh[19] to the Aūzbegs. But as soon as that very Aūzbeg heard of Babur and other alliance of Mīrzās marching against him, he rushed away to Samarkand.

In the meantime, Babur was finding the Mīrzās to not be as good fighters as they were as good for parties.[*]

> The Mīrzās were good enough as company and in social matters, in conversation and parties, but they were strangers to war, strategy, equipment, bold fight and encounter.

Now, while Babur and Mīrzās were on the Murghāb, the message came that Ḥaq-naẕīr Chapā along with his half a thousand men was invading the vicinity of Chīchīk-tū. But to their pity, Mīrzās couldn't send even the lightest of troops to defend this invasion of raiders. This must be noted that the distance between Murghāb and Chīchīk-tū was just around fifty-five miles. Babur has asserted in *Baburnama* that though he wanted to lead at this point, he wasn't given the opportunity.[†]

> I asked the work; they, with a thought for their own reputation, would not give it to me.

---

[*] Babur, Abdul Rahim Khan-I-Khanan (trans.), *Tuzk-e Babri*, Delhi: Akbar, 1589, p. Folio 187b. This manuscript is available in National Museum, New Delhi. The Persian translation was done from the original Turkic manuscript of Babur. This was translated by author from the copy kept at National Museum, New Delhi.

[†] Ibid, p. Folio 188.

Almost a year had passed since Shaybāni Khān had retired. Winter was knocking at the door. The Mīrzās decided to it at a convenient place and from where they could congregate again in the coming summers with the mission to deter their enemy.

The Mīrzās tried to persuade Babur to pass the winters in Khurāsān. But both Kābul and Ghaznī were now full of people with ill temperament, who only caused turbulence in the eyes of Babur and his well-wishers. Those people and hordes included the Turks, Moghūls, Afghāns and Hazāra. Apart from these troubles as seen by Babur's well-wishers, other hurdles like a mountain road full of snow would have made hard the seven-week-long journey. Hence one of Babur's well-wishers thoroughly opposed this proposal.

Eventually, Babur rejected the proposal but the more he insisted, the Mīrzās urged more. When nothing could be concluded, Badī'u'z-zamān Mīrzā, Abū'l-muḥsin Mīrzā and Muẕaffar Mīrzā came to see Babur in his tent itself. Babur, who respected them for their Timurid lineage, couldn't refuse at all. That apart, Babur also thought that in the whole of the world (as he knew), no town matched the splendour of Herī which had prospered under the rule of Sulṯān Husayn Mīrzā. He has mentioned the splendour to have grown by almost twenty times what it was before Sulṯān Husayn's rule. Babur consented to stay back.

On the other hand, Abū'l-muḥsin went back to Marv, Ibn-i-ḥusayn rode to Tūn, Badī'u'z-zamān and Muẕaffar set off for Herī. Babur followed the latter cruising on the road of Chihil-dukhtarān and Tāsh-rabāt.

Babur's paternal-aunt Pāyanda Sulṯān Begum, Khadīja Begum, Apāq Begum, daughters of Sulṯān Abū-sa'īd Mīrzā were gathered together waiting to see him at Sulṯān Ḥusayn Mīrzā's catacomb. As the custom and tradition wanted, Babur bent the knee to Pāyanda Sulṯān Begum. Next, he had an interview with Apāq Begum, but notably, he didn't bend his knee here.[20] Then he went to Khadīja Begum and bent the knee to her too.

He sat there during the reading of the Qur'ān. Babur along with other begums went to the southern college, where Khadīja Begum's tent was pitched. The eateries had been placed too. After having the food, Babur and others went to the tent of Pāyanda Sulṯān Begum and spent the night there.

Babur and other's camp was arranged in the New Year's Garden. He also spent the night at the camp, the after he visited the begums. But the place didn't give Babur the comfort as expected and after complaining he was assigned to stay in the residence of 'Alī-sher Beg. He stayed there for the complete stay of Herī. During the whole stay, he regularly took the audience of Badī'u'z-zamān Mīrzā at the beautiful New Year's Garden.

In a few days, Muẓaffar Mīrzā had got himself settled down in the white garden. He invited Babur to his quarter. Babur arrived with Jahāngīr Mīrzā. Even Khadīja Begum was present. They had a good meal after which Muẓaffar Mīrzā took Babur to Ṭarab-khāna (a place built by Babur Mirza*) where a wine party was organized. The place known as the joy-house was a two-storied adobe built in the middle of a small garden. Babur has given a good description of the place:†

> Great pains have been taken with its upper story; this has a retreat in each of its four corners, the space between each two retreats being like a shāh-nīshīn;[21] in between these retreats and shāh-nīshīns is one large room on all sides of which are pictures which, although Bābur Mīrzā built the house, were commanded by Abū-sa'īd Mīrzā and depict his own wars and encounters.
>
> Two divans had been set in the north shāh-nīshīn, facing each other, and with their sides turned to the north.

Of the four divans mentioned, on one sat Muẓaffar Mīrzā and Babur. On the second one Sulṭān Mas'ūd Mīrzā and Jahāngīr Mīrzā. Babur's place was elevated out of honour. The cups and mugs were oozing with wine. The cupbearers kept serving it to the guests and soon most of them turned high. They drank as if they were thirsty for it since forever.

* Abul-Qasim Babur Mirza was a Timurid ruler in Khurasan (1449–1457). He was great-grandson of Amir Timur and the son of Ghiyath-ud-din Baysunghur ibn Shah Rukh Mirza.

† Babur, Abdul Rahim Khan-I-Khanan (trans.), *Tuzk-e Babri*, Delhi: Akbar, 1589, p. Folio 189. This manuscript is available in National Museum, New Delhi. The Persian translation was done from the original Turkic manuscript of Babur. This was translated by author from the copy kept at National Museum, New Delhi.

Babur, a teetotaller, was forced to drink this time. Babur didn't touch wine until AD 1511, when he was thirty years old.*

> Though up till then I had not committed the sin of wine-drinking and known the cheering sensation of comfortable drunkenness, I was inclined to drink wine and my heart was drawn to cross that stream. I had had no inclination for wine in my childhood; I knew nothing of its cheer and pleasure. If, as sometimes, my father pressed wine on me, I excused myself; I did not commit the sin. After he died, Khwāja Qāẓī's right guidance kept me guiltless; as at that time I abstained from forbidden viands, what room was there for the sin of wine? Later on, when, with the young man's lusts and at the prompting of sensual passion, desire for wine arose, there was no-one to press it on me, no-one indeed aware of my leaning towards it; so that, inclined for it though my heart was, it was difficult of myself to do such a thing, one thitherto undone. It crossed my mind now, when the Mīrzās were so pressing and when too we were in a town so refined as Herī, 'Where should I drink if not here? here where all the chattels and utensils of luxury and comfort are gathered and in use.' So saying to myself, I resolved to drink wine; I determined to cross that stream; but it occurred to me that as I had not taken wine in Badī'u'z-zamān Mīrzā's house or from his hand, who was to me as an elder brother, things might find way into his mind if I took wine in his younger brother's house and from his hand. Having so said to myself, I mentioned my doubt and difficulty.

After Babur's resistance and explanation, they said, 'Both the excuse and the obstacle are reasonable.' Having said so they didn't force Babur anymore to drink. But they settled on a condition that Babur must drink whenever he would be in the company of the elder and the younger Mirzas.

Lots of musicians were present on the occasion. They have been named in the *Baburnama*—Ḥāfiẓ Ḥājī, Jalālu'd-dīn Maḥmūd the flautist and Ghulām shādī's younger brother, Ghulām bacha

* Babur, Abdul Rahim Khan-I-Khanan (trans.), *Tuzk-e Babri*, Delhi: Akbar, 1589, p. Folio 160. This manuscript is available in National Museum, New Delhi. The Persian translation was done from the original Turkic manuscript of Babur. This was translated by author from the copy kept at National Museum, New Delhi.

the Jews' harpist. Ḥāfiẓ Ḥājī presented a beautiful song calmly and melodiously. Babur criticized the Samarkandi singer Mīr Jān by describing his songs as harsh, loud and out of tune. He was brought in by Jahāngīr. According to Babur, Khurāsānīs were well-mannered people and hence, despite the singing being so unpleasant, none rose to make him stop singing. This perhaps was also because of the consideration for the Mīrzā.

The sun had retired and the time for the evening prayers had come. Post the prayers, they all left the Ṯarab-khāna and went to the new house in Muẕaffar Mīrzā's winter quarters. The alcohol was served there too the very night and one Yūsuf-i-'alī danced quite a bit once he was high. He was a master of music and a great dancer. The party was warm and comforting as the night passed. Muẕaffar Mīrzā gifted Babur a lambskin surtout, a sword belt and a grey horse. Two of Mīrzā's slaves, Big Moon and Little Moon indulged in offensive acts on the drunken night. Everyone left after the party concluded, except Babur.

When Qāsim Beg heard of Babur being forced to drink, he got a bit anxious and offended. He soon sent someone to Ẕū'n-nūn Beg. The man carried some advice for both Ẕū'nnūn and Muẕaffar Mīrzā. The message was harsh and diplomatic, but impactful and plain enough. Thereupon, the Mīrzās never pressed Babur to have wine again. When Badī'u'z-zamān Mīrzā heard of Muẕaffar hosting a party for Babur, he called Babur and some of his trusted men to a feast arranged in the Maqauwī-khāna in a beautiful garden of the region. The trusted men were not so open to alcohol as well.

Babur has written about this awkward situation:*

> Those about me could never drink (openly) on my own account; if they ever did drink, they did it perhaps once in forty days, with door strap fast and under a hundred fears. Such as these were now invited; here too they drank with a hundred precautions, sometimes calling off my attention, sometimes making a screen of their hands, notwithstanding that I had given them permission to follow common

---

* Babur, Abdul Rahim Khan-I-Khanan (trans.), *Tuzk-e Babri*, Delhi: Akbar, 1589, p. Folio 190. This manuscript is available in National Museum, New Delhi. The Persian translation was done from the original Turkic manuscript of Babur. This was translated by author from the copy kept at National Museum, New Delhi.

> custom, because this party was given by one standing to me as a father or elder brother. People brought in weeping-willows (. . .)

At the feast, a goose was being roasted in front of Babur. But Babur never craved the meat of birds and showed no excitement, unlike the others. After sometime Badī'u'z-zamān Mīrzā asked Babur, 'Do you not like it?'

Babur said slowly with a smile, 'I am a poor carver.'

And then, with a smile, Mīrzā offered the roasted bird to Babur.

The feast ended and Mīrzā happily offered Babur an enamelled waist-dagger, a *chārqāb*,[22] and a horse.

For the whole, the long stay in Herī Yūsuf-i-'alī Kūkūldāsh happened to become Babur's guide for the excursion. Babur roamed around almost the whole of the town in those forty days except for a place—Sulṭān Ḥusayn Mīrzā's almshouse, which nevertheless wasn't a famous spot according to Babur. He has recorded the places he visited in the *Baburnama*:[*]

> I saw the Gāzur-gāh, 'Alī-sher's Bāghcha (Little-garden), the Paper-mortars, Takht-astāna (Royal-residence), Pul-i-gāh, Kahad-stān, Naẓar-gāh-garden, Ni'matābād (Pleasure-place), Gāzur-gāh Avenue, Sulṭān Aḥmad Mīrzā's Ḥaẓirat, Takht-i-safar, Takht-i-nawā'ī, Takht-i-barkar, Takht-i-Ḥājī Beg, Takht-i-Bahā'u'd-dīn 'Umar, Takht-i-Shaikh Zainu'd-dīn, Maulānā 'Abdu'r-raḥmān Jāmī's honoured shrine and tomb, Namāz-gāh-i-mukhtār, the Fish-pond, Sāq-i-sulaimān, Bulūrī (Crystal) which originally may have been Abū'l-walīd, Imām Fakhr, Avenue-garden, Mīrzā's Colleges and tomb, Guhār-shād Begum's College, tomb, and Congregational Mosque, the Ravens'-garden,New-garden, Zubaida-garden, Sulṭān Abū-sa'īd Mīrzā's White-house outside the 'Iraq-gate, Pūrān, the Archer's-seat, Chargh (hawk)-meadow, Amīr Wāḥid, Mālān-bridge, Khwāja-tāq, White-garden, Ṭarab-khāna, Bāgh-i-jahān-ārā, Kūshk, Maqauwī-khāna, Lily-house, Twelve-towers, the great tank to the north of Jahān-ārā and the four dwellings on its four sides, the five

[*] Babur. Tuzk-e Babri. (trans.) Abdul Rahim Khan-I-Khanan. illuminated. Delhi: Akbar, 1589. p. Folio 191b. This manuscript is available in National Museum, New Delhi. The Persian translation was done from the original Turkic manuscript of Babur. This was translated by author from the copy kept at National Museum, New Delhi.

> Fort-gates, viz. the Malik, 'Irāq, Fīrūzābād, Khūsh and Qībchāq Gates, Chārsū, Shaikhu'l-islām's College, Maliks' Congregational Mosque, Town-garden, Badī'u'z-zamān Mīrzā's College on the bank of the Anjīl-canal, 'Alī-sher Beg's dwellings where we resided and which people call Unsīya (Ease), his tomb and mosque which they call Qudsīya (Holy), his College and Almshouse which they call Khalāṣīya and Akhlāṣīya (Freedom and Sincerity), his Hot-bath and Hospital which they call Ṣafā'īya and Shafā'īya. All these I visited in that space of time.

Babur Gets Engaged to Ma'ṣūma Sulṭān and Leaves Khurāsān

Sulṭān Aḥmad Mīrzā's mother Ḥabība Sulṭān Begum, had brought her youngest daughter Ma'ṣūma Sulṭān begum to Herī. One fine day when Babur visited his Ākā, Ma'ṣūma Sulṭān begum too arrived there with her mother. She was immensely infatuated with Babur at first sight. Discussions around engagement happened with Pāyanda Sulṭān Begum and Habība Sulṭān Begum. It was finally settled between them that Habība Sulṭān Begum should bring her daughter to Kābul after Babur had reached there.

Muḥammad Barandūq Beg and Ẕū'n-nūn Arghūn had been insisting Babur spend the winters there, but no arrangements for same were made. Finally, the bad winters had arrived. The thick sheet of snow lay on the mountains between Babur and Kābul. Babur was becoming increasingly anxious about Kābul. No arrangements were made to face the cold till that point. No quarters were allocated either, so Babur decided to make a move from Herī.

Losing all hope, Babur along with his men got out of town on 24 December of AD 1506. On the pretext of finding the winter quarters, Babur and his men went near Bādghīs. They were riding so slow that the moon of Ramzan could be seen only a few marches beyond the Langar of Mīr Ghiyāṣ.[23] Many of Babur's men had been absent on various occasions but now almost all had come out. Some of them joined Babur, while some followed him to Kābul after three weeks. Some stayed back in Herī submitting themselves to the service of Mīrzās. One among them was Sayyidīm 'Alī the gate-ward who went on to become Badī'u'z-zamān Mīrzā's retainer. Babur's behaviour towards him had been exceptional given that he had not been so generous to any servant of Khusrau Shāh. He had been given Ghaznī at the time when Jahāngīr Mīrzā abandoned it. But when he became the retainer of Badī'u'z-zamān Mīrzā, he gave the responsibility of Ghaznī to his younger brother Dost-i-anjū Shaikh.*

> There were in truth no better men amongst Khusrau Shāh's retainers than this man Sayyidīm 'Alī the gate-ward and Muḥibb-i-'alī the armourer. Sayyidīm was of excellent nature and manners, a bold swordsman, a singularly competent and methodical man. His house was never without company and assembly; he was greatly generous, had wit and charm, a variety of talk and story, and was a sweet-natured, good-humored, ingenious, fun-loving person. His fault was that he practiced vice and pederasty. He may have swerved from the Faith; may also have been a hypocrite in his dealings; some of what seemed double-dealing people attributed to his jokes, but, still, there must have been a something!

But when Badī'u'z-zamān Mīrzā had let Shaybāni Khān take control of Herī, he had gone to Shāh Beg. By doing so, he had disposed Sayyidīm 'Alī into Harmand. It was a double deal struck between the Mīrzā and Shāh Beg.

Babur and his men guided themselves past the border villages of Gharjistān[24] to Chach-charān[25] the Langar of Mīr Ghiyāṣ. There lay a continuous thick blanket of snow right from the almshouse to Gharjistān. It kept deepening as they moved further. Near the Chach-charān the snow reached the horses' knees.

Chach-charān was now in control of Ẕū'n-nūn Arghūn. When Babur and his men reached, Ẕū'nnūn's retainer Mīr Jān-aīrdī was in control of the place. Babur took the whole provision store of Ẕū'n-nūn Beg as payment.

They began to march further but only to find the route turning worse. The snow now reached above the stirrup. Babur has said in the *Baburnama* that, 'indeed in many places the horses' feet did not touch the ground'.

---

* Babur, Abdul Rahim Khan-I-Khanan (trans.), *Tuzk-e Babri*, Delhi: Akbar, 1589, p. Folio 192b. This manuscript is available in National Museum, New Delhi. The Persian translation was done from the original Turkic manuscript of Babur. This was translated by author from the copy kept at National Museum, New Delhi.

Babur consulted with his best minds at the Langar of Mīr Ghiyāṣ about the route for return to Kābul. They all reached an agreement and said, 'It is winter, the mountain-road is difficult and dangerous; the Qandahār road, though a little longer, is safe and easy.' But Qāsim Beg opposed the proposition. He said, 'That road is long; you will go by this one.' Finally, they decided to take the mountain road.

A Pashāī named Pīr Sulṭān was Babur's guide during this time.

Brief About Pashāī

The pashai are a Dardic ethnolinguistic group who primarily reside in eastern Afghanistan. They are the descendants of a Rig Vaidik Gāndhārī tribe and currently, their population is estimated to be around half a million. They are considered to be the oldest ethnic minority in Afghanistan.

As of now, they are currently concentrated in the northern parts of Laghman and Nangarhar. Few also lie in the parts of Kunar, Kapisa, Parwan, Nuristan, and Panjshir. Most of the Pashai consider themselves Pashtuns speaking a special language, and few are bilingual in Pashto. They are also found in the Chitral district of north-western Pakistan.

The documentation of many experts shows that the Pashai people practised Hindu and Buddhist faiths.[*] They stayed in Kunar and Laghman valleys near Jalalabad in north-eastern Afghanistan until they were displaced to a less fertile mountainous region by successive waves of immigration by Ghilji Pashtuns.[†] Interestingly, Marco Polo came across this part of the world in the thirteenth century and he writes, 'You must know that ten days' journey to the south of Badashan there is a Province called PASHAI, the people of which have a peculiar language, and are Idolaters, of a brown complexion. They are great adepts in sorceries and the diabolic arts. The men wear earrings and brooches of gold and silver set with stones and pearls.

---

[*] James B. Minahan, *Ethnic Groups of North, East, and Central Asia: An Encyclopedia*, Santa Barbara: ABC-CLIO, 2014, p. 217

[†] Christine Noelle, *State and Tribe in Nineteenth-Century Afghanistan, The Reign of Amir Dost Muhammad Khan (1826-1863)*, Abingdon-on-Thames: Taylor & Francis, 2012, p. 161.

They are a pestilent people and a crafty; and they live upon flesh and rice. Their country is very hot.'*

Currently, the majority of Pashai follow Sunni Islam and get referred to as Kohistani.† Abu'l-Fath Jalal-ud-din Muhammad Akbar, (the Tīmūrid King popularly known as Akbar) had sent his younger brother Mirza Muhammad Hakim, to wage a war against the Kafirs (infidels) of Katwar in AD 1582.‡ He was a staunch adherent of the missionary-minded Naqshbandi Sufi order and a semi-independent governor of Kābul. The *Sifat-nama* gives Muhammad Hakim the epithet of Darvis Khan Gazi. This clearly speaks aloud of his spirit to war against the Kafirs. His invasions ranging from Laghman to Alishang, led to the conversion of around seventy valleys to Islam. After having conquered the Tajau and Nijrau valleys in the Panjshir area, the Jihadis established a fort at Islamabad at the confluence of the Alishang and Alingar rivers. They continued raiding up to Alishang and made their last effort against the non-Muslims of Alingar, fighting up to Mangu (the modern border between Pashai and Ashkun-speaking areas).§

Babur's Narrative Continues

But somehow, Pīr Sulṭān failed to guide Babur and his men through. Maybe his old age had become taxing, or the deep snow had an impact. This failure robbed Qāsim Beg's peace—as the very route was suggested by him—and Babur had chosen it although the majority had a different opinion. To not lose respect, he along with his son dismounted from the horse. They began to trample the snow down. Eventually, a faint footprint on the road appeared, and he took the lead.

---

* Marco Polo, *The Travels of Marco Polo*, (trans.) Henry Yule, Edinburgh: Oliver and Boyd, 1845, p. 235.

† Barbara A. West, *Encyclopedia of the Peoples of Asia and Oceania*, s.l.: Infobase Publishing, 2010, p. 646.

‡ Henry Miers Elliot, *The History of India, As Told by Its Own Historians: The Muhammadan Period*, (ed.) John Dawson, London: Trübner & Co, 1873. Vol. 5, pp. 423-8.

§ Alberto M. Cacopardo, Augusto S. Cacopardo, *Gates of Peristan: History, Religion and Society in the Hindu Kush*, s.l.: University of Michigan, 2001, p. 32.

They kept on riding, hoping to reach their destination the quickest possible way. But the destiny had other plans. The winter snow kept turning deeper. One, it was so deep, and the way became so uncertain that they couldn't even take a stride. No help could come then. They had no choice but to return to a place where they could at least find food and supplies. They dismounted at such a place. There, Babur sent out around seventy good men down to valley to find a Hazāra, who could show them the right road ahead. Babur was hoping that someone would be wintering down in the valley. But against Babur's hope, no one was found.

Once more Babur had to look upon Sulṭān Pashāī to show the road. Putting his faith in Allah, Babur under his guidance, took the same road. They reached back from where they had lost.

It has been mentioned in the *Baburnama* that it was one of the most stressful phases of his life, during which abundant misery had befallen him. He composed the following couplet expressing this phase of stress:*

Is there one cruel turn of Fortune's wheel unseen of me?
Is there a pang, a grief my wounded heart has missed?

The path was indeed very tough. They kept on riding for nearly a week, crushing away the thick sheet of snow on the way. They could hardly cover a score of miles by then.

Babur led the horrific path along with his other fifteen trusted strong households. Those included Qāsim Beg, his sons Tīngrī-bīrdī and Qaṃbar-i-'alī and two or three of their retainers. They would walk around seven to eight yards, stamping the snow down at each step and they would sink to almost their breast. After those few steps, the leading man would stand still, exhausted and consumed by the terrific labour. Then the second one would follow, and the process would go on and on. By the time fifteen to twenty men would have stamped the snow down, it became at least feasible enough to ride a horse over it. However, the horse would sink to the stirrups

---

* Babur, Abdul Rahim Khan-I-Khanan (trans.), *Tuzk-e Babri*, Delhi: Akbar, 1589, p. Folio 193b. This manuscript is available in National Museum, New Delhi. The Persian translation was done from the original Turkic manuscript of Babur. This was translated by author from the copy kept at National Museum, New Delhi.

and couldn't do more than a dozen of steps or so. Then that horse would be set aside and the other would be made to follow the same procedure. After those fifteen to twenty men would have stamped the snow and had led horses, the remaining troop would slog in the beaten track.

Babur had clearly understood the value of the hardship. He has mentioned, 'It was not a time to urge or compel! The man with will and hardihood for such tasks does them by his own request!'

Stamping the snow down this way, Babur and his men got out from there finally and in next four days reached to a cave known as the Khawāl-i-qūtī below the Zirrīn pass.

Perhaps, it was just very right time when Babur and his men made to the cave. The very night, the snowstorm came so ferociously that it only projected end of every man's life.*

> That night the snow fell in such an amazing blizzard of cutting wind that every man feared for his life.

The snowstorm had become too violent by the time they had reached the cave. Babur and his men dismounted at the orifice of the cave. Babur has described the situation as follows:

> Deep snow! a one-man road! and even on that stamped-down and trampled road, pitfalls for horses! the days at their shortest!

Hence people kept arriving in batches. The first batch along with Babur had reached in the daylight although the environs appeared extremely gloomy and scary. The second batch arrived in time for the evening prayer and the batches kept coming till the night. Many couldn't make it to the cave and dismounted wherever they could. They all feared for their lives on this ghostly night of the sharpest storm. Dawn had broken yet many still lay in the saddle.

The snow blanket had made the cave appear smaller than its size. Babur took a shovel and carved out a place near the cave's mouth

---

* Babur, Abdul Rahim Khan-I-Khanan (trans.), *Tuzk-e Babri*, Delhi: Akbar, 1589, p. Folio 194. This manuscript is available in National Museum, New Delhi. The Persian translation was done from the original Turkic manuscript of Babur. This was translated by author from the copy kept at National Museum, New Delhi.

for about the size of a Namaz mat. He had dug the place hard till his breast, yet there was no trace of ground whatsoever. Babur took shelter within that shovelled space. His people kept asking him to come inside the cave, but he refused and chose to stay in what he had dug. His mind was lost in a thought which read as below:*

> Some of my men in snow and storm, I in the comfort of a warm house! the whole horde outside in misery and pain, I inside sleeping at ease! That would be far from a man's act, quite another matter than comradeship! Whatever hardship and wretchedness there is, I will face; what strong men stand, I will stand; for, as the Persian proverb says, to die with friends is a nuptial.

Babur calmly sat in that snowstorm in the dugout place till the bedtime prayer. The layer of snow, no thinner than four hands had covered his head and back. The storm raged till the point where one couldn't see clearly or hear, for even eyes or ears were coated with the layer of snow. He shivered lightly even though the thickest possible clothes covered him. The cold had begun to affect Babur's ears badly.

The time for the night prayers had arrived. Someone looked thoroughly and carefully inside and shouted aloud, 'It is a very roomy cave with a place for everybody.' Hearing so, Babur was delighted and wanted to smile, but the acute storm didn't let him. Babur shook away the snow and asked his men around him to get inside. The cave indeed had a place for around five dozen men. People stormed in and brought out their rations, cold meat, parched grain, along with whatever they had. It was a great feeling to have stayed in such a chilled skin-piercing, stormy environment in a warm, cozy and quiet space.

The next day the storm had gone away, and it wasn't snowing at all. Babur and his men started early. They again embarked on the daunting journey by making a way by stamping the snow. The proper road which they saw seemed to be making a detour up through the mountain flank, snaking even higher. They thought it was the Zirrīn

---

* Babur, Abdul Rahim Khan-I-Khanan (trans.), *Tuzk-e Babri*, Delhi: Akbar, 1589, p. Folio 194b. This manuscript is available in National Museum, New Delhi. The Persian translation was done from the original Turkic manuscript of Babur. This was translated by author from the copy kept at National Museum, New Delhi.

pass. They took the road and went straight to the bottom of valley.[26] By night, they could reach the further side of the Bakkak Pass. They spent the night in the mouth of the valley. This night too was not ready to give respite from the mighty cold. The saga of distress and suffering was to continue. The hands and legs of most of the men had been frost-bitten.

The next morning, with trust in Allah, they rode straight down. The slope was bad with sudden falls and certainly, it didn't look like the correct one. By the time of evening prayer, they were able to get out of the valley.

Babur saw this as a great achievement and he wrote about it in the *Baburnama*:*

> No long-memoried old man knew that any-one had been heard of as crossing that pass with the snow so deep, or indeed that it had ever entered the heart of man to cross it at that time of year. Though for a few days we had suffered greatly through the depth of the snow, yet its depth, in the end, enabled us to reach our destination. For why? How otherwise should we have traversed those pathless slopes and sudden falls? All ill, all good in the count, is gain if looked at aright!

When the people of Yaka-aūlāng heard of Babur's arrival, they happily offered their warm houses. They also offered fat sheep, clean water and grass and corn for the horses. They also supplied wood and dung to ignite the fire. It was a beautiful relief to Babur and his men who had come from the perilous snowstorm trip of mountain roads. They stayed there for a day and on the next morning, they left for Yīghāch, which was only twelve miles from there. The following day—14 February of AD 1507—was Babur's twenty-fourth birthday and a Ramẕān feast. Babur and his party went on through Bamyan, crossed by Shibr-tū and dismounted before reaching Janglīk.

* Babur, Abdul Rahim Khan-I-Khanan (trans.), *Tuzk-e Babri*, Delhi: Akbar, 1589, p. Folio 195b. This manuscript is available in National Museum, New Delhi. The Persian translation was done from the original Turkic manuscript of Babur. This was translated by author from the copy kept at National Museum, New Delhi.

Babur's Second Raid on the Turkmān Hazāras

Babur was expecting the Turkmān Hazāras with their families to have made their winter quarters upon the road[27] he had taken. Babur also believed that they had no clue about his arrival. When he along with his men arrived near their tents and cattle pens, they seemed to have gone out to ruin and plunder (according to Babur). Their children, wives and tents remained abandoned. Babur soon heard the news that they were shooting arrows in a narrow passage and not letting anyone pass. Babur has written a poem referring to this incident:*

They saw the blackness of the foe;
Stood idle-handed and amazed;
I arriving, went swift that way,
Pressed on with shout, "Move on! move on!"
I wanted to hurry my men on,
To make them stand up to the foe.
With a "Hurry up!" to my men,
I went on to the front.
Not a man gave ear to my words.
I had no armour nor horse-mail nor arms,
I had but my arrows and quiver.
I went, the rest, maybe all of them, stood,
Stood still as if slain by the foe!
Your servant you take that you may have use
Of his arms, of his life, the whole time;
Not that the servant stand still
While the beg makes advance to the front;
Not that the servant take rest
While his beg is making the rounds.
From no such a servant will come
Speed, or use in your Gate, or zest for your food.
At last I charged forward myself,

* Babur, Abdul Rahim Khan-I-Khanan (trans.), *Tuzk-e Babri*, Delhi: Akbar, 1589, p. Folio 196. This manuscript is available in National Museum, New Delhi. The Persian translation was done from the original Turkic manuscript of Babur. This was translated by author from the copy kept at National Museum, New Delhi.

Herding the foe up the hill;
Seeing me go, my men also moved,
Leaving their terrors behind.
With me they swift spread over the slope,
Moving on without heed to the shaft;
Sometimes on foot, mounted sometimes,
Boldly we ever moved on,
Still from the hill poured the shafts.
Our strength seen, the foe took to flight.
We got out on the hill; we drove the Hazāras,
Drove them like deer by valley and ridge;
We shot those wretches like deer;
We shared out the booty in goods and in sheep;
The Turkmān Hazāras' kinsfolk we took;
We made captive their people of sorts (qarā);
We laid hands on their men of renown;
Their wives and their children we took.

Babur himself took a few of Hazāras' sheep as booty and gave their charge to Yārak Ṭaghāī. Passing by the ridge and valley, driving the horses and sheep at the front, Babur and his men went to Tīmūr Beg's Langar. They dismounted there. Babur had caught around fifteen Hazāras (he addresses them as thieves in the *Baburnama*). He tortured them in various ways before killing them. Babur believed that killing them would let out a strong warning message to all highwaymen and robbers.

But Qāsim Beg did something that annoyed Babur. He showed compassion and let those fifteen captives go free. Babur composed the following poem in *Baburnama* for this incident:*

To do good to the bad is one and the same
As the doing of ill to the good;
On brackish soil no spikenard grows,
Waste no seed of toil upon it.

* Babur, Abdul Rahim Khan-I-Khanan (trans.), *Tuzk-e Babri*, Delhi: Akbar, 1589, p. Folio 197b. This manuscript is available in National Museum, New Delhi. The Persian translation was done from the original Turkic manuscript of Babur. This was translated by author from the copy kept at National Museum, New Delhi.

The rest of the prisoners were released on compassionate grounds as well.

While Babur was busy raiding the Turkmān Hazāras, news of political turbulence came from Kābul. Muḥammad Ḥusain Mīrzā Dūghlāt and Sulṭān Sanjar Barlās had come over to the Moghūls left in Kābul. They declared Mīrzā Khān (Wais) the Padishah. They laid siege to the fort and spread a rumour that Badī'u'z-zamān Mīrzā and Muẕaffar Mīrzā had made Babur a prisoner in Fort Ikhtiyāru'd-dīn (also known as Ālā-qūrghān). But people in command, including Mullā Bābā of Pashāghar, Khalīfa, Muḥibb-i-'alī the armourer, Aḥmad-i-yūsuf and Aḥmad-i-qāsim were able to strengthen the fort and didn't let it fell.

Without wasting a single moment, Qāsim Beg's servant, Muhammad of Andijān, a Tūqbāī was sent to the begs of Kābul from Timur's Langar. He had a written message to deliver:*

> When we are out of the Ghūr-bund narrows, we will fall on them suddenly; let our signal to you be the fire we will light directly we have passed Minār-hill; do you in reply light one in the citadel, on the old Kūshk (kiosk), now the Treasury, so that we may be sure you know of our coming. We will come up from our side; you come out from yours; neglect nothing your hands can find to do!

Babur and his men began to ride the very next dawn from the langar and dismounted around Ushtur-shahr. By the next morning, they passed the Ghūr-bund narrows and dismounted at the bridgehead. They made the horses drink water and rest for a while before resuming the journey to Kābul around the mid-day prayer. The snow was completely absent till they reached the Toll Gate (Annette Susannah Beveridge has also translated *tūtqāwal* as Toll Gate). The more they proceeded beyond the tool the more the snow deepened. Between the node of Ẕamma-yakhshī and Minār, the piercing cold was such that Babur had never experienced before.

---

* Babur, Abdul Rahim Khan-I-Khanan (trans.), *Tuzk-e Babri*, Delhi: Akbar, 1589, p. Folio 197b. This manuscript is available in National Museum, New Delhi. The Persian translation was done from the original Turkic manuscript of Babur. This was translated by author from the copy kept at National Museum, New Delhi.

When they drew closer, Babur thought of sending the missive to the begs again through Aḥmad, the messenger, and Qarā Aḥmad. The message read:*

> Here we are at the time promised; be ready! Be bold!

They crossed the Minār hill and dismounted on the skirt. The cold experienced during the journey had affected them—the chill continued unabated. They ignited fire to warm themselves and fight the cold for some time. It must be noted that it was not the signal fire for the begs but only lit for the purpose of warming themselves.

As the dawn cracked again after the last night's survival, they left from the Minār hill. The snow worsened towards Kābul. Horses were buried knee-deep. They had to ride in a single file for the whole way on this road.

But like every cloud has a silver lining, their ride in a single file made them highly undiscoverable. By the time they reached Bībī Māh-rūī (Lady Moon-face), they could see the blaze of fire on the citadel, giving them the signal that the begs were looking out for them.

They reached the Sayyid Qāsim's bridge. The men on the right, including Sherīm Ṭaghāī, were told to move towards Mullā Bābā's bridge. Those on the left and centre were told to go ahead on the Bābā Lūlī road. Within the Khalīfa's garden existed a small garden made by Aūlūgh Beg Mīrzā for a langar (almshouse). Although there was no trace of trees or shrubs that existed earlier, the walls stood unblemished. Mīrzā Khān was seated in this garden. Muḥammad Ḥusain Mīrzā was lying in the Aūlūgh Beg Mīrzā's great Bāgh-i-bihisht. Babur had gone as far along the lane of Mullā Bābā's garden, which turned to the burial ground. He encountered four men—Lord of the Gate Sayyid Qāsim, Qāsim Beg's son Qaṃbar-i-'alī, Sher-qulī the scout and one from the latter's band namely Sulṭān Aḥmad Moghūl—hurrying towards Mīrzā Khān's quarters. They were beaten badly and forced to turn away. The commotion alerted Mīrzā Khān, and he fled.

* Khan-Khana, Abdul Rahim, (trans.). illuminated. s.l.: Akbar. p. Folio 198. This manuscript is available in National Museum, New Delhi. The Persian translation was done from the original Turkic manuscript of Babur. This was translated by author from the copy kept at National Museum, New Delhi.

Several had sided with Mīrzā Khān. Even, Muhammad Ḥusain, the younger brother of Abū'l-ḥasan the armourer, had joined the service of Mīrzā Khān.

Muhammad Ḥusain jumped at Sher-qulī, one among those four and threw him down. Husain tried to slash Sher. He was about to behead him when Sher-qulī somehow just managed to free himself. The four so-called warriors were wounded badly and came running to Babur.

Babur's horsemen were blocked in the narrow lane and were unable to make a move in any direction. But Babur was keen for the action and yelled, 'Get off and make a way out.' His call energized the men who were stuck. After hearing him, Nāṣir Dost, Khwāja Muḥammad 'Alī the librarian, Bābā Sher-zād, Shāh Maḥmūd and their followers got off and pushed forward, clearing the way. They fought a good battle there. Babur kept waiting for the begs but they never came as a strong force. They began to drop in ones and twos, but Babur and his men had already pushed the enemy away.

Aḥmad-i-yūsuf had reached Mīrzā Khān's quarters before Babur headed to Chār-bāgh. He accompanied Babur to the Chār-bāgh, where Mīrzā Khān had been. But by the time they both reached the spot, Mīrzā had already fled. At the Gate of the Garden, Babur found Dost of Sar-i-pul standing with a sword in his hand whom he had promoted as Kotwal from a foot soldier for his bravery while leaving from Kābul the last time.

Although Babur still had cuirass put on, he had neither fastened the gharīcha nor had he had put on the rudder. He attacked Babur's unprotected arm with the sword. However, he survived. Babur has said:*

> Whether he did not recognize me because of change wrought by cold and snow, or whether because of the flurry of the fight, though I shouted 'Hāī Dost! Hāī Dost!' and though Aḥmad-i-yūsuf also shouted, he, without a 'God forbid!' brought down his sword on

* Babur, Abdul Rahim Khan-I-Khanan (trans.), *Tuzk-e Babri*, Delhi: Akbar, 1589, p. Folio 199. This manuscript is available in National Museum, New Delhi. The Persian translation was done from the original Turkic manuscript of Babur. This was translated by author from the copy kept at National Museum, New Delhi.

my unprotected arm. Only by God's grace can it have been that not a hairbreadth of harm was done to me.

And he has composed a couplet:

If a sword shook the Earth from her place,
Not a vein would it cut till God wills.

Babur has mentioned that it was only the virtue of the prayer that he often repeated, that made Allah avert the danger, turning the evil aside:[28]

> O my God! Thou art my Creator; except Thee there is no God. On Thee do I repose my trust; Thou art the Lord of the mighty throne. What God wills comes to pass; and what he does not will comes not to pass; and there is no power or strength but through the high and exalted God; and, of a truth, in all things God is almighty; and verily He comprehends all things by his knowledge and has taken account of everything. O my Creator! as I sincerely trust in Thee, do Thou seize by the forelock all evil proceeding from within myself, and all evil coming from without, and all evil proceeding from every man who can be the occasion of evil, and all such evil as can proceed from any living thing, and remove them far from me; since, of a truth, Thou art the Lord of the exalted throne!

Leaving that garden, Babur rushed to the quarters of Muhammad Ḥusain Mīrzā. It lied in Bāgh-i-bihisht. But even he had run away and hid. He found eight men waiting to fight him and his men at the garden wall. Babur dealt with them very strongly. He was about to chop off one of the men's heads, but he recognized him. He appeared to be Mīrzā Khān's foster-brother, Tūlik Kūkūldāsh. Babur's sword fell on his shoulder and he couldn't behead him.[29]

When Babur reached the gate of Muḥammad Ḥusain Mīrzā's quarters, a Moghūl on the roof drew his bow aiming at Babur's face. Babur saw and immediately recognized him as one of his own servants. Just then the people from all the sides began to shout at once.

'Hāi! hāi! it is the Padishah.'

Suddenly, the arrow was shot but at a different target. The Moghūl ran away. Babur was suspicious of this occurrence:*

> The affair was beyond the shooting of arrows! His Mīrzā, his leaders, had run away or been taken; why was he shooting?

Sulṭān Sanjar Barlās was brought to Babur as a captive, being led by a rope tied around his neck. Babur couldn't believe that he had a part in the mutiny given that he won good favour in the past.

He wept and said, 'Hāi! what fault is in me?'

Babur and Sanjar exchanged a few words for a while. Babur did not appear initially in any mood to let him go at ease. But ultimately, Babur gave amnesty to him.†

> But as he was the sister's son of my Khān dada's mother, Shāh Begum, I gave the order, 'Do not lead him with such dishonor; it is not death.'

Now they left the place, but Babur hadn't forgotten about Mīrzā Khān. He sent one of the begs of fort, Aḥmad-i-qasim Kohbur to pursue Mīrzā Khān.

After leaving Bāgh-i-bihisht, Babur went to visit Shāh begum and Mihr Nigār Khānum. They were settled in the tents by the side of the garden.

Babur took the riot and plunder caused by townspeople and the black bludgeoners very seriously. He decided to catch those people from each corner of the town. Babur sent his men to fight them out and they were shown a way away right then.‡

Babur approached with reverence and gallantry to have an interview with Shāh Begum and Mihr Nigār Khānum. Both appeared ashamed from within and seemed that they couldn't excuse themselves

---

* Babur, Abdul Rahim Khan-I-Khanan (trans.), *Tuzk-e Babri*, Delhi: Akbar, 1589, p. Folio 199b. This manuscript is available in National Museum, New Delhi. The Persian translation was done from the original Turkic manuscript of Babur. This was translated by author from the copy kept at National Museum, New Delhi.

† Ibid.

‡ As per the note 1235 of Annette Susannah Beveridge, this was probably done by Babur for the protection of the two women.

for whatever had transpired. Their guilt prevented them from expressing their affection for Babur. In short, the scenario appeared a bit awkward.[30]

Babur has expressed discontent about the scenario:*

> I had not expected this (disloyalty) of them; it was not as though that party, evil as was the position it had taken up, consisted of persons who would not give ear to the words of Shāh Begum and Khānum; Mīrzā Khān was the Begum's grandson, in her presence night and day; if she had not fallen in with the affair, she could have kept him with her.
>
> Twice over when fickle Fortune and discordant Fate had parted me from throne and country, retainer and following, I, and my mother with me, had taken refuge with them and had had no kindness soever from them. At that time my younger brother (i.e., cousin) Mīrzā Khān and his mother Sulṭān-nigār Khānum held valuable cultivated districts; yet my mother and I, —to leave all question of a district aside, —were not made possessors of a single village or a few yokes of plough-oxen. Was my mother not Yūnas Khān's daughter? Was I not his grandson?
>
> In my days of plenty I have given from my hand what matched the blood-relationship and the position of whatsoever member of that (Chaghatāī) dynasty chanced down upon me. For example, when the honored Shāh Begum came to me, I gave her Pamghān, one of the best places in Kābul, and failed in no sort of filial duty and service towards her. Again, when Sulṭān Sa'īd Khān, Khān in Kāshghar, came (914 AH) with five or six naked followers on foot, I looked upon him as an honored guest and gave him Mandrāwar of the Lamghān tūmāns. Beyond this also, when Shāh Ismā'īl had killed Shaybāni Khān in Marv and I crossed over to Qūndūz (916 AH-1511 AD), the Andijānīs, some driving their (Aūzbeg) dāroghas out, some making their places fast, turned their eyes to me and sent me a man; at that time I trusted those old family servants to that same Sulṭān Sa'īd Khān, gave him a force, made him Khān and sped

* Babur, Abdul Rahim Khan-I-Khanan (trans.), *Tuzk-e Babri*, Delhi: Akbar, 1589, p. Folio 200. This manuscript is available in National Museum, New Delhi. The Persian translation was done from the original Turkic manuscript of Babur. This was translated by author from the copy kept at National Museum, New Delhi.

him forth. Again, down to the present time (circa 934 AH) I have not looked upon any member of that family who has come to me, in any other light than as a blood-relation. For example, there are now in my service Chīn-tīmūr Sulṭān; Aīsān-tīmūr Sulṭān, Tūkhtā-būghā Sulṭān, and Bābā Sulṭān;[31] on one and all of these I have looked with more favor than on blood-relations of my own.

I do not write this in order to make complaint; I have written the plain truth. I do not set these matters down in order to make known my own deserts; I have set down exactly what has happened. In this History I have held firmly to it that the truth should be reached in every matter, and that every act should be recorded precisely as it occurred. From this it follows of necessity that I have set down of good and bad whatever is known, concerning father and elder brother, kinsman and stranger; of them all I have set down carefully the known virtues and defects. Let the reader accept my excuse; let the reader pass on from the place of severity!

Babur sent letters of victory to all the countries, clans and retainers. Then he and his men rode to the citadel.

The time had come for Babur to catch hold of those whom he considered rebels. He heard that Muhammad Ḥussayn Mīrzā had run into the Khānum's bedroom and had fastened himself into the bundle of bedding. Babur appointed Mīrīm Dīwān along with some important begs of the fort to capture Ḥussayn Mīrzā. Mīrīm Dīwān rushed into the place shouting abusive words and got hold of the hiding Ḥussayn Mīrzā. He was brought in front of Babur in the citadel.

Babur has claimed to be generous in these circumstances. According to *Baburnama*, he rose at once to receive the Mīrzā. He showed the usual admiration and didn't wear harshness even on his face. But Babur certainly wanted to do worse, but he didn't for some obvious reasons as he sees:*

If I had had that Muhammad Ḥussayn Mīrzā cut in pieces, there was the ground for it that he had had part in base and shameful action,

* Babur, Abdul Rahim Khan-I-Khanan (trans.), *Tuzk-e Babri*, Delhi: Akbar, 1589, p. Folio 201b. This manuscript is available in National Museum, New Delhi. The Persian translation was done from the original Turkic manuscript of Babur. This was translated by author from the copy kept at National Museum, New Delhi.

> started and spurred on mutiny and treason. Death, he deserved with one after another of varied pain and torture, but because there had come to be various connection between us, his very sons and daughters being by my own mother's sister Khūb Nigār Khānum, I kept this just claim in mind, let him go free, and permitted him to set out towards Khurāsān.

But as Babur has claimed in *Baburnama*, he did not keep the worth of the amnesty given by the former:

> The cowardly ingrate then forgot altogether the good I did him by the gift of his life; he blamed and slandered me to Shaybāni Khān. Little time passed, however, before the Khān gave him his deserts by death.

And he writes the below couplet:

> Leave thou to Fate the man who does thee wrong,
> For Fate is an avenging servitor.

Babur sent Aḥmad-i-qāsim Kohbur with a party of braves in the pursuit of Mīrzā Khān. Finally, he was caught in the low hills of Qargha-yīlāq. He tried his best to run away but failed. He was brought in front of Babur, who was seated on the north-east porch, of the old courthouse. Looking at him Babur said, 'Come! let's have a look at one another.'

As per the custom, twice before he could bend the knee and come forward, he fell because of the distress he was in. But he picked himself and came up to Babur. Both looked at each other. Babur placed him by his side. Sherbet was served which he initially denied taking. Upon insistence, he feared that it was poisoned. Babur smiled, took the sherbet and drank it one gulp.

Yet those who had accompanied him (soldiers, peasants, Moghūls and Chaghatāīs) were in suspense. They feared that Mīrzā Khān would be assassinated. But Babur simply ordered Mīrzā Khān to live in his elder sister's house for a few days. His well-wishers, who feared for his life in Kābul, kept insisting on his release. A few days later he was allowed to move to Khurāsān.

Once they were released, Babur went for an excursion to Bārān,[32] Chāsh-tūpa, and the skirt of Gul-i-bahār. Babur claims that the open land of Bārān, the plain of Chāsh-tūpa, and the skirt of Gul-i-bahār were more beautiful in spring than any part of Kābul. Babur saw various kinds of tulips appearing, which he counted to be thirty-four in number. He has written couplets in praise of those places:*

Kābul in Spring is an Eden of verdure and blossom;
Matchless in Kābul the Spring of Gul-i-bahār and Bārān.
He also composed the below limerick on the excursion:
My heart, like the bud of the red, red rose,
Lies fold within fold aflame;
Would the breath of even a myriad Springs
Blow my heart's bud to a rose?

Babur found a few places over there very similar like those for the spring excursions, hawking or bird-shooting in Kābul and Ghaznī.

That year, the begs of Badakhshān—Muhammad the armourer, Mubārak Shāh, Zubair Jahāngīr etc.—were furious with Nāṣir Mīrzā and his followers. They brought out an army of soldiers on horses and those on feet. They were arrayed on the plains by the edge of Kūkcha-water and soon they began to move towards Yaftal and Rāgh, near Khamchān, taking the route of lower hills. Nāṣir Mīrzā came to fight back—he was inexperienced, and so were the begs by his side. The lack of experience was evident as they arrived to battle at lower hills, a battlefield which was contoured in various ways.

The Badakhshīs had several men on foot who were ready to counter the Mīrzā's horse and his allies multiple times over. The Mīrzā and his men couldn't face them and were beaten and plundered . . . almost stripped bare.

The defeated ones, about eighty men, took the road through Ishkīmīsh and Nārīn to Kīlā-gāhī. They got out on the Āb-dara road, making a crossing at Shibr-tū, and made their way to the Kābul. They appeared worn-out, naked and famished.

* Babur, Abdul Rahim Khan-I-Khanan (trans.), *Tuzk-e Babri*, Delhi: Akbar, 1589, p. Folio 202b. This manuscript is available in National Museum, New Delhi. The Persian translation was done from the original Turkic manuscript of Babur. This was translated by author from the copy kept at National Museum, New Delhi.

This conflict delighted Babur for a few obvious personal reasons:

> That was a marvelous sign of the Divine might! Two or three years earlier the Mīrzā had left the Kābul country like a foe, driving tribes and hordes like sheep before him, reached Badakhshān and made fast its forts and valley-strongholds. With what fancy in his mind had he marched out? Now he was back, hanging the head of shame for those earlier misdeeds, humbled and distraught about that breach with me!

Nāṣir Mīrzā was sceptical about how he would be received for he was aware of his misdeeds. But to his surprise, Babur didn't show him any displeasure. Instead, with a smile, he enquired about his well-being.

On 13 May AD 1507, Babur rode out of Kābul. He was intending to overrun the Ghiljīs. But when Babur had dismounted at Sar-i-dih, he was told that several Mahmands (Afghāns) were lying in Masht and Sih-kāna around five miles from his location. It was then that the begs of Babur yelled in agreement, 'The Mahmands must be over-run.'

Babur replied, 'Would it be right to turn aside and raid our own peasants instead of doing what we set out to do? It cannot be.'[33]

Riding from Sar-i-dih, Babur crossed the plain of Kattawāz in the ghastly dark of the night. At one stretch of the land, there appeared no mountain or hill. Nor the road appeared known. None agreed to lead, prompting Babur to take up the task. He had been on this route on several occasions earlier. Reminiscing on the lingering memories of the past journeys, he began to lead. By the grace of Allah, as Babur has written, his guidance proved to be right. They went straight to the Qīāq-tū and the Aūlābā-tū torrent. They reached the Khwāja Ismā'īl Sirītī road which crossed the two torrents and where the Ghiljīs were stationed. Babur and his men dismounted near the torrent. They slept and let the horse rest too till dawn. They resumed their march. Sun had elevated to a good height before they could get out of those low hills. The Ghiljīs were lying at the bottom of the valley and the plains quite a few miles away. Once Babur was out of the plain, he could see the darkness in the sky caused by the smoke of fire started by the Ghiljīs.

Suddenly, Babur and his army began to gallop. Perhaps they wanted to hurry the conquest for some reason. They shot many arrows at the Ghiljīs, subsequently conquering tribe. It would have been very difficult to get 6000 galloping soldiers in control and hence Babur chose to go with the flow. The raid was a success. Babur was quite delighted to have extorted way more sheep in this raid than any other in the recent past.

Babur's men loaded the spoils and began to ride back. But in the tourney, the Afghāns men kept coming, trying to provoke a fight. Babur and his men spared none. All were slaughtered and yet again a tower of skulls was set up.

Babur talks of only one loss in this battle. It was Dost the Kotwal on whose feet an arrow had pierced. He couldn't survive till Babur's troop reached Kābul.

Marching from Khwāja Ismā'īl, Babur and his men dismounted once more at Aūlābā-tū. Some of the begs and households of Babur were instructed to go forward and carefully separate one-fifth[34] of the enemy's spoils. Babur was quite favourable to Qāsim Beg and other allied begs. He writes in the *Baburnama*:[*]

> By way of favor, we did not take the Fifth from Qāsim Beg and some others. From what was written down, the Fifth came out at 16,000, that is to say, this 16,000 was the fifth of 80,000 sheep; no question however but that with those lost and those not asked for, a lakh (100,000) of sheep had been taken.

The very next day, they rode out of the camp and formed a hunting circle on the plain of Kattawāz, where there were abundant fat deer and wild ass. They were killed in droves. Babur ran after a wild ass and shot an arrow as he got close, but it did not hit the target. He kept shooting, but the animal didn't stop despite being wounded twice. However, it had slowed down. Babur ran closer and hacked it at the scruff of its neck behind the ears and chopped through the windpipe. The ass paused and died turning over right then. As Babur has explained, this wild ass was a fatter one and its rib may be close to the length of a yard. Babur shot many other wild asses too. Finally, all

[*] Babur, Abdul Rahim Khan-I-Khanan (trans.), *Tuzk-e Babri*, Delhi: Akbar, 1589, p. Folio 203b. This manuscript is available in National Museum, New Delhi. The Persian translation was done from the original Turkic manuscript of Babur. This was translated by author from the copy kept at National Museum, New Delhi.

those hunted wild asses and were brought down at a place and Babur observed that none were as fat as his first kill.

With the raid and hunt done, Babur along with his men set out to Kābul.

Shaybāni Khān Moves to Khurāsān

Bad times for Babur were set to begin again. His old foe, Shaybāni Khān had got an army to horses at the end of last year to go from Samarkand against Khurāsān. But his march hastened a bit as a servant of Shāh Manṣūr (in Andikhūd) came to Shaybāni Khān. Babur has described Shāh Manṣūr as a traitor to salt, a vile wretch who said, 'I have sent a man to the Aūzbeg,' when the Khān was approaching Andikhūd. Relying on the words of Shāh Manṣūr, he bejewelled himself, stuck up a tassel on his head, and went out, bearing gift and tribute. But then the leaderless Aūzbegs decanted down on him from all the sides, and turned him upside down, ravishing not only his people but also the offerings of all sorts.

Vacillation of the Khurāsān Mīrzās

Along with their army, Badī'u'z-zamān Mīrzā, Muẕaffar Mīrzā, Muḥammad Barandūq Barlās and Ẕū'n-nūn Arghūn were lying in Bābā Khākī. They had neither decided to fight nor settled to secure the fort of Herī. They sat lazily, baffled, equivocal and certainly uncertain about the next step. But among all, Muhammad Barandūq Barlās was thinking otherwise and in Babur's opinion he appeared to be a knowledgeable man.

He said, 'You let Muẕaffar Mīrzā and me make the fort fast, let Badī'u'z-zamān Mīrzā and Ẕū'n-nūn Beg go into the mountains near Herī and gather in Sulṭān 'Alī Arghūn from Sīstān and Zamīn-dāwar, Shāh Beg and Muqīm from Qandahār with all their armies, and let them collect also what there is of Nikdīrī and Hazāra force; this done, let them make a swift and telling move. The enemy would find it difficult to go into the mountains and could not come against the (Herī) fort because he would be afraid of the army outside.'

Babur has said that he found Muhammad Barandūq Barlās' strategy very practical.

According to Babur, although Ẕū'n-nūn Arghūn was brave, he was a mean man. He had strength but was highly materialistic by nature. Babur has said that he was far from being businesslike or judicious. Rather he was a shallow a bit of a fool. When both younger and elder brothers became joint rulers in Herī, Badī'u'z-zamān Mīrzā became the chief authority in the presence of Ẕū'n-nūn Arghūn. And now he didn't want Muhammad Barandūq Beg to remain inside the town of Herī town. Being a man with charm for materials he himself wanted to be there with Muhammad gone. As Babur has stated:*

> Is there a better sign of his shallow-pate and craze than that he degraded himself and became contemptible by accepting the lies and flattery of rogues and sycophants?

Babur gave the particulars as under:

> While he was so dominant and trusted in Herī, certain Shaikhs and Mullās went to him and said, 'The Spheres are holding commerce with us; you are styled Hizabru'l-lāh (Lion of God); you will overcome the Aūzbeg.' Believing these words, he put his bathing-cloth round his neck and gave thanks. It was through this he did not accept Muḥammad Barandūq Beg's sensible counsel, did not strengthen the works (aīsh) of the fort, get ready fighting equipment, set scout or rearward to warn of the foe's approach, or plan out such method of array that, should the foe appear, his men would fight with ready heart.

Shaybāni Khān Takes Hold of Herī

It was the month of Muharram of AD 1507 (May-June) when Shaybāni Khān passed through Murghāb towards Sīrkāī. The news reached the ears of the Mīrzās, upsetting them. They couldn't act the

* Babur, Abdul Rahim Khan-I-Khanan (trans.), *Tuzk-e Babri*, Delhi: Akbar, 1589, p. Folio 205b. This manuscript is available in National Museum, New Delhi. The Persian translation was done from the original Turkic manuscript of Babur. This was translated by author from the copy kept at National Museum, New Delhi.

way that they should have—they essentially failed to assemble the troops. Babur has written, 'Dreamers, they moved through a dream!'

Ẕū'n-nūn Arghūn was glorified by flattery around him. In his foolishness, he went to Qarā-rabāṭ with hardly 150 men to face the massive giant army of half a lakh Aūzbegs. Ẕū'n-nūn Arghūn was eventually captured, and his head was chopped.

Mīrzās' mothers, elder and younger sisters, wives and treasure were in Fort Ikhtiyāru'd-dīn at Ālā-qūrghān. The sluggish Mīrzās reached the town at night and let their horses rest till before resuming in the dawn. Look at the irony, they didn't even think once to strengthen the fort and ran away leaving their mothers, sisters, wives and children for the Aūzbeg's to capture.

Within Ālā-qūrghān, Sulṭān Ḥusaayn Mīrzā's had a harem with Pāyanda Sulṭān Begum and Khadīja Begum heading it. The harems of Badī'u'z-zamān Mīrzāand Muẕaffar Mīrzā too were placed within this place along with their little children, treasure, and households.

Indeed, the Mīrzās had acted cowardly and foolishly by not securing the fort, and neither had any reinforcement arrived. But 'Āshiq-i-muḥammad Arghūn, the younger brother of Mazīd Beg showed courage and fled from the army on foot to get into the fort. Amīr Umar Beg's son, 'Alī Khān (Turkmān), Shaikh 'Abdu'l-lāh, Mīrzā Beg Kāī-khusraūī, and Mīrak Gūr the dīwān too barged into the fort to prepare it for the upcoming conflict.

Trouble arrived within three days—Shaybāni Khān had come. And with him had come treachery of the people. Many notables, including Shaikhu'l-islām came out in support of the Khān and handed over the keys of the outer fort. But there was one man, 'Āshiq-i-muḥammad (discussed in the paragraph above), who had abandoned the Tīmūrids to save the fort. He held the fort for almost seventeen days and finally on the eighteenth day the breach occurred, when a mine was fired from the horse-market outside. It was devastating to see the watch tower fall.

The fort had fallen.

After Shaybāni Khān took Herī, he misbehaved with every woman and the children. His five days of stay had earned him a bad reputation, according to Babur. In his eyes, one of Shaybāni Khān's first improper deeds in Herī was to make Khadīja Begum miserable. The despicable (in the eyes of Babur), paymaster Shāh Manṣūr, was tasked with holding her. He looted her in every way possible. Then

Shaybāni Khān, let 'Abdu'l-wahhāb Moghūl plunder the revered and virtuous Shaikh Pūrān. Each of his children was taken as a slave by someone or other. Shaybāni Khān got a band of poets detained by Mullā Banā'ī. This matter is well captured in a Persian verse and was quite well known in Khurāsān. *

> Except 'Abdu'l-lāh the stupid fool (kīr-khar),
> Not a poet to-day sees the color of gold;
> From the poets' band Banā'ī would get gold,
> All he will get is kīr-khar.

Shaybāni Khān had direct possession of Herī now. He took Khānzāda Khānum, Muẕaffar Mīrzā's wife. Babur has mentioned that Shaybāni did so disregarding the Muslim law.[35] Babur has denounced Shaybāni's illiteracy about Islamic law but also talks about how actually the scholars are misguided on this account as well. He instructed his own version of Qu'ran to Qāẓī Ikhtiyār and Muḥammad Mīr Yūsuf, the two well-known expert *mullās* of Herī.

It did not end here.

He took a pen and corrected the writings of Mullā Sulṭān 'Alī of Mashhad and the drawing of Bihzād. Babur has made a satirical comment in the *Baburnama* about the situation:†

> In a few days, Shaybāni had composed some tasteless couplet, he would have it read from the pulpit, hung in the square, and for it accept the offerings of the townspeople!

Babur has noted that Shaybāni Khān was an early riser who wouldn't miss any of the five prayers. He would recite the Qur'an with utmost glory but his acts and deeds were as absurd, impudent and heathenish as those just named.

A couple of weeks had passed since Shaybāni Khān had taken possession of Herī. He went to Pul-i-sālār and sent Tīmūr Sulṭān and 'Ubaid Sulṭān with an army against Abū'l-muḥsin Mīrzā and Kūpuk

---

* Babur, Abdul Rahim Khan-I-Khanan (trans.), *Tuzk-e Babri*, Delhi: Akbar, 1589, p. Folio 206. This manuscript is available in National Museum, New Delhi. The Persian translation was done from the original Turkic manuscript of Babur. This was translated by author from the copy kept at National Museum, New Delhi.

† Ibid. p. Folio 215.

Mīrzā. Both were happily seated in Mashhad carefree and unaware of the trouble that was set to come. Both the Mirzas once thought of making the fort of Qalāt secure, but before they could act, the reaction had already occurred. The Aūzbegs were approaching. Both planned to induce a forced march against the Aūzbegs along a different route. This would have been a great idea but to their disappointment, while they remained seated in Mashhad with nothing decided, the Sulṭāns arrived.

After a bout of helplessness and cluelessness in dealing with this occasion, they decided to array the soldiers and give a fight. In the conflict, Abū'l-muḥsin Mīrzā was beaten and badly injured. Kūpuk Mīrzā charged at his brother's assailants with a handful of his men. But the Aūzbegs proved to be heftier, and they carried both brothers away. Soon the brothers were dismounted and were made to sit on the ground. Knowing well that what would follow, both embraced and kissed each other farewell. Abū'l-muḥsin showed courage by throwing a few words of hope but it didn't change the dismayed face of Kūpuk Mirza. They were decapitated and their heads were carried to Shaybāni Khān in Pul-i-Sālār.

Babur Sets Out for Qandahār

Shaybāni's terror reigned high within the whole Tīmūrid clan. Shāh Beg and his younger brother Muḥammad Muqīm, perplexed by the probable attack by Shaybāni, sent envoys to Babur. Those envoys carried letters reminding them of duty, a sign of amity and good wishes. In one of the letters personally written by Muqīm, he explicitly invited Babur to stand by them. By reading the letters and messages conveyed by the envoys, Babur was convinced that the Shāh Beg and Muqīm were looking upon him with hope. Babur went on to consult with the begs and counsellors. It was concluded in the following manner:*

> We were to get an army to horse, join the Arghūn begs and decide in accord and agreement with them, whether to move into Khurāsān or elsewhere as might seem good.

* Babur, Abdul Rahim Khan-I-Khanan (trans.), *Tuzk-e Babri*, Delhi: Akbar, 1589, p. Folio 207b. This manuscript is available in National Museum, New Delhi. The Persian translation was done from the original Turkic manuscript of Babur. This was translated by author from the copy kept at National Museum, New Delhi.

Ḥabība Sulṭān Begum (Babur addressed her as aunt) met the convoy of Babur in Ghaznī. She had come from Herī accompanied by Khusrau Kūkūldāsh, Sulṭān Qulī Chūnāq and Gadāī Balāl to make arrangements to bring her daughter Maṣ'ūma Sulṭān Begum. They too were seeking refuge in the might of Babur after having not been given a place with Ibn-i-ḥusain Mīrzā and Abū'l-muḥsin Mīrzā.

Babur's army came across a mass of traders from Hindustan in Qalāt. Perhaps they were stuck because of the riads of Aūzbegs. Babur's men were of clear opinion that they should be plundered for they were in enemies' territory, but Babur didn't approve of it. He says, 'What is the traders' offence? If we, looking to God's pleasure, leave such scrapings of gain aside, the Highest God will apportion our reward. It is now just as it was a short time back when we rode out to raid the Ghiljī; many of you then were of one mind to raid the Mahmand Afghāns, their sheep and goods, their wives, and families, just because they were within five miles of you! Then as now, I did not agree with you. On the very next day the Highest God apportioned you more sheep belonging to Afghān enemies than had ever before fallen to the share of the army.'

Having said that Babur went ahead to collect a small *peshkash* (offering) which was taken from each trader after dismounting on the other side of Qalāt. It was then that the following two Mīrzās joined them fleeing from Qandahār:

a) Mīrzā Khān (Wais) who post defeat in Kābul had been allowed to go into Khurāsān.
b) 'Abdu'r-razzāq Mīrzā who had stayed on in Khurāsān when Babur had left.

As a surprise, the mother of Jahāngīr Mīrzā's son Pīr-i-Muḥammad, (a grandson of Pahār Mīrzā) had come with them and waited on Babur[36]. Then Babur sent a messenger with letters to Shāh Beg and Muqīm:[*]

[*] Babur, Abdul Rahim Khan-I-Khanan (trans.), *Tuzk-e Babri*, Delhi: Akbar, 1589, p. Folio 208. This manuscript is available in National Museum, New Delhi. The Persian translation was done from the original Turkic manuscript of Babur. This was translated by author from the copy kept at National Museum, New Delhi.

> Here we are at your word; a stranger-foe like the Aūzbeg has taken Khurāsān; come! let us settle, in concert and amity, what will be for the general good.

But their actions were in total discord with the letter of invitation to Babur. They were ill-mannered and rude as Babur has stated. To show the vulgarity (as Babur has said) Shāh Beg stamped his letter to Babur in the middle of its reverse.[37] Perhaps he would have forgotten all their ill manners and rude answers, but there was something which prevented Babur from doing so. He quotes the below line with this context in *Baburnama*:

> A strife-stirring word will accomplish the downfall of an ancient line.

Babur says that they acted shabbily towards households, families and the hordes for around four decades.

Babur and his men moved on to Guzar steadily.[38] Babur again tried for a deliberate truce with the Arghūns. But they paid no heed. Now he was sure that the battle was inevitable. The very next day Babur asked his men to array for the war and put on their mail. Beautifully arrayed on right and left, they marched for Qandahār.

The Battle of Qandahār

Shāh Beg and Muqīm had seated themselves under an awning set in front of the maze of the Qandahār hill. It was the same place where Babur had a rock residence carved out. Muqīm's men pushed forward through the array of trees. There was one Ṯūfān Arghūn, who was known to be a close ally of Babur's enemy. He had fled to join Babur's army when they were near Shahr-i-ṣafā. He knew quite a few secrets which would help Babur in this battle.

One 'Ashaqu'l-lāh was briskly leading eight soldiers. They were all prepared to bring all troubles to Babur. But Ṯūfān joined the party. He took on 'Ashaqu'l-lāh and his eight with all his might all alone. Perhaps he saw this as a big chance to prove his loyalty to Babur. After clashing the swords for long, 'Ashaqu'l-lāh was unhorsed and beheaded by Ṭūfān. The head was brought to Babur which he accepted as a great omen.

Babur was clear that a proper battle could not be fought within the suburbs and trees and accordingly, he led his troop to the skirts of hill. They reached a meadow on the Qandahār side of the torrent, opposite Khalishak. Just when they had dismounted and settled for camping, Sher Qulī the scout brought the news of a strongly arrayed enemy making a move towards them.

Perhaps the time wasn't right for Babur. The whole army, after the long march from Qalāt, was extremely exhausted, down with thirst and hunger. Hence, most of them had scattered looking for cattle, sheep, grain and other victuals. But they had to respond to the enemy. Babur did not bother collecting the scattered men and marched ahead to face the enemy. Babur and his men ran the fastest they could. Babur has claimed that although his army comprised less than a couple of thousand men, he had to gallop ahead with half of that number. As mentioned in *Baburnama*, despite having way fewer men, they were organized, posted and arrayed in one of the best strategies that Babur ever made. Babur had selected a few warriors for his immediate command in a group of tens and fifties. Each ten and fifty was decorated under a leader who knew the post in the right or left of the centre for his ten or his fifty.[39] About this situation, Babur has said:*

> They were the one who knew the role of each one the battle and was there on the observant watch; so that, after mounting, the right and left, right and left hands, right and left sides, charged right and left without the trouble of arraying them or the need of a tawāchī.
>
> The right wing (barānghār) was Mīrzā Khān (Wais), Sherīm Ṭaghāī, Yārak Ṭaghāī with his elder and younger brethren, Chilma Moghūl, Ayūb Beg, Muḥammad Beg, Ibrāhīm Beg, 'Alī Sayyid Moghūl with his Moghūls, Sulṭān Qulī chuhra, Khudā-bakhsh and Abū'l-ḥasan with his elder and younger brethren.

* Babur, Abdul Rahim Khan-I-Khanan (trans.), *Tuzk-e Babri*, Delhi: Akbar, 1589, p. Folio 209-10b. This manuscript is available in National Museum, New Delhi. The Persian translation was done from the original Turkic manuscript of Babur. This was translated by author from the copy kept at National Museum, New Delhi.

The left (jawānghār) was 'Abdu'r-razzāq Mīrzā, Qāsim Beg, Tīngrī-bīrdī, Qambar-i-'alī, Aḥmad Aīlchī-būghā, Ghūrī Barlās, Sayyid Ḥusain Akbar, and Mīr Shāh Qūchin.

The advance (aīrāwal) was Nāṣir Mīrzā, Sayyid Qāsim Lord of the Gate, Muḥibb-i-'alī the armourer, Pāpā Aūghulī (Pāpā's son?), Allāh-wairan Turkmān, Sher Qulī Moghūl the scout with his elder and younger brethren, and Muḥammad 'Alī.

In the centre (ghūl), on my right hand, were Qāsim Kūkūldāsh, Khusrau Kūkūldāsh, Sulṭān Muḥammad Dūldāī, Shāh Maḥmūd the secretary, Qūl-i-bāyazīd the taster, and Kamāl the sherbet-server; on my left were Khwāja Muḥammad 'Alī, Nāṣir's Dost, Nāṣir's Mīrīm, Bābā Sher-zād, Khān-qulī, Walī the treasurer, Qūtlūq-qadam the scout, Maqsūd the water-bearer (sū-chī), and Bābā Shaikh. Those in the centre were all of my household; there were no great begs; not one of those enumerated had reached the rank of beg. Those inscribed in this būī were Sher Beg, Ḥātim the Armoury-master, Kūpuk, Qulī Bābā, Abū'l-ḥasan the armourer;—of the Moghūls, Aūrūs (Russian) 'Alī Sayyid, Darwīsh-i-'alī Sayyid, Khūsh-kīldī, Chilma, Dost-kīldī, Chilma Tāghchī, Dāmāchī, Mindī;—of the Turkmāns, Manṣūr, Rustam-i-'alī with his elder and younger brother, and Shāh Nāẓir and Sīūndūk.

The enemy was in two divisions, one under Shāh Shujā' Arghūn, known as Shāh Beg and hereafter to be written of simply as Shāh Beg, the other under his younger brother Muqīm.

Some estimated the dark mass of Arghūns at 6 or 7000 men; no question whatever but that Shāh Beg's own men in mail were 4 or 5000. He faced our right, Muqīm with a force smaller may-be than his brother's, faced our left. Muqīm made a mightily strong attack on our left, that is on Qāsim Beg from whom two or three persons came before fighting began, to ask for reinforcement; we however could not detach a man because in front of us also the enemy was very strong.

Babur and his men commenced the attack without any delay. The Arghūn enemies fell suddenly on Babur's van. They turned it back and bumped it into their centre. The enemy shot many arrows. As soon as the first phase of arrows ended, Babur and his men advanced. Just then a man came in front of Babur, dismounted and targeted him with his arrow. Babur moved briskly and thwarted the move. The man's many attempts failed and he rode back pushing away. Babur felt that it was probably Shāh Beg himself.

The battle was turning intense with each passing moment. During the fight, Pīrī Beg Turkmān[40] and five of his brethren surrendered and turned their faces from the foe with a turban in hand. They were now against Babur.

Babur was a bit anxious with the prevailing situation, and he knew very well that whatever it may take the first thing was to overcome the foe. The battle had intensified, leaving Babur extremely exhausted. On the left, Babur's troops had gone as far as the irrigation channel surrounded by a tangle of trees. Muqīm was positioned on the opposite end with more men than Babur.

Babur has mentioned in the *Baburnama* that what Allah did was right.

Around three or four tree-tangled water channels flowing towards Qandahār lay between Babur's troop and Muqīm. They were exactly at crossings and allowed no passage at all. Ḥalwāchī Tarkhān went in the water with Tīngrī-bīrdī and Qaṃbar-i-'alī who had got wounded. An arrow stuck Qāsim Beg's forehead while it hit Ghūrī Barlās just above the eyebrow that came out of his cheek. Babur has said that despite massive losses his army was giving a good fight. They had crossed those channels towards the maze of Murghān-koh (Birds' hill). Babur saw someone running away on a grey tīpūchāq along the skirt of the hill. He again thought that it was Shāh Beg.

Babur's men fought well and beat their opponents despite the weaker initial odds. Most of them were unhorsed. Not many were left on Babur's side either. Babur counted them to be eleven, including 'Abdu'l-lāh the librarian. Babur observed that Muqīm was holding onto his ground by fighting hard. Ignoring the fewness of men left out of thousands, putting their trust in Allah, they began beating the nagarets and moved ahead to face Muqīm with full force. Babur has composed bilingual verses about this battle:*

* Babur, Abdul Rahim Khan-I-Khanan (trans.), *Tuzk-e Babri*, Delhi: Akbar, 1589, p. Folio 211. This manuscript is available in National Museum, New Delhi. The Persian translation was done from the original Turkic manuscript of Babur. This was translated by author from the copy kept at National Museum, New Delhi.

(Turkī) For few or for many God is full strength;
No man has might in His Court.
(Arabic) How often, God willing it, a small force has vanquished a large one!

The empowering sound of nagarets and the powerful approach of Babur's men weakened Muqīm mentally. He forgot his plan of action and chose to flee. Babur has thanked Allah for this.

The victorious Babur with the remaining men moved towards Qandahār. He dismounted in Farrukh-zād Beg's Chārbāgh. Babur has said that no trace of that park was found at the time he was writing these passages.

Babur's Entry in Qandahār

Shāh Beg and Muqīm had already run away towards Shāl, Quetta and Zamīn-dāwar, respectively and didn't even attempt to enter Qandahār. No one was left to defend the fort. Of course, people like Aḥmad 'Alī Tarkhān along with other brethren of Qulī Beg Arghūn were present inside the fort, but Babur was sure that they would do nothing.

Despite all the flaws, they all had a very good relationship with Babur. He sat in a meeting with them to make important arrangements for the way forward. They rightly sought protection for the women and children of their brethren. Babur granted what they requested and on top also bestowed favours. Once the parley was done, they opened the Māshūr Gate of the town. But the populace without a leader was quite reactionary. They didn't let the other gates open for Babur. He couldn't tolerate it, went ahead with a few households and killed three of the civilians mercilessly to set an example for the rebels (a typical Tīmūrid trait).

Having set the populace in order, it was time for Babur to collect as much of spoils as he could. He began plundering from Muqīm's treasury which was in the outer fort. When Babur arrived, his aide 'Abdu'r-razzāq Mīrzā was just dismounting there. Babur handed over a few things to him and assigned Dost-i-Nāṣir Beg, Qul-i-bāyazīd and Muḥammad Bakhshī of the booty. Having done so Babur rushed to the citadel and appointed Khwāja Muḥammad 'Alī, Shāh Maḥmūd and Ṯaghāī Shāh Bakhshī as in charge of Shāh Beg's treasury. He sent Nāṣir's Mīrīm and Maqṣūd to keep the house of Ẕū'n-nūn's Dīwān Mīr Jān for Nāṣir Mīrzā. The house of Shaikh Abū-sa'īd Tarkhānī was kept for Mīrzā Khān and one house[41] was also kept for 'Abdu'r-razzāq Mīrzā.

There was no trace of any money, and no one had any clue as such. That very night, when Babur and his men stayed in the citadel, Shāh Beg's slave Saṃbhal was captured and brought in. Babur handed him over to someone as a slave. But as no one kept a watch on him, he managed to escape. The next day, Babur rode back to his camp in Farrukh-zād Beg's Chārbāgh.

Having finished the battle, Babur had to set the administration right. He handed over the country of Qandahār to Nāṣir Mīrzā. The treasures had been set in order and loaded in the carriages. Nāṣir Mīrzā carried loads of white tankas off a string of camels at the citadel treasury to keep them. Babur has mentioned that he did not demand it back and just gave it to him.

Having conquered Qandahār, Babur moved out. He and his troops dismounted in the meadows of Qūsh-khāna. He let his army rest after the long battle. Babur went for an excursion. When he returned to the camp, he found it unrecognizable. It seemed like another camp. The spoils from the battle had completely transformed it. He has described it as follows:*

> It was another camp! not to be recognized! Excellent tīpūchāqs, strings and strings of he-camels, she-camels, and mules, bearing saddlebags (khurzīn) of silken stuffs and cloth, —tents of scarlet (cloth) and velvet, all sorts of awnings, every kind of workshop, ass-load after ass-load of chests! The goods of the elder and younger (Arghūn) brethren had been kept in separate treasuries; out of each had come chest upon chest, bale upon bale of stuffs and `clothes-in-wear (artmāq artmāq), sack upon sack of white tankas. In aūtāgh

* Babur, Abdul Rahim Khan-I-Khanan (trans.), *Tuzk-e Babri*, Delhi: Akbar, 1589, p. Folio 212. This manuscript is available in National Museum, New Delhi. The Persian translation was done from the original Turkic manuscript of Babur. This was translated by author from the copy kept at National Museum, New Delhi.

> and chādar (lattice-tent and pole-tent) was much spoil for every man soever; many sheep also had been taken but sheep were less cared about!

Babur handed over everything to Qāsim Beg Muqīm's retainers in Qalāt, namely Qūj Arghūn and Tāju'd-dīn Maḥmūd, all their goods and spoils. Babur knew Qāsim Beg very well and as a wise one, he continually advised Babur to stay longer near Qandahār. Babur finally marched away. Now that Babur had bestowed Qandahār on Nāṣir Mīrzā he was permitted to go there while Babur cruised for Kābul.

Babur has mentioned that since there was no point in distributing the spoils near Qandahār,[42] it was done at the Qarā-bāgh. Babur was delayed there for a couple of days as it was important to not move ahead without getting the measure of the spoils they had got. Since they had got hold of a huge number of coins it wasn't going to be feasible to count them and hence, they were apportioned by weighing them in scales. The households, retainers and the begs of all the ranks kept on loading up ass-load after ass-load of satchels full of white tankas. They also paid their soldiers for this spoil.

He returned to Kābul with added honour and of course, he was extremely happy to with the goods and treasure. His reputation had gotten highly elevated. Upon returning, Babur married (in AD 1507) his uncle Sulṭān Aḥmad Mīrzā's daughter Ma'ṣūma Sulṭān Begum. He had asked her for marriage at Khurāsān and had brought her here from there.

Shaybāni Khān at Qandahār

Within a few days after the glorious victory of Qandahār, a servant of Nāṣir Mīrzā brought bad news. Shaybāni Khān had laid siege to Qandahār. It was Muqīm who after having fled to Zamīn-dāwar went further to see Shaybāni Khān. A servant of Shāh Beg's too had been to see Shaybāni Khān. They both instigated and requested Shaybāni to come, and he didn't deny it. He swiftly entered Qandahār by the mountain road.[43] Shaybāni was also expecting to find Babur there. Perhaps this was the fear for which Qāsim Beg was insisting on Babur's exit from the vicinity of Qandahār at the earliest. For this instance, Babur has mentioned following verse in *Baburnama*:*

(Persian) What a mirror shews to the young man,
A baked brick shews to the old one!

Shaybāni Khān besieged Nāṣir Mīrzā in Qandahār as soon as he arrived.

The news had left people in Kābul petrified. Hearing the news Babur immediately summoned the begs for counsel. His discussion went as follows:†

> Strangers and ancient foes, such as are Shaybāni Khān and the Aūzbegs, are in possession of all the countries once held by Tīmūr Beg's descendants; even where Turks and Chaghatāīs survive in corners and border-lands, they have all joined the Aūzbeg, willingly or with aversion; one remains, I myself, in Kābul, the foe mightily strong, I very weak, with no means of making terms, no strength to oppose; that, in the presence of such power and potency, we had to think of some place for ourselves and, at this crisis and in the crack of time there was, to put a wider space between us and the strong foeman; that choice lay between Badakhshān and Hindustan and that decision must now be made.

Qāsim Beg and Sherīm Ṭaghāī agreed for Badakhshān[44] while many other households beg including Babur preferred going towards Hindustan to accomplish an unfinished dream of Tīmūr.

Qandahār was taken and Babur had bestowed Qalāt and the country of Turnūk (Tarnak) on 'Abdu'r-razzāq Mīrzā. Accordingly, Babur had left him in Qalāt. By this time, the Aūzbegs had completely besieged Qandahār. Babur had no choice, given the fear of Shaybāni Khān, but to return to Kābul. By the time he reached, Babur was all

* Babur, Abdul Rahim Khan-I-Khanan (trans.), *Tuzk-e Babri*, Delhi: Akbar, 1589, p. Folio 213. This manuscript is available in National Museum, New Delhi. The Persian translation was done from the original Turkic manuscript of Babur. This was translated by author from the copy kept at National Museum, New Delhi.
† Ibid.

set to march out for Hindustan. He took to opportunity to pass on the charge of Kābul to him.

Now the land of Badakhshān was without a ruler or ruler's heir. Mīrzā Khān was eager enough to go there. Babur has mentioned in *Baburnama* that it was Mīrzā's relationship with Shāh Begum,[45] along with her approval, which pushed him to go there. Babur permitted him to go, and the honourable begum too joined him. Babur badly wanted his maternal aunt Mihr-nigār Khānum to be with him as a blood relation, but she too was keen to go to Badakhshān. She went to Badakhshān.

The Second Start for Hindustan

In September of AD 1507 (first Jumada), Babur began to execute the plan of going to Hindustan. They began by marching out of Kābul, taking the road through little Kābul and going down by Sūrkh-rabāṭ to Qūrūq-sāī.

Babur has previously talked of Afghān thieves living between Kābul and Lamghān (Ningnahār), who had caused trouble for long. It had come to Babur's notice that the thieves' misdeed had multiplied as they heard of his march towards Hindustan. One fine morning, when Babur and his men marched from Jagdālīk, the Afghans located between it and Lamghān were ready to block the pass. Accordingly, they arrayed on the mountain to the north and advanced with a loud sound of tambour holding shining swords in their hands. As Babur and his men took the pass, he instructed them to keep moving and pushed along the mountainside. The Afghāns stood firm at their ground and were so well organized that they would not let even one arrow fly. They soon took up the fight with Babur's men.

Babur has not given the details of this fight in the *Baburnama*, but he has hinted that the Afghāns were brutally beaten. Babur's army brutalized them with an intense shower of arrows. Most Afghāns were caught and brought to Babur, and he ordered the execution of each of them to set an example. Then, he resumed his march and dismounted not before reaching the Adīnapūr-fort in the Nangarhār tūmān.

Babur was clueless about where he would go, camp and stay en route Hindustan. He had just marched up and down, camping in places never heard of before.

Autumn arrived and with it, the rice was harvested by the lowlanders.

It was late in the autumn; most lowlanders had carried in their rice. He was informed by the local people that the Kafirs[46] living up the water of the ‘Alīshang tūmān grew massive quantity of rice. Babur thought that it would be a great idea to collect rice for winter supplies for his army from there. Thus, Babur rode out of the Nangarhār-dale crossed the Bārān River at Sāīkal. They rode very swiftly and reached as far as Pūramīn Valley, the place which was full of rice cultivation located at the bottom of hill. Babur's soldiers collected a huge mass of rice after threatening the Kafirs. Most ran away without resistance, and those who resisted were put to death. Babur had sent out a few men to look out on a maze of the Pūranīm valley. While they were making a return, a few Kafirs rushed from the hill above and began to shoot arrows endlessly. In this fight, Qāsim Beg's son-in-law Pūrān fell prey. They attacked him with an axe but few of Babur's men stood and helped him flee to save his life. Somehow, they were able to cope with the situation and spent the night in the rice fields of Kafirs. The next day, they returned to the camp collecting a huge mass of provisions looted from the Kafir's properties.

Babur had reached all the way till Mandrāwar only to realize that it was not desirable to go into Hindustan at that time. Babur has not mentioned the detailed reason for abandoning his mission.

He sent Mullā Bābā of Pashāghar along with a few men back to Kābul and he marched to Atar and Shīwa where he stayed for a few days. He then visited Kūnār and Nūr-gal. From Kūnār he went back to camp riding on a raft. Babur was extremely pleased sitting on a raft:*

> It was the first time I had sat on one; it pleased me much, and the raft came into common use thereafter.

* Babur, Abdul Rahim Khan-I-Khanan (trans.), *Tuzk-e Babri*, Delhi: Akbar, 1589, p. Folio 214b. This manuscript is available in National Museum, New Delhi. The Persian translation was done from the original Turkic manuscript of Babur. This was translated by author from the copy kept at National Museum, New Delhi.

Shaybāni Khān Leaves Qandahār

While Babur had abandoned his plan for Hindustan, Mullā Bābā of Farkat arrived with some news. Shaybāni Khān had not been able to take the citadel despite taking the outer fort of Qandahār and he chose to retire. He also brought the news that Nasir Mīrzā had gone to Ghaznī after leaving Qandahār.

Shaybāni Khān's arrived in Qandahār just a few days after Babur had departed. It was so shocking that the garrison couldn't even attempt to secure the outer fort. He took it away but his all attempts to take control of the citadel kept failing although he assaulted the place using mines multiple times. But there came a time when Shaybāni's fate had smiled, and the citadel was almost lost. The situation had turned anxious and four people responsible for external security, Khwāja Muḥammad Amīn, Khwāja Dost Khāwand, Muḥammad 'Alī, a foot-soldier, and Shāmī jumped down the walls and ran away. The citadel was all set to surrender, and it was then that Shaybāni interrupted peace. Babur has mentioned why it happened the way it did:*

> It appears that before he went there, he had sent his ḥaram to Nīrah-tū,[47] and that in Nīrahtū some-one lifted up his head and got command in the fort; the Khān therefore made a sort of peace and retired from Qandahār.

Babur was back to Kābul by the Bād-i-pīch road abandoning the project of Hindustan yet again, which was in the middle of winter. Babur had ordered an inscription to be cut on a stone above Bād-i-pīch mentioning the date of transit and the crossing of the pass.[48] It was Ḥāfiẓ Mīrak who wrote the inscription. Babur has complained in the *Baburnama* that Ustād Shāh Muhammad did not perform the cutting of stone properly because of haste.

---

* Babur, Abdul Rahim Khan-I-Khanan (trans.), *Tuzk-e Babri*, Delhi: Akbar, 1589, p. Folio 215. This manuscript is available in National Museum, New Delhi. The Persian translation was done from the original Turkic manuscript of Babur. This was translated by author from the copy kept at National Museum, New Delhi.

In the meantime, Babur had already bestowed Ghaznī on Nāṣir Mīrzā, Nangarhār tūmān Mandrāwar, Nūr valley, Kūnār and Nūrgal to 'Abdu'r-razzāq Mīrzā.

Padishah Babur Becomes Father

Till this very time, every ruler from Tīmūr Beg's legacy was addressed as Mīrzā. Babur brought a change. He instructed people to address him as Padishah.[49]

On 6 March of AD 1508, on the fourth day of the last month of Ẕū'l-qa'da, when the sun lay in Pisces, Babur became father to Humāyūn, his first living child, in the citadel of Kābul. The date of his birth was first found by the poet Maulānā Masnadī along with his name, Sulṭān Humāyūn Khān.[50] It is also recorded by a minor poet of Kābul found in Shāh-i-fīrūs-qadr (Shāh of victorious might).

Babur has mentioned that his first child received the name Humāyūn six days after his birth. Babur organized a feast of nativity at Chārbāgh. Babur showered gifts and a huge mass of white tankas over all his begs, small and great alike—it was never done before. Babur has written, 'It was a first-rate feast!'

Even as happiness was re-entering Babur's life, a new trouble was brewing as well. In May of AD 1508, a Moghūl rebellion had picked up.

Once Babur was back from the raids, Qūj Beg, Faqīr-i-'alī, Karīm-dād and Bābā Chuhra were conspiring to desert him. Babur received intel on the conspiracy and sent people to catch a duo that was found just below Astarghach. Their rebellious words were reported to Babur which were no different from what they spoke during the lifetime of Jahāngīr Mirza.[51]

Babur ordered their execution amid the bazaar. Accordingly, they were captured, tied by rope and taken to public places. They were just about to be hanged when Khalifa came with Qāsim Beg's message. He had appealed to Babur to pardon them for their offences. Maintaining a sense of respect for Qāsim, Babur let them go away with the *act of being hung to death* yet ordered them to be kept in jail.

Now there was news about Khusrau Shāh's retainers from Ḥiṣār and Qūndūz. They joined hands with the headmen of the Moghūls, Chilma, 'Alī Sayyid, Sakma, Sher-qulī and Aīkū-sālam. They were also joined by Khusrau Shāh's favourite Chaghatāī retainers under Sulṯān 'Alī chuhra and Khudabakhsh, along with 3000 brave Turkmān soldiers led by Sīūndūk and Shāh Naẕar.[52] A mutiny was raised against Babur. They had congregated in front of Khwāja Riwāj, right from the Sūng-qūrghān meadow to the Chālāk. 'Abdu'r-razzāq Mīrzā, too joined them while coming from Nīng-nahār.[53]

It is interesting to note that Babur was apprised about the matter earlier, too. Muḥibb-i-'alī, the armourer, had passed on the message of this assembly to Khalifa and Mullā Bābā twice, and on both occasions, a hint was given to Babur. But Babur ignored it, thinking the matter to be implausible. He gave no attention.

One fine night around night-time prayer, Babur was seated in the audience hall of the Chār-bāgh. Mūsa Khwāja came running and whispered in his ear, 'The Moghūls are really rebelling! We do not know for certain whether they have got 'Abdu'r-razzāq to join them. They have not settled to rise to-night.'

The news had left Babur badly disturbed. He went running towards the harems in the Yūrūnchqa-garden and the Bāgh-i-khilwat. Babur saw a page, servitor and messenger nearing them. He was assured of a safe environment there and moved away. Babur, accompanied by the chief slave, went towards the town and along the trench. Babur went riding to the Iron Gate where Khwāja Muḥammad 'Alī[54] met him while coming by the bazaar road from the opposite direction.

Summary of Babur's Twenty-Five Years

A lot transpired in twenty-five years of Babur's life. He lost his father at the age of eleven and got the responsibility of ruling Ferghana with a hostile rebellious situation all around. While his uncles tried their best to dethrone him, his maternal grandmother Aisan Duglat Begum could make him stand firm. He always desired to gain Samarkand which he did for a brief period but eventually, it slipped away. It was in the quest to retain Samarkand that he lost his sister to his old Uzbek foe, Shaybāni Khān. When life began to turn even more miserable, Babur had to take refuge in Tashkent, which was ruled by his maternal uncle. But Babur gained no comfort even there. Finally with the short-lived victories and much of miseries for a decade since having become the ruler of Ferghana, Babur reached Kābul in

AD 1504 which was once ruled by his paternal uncle Ulugh Beg-II who had died leaving behind only an infant as heir and Mukin Beg had shown the authority to rule. Babur established his supremacy and would stay there until finally making an entry in Hindustan in AD 1526. Babur's approach and stay in Kābul had been a bloody one. We observe the trait of Timur reflecting deeply in Babur where he keeps slaughtering and making pyramids of skulls.

In AD 1505, when revenues had gone extremely low in the newly established mountain kingdom, Babur decided to enter Hindustan for the first time, but the expedition ended at the crossing of Khyber Pass. The same year he united with Sulṭān Husayn Mirza Bayqarah of Herat, who was a fellow Tīmūrid and distant relative, against their common enemy, the Uzbek Shaybāni. But as Husayn Mirza died in AD 1506, the venture against Shaybāni failed as the former's son showed no interest in going to war. Yet, Babur chose to stay in Herat after being invited by the two Mirza brothers. He stayed there for around two months and then had to leave because the resources had begun to diminish completely. Later, whatever was leftover, was overrun by the old foe Shaybāni. Eventually, the Mirza brothers fled. Now that Herat was gone, Babur remained the only reigning Tīmūrid ruler. Many princes of the clan came to Babur to gain refuge in Kābul as Shaybāni had been invading the western parts. Eventually, looking at the prevailing situations, Babur assumed the title of 'Padishah', among the Tīmūrids. In my opinion, this title was not of much significance as most of the ancestral land was taken and even Kābul had been witnessing Shaybāni Khān's threat.

Given the circumstances, Babur decided to make a second attempt at one of his most desired lands, Hindustan only to fail again. Humayun was born after the failure of this mission.

While studying the *Baburnama*, I observed an interesting point. Babur has not chronicled his life for around eleven years, and one needs to rely upon other sources to juxtapose a case for continuity in the biography. I have explained about this gap in the next section.

But this gap has also allowed me to bring a halt to the tale of the pioneer of the second Tīmūrid colonization. The tale of Babur post-Humayun's birth and the latter's life will be addressed in the next volume of this series. The next volume would show us a drastically different Babur. It would capture all the realities of his attempt to wage jihad against the *Kafirs* of Hindustan and detailed account of the loot.

Author's Note on Absence of Records Between AD 1508 to AD 1519

A careful reading of the *Baburnama* and Gulbadan's *Humāyūnnāma** shows that Babur was compiling the chronicles of AD 1509 not long before his illness and consequent death. It is evident that the records between AD 1509 and AD 1519 are completely missing, or one can say that there is a broken thread in his autobiography. Annette Susannah Beveridge writes, 'there is a lacuna of narrative extending over nearly eleven years'.

William Erskine has spoken about this period in his book, *History of India* while penning part of Babur's biography. But he ignores to use other firsthand sources like *Habību's-siyar* and *Tārīkh-i-rashīdī*. Abel Pavet de Courteille did translate the *Baburnama* from the Chagatai text, but he too does not cover this unchronicled patch. Most of the academicians who have tried to dwell over this patch of Babur's life have made it highly sympathetic. This is something which even Annette Susannah Beveridge has pointed out. Extreme balance is needed while dealing with especially the first seven years of the non-chronicled period. It is because secondary sources do tell us that Babur was involved in bitter conflicts between the Shi'a and Sunni. So, I am going to attempt to present a brisk summary (in the appendix) of events based on the reading of *Baburnama* translated by Annette Susannah Beveridge. She has used sources which have been not used by William Erskine.

This must be admitted that no other recent contemporary source tells the tale of Babur's life for this period as Babur himself would have narrated. More than anything, the biggest problem that I see for the secondary sources is that almost all of them do not have the central theme of Babur's biography. Among the best-known sources *Ḥabību's-siyar of Khwānd-amīr* and *Tārīkh-i-rashīdī* of *Ḥaidar Mīrzā Dūghlāt*'s top the list. The former was completed nominally seven

* Gulbadan, *The History of Humāyūn (Humāyūn-nāma)*, (ed.) Annette Susannah Beveridge. (trans.) Annette Susannah Beveridge, London: Royal Asiatic Society, 1902, p. 225.

years before (AD 1524 to AD 1525) the death of Babur. Lots of matter was added by Khwānd-amīr after he came to Hindustan in AD 1538. *Tārīkh-i-rashīdī* was completed under Humāyūn in AD 1547, just three years before the author was killed at the hands of Kashmiris. One can say that his work is one of the most important sources for everyone who is especially interested in studying Babur. I come to this belief considering how close he was to Babur's family. He stayed in Babur's protection from when he turned eleven to when he turned thirteen. For the next nineteen years, he served under Sa'īd Khān in Kāshghar, who happened to be a mutual cousin between Babur and him. When Khān died he went on to serve Babur's sons Kāmrān and Humāyūn in Hindustan.

Annette Susannah Beveridge also indicates a piece of literature called *Sūlūku'l-mulūk* published by a Sunnī centre of Aūzbegs. It was written by *Faẓl bin Ruzbahān Isfahānī* at the orders of 'Ubaidu'l-lāh Khān Aūzbeg. It is a treatise on Islamic law and was written to fulfil the vow that the latter had made before attacking Babur in AD 1512 at the shrine of Khwāja Aḥmad Yasawī (in Ḥaẓrat Turkistān). The vow was that if he would turn victorious against Babur he would conform exactly with the divine (Islamic) law and uphold it in Māwarā'u'n-nahr (Transoxiana). The preface of this text talks of the spread of sacrilege in Transoxiana because of Babur's invasions.

Before jumping into the works of *Firsihta*, I thought it would be great to dwell on his own sources as he was writing almost a century and a half after Babur's death. It was the *Tārīkh-i Ḥājī Muḥammad 'Ārif Qandahārī* that appears frequently in the writing. This becomes an important source because he belonged to Qandahār where Babur had enough adventure during his unchronicled years. The author was also the witness of Bairām Khān-i-khānān's assassination on 31 January of AD 1561. He was the servant of the assassinated. Unfortunately, even though all his records around Akbar survive, there is no manuscript concerning Babur's period.

Then we have a Shia source called *Lubbu't-tawārīkh* by *Yahya Kazwīnī* written in AD 1541. But it gives us only a brief account of Babur's life. It was commissioned by *Shāh Ismā'īl Ṣafawī's* son *Bahrām*. We have one more Shia source published by the Ṣafawī Center. It is called *Tārīkh-i-'ālam-arāī* and was written by Mīr

Sikandar. It was completed in AD 1616. One can get a brief account of how Babur dealt with Shāh Ismā'īl in this source.

One of the most important sources for Babur's unchronicled years however in my opinion can be Firishta's *Tārīkh-i-firishta*. It was finished in the first quarter of the seventeenth century and was commissioned by Jahāngīr (Babur's great-grandson). While studying the works of William Erskine, I observed that he has referred frequently to *Tārīkh* by Khwāfī Khān. It can be considered as a tertiary source as it was commissioned by Aurangzeb, based on Firishta's works. It gives us only the summary of Babur's period. One can also refer to *Tārīkh-i-badāyūnī* by Shaikh 'Abdu'l-qādir and *Tārīkh-i-sind* by Mīr Ma'ṣūm.

To avoid injustice for the readers, I have put a narrative around the unchronicled years based on *Baburnama* translated by Annette Susannah Beveridge in Appendix B.

Epilogue

Three Invaders from Tramontana and Jihad

Babur has mentioned in the *Baburnama* about two invaders from Tramontana, from the time of Prophet Muhammad's demise, who have ruled and conquered Hindustan as below:

a) Mahmud of Ghaznī
b) Muhammad of Ghor

Babur says that the first one's descendants sat long on the seat of government in Hindustan and the second one's slaves and dependents royally shepherded the seat. He considered himself to be the third one.

Babur saw it as his legal right to sit on the throne of Hindustan, drawing inspiration from the Timur's conquest of north-western India. Nevertheless, his actions in days to come (detailed discussion in volume 2) do tell us that jihad and victory of Islam was indeed his main motive once he entered Hindustan. Below is a discussion as the prelude of the Battle of Khanwa in Babur's own words:*

* Babur. Tuzk-e Babri. (trans.) Abdul Rahim Khan-I-Khanan. illuminated. Delhi: Akbar, 1589. p. Folio 318b. This manuscript is available in National Museum, New Delhi. The Persian translation was done from the original Turkic manuscript of Babur. This was translated by author from the copy kept at National Museum, New Delhi.

(March 17th, 1527) On Saturday the 13th day of the second Jumāda of the date 933, a day blessed by the words, God hath blessed your Saturday, the army of Islām was encamped near the village of Kānwa, a dependency of Bīāna, hard by a hill which was four miles from the enemies of the Faith. When those accursed infidel foes of Muḥammad's religion heard the reverberation of the armies of Islām, they arrayed their ill-starred forces and moved forward with one heart, relying on their mountain-like, demon-shaped elephants, as had relied the Lords of the Elephant[1] who went to overthrow the sanctuary (ka'ba) of Islām.

Having these elephants, the wretched Hindus
Became proud, like the Lords of the Elephant;
Yet were they odious and vile as is the evening of death,
Blacker than night, outnumbering the stars,
All such as fire is but their heads upraised
In hate, as rises its smoke in the azure sky,
Ant-like they come from right and from left,
Thousands and thousands of horse and foot.

They advanced towards the victorious encampment, intending to give battle. The holy warriors of Islām, trees in the garden of valor, moved forward in ranks straight as serried pines and, like pines uplift their crests to heaven, uplifting their helmet-crests which shone even as shine the hearts of those that strive in the way of the Lord; their array was like Alexander's iron-wall, and, as is the way of the Prophet's Law, straight and firm and strong, as though they were a well-compacted building; and they became fortunate and successful in accordance with the saying, They are directed by their Lord, and they shall prosper.

In that array no rent was frayed by timid souls;
Firm was it as the Shāhanshāh's resolve, strong as the Faith;
Their standards brushed against the sky;
Verily we have granted thee certain victory.

Obeying the cautions of prudence, we imitated the ghāzīs of Rūm by posting matchlockmen (tufanchīān) and cannoneers (ra'd-andāzān)

> along the line of carts which were chained to one another in front of us; in fact, Islām's army was so arrayed and so steadfast that primal Intelligence and the firmament ('aql-i-pīr u charkh-i-aṣīr) applauded the marshalling thereof. To affect this arrangement and organization, Niẓāmu'd-dīn 'Alī Khalīfa, the pillar of the Imperial fortune, exerted himself strenuously; his efforts were in accord with Destiny, and were approved by his sovereign's luminous judgment.

History is an open book. Babur's tale is available—with primary sources—for consumption in an easy way. I hope that the next volume will bring forth a lot more information about the founder of the so-called Moghūl Empire.

Appendix A

Economic Conditions in Tīmūrid Colonization

Table A.1: World Population: Twenty Countries and Regional Totals, AD 1–2003 (Maddison, 2007)

	1	1000	1500	1600	1700	1820	1870	1913	1950	1973	2003
Austria	500	700	2,000	2,500	2,500	3,369	4,520	6,767	6,935	7,586	8,163
Belgium	300	400	1,400	1,600	2,000	3,434	5,096	7,666	8,639	9,738	10,331
Denmark	180	360	600	650	700	1,155	1,888	2,983	4,271	5,022	5,394
Finland	20	40	300	400	400	1,169	1,754	3,027	4,009	4,666	5,204
France	5,000	6,500	15,000	18,500	21,471	31,250	38,440	41,463	41,829	52,157	60,181
Germany	3,000	3,500	12,000	16,000	15,000	24,905	39,231	65,058	68,375	78,950	82,398
Italy	8,000	5,000	10,500	13,100	13,300	20,176	27,888	37,248	47,105	54,797	57,998
Netherlands	200	300	950	1,500	1,900	2,333	3,610	6,164	10,114	13,438	16,223
Norway	100	200	300	400	500	970	1,735	2,447	3,265	3,961	4,555
Sweden	200	400	550	760	1,260	2,585	4,169	5,621	7,014	8,137	8,970
Switzerland	300	300	650	1,000	1,200	1,986	2,655	3,864	4,694	6,441	7,408
UK	800	2,000	3,942	6,170	8,565	21,239	31,400	45,649	50,127	56,210	60,095
12 country total	**18,600**	**19,700**	**48,192**	**62,580**	**68,796**	**114,571**	**162,386**	**227,957**	**256,377**	**301,103**	**326,920**
Portugal	400	600	1,000	1,100	2,000	3,297	4,327	5,972	8,443	8,976	10,480
Spain	3,750	4,000	6,800	8,240	8,770	12,203	16,201	20,263	28,063	34,837	40,217
Other	2,300	1,260	1,340	1,858	1,894	2,969	4,590	6,783	12,058	13,909	16,987
Total western Europe	**25,050**	**25,560**	**57,332**	**73,778**	**81,460**	**133,040**	**187,504**	**260,975**	**304,941**	**358,825**	**394,604**
Eastern Europe	**4,750**	**6,500**	**13,500**	**16,950**	**18,800**	**36,457**	**53,557**	**79,530**	**87,637**	**110,418**	**121,434**
Former USSR	**3,900**	**7,100**	**16,950**	**20,700**	**26,550**	**54,765**	**88,672**	**156,192**	**179,571**	**249,712**	**287,601**
US	680	1,300	2,000	1,500	1,000	9,981	40,241	97,606	152,271	211,909	290,343
Other western offshoots	440	570	800	800	750	1,250	5,847	13,795	24,186	38,932	55,890
Total western offshoots	**1,120**	**1,870**	**2,800**	**2,300**	**1,750**	**11,231**	**46,088**	**111,401**	**176,457**	**250,841**	**346,233**
Mexico	2,200	4,500	7,500	2,500	4,500	6,587	9,219	14,970	28,485	57,557	103,718
Other Latin America	3,400	6,900	10,000	6,100	7,550	15,004	31,180	65,965	137,453	250,316	437,641
Total Latin America	**5,600**	**11,400**	**17,500**	**8,600**	**12,050**	**21,591**	**40,399**	**80,935**	**165,938**	**307,873**	**541,359**
Japan	**3,000**	**7,500**	**15,400**	**18,500**	**27,000**	**31,000**	**34,437**	**51,672**	**83,805**	**108,707**	**127,214**
China	59,600	59,000	103,000	160,000	138,000	381,000	358,000	437,140	546,815	881,940	1,288,400
India	75,000	75,000	110,000	135,000	165,000	209,000	253,000	303,700	359,000	580,000	1,049,700
Other east Asia	11,400	21,100	37,600	43,600	50,700	64,228	89,506	145,893	333,310	565,057	1,018,844
West Asia	19,400	20,000	17,800	21,400	20,800	25,147	30,290	38,956	59,847	112,918	249,809
Total Asia (excl. Japan)	**165,400**	**175,100**	**268,400**	**360,000**	**374,500**	**679,375**	**730,796**	**925,689**	**1,298,972**	**2,139,915**	**3,606,753**
Africa	**17,000**	**32,300**	**46,610**	**55,320**	**61,080**	**74,236**	**90,466**	**124,697**	**228,181**	**390,202**	**853,422**
World	**225,820**	**267,330**	**438,492**	**556,148**	**603,190**	**1,041,695**	**1,271,919**	**1,791,091**	**2,525,502**	**3,916,493**	**6,278,620**

This table gives us interesting feedback. Till AD 1000 (before the Turkic footprint), the population growth has been neutral. Especially from AD 1500, we say exponential population growth.

Table A.2: Rate of Growth of World Population: 20 Countries and Regional Totals, AD 1 to AD 2003 (annual average compound growth rates) (Maddison, 2007)

	1–1000	1000–1500	1500–1820	1820–70	1870–1913	1913–50	1950–73	1973–20
Austria	0.03	0.21	0.16	0.59	0.94	0.07	0.39	0.24
Belgium	0.03	0.25	0.28	0.79	0.95	0.32	0.52	0.20
Denmark	0.07	0.10	0.20	0.99	1.07	0.97	0.71	0.24
Finland	0.07	0.40	0.43	0.81	1.28	0.76	0.66	0.36
France	0.03	0.17	0.23	0.42	0.18	0.02	0.96	0.48
Germany	0.02	0.25	0.23	0.91	1.18	0.13	0.63	0.14
Italy	−0.05	0.15	0.20	0.65	0.68	0.64	0.66	0.19
Netherlands	0.04	0.23	0.28	0.88	1.25	1.35	1.24	0.63
Norway	0.07	0.08	0.37	1.17	0.80	0.78	0.84	0.47
Sweden	0.07	0.06	0.48	0.96	0.70	0.60	0.65	0.33
Switzerland	0.00	0.15	0.35	0.58	0.88	0.53	1.39	0.47
UK	0.09	0.14	0.53	0.79	0.87	0.25	0.50	0.22
12 country average	**0.01**	**0.18**	**0.27**	**0.70**	**0.79**	**0.32**	**0.70**	**0.27**
Portugal	0.04	0.10	0.37	0.55	0.75	0.94	0.27	0.52
Spain	0.01	0.11	0.18	0.57	0.52	0.88	0.94	0.48
Other	−0.06	0.01	0.25	0.88	0.91	1.57	0.62	0.67
Total western Europe	**0.00**	**0.16**	**0.26**	**0.69**	**0.77**	**0.42**	**0.71**	**0.32**
Eastern Europe	**0.03**	**0.15**	**0.31**	**0.77**	**0.92**	**0.26**	**1.01**	**0.32**
Former USSR	**0.06**	**0.17**	**0.37**	**0.97**	**1.33**	**0.38**	**1.44**	**0.47**
USA	0.06	0.09	0.50	2.83	2.08	1.21	1.45	1.06
Other western offshoots	0.03	0.07	0.14	3.13	2.02	1.53	2.09	1.21
Total western offshoots	**0.05**	**0.08**	**0.44**	**2.86**	**2.07**	**1.25**	**1.54**	**1.08**
Mexico	0.07	0.10	−0.04	0.67	1.13	1.75	3.11	1.98
Other Latin America	0.07	0.07	0.13	1.47	1.76	2.00	2.64	1.88
Total Latin America	**0.07**	**0.09**	**0.07**	**1.26**	**1.63**	**1.96**	**2.72**	**1.90**
Japan	**0.09**	**0.14**	**0.22**	**0.21**	**0.95**	**1.32**	**1.14**	**0.53**
China	0.00	0.11	0.41	−0.12	0.47	0.61	2.10	1.27
India	0.00	0.08	0.20	0.38	0.43	0.45	2.11	2.00
Other east Asia	0.06	0.12	0.17	0.67	1.14	2.26	2.32	1.98
West Asia	0.00	−0.02	0.11	0.37	0.59	1.17	2.80	2.68
Total Asia (excl. Japan)	**0.01**	**0.09**	**0.29**	**0.15**	**0.55**	**0.92**	**2.19**	**1.76**
Africa	**0.06**	**0.07**	**0.15**	**0.40**	**0.75**	**1.65**	**2.36**	**2.64**
World	**0.02**	**0.10**	**0.27**	**0.40**	**0.80**	**0.93**	**1.93**	**1.59**

Table A.3: Share of World GDP: Twenty Countries and Regional Totals, AD 1 to AD 2003 (per cent of the world total) (Maddison, 2007)

	1	1000	1500	1600	1700	1820	1870	1913	1950	1973	2003
Austria	0.2	0.2	0.6	0.6	0.7	0.6	0.8	0.9	0.5	0.5	0.4
Belgium	0.1	0.1	0.5	0.5	0.6	0.7	1.2	1.2	0.9	0.7	0.5
Denmark	0.1	0.1	0.2	0.2	0.2	0.2	0.3	0.4	0.6	0.4	0.3
Finland	0.0	0.0	0.1	0.1	0.1	0.1	0.2	0.2	0.3	0.3	0.3
France	2.2	2.3	4.4	4.7	5.3	5.1	6.5	5.3	4.1	4.3	3.2
Germany	1.2	1.2	3.3	3.8	3.7	3.9	6.5	8.7	5.0	5.9	3.9
Italy	6.1	1.9	4.7	4.3	3.9	3.2	3.8	3.5	3.1	3.6	2.7
Netherlands	0.1	0.1	0.3	0.6	1.1	0.6	0.9	0.9	1.1	1.1	0.9
Norway	0.0	0.1	0.1	0.1	0.1	0.1	0.2	0.2	0.3	0.3	0.3
Sweden	0.1	0.1	0.2	0.2	0.3	0.4	0.6	0.6	0.9	0.7	0.5
Switzerland	0.1	0.1	0.2	0.2	0.3	0.3	0.5	0.6	0.8	0.7	0.4
UK	0.3	0.7	1.1	1.8	2.9	5.2	9.0	8.2	6.5	4.2	3.1
12 country total	**10.6**	**7.0**	**15.5**	**17.1**	**19.1**	**20.5**	**30.5**	**30.8**	**24.1**	**22.8**	**16.5**
Portugal	0.2	0.2	0.2	0.2	0.4	0.4	0.4	0.3	0.3	0.4	0.4
Spain	1.8	1.5	1.8	2.1	2.0	1.8	1.8	1.5	1.2	1.7	1.7
Other	1.2	0.4	0.3	0.3	0.3	0.3	0.4	0.5	0.6	0.7	0.7
Total western Europe	**13.7**	**9.1**	**17.8**	**19.8**	**21.9**	**23.0**	**33.1**	**33.0**	**26.2**	**25.6**	**19.2**
Eastern Europe	**1.9**	**2.2**	**2.7**	**2.8**	**3.1**	**3.6**	**4.5**	**4.9**	**3.5**	**3.4**	**1.9**
Former USSR	**1.5**	**2.4**	**3.4**	**3.4**	**4.4**	**5.4**	**7.5**	**8.5**	**9.6**	**9.4**	**3.8**
USA	0.3	0.4	0.3	0.2	0.1	1.8	8.9	18.9	27.3	22.1	20.6
Other western offshoots	0.2	0.2	0.1	0.1	0.1	0.1	1.2	2.4	3.4	3.3	3.1
Total western offshoots	**0.4**	**0.6**	**0.5**	**0.3**	**0.2**	**1.9**	**10.0**	**21.3**	**30.6**	**25.3**	**23.7**
Mexico	0.8	1.5	1.3	0.3	0.7	0.7	0.6	0.9	1.3	1.7	1.8
Other Latin America	1.3	2.3	1.7	0.8	1.0	1.4	1.9	3.5	6.5	6.9	5.8
Total Latin America	**2.1**	**3.8**	**2.9**	**1.1**	**1.7**	**2.1**	**2.5**	**4.4**	**7.8**	**8.7**	**7.7**
Japan	**1.1**	**2.7**	**3.1**	**2.9**	**4.1**	**3.0**	**2.3**	**2.6**	**3.0**	**7.8**	**6.6**
China	25.4	22.1	24.9	29.0	22.3	32.9	17.1	8.8	4.6	4.6	15.1
India	32.0	28.1	24.4	22.4	24.4	16.0	12.1	7.5	4.2	3.1	5.5
Other east Asia	4.6	7.5	8.4	7.4	7.7	5.2	4.8	4.5	4.8	5.2	9.6
West Asia	9.6	10.3	4.2	3.8	3.3	2.2	2.0	1.5	2.0	3.4	3.6
Total Asia (excl. Japan)	**71.7**	**67.9**	**61.8**	**62.6**	**57.7**	**56.4**	**36.0**	**22.3**	**15.6**	**16.4**	**33.9**
Africa	**7.6**	**11.4**	**7.8**	**7.0**	**6.9**	**4.5**	**4.1**	**2.9**	**3.8**	**3.4**	**3.2**
World	**100.0**	**100.0**	**100.0**	**100.0**	**100.0**	**100.0**	**100.0**	**100.0**	**100.0**	**100.0**	**100.0**

What we can observe from this table is that till AD 1000, India's GDP share was the highest in the world. In fact, at a certain time, it was almost one-third of the world. When the Tīmūrid Empire was established in Hindustan, the latter's GDP share was 24.4 per cent (only slightly lesser than China). It means Hindustan was already the richest country before Babur arrived. It washes away the argument that Hindustan was made richer by the Tīmūrids (known as Moghūls). In fact, the world GDP share of Hindustan fell below China for the first time drastically in AD 1600 when Akbar was the ruler. The fall of GDP following the Tīmūrid period shall never recover in future. This is also true that the fall was massive during the era of British colonialism and despite being lower than in the earlier period the GDP share was almost neutral throughout the Tīmūrid period. But does it mean that people were richer during the Tīmūrid colonialism than those in British Colonialism? The answer can be obtained from table A.4.

Table A.4: Rate of Growth of World per Capita GDP: Twnry Countries and Regional Averages, AD 1 to AD (annual average compound growth rates)*

	1–1000	1000–1500	1500–1820	1820–70	1870–1913	1913–50	1950–73	1973–2003
Austria	0.00	0.10	0.17	0.85	1.45	0.18	4.94	2.14
Belgium	−0.01	0.14	0.13	1.44	1.05	0.70	3.54	1.87
Denmark	0.00	0.12	0.17	0.91	1.57	1.56	3.08	1.70
Finland	0.00	0.03	0.17	0.76	1.44	1.91	4.25	2.07
France	−0.01	0.11	0.14	1.01	1.45	1.12	4.04	1.72
Germany	0.00	0.10	0.14	1.08	1.61	0.17	5.02	1.58
Italy	−0.06	0.18	0.00	0.59	1.26	0.85	4.95	1.98
Netherlands	0.00	0.12	0.28	0.81	0.90	1.07	3.45	1.67
Norway	0.00	0.08	0.09	1.06	1.38	2.18	3.25	2.81
Sweden	0.00	0.11	0.17	0.66	1.46	2.12	3.06	1.57
Switzerland	0.00	0.09	0.17	1.32	1.66	2.06	3.08	0.67
UK	0.00	0.12	0.27	1.26	1.01	0.93	2.42	1.93
12 country average	−0.03	0.13	**0.14**	**1.04**	**1.33**	**0.84**	**3.92**	**1.77**
Portugal	−0.01	0.07	0.13	0.11	0.58	1.39	5.45	2.26
Spain	−0.01	0.08	0.13	0.36	1.25	0.17	5.60	2.70
Other	−0.03	0.03	0.13	0.74	1.37	0.87	4.89	2.78
Total western Europe	**−0.03**	**0.12**	**0.14**	**0.98**	**1.33**	**0.76**	**4.05**	**1.87**
Eastern Europe	**0.00**	**0.04**	**0.10**	**0.63**	**1.39**	**0.60**	**3.81**	**0.87**
Former USSR	**0.00**	**0.04**	**0.10**	**0.63**	**1.06**	**1.76**	**3.35**	**−0.38**
USA	0.00	0.00	0.36	1.34	1.82	1.61	2.45	1.86
Other western offshoots	0.00	0.00	0.20	2.19	1.76	1.21	2.60	1.80
Total western offshoots	**0.00**	**0.00**	**0.34**	**1.41**	**1.81**	**1.56**	**2.45**	**1.85**
Mexico	0.00	0.01	0.18	−0.24	2.22	0.85	3.17	1.29
Other Latin America	0.00	0.00	0.15	0.05	1.77	1.54	2.47	0.70
Total Latin America	**0.00**	**0.01**	**0.16**	**−0.04**	**1.86**	**1.41**	**2.60**	**0.83**
Japan	**0.01**	**0.03**	**0.09**	**0.19**	**1.48**	**0.88**	**8.06**	**2.08**
China	0.00	0.06	0.00	−0.25	0.10	−0.56	2.76	5.99
India	0.00	0.04	−0.01	0.00	0.54	−0.22	1.40	3.14
Other east Asia	0.00	0.05	0.01	0.09	0.82	−0.24	2.89	3.23
West Asia	0.02	−0.01	0.01	0.40	0.79	1.45	4.47	0.65
Total Asia (excl. Japan)	**0.00**	**0.04**	**0.00**	**−0.10**	**0.43**	**−0.08**	**2.87**	**3.88**
Africa	**−0.01**	**−0.01**	**0.00**	**0.35**	**0.57**	**0.91**	**2.02**	**0.32**
World	**0.00**	**0.05**	**0.05**	**0.54**	**1.31**	**0.88**	**2.91**	**1.56**

* Agnus Maddison, *Contours of the World Economy, 1–2030AD*, New York: Oxford University Press, 2007.

This table gives us a pertinent and interesting insight into the financial condition of subjects under the Tīmūrid rule. If we refer to Table A.3, it is clear that although the wealth of Hindustan wasn't drastically low as compared to the past (although it dropped), the GDP/capita growth was negative between AD 1500 and AD 1820. It was negative twice from AD 1913 to AD 1950. Of course, this is a very well-acknowledged fact that Bharat under British colonialism had people turning poor although the ruling government kept accumulating wealth. The same cannot be denied about what the Tīmūrid colonialists were doing. This is well supported by many statements by various foreign travellers and court historians of that time. People would be surprised to know how systematically the Tīmūrids drained Indian wealth, including the huge money spent on Hajj and to please the Amirs of Mecca. After his victory over the Lodi, Babur owned massive wealth. Perhaps, he was awestruck looking at so much wealth. Persian historian Firishta (of the sixteenth and seventeenth centuries) has said:

> *Babur left himself stripped so bare by his far-flung largess that he was nick-named Qalandar.*

Although this matter will be dealt with in much detail in upcoming volumes, here I am just going to give a glimpse of the wealth drain by the Tīmūrids right from Babur. The *Baburnama* has spoken in detail about the looted wealth:*

> May 12th, on Saturday the 29th of Rajab the examination and distribution of the treasure were begun. To Humāyūn were given 70 lakhs from the Treasury, and, over and above this, a treasure house was bestowed on him just as it was, without ascertaining and writing down its contents. To some begs 10 lakhs were given, 8, 7, or 6 to others. Suitable money-gifts were bestowed from the Treasury on the whole army, to every tribe there was, Afghān, Hazāra, 'Arab, Bīlūch, etc. to each according to its position. Every trader and student, indeed every man who had come with the army, took ample portion and

* Ghāzī, Ẓahiru'd-dīn Muḥammad Bābur Pādshāh, *The Babur-nama in English* (Memoirs of Babur), translated from the original Turki Text of Ẓahiru'd-dīn Muḥammad Bābur Pādshāh Ghāzī. (ed.) Annette Susannah Beveridge. (trans.) Annette Susannah Beveridge. London: Luzac and Co, 1922. pp. 522-525.

> share of bounteous gift and largess. To those not with the army went a mass of treasure in gift and largess, as for instance, 17 lakhs to Kāmran, 15 lakhs to Muḥammad-i-zamān Mīrzā, while to 'Askarī, Hindāl and indeed to the whole various train of relations and younger children went masses of red and white (gold and silver), of plenishing, jewels, and slaves. Many gifts went to the begs and soldiery on that side (Tramontana). Valuable gifts (saughāt) were sent for the various relations in Samarkand, Khurāsān, Kāshghar and 'Irāq. To holy men belonging to Samarkand and Khurāsān went offerings vowed to God (nuẕūr); so too to Makka and Madīna. We gave one shāhrukhi for every soul in the country of Kābul and the valley-side of Varsak, man and woman, bond and free, of age or non-age.

With time, Babur's people had begun to show discontent about staying in Hindustan and hence he called a council to resolve the matter. He has written about it in the *Baburnama*:*

> When I knew of this unsteadiness amongst (my) people, I summoned all the begs and took counsel. Said I, "There is no supremacy and grip on the world without means and resources; without lands and retainers' sovereignty and command (Padishahlīq u amīrlīq) are impossible. By the labors of several years, by encountering hardship, by long travel, by flinging myself and the army into battle, and by deadly slaughter, we, through Allah's grace, beat these masses of enemies so that we might take their broad lands. And now what force compels us, what necessity has arisen that we should, without cause, abandon countries taken at such risk of life? Was it for us to remain in Kābul, the sport of harsh poverty? Henceforth, let no well-wisher of mine speak of such things! But let not those turn back from going who, weak in strong persistence, have set their faces to depart!" By these words, which recalled just and reasonable views to their minds, I made them, willy-nilly, quit their fears.

Interestingly, when Khwāja Kalān decided to leave Hindustan, Babur lured him with many gifts and territories. Babur has said:†

* Ibid.
† Ibid.

I bestowed on him Ghaznī, Girdīz and the Sulṭān Mas'ūdī Hazāra, gave also the Hindustan pargana of G'hūram, worth 3 or 4 lakhs. It was settled for Khwāja Mīr-i-mīrān also to go to Kābul; the gifts were put into his immediate charge, under the custody of Mullā Ḥasan the banker (ṣarrāf) and Tūka Hindū.

When Sulṭān Ibrāhīm Lodi had appointed several amīrs under Muṣṭafa Farmūlī and Fīrūz Khān Sārang-khānī, to act against the rebel amīrs of the east, one Muṣṭafa had fought and drubbed them thoroughly. He died just before Babur defeated Ibrāhīm. His younger brother Shaikh Bāyazīd then had led the men. After the victory, Shaikh Bāyazīd along with Fīrūz Khān, Maḥmūd Khān Nuḥānī and Qāẓī Jīā had come to serve. Babur was very happy. In his happiness, he showered them with abundant kindness and favour. He gave Fīrūz Khān one krūr, forty-six lakhs and five thousand tankas from Jūnpūr. Shaikh Bāyazīd was given one krūr, forty-eight lakhs, and fifty thousand tankas from Awadh. Babur granted ninety lakhs and thirty thousand tankas to Maḥmūd Khān from Ghāzīpūr (originally Gadhipur) and finally, Qāẓī Jīā was granted Rs 23 lakh.

Once, post the victory on Lodis, an 'Īd celebration party was thrown at a place which was once the Ibrāhīm's private apartment. Babur bestowed several gifts:*

1. Two items (*rā*'s) of tīpūchāq horses with saddles.
2. Sixteen items (*qabẓa*) of poniards, set with jewels, etc.
3. Eight items (*qabẓa*) of purpet over-garments.
4. Two items (*tob*) of jewelled sword belts.
5. Items (*qabẓa*) of broad daggers (*jamd'kar*) set with jewels.
6. Twenty-five items of jewelled hangers (*Khānjar*).
7. Items of gold-hilted Hindī knives (*kārd*).
8. Fifty-one pieces of purpet.

* Ghāzī, Ẓahiru'd-dīn Muḥammad Bābur Pādshāh, *The Babur-nama in English* (Memoirs of Babur), translated from the original Turki Text of Ẓahiru'd-dīn Muḥammad Bābur Pādshāh Ghāzī, (ed.) Annette Susannah Beveridge, (trans). Annette Susannah Beveridge, London: Luzac and Co, 1922. pp. 527-528.

It is very clearly established from Babur's writing that he was on a campaign to drain away the Indian wealth as he could for the benefit of his people who certainly were not Indians.

One thing remained constant throughout the reign—the investments of Hajj. On average, around 15,000 pilgrims visited Mecca annually to perform Hajj during the Tīmūrid (distorted as Moghūls) era. The official Tīmūrid records tell us that the Tīmūrids sponsored the pilgrimage at public expense with gold, goods and rich presents merely with the desire to stand out as defenders of Islam. The major sponsorship began with the period of Abu'l-Fath Jalal-ud-din Muhammad Akbar when he conquered Gujarat in AD 1573. This victory had given him access to the port of Surat. An imperial proclamation in this regard stated:*

> The traveling expenses of anybody who might intend to perform the pilgrimage to the Sacred Places should be paid.

According to Wollebrant Geleynssen, it was in AD 1576, that a Hajj caravan under the Tīmūrid (distorted as Moghūls) patronage left Agra with a huge donation amount of Rs 6 lakh. I do not have records of this time but for AD 1637, the daily wages were as follows:†

Category of Employees	**Wages in Rupees**
Washer man	5.0
Groom	4.5
Servant of chief factor, Geleynssen	4.5
Torchbearer	4.0
Servant of factor, Barentsen	3.5
Chariot driver	3.5
Gatekeeper	3.5
Peons	3.5*
Luggage boy of Geleynssen	2.5
Keeper of the graveyard	2.0
Writer of letters in Persian	0.5
Barber	0.5

* Each

* John Slight, *The British Empire and the Hajj*, s.l.: Harvard University Press, 2015.

† Najaf Haider, *Structure and Movement of Wages in the Mughal Empire*, 2008.

So, it means that this donation sent out in AD 1576 to Hajj was equivalent to at least a salary of around six lakh people on an average. The population of India in that period was 1,35,000. This means that if each Indian earned Rs 4.88 every month—the sum would have been equal to what was invested for the Hajj of AD 1576.

Just the very next year another caravan left for Mecca with a bounty of Rs 5 lakh and Rs 1 lakh for the Sherif of Mecca who was known to be descendent of Prophet Muhammad's grandson Hasan ibn Ali. When these gigantic amounts came to Mecca, the Muslim world flocked over here desperately to claim whatever they could in name of alms.* †

The records do tell us that Akbar was trying hard to become the Caliph, a syndrome from which even Timur suffered. When things were not working just by wasting much Indian wealth over the Muslim world, in AD 1579, he insisted the Ulemas to sign a document to let him use the title 'Padshah-i Islam' and attempted to be presented as the Khalifa. He had begun to lead the Friday prayers, taking the precedents from the Abbassid rulers. But finally, in AD 1581–82, the Ottomans showed him a way out.‡Three years later, he established Din-E-Illahi. The aspiration to lead with religion was deeply embedded in the Tīmūrid psyche.

After Akbar came Jahangir. He resumed the tradition of patronage for Hajj. An amount of Rs 2 lakh was allocated for Hajj.§He has mentioned it in his autobiography, *Tarikh-i-Salim Shahi*:¶

> During the reign of my father, the ministers of religion and students of law and literature, to the number of two and three thousand, in the principal cities of the empire, were already allowed pensions from the state; and to these, in conformity with the regulations established by my father, I directed Miran Sadr Jahan one of the noblest among the Seyeds of Herat, to allot a subsistence corresponding with their

* John Slight, *The British Empire and the Hajj*, s.l.: Harvard University Press, 2015.

† David Thomas, John A. Chesworth, *Christian-Muslim Relations. A Bibliographical History*, Volume 6, Western Europe (1500–1600), 2015.

‡ John Slight, *The British Empire and the Hajj*, s.l.: Harvard University Press, 2015.

§ Ibid

¶ Jahangir, *Tarikh-i Salim Shahi*, s.l.: Sushil Gupta, 1952.

> situation; and this is not only to the subjects of my own realms, but to foreigners – to natives of Persia, Roum, Bokhara, and Azerbaijan, with strict charge that this class of men should not be permitted either want or inconvenience of any type.

Despite having claimed to be highly non-religious in nature, Jahangir too did his part of sending out Indian wealth to Mecca. He had sent an amber candlestick covered with a network of gold, ornamented with gems and diamonds by his artisans of the court. The cost of this beautiful piece as per records was Rs 2.50 lakh.* In AD 1650, a diamond-studded candlestick along with a 300-carat diamond was sent to Mecca.†

If we move further, Aurangzeb can be deemed one of the grandest donors for Muslim lands. Between AD 1661 and AD 1667, Aurangzeb welcomed the kings of Persia, Bukhara, Kashgar, Balkh, Urganj, and Shahr-i-Nau and the Turkish governors of Basra (in Iraq).

Sir Richard Burn, the editor of *Cambridge History of India,* has stated:‡

> His policy was to dazzle the eyes of these princes by lavish gift of presents to them and to their envoys, and thus induce the outer Muslim world to forget his treatment of his father and brothers. The fame of India as a soft milch cow spread throughout the middle and near East, and the minor embassies were merely begging expeditions.

Records state that around Rs 30 lakh were spent by Aurangzeb between AD 1661 and AD 1667. He had also distributed a large sum annually at Mecca. He had sent a gift of Rs 10 lakh to Abdullah Khān. He was the deposed king of Kashgar and had been granted refuge by Aurangzeb in AD 1668.§

The cashflow to Mecca continued flawlessly under Aurangzeb through his agents. It is very interesting to note that this wealth

---

* Radhakamal Mukerjee, *The Economic History of India*, 1600–1800. s.l.: Kitab Mahal, 1967.

† John Slight, *The British Empire and the Hajj*, s.l.: Harvard University Press, 2015.

‡ Lt Colonel Sir Wolseley Haig, *The Cambridge History of India*, (ed.) Sir Richard Burn, Cambridge: Cambridge University Press, 1937. Vol. IV, p. 229

§ Ibid.

export of Tīmūrids was a one-way street. Nothing substantial came as a return. This is very well described by the seventeenth-century travelogue of François Bernier.

In AD 1664, the Christian monarch of Ethiopia sent an embassy to Aurangzeb. The embassy was represented by two ambassadors. One of them was Murat, an Armenian Christian while the other one was a Muslim merchant (name unknown). On arrival, they brought a mule skin, the horn of Ox, and a few ravenous and half-naked African slaves:*

Having received them, Aurangzeb gifted back the following:

a) A brocade sash
b) A silken and embroidered girdle
c) A turban of the same materials and workmanship

Not only that, but Aurangzeb also ordered for complete maintenance of those ambassadors in the city of Agra at public expense. On a later audience, he once again gifted them very well. He gave both another sash along with a present of Rs 6000. But what is interesting to note here is that he divided money unequally based on religion. The Muslim merchant received Rs 4000 while Murat received only Rs 2000.†

Here, the merchant fooled Aurangzeb the best he could. The cunning one promised Aurangzeb that once he reaches home, he would urge the monarch of Ethiopia to permit the repair of a mosque destroyed by the Portuguese. Being lured by him, Aurangzeb gave ambassadors an extra Rs 2000 expecting the mosque to be repaired in Ethiopia.‡

We then get details about an embassy that had come from the Aūzbeg Tatars. They had brought the following:

a) some boxes of lapis-lazuli
b) a few long-haired camels

* François Bernier, *Travels in the Mogul Empire*, AD *1656–1668*, (ed.) Archibald Constable and Vincent A Smith, (trans.) Archibald Constable, London, Edinburgh, Glasgow, New York, Toronto, Melbourne, Bombay: Humphrey Milford, Oxford University Press, 1891. pp. 136–139.
† Ibid
‡ Ibid, pp. 140–41.

c) several horses
d) some camel loads of fresh fruit, such as apples, pears, grapes, melons, and many loads of dry fruit.

Bernier described the Aūzbeg Tatars as being remarkable for the 'filthiness of their persons'. He has also said, 'There are probably no people more narrow-minded, sordid, or unclean than the Aūzbeg Tatars.'

Here again, Aurangzeb took no offense with respect to his general attitude just because the embassies were Muslim. He showered them the best of favours and honour in front of all courtiers. He presented each one with two rich shashes and Rs 8000 in cash. He also presented a big number of the richest and most exquisitely shaped brocades, several fine linens, silk material interwoven with gold and silver, a few carpets, and two daggers set with precious stones.*

While he was generous to these Muslim embassies, on the contrary, he was fond of hanging the tax-defaulting Indian subjects to trees.

A statement from Bernier gives complete clarity on why the GDP of the Sulṭānate remained almost constant while GDP/capita growth turned negative. Bernier writes:†

> Gold and silver are not in greater plenty here than elsewhere; on the contrary, the inhabitants have less the appearance of a moneyed people than those of many other parts of the globe.

Bernier informs us about the Aurangzeb's period by stating as below:‡

> Labourers perish due to bad treatment from Governors. Children of poor are carried away as slaves. Peasantry abandon the country driven by despair. As the land throughout the whole empire is considered the property of the sovereign, there can be no earldoms, marquisates, or duchies. The royal grants consist only of pensions,

* Ibid.
† Ibid, p. 223
‡ Ibid, p. 205

> either in land or money, which the king gives, augments, retrenches or takes away at pleasure.
>
> The artisans who manufactured the luxury goods for the Mughal aristocracy were almost always on starvation wages.

It is crucial to note that the price of goods produced by these artisans was determined by the buyers. When they failed to comply with the price standards as set, they were ought to face imprisonment or death. We are told by Bernier that the weavers who spun the world's finest brocades and garments went about half-naked.

English Ambassador Thomas Roe who had visited the court of Jahangir had observed a similar aspect. He was amazed looking at the diamonds, pearls and rubies displayed in the court of Tīmūrids but at the same time, the impoverished life of common people caught his eyes too along the route from Surat to Delhi.[*]

The 'Introduction' section of this book has details of how Shah Jahan had created the famine of AD 1620–32. Just bear that in mind and note the following.

Shah Jahan had organized a grand feast on Nauroz in AD 1628. All the elites were part of the celebrations. Shah Jahan gifted each member of royalty with abundant gifts and titles as below:

> The imperial consort, Mumtaz Mahal received Rs fifty lakh from the treasury. Jahan Ara, Shah Jahan's daughter from Mumtaz was granted twenty lakh, and her sister Raushan Ara, received a sum of five lakh.

The records tell us that in this period, Shah Jahan had spent Rs 1.6 crore from the public treasury only for granting the rewards and pensions.[†]

But after having engineered the massive famine can you imagine the aid he gave to the survivors? We are told that corpses piled up all along the highways as millions marched looking for the food. Fathers

---

[*] Sir Thomas Roe, *The Embassy of Sir Thomas Roe to India, 1615-19: As Narrated in His Journal and Correspondence*, (ed.) William Foster, London: Hakluyt Society, 1899. Vol. I, p. 46

[†] S.M. Jaffar, *The Mughal Empire from Bābar to Aurangzeb*, s.l.: University of Michigan, 2008.

looked for opportunities to sell their sons as slaves, hoping they find some nourishment, but such was the wrath of famine that there were no takers. The mothers along with their daughters drowned in the rivers.

Shah Jahan distributed a famine relief fund of Rs 1 lakh which was merely 2 per cent of what he had gifted Mumtaz on the eve of Nauroz. The annual maintenance of Mumtaz was Rs 1 crore and his imperial treasury had sum of Rs 6 crore in cash. The famous Peacock Throne on which he sat was valued to be around Rs 3 crores in that period.

Angus Madison gives us some interesting records.*

The total expense of the Tīmūrid (distorted as Moghūls) State, and associated autonomous princelings and chiefs was anything between 15-18 per cent of the national income.

He estimates that around twenty-one million people (out of a total population of approximately 150 million) constituted the predatory Tīmūrid (distorted as Mughal) ecosystem—the court, family, army, harems, servants, slaves, and eunuchs who produced nothing and only consumed.

He writes, 'As far as the economy was concerned, the Moghūl state apparatus was parasitic.' According to him, the state was a regime of warlord predators which was lesser efficient than European feudalism.

He further writes, 'The Moghūl state and aristocracy put their income were largely unproductive. Their investments were made in two main forms: hoarding precious metals and jewels.'

Bharat had always been primarily agrarian in nature and the Tīmūrid Empire systematically destroyed it. American Historian J.F. Richards writes in his work *Fiscal States in Mughal and British India*:†

> The Mughal dynasty's wealth and power was based upon its ability to tap directly into the agrarian productivity of the Indian sub-continent.

---

* Angus Maddison, *The World Economy, A Millenial Perspective*. s.l.: OECD. p. 109.

† J.F.Richards, *Fiscal States in Mughal and British India*, Francisco Comín Comín, (ed.) Francisco Comín Comín, Patrick K. O'Brien Bartolomé Yun-Casalilla, *The Rise of Fiscal States, A Global History, 1500–1914*, Cambridge, New York, Melbourne, Madrid, Cape Town, Singapore, Sao Paulo, Delhi, Mexico City: Cambridge University Press, 2012, 17, p. 410.

Trade, manufacture and other taxes were much less important to the imperial revenues than agriculture, most estimates putting them at less than 10% of the total.

Let us again come back to the writings of Bernier:*

Of the vast tracts of country constituting the empire of Hindoustan, many are little more than sand, or barren mountains, badly cultivated and thinly peopled; and even a considerable portion of the good land remains untilled from want of labourers; many of whom perish in consequence of the bad treatment they experience from the Governors.

These poor people, when incapable of discharging the demands of their rapacious lords, are not only often deprived of the means of subsistence, but are bereft of their children, who are carried away as slaves. Thus it happens that many of the peasantry, driven to despair by so execrable a tyranny, abandon the country, and seek a more tolerable mode of existence, either in the towns, or camps; as bearers of burdens, carriers of water, or servants to horsemen. Sometimes they fly to the territories of a Raja, because there they find less oppression, and are allowed a greater degree of comfort.

The truth is that in the opinion of all scholarly works. the Tīmūrids (distorted as Moghūls) have been shown as greedy rulers. In the words of Tapan Raychaudhuri (*State and the Economy: The Mughal Empire*), 'The Mughal state was an insatiable Leviathan.'† If one goes through essays in *The Cambridge Economic History of India* edited by Raychaudhuri and Irfan Habib,‡ it becomes very evident that the Tīmūrids were extortionist and an extraction machinery. They took away the entire surplus from the peasants.

As per Angus Maddison, the irrigation system was poor. He has said, '(. . .) but in the context of the economy as a whole these were

* François Bernier, *Travels in the Mogul Empire*, AD *1656–1668*, (ed.) Archibald Constable and Vincent A Smith, (trans.) Archibald Constable, London, Edinburgh, Glasgow, New York, Toronto, Melbourne, Bombay: Humphrey Milford, Oxford University Press, 1891.

† Tapan Raychaudhuri, *The State and the Economy, The Mughal Empire*; (ed.) Irfan Habib Tapan Raychaudhuri, *The Cambridge Economic History of India*, Cambridge, New York, New Rochelle, Melbourne, Sydney: Cambridge University Press, 1987, Vol. 1, VII.1, p. 173.

‡ Tapan Raychaudhuri, Irfan Habib, *Cambridge Economic History of India*, s.l.: Cambridge University Press, 1987.

unimportant and probably did not cover more than 5 percent of the cultivated land of India.'*

In the last years of the decade of the 1780s, Hasan Raza Khān, the chief minister of Awadh had contributed a sum of Rs 5 lakh for the construction of Hindiya Canal (Iran) which was completed in AD 1803, bringing water for Najaf. Not to forget that this was the period when the Marathas had weakened them completely, but despite that they were able arrange such a huge fund for something to be built in distant Muslim land.

Lahore-based historian Khaled Ahmed has said, 'So big was the diversion of the water from the Euphrates that the river changed course. The canal became a virtual river and transformed the arid zone between the cities of Najaf and Karbala into fertile land that attracted the Sunni Arab tribes to settle there and take to farming.'

So, while the Tīmūrids didn't build any canal in India, for their prominent stay of around three centuries, they built one that brought a complete change to the destiny of some place in Arabia. They did so in the worst of their periods when both British and Marathas were at their neck badly. It means that they were able to extract money from the subjects and that was in the 1780s when the Mughal Empire was a vassal of the Marathas, and the British had captured large swaths of its eastern territories. If it doesn't mean that the Tīmūrids were desperate to use Indian money for Muslim causes outside India, then I'm unsure of what needs to be said. I'll again quote Khaled Ahmed. He has said, 'The custodian of the seminarian complex of Najaf and the mausoleum of Caliph Ali is a Pakistani grand ayatollah, appointed to his top position in deference to the fact that Najaf and Karbala were developed as a habitable economic zone by the Shia rulers of North India.'†

Well, all these anecdotes from the pages of history make us understand that while the GDP share of the Sulṭānate never dropped much though GDP/capita growth turned negative.

---

* Agnus Maddison, *The World Economy*, A Millenial Perspective. s.l.: OECD. p. 109.

† Khaled Ahmed, *The Lucknow Connection*, s.l.: *The Indian Express*.

Table A.5: Revenues of Hindustan Babur drew in AD 1528:*

Sarkārs.	Krūrs.	Laks.	Tankas.
Trans-sutluj:--Bhīra, Lāhūr, Sīālkūt, Dībālpūr, etc.	3	33	15,989
Sihrind	1	29	31,985
Ḥiṣār-fīrūza	1	30	75,174
The capital Dihlī and Mīān-dū-āb	3	69	50,254
Mīwāt, not included in Sikandar's time	1	69	81,000
Bīāna	1	44	14,930
Āgra		29	76,919
Mīān-wilāyat (Midlands)	2	91	19
Gūālīār	2	23	57,450
Kālpī and Sehoṇda (Seondhā)	4	28	55,950
Qanauj	1	36	63,358
Saṃbhal	1	38	44,000
Laknūr and Baksar	1	39	82,433
Khairābād		12	65,000
Aūd (Oude) and Bahraj (Baraich)	1	17	1,369
Jūnpūr	4	·0	88,333
Karra and Mānikpūr	1	63	27,282
Bihār	4	5	60,000
Sāran	1	10	17,506½
Sarwār	1	55	18,373
Champāran	1	90	86,060
Kandla	1	43	30,300
Tirhut from Rāja Rup-narāīn's tribute, silver	1	43	55,000
black (i.e. copper)	1	27	50,300
Rantanbhūr from Būlī, Chātsū, and Malarna		20	00,000
Nagūr	--	--	--
Rāja Bikrāmajīt in Rantanbhūr	--	--	--
Kalanjarī	--	--	--
Rāja Bīr-sang-deo (or, Sang only)	--	--	--
Rāja Bikam-deo	--	--	--
Rāja Bikam-chand	--	--	--

* Annette Susannah Beveridge, Ẓahiru'd-dīn Muḥammad Bābur Pādshāh Ghāzī, Bābur, *The Bābur-nāma in English*, London: Luzac, 1922, p. 189.

Appendix B

Events of Unchronicles Years (based on the *Baburnama* translation by Annette Susannah Beveridge)*

2 May of AD 1508 to 21 April of AD 1509

The mutiny, of which an account begins in *Baburnama*, was crushed vehemently. It was a victory of 500 loyalists over 3000 rebels. Beveridge finds one factor of success being the Bābur's defeat in single combat of five champions of his adversaries.[1] The turbulence was not there to stay for long. By the month of Sha'bān (November) Kābul was at peace. It was the time when twenty-year-old Sulṭān Sa'īd Khān Chaghatāī had arrived there. After having seen a series of setbacks he was seeking his cousin's protection. Sulṭān Sa'īd was defeated at the hands of his own brother Manṣūr at Almātū. He had almost defeated death. While being in Ferghana he was commanded by Shaybāni. He took a winter journey through Qarā-tīgīn to see Mīrzā Khān in Qilā'-i-ẕafar. But he was refused of an offer to replace feeble Mīrzā. And hence having lost all hopes he came to Kābul. He presented himself a destitute fugitive and enjoyed a freedom from care which was never known by him earlier.† The year of AD 1508 was incurable to Ḥaidar

* Ibid, p. 350

† Mirza Muhammad Haidar Dughlt, *A History of the Moghuls of Central Asia: The Tarikh-i-Rashidi*, (trans.) N. Elias and Sir Edward Denison Ross, New York: Cosimo Inc., 2008. p. 226.

and Babur's family. Shaybānī murdered Muḥammad Ḥusain Mīrzā, other Dūghlāt Sulṭāns, Sulṭān Maḥmūd Khān and along with his six sons,.

21 April of AD 1509 to 11 April of AD 1510

The summers of AD 1509 began with hostilities between Shāh Ismā'īl Ṣafawī and Muḥammad Shaybānī Khān Aūzbeg. This was a piece of news which must have excited keen interest in Kābul.

The year would embark an occurrence of great importance in Turco-Mongol History. The personal acquaintance between Babur and his sympathetic biographer Ḥaidar Mīrzā Dūghlāt had just begun. Ḥaidar had escaped the protection of a kinsman; while he was just eleven. It is then that Shaybāni had attempted to kill him but he was saved by the servants of Mīrzā Khān (then located in Badakhshān). Mīrzā Khān sent Haidar to Bābur for the greater security of Kābul.*

11 April of AD 1510 to 31 March of AD 1510

a) News of the battle of Merv
Around six months passed at peace in Kābul. But a news sent by Mīrzā Khān (Wāis) in the month of Ramẓān (December) brought the turbulence. Ismā'īl had defeated Shaybāni near Merv.[2] 'It is not known,' wrote the Mīrzā, 'whether Shāhī Beg Khān has been killed or not. All the Aūzbegs have crossed the Amū. Amīr Aūrūs, who was in Qūndūz, has fled. About 20,000 Moghūls, who left the Aūzbeg at Merv, have come to Qūndūz. I have come there.' ThenMīrzā Khān invited Bābur to join him in the quest to recover their ancestral territories.†

b) Bābur's campaign in Transoxiana begins
The Mīrzā's letter had travelled through passes blocked by snow. Babur took the one winter-route through Āb-dara going at the maximum speed he could, and kept the Ramẓān Feast in Bamiyan. He reached Qūndūz in Shawwāl (January of AD 1511).

---

* Ibid, p. 227
† Ibid, p. 237.

The feast's description by Ḥaidar seems likely to have been recorded because he had read Babur's own remark, made in Ramzan (June of AD 1527).

c) Moghūl affairs

As mentioned by Mīrzā Khān in the letter, just outside Qūndūz stood the Moghūls who had come from Merv most likely as the reinforcement. They had served Babur's uncles Mahmūd and Ahmad. When Shaybānī defeated the two Khāns at Akhsī in AD 1502 those Moghūlswere compelled by him to migrate into Khurāsān to places remote from Moghūlistān. Many among them had served in Kāshghar but had neverserved a Tīmūrid Mīrzā before. As Shaybāni died, they became free and came east. This was a Moghūl army without any Khān. They numbered to around 20,000 and were fully equipped with arms. On the other hand, Chaghatāīs were not more than 5,000. Along with Moghūls from Kābul they used the opportunity for making a return to a more amiable location with an able leadership. They saw in Qūndūz a legitimate Khāqān to lead them. The two branches of Moghūls were being led bySherīm Taghāī and Ayūb Begchīk.They proffered the Moghūl Khānship to Sa'īd and at the same time proposed to set Babur aside.Perhaps they even conspired to kill him but same won't happen given the way Babur dealt with the matter.

It's unlikely that when they made their offer, they envisioned establishing themselves in the limited territory of Kābul. What they appeared to desire was what Babur granted them: Sa'īd as their Khāqān and permission to travel north with him.

On the other hand Sa'īd in the name of justice and gratitude had rejected their offer to incur any harm to Babur. He appealed to serve under Babur's command, where they could maintain their friendship for their mutual benefit. The decision was finalized when Babur responded to an urgent plea for assistance from Haider's uncle in Andijan by dispatching him there. It was on the May 13 of AD 1511 (the 14th of Safar) that Haider was appointed as a Khān and began his journey. Most of the Moghūls accompanied him, although not all of them, as records indicate that even individuals like Ayūb Begchīk from Merv continued to be associated with Babur on several later occasions.

d) Babur's use of the phrase 'I made him Khān'* echoes a similar appointment mentioned earlier,† where Abu-sa'id of Yunas was appointed as Khān of the Moghūls. In both cases, it appears that the Tīmūrid Mīrzā appointed the Chaghatāī Khān as the leader of the Moghūls.

e) First attempt on Ḥiṣār
Following a brief stay in Qūndūz, Babur proceeded towards Ḥiṣār, where the Aūzbeg sulṭāns Mahdī and Ḥamza were situated. They ventured out to Wakhsh with the intention of meeting him, but due to a misunderstanding, no confrontation occurred, and both parties withdrew.‡

f) Intercourse between Babur and Ismā'īl Ṣafawī
While Babur was residing in Qūndūz, his sister Khān-zāda arrived there safely, escorted by the Shāh's troops. This was after the battle of Merv, in which her successive husbands, Shaybāni and Sayyid Hādī, had perished. Accompanying her was an emissary from Isma'il, extending gestures of friendship and goodwill with the aim of soliciting Persian support for Babur. In response to these courtesies, Babur dispatched Mīrzā Khān with expressions of gratitude and gifts. According to Haidar, Mīrzā Khān also conveyed assurances of their good intentions and a request for military aid. The reception was warm, and the request for assistance was granted, albeit under stringent conditions, as later events would reveal.

31 March of AD 1511 to 9 March of AD 1512

a) Second attempt on Ḥiṣār
In this year, Babur once more advanced towards Ḥiṣār. He established his position at the Pul-i-sangīn (Stone Bridge) on the Sūrkh-āb, a place where his ancestor Tīmūr had previously

* Refer Folio 200b of *Baburnama*.

† Refer Folio 10b of *Baburnama*.

‡ Mirza Muhammad Haidar Dughlt, *A History of the Moghuls of Central Asia: The Tarikh-i-Rashidi*, (trans.) N. Elias and Sir Edward Denison Ross, New York: Cosimo Inc., 2008. p. 238.

achieved remarkable success against formidable odds. He remained stationed there for a month, awaiting reinforcements. On the opposite side of the river, the Aūzbeg sulṯāns confronted him, presumably also expecting reinforcements. They initiated their move when they deemed themselves sufficiently strong to launch an attack, either by augmenting their own forces or upon learning that Babur had not significantly bolstered his own. It is possible to speculate that in the latter scenario, Babur had hoped for more substantial reinforcement than he actually received. He seems to have left Qūndūz before Mirzā Khān returned from his mission to Ismā'īl, expecting Persian support to arrive with Mirzā Khān. At Pul-i-sangīn, where Mirzā Khān joined him in time for the battle, Babur likely drew strength from Mirzā Khān's followers and a few, if any, foreign auxiliaries. These speculations find support in what Khwānd-amīr relates about the conditions under which the Shah's primary contingent was dispatched, and he indicates that it did not depart until after the Shah had received news of the battle at Pul-i-sangīn.

At the end of the month-long waiting period, one morning, the Aūzbegs swam across the Sūrkh-āb below the bridge. In the afternoon of the same day, Babur withdrew to more favourable terrain within the mountain strongholds of a local Āb-dara. In the ensuing desperate confrontation, the Aūzbegs suffered a decisive defeat, incurring substantial casualties. They were pursued to Darband-i-ahanīn (Iron Gate) on the Ḥiṣār border, as they were en route to join a substantial force assembled at Qarshī under Kūchūm Khān, the successor to Shaybāni as Aūzbeg Khāqān. The battle is eloquently described by Ḥaidar, who was then a 12-year-old boy with a keen eye witnessing his own inaugural battle, fought against adversaries who had made him the last male survivor of his lineage. In the evening following the victory, Mahdī, Ḥamza, and Ḥamza's son Mamak were presented before Babur. As recounted by Ḥaidar, Babur dealt with them in a manner akin to what they had previously done to the Moghūl Khāqāns and Chaghatāī Sulṯāns, exacting a measure of vengeance in blood for the lives of numerous kinsmen.

b) Persian reinforcement

After the battle, Babur relocated near Ḥiṣār, where he was joined by numerous local tribesmen. Some time later, a substantial force of troops from Ismā'īl, led by Aḥmad Beg Ṣafawī, 'Alī Khān Istiljū, and Shāhrukh SultanSulṭān Afshār, Ismā'īl's keeper of the seal, joined him. The details provided by Khwānd-amīr regarding the dispatch of this reinforcement help establish the sequence of events and shed light on the terms Babur had to meet for his auxiliaries. Babur reported his victory over Mahdī and Ḥamza to the Shah and simultaneously made promises. He pledged that if he, with the Shah's assistance, reconquered the rest of Transoxiana, he would include the Shah's name in the khuṭba, inscribe it on coins alongside those of the Twelve Imāms, and work to diminish the power of the Aūzbegs. These commitments appear to have been a response to a demand, and they were likely imposed rather than voluntarily offered. Khwānd-amīr notes that when Ismā'īl fully grasped the significance of Babur's letter (indicating that his conditions for assistance had been accepted), he dispatched the troops under the three mentioned commanders.

Persian leaders recommended a direct move on Bukhārā and Samarkand, a plan that Babur's advisors supported. According to Ḥaidar, they argued that Bukhārā was then devoid of troops and filled with unprepared individuals. 'Ubaid Khān had taken refuge in Qarshī, and it was decided not to assault him but to proceed onward and camp one stage beyond the town. This plan was executed, and as scouts reported 'Ubaid Khān's departure from Qarshī and his hasty journey to Bukhārā, his own territory, swift and immediate pursuit followed. Over the span of 100 miles along the caravan road, they chased him into Bukhārā and beyond, compelling him and his garrison, as they fled, to surrender their plunder in the open expanse of Turkistān. Many sulṭāns had congregated in Samarkand, possibly including fugitives who had escaped from Pul-i-sangīn, such as Tīmūr, its governor. Overwhelmed by Babur's second triumph, they dispersed into Turkistān, thereby leaving him with an unobstructed path.

c) Samarkand re-occupied and relations with Ismā'īl Ṣafawī

At this point, Babur likely entertained the hope of being able to do away with his risky associates, as he dismissed them upon his arrival in Bukhārā, expressing gratitude and presenting them with gifts for their contributions. Ḥaidar, who was present during this period, specifies Bukhārā as the location for this event.* From Bukhārā, Babur proceeded to Samarkand. It was in mid-Rajab (corresponding to October of AD 1511), approximately ten months after departing from Kābul and after nine years of absence, that he re-entered the city. Samarkand was adorned for his reception, and the townspeople warmly welcomed him with great enthusiasm.[3]

Over the course of eight months, it became evident that Babur was powerless to maintain his control against the formidable forces aligned against him. These forces consisted of the consolidated military might of the Aūzbegs, driven by Sunnī zeal, intensified by their aversion to being under the rule of a Shī'a suzerain. Both as a Sunnī himself and as someone who had not previously acknowledged a suzerain, Babur found himself in an uncomfortable position. He was aware of the dangers inherent in his alliance with Ismā'īl. Furthermore, he recognized that these risks were escalating as news of Ismā'īl's fervent cruelty towards pious and erudite Sunnīs, especially in Herat, spread throughout Transoxiana.

Babur exhibited a desire for emancipation, both during the period when he not only dismissed his Persian allies but also treated the envoy, Muhammad Jān, with such indifference. Muhammad Jān, who held the title of Najm Ṣ̤ānī's Lord of the Gate, felt slighted and reported that Babur displayed arrogance, opposition, and an unwillingness to fulfil his commitments. This sentiment continued later when Babur made a fervent but unassisted attempt to conquer 'Ubaid Khān and suffered defeat. It exemplifies the Shah's perspective on his suzerain relationship with Babur that, upon hearing Muhammad Jān's report, he instructed Najm Ṣ̤ānī to discipline the offending party.

In the meantime, it appears that the Shāh's stipulations were implemented in Samarkand, clearly demonstrating Babur's

* Mirza Muhammad Haidar, *A History of the Moghuls of Central Asia: The Tarikh-i-Rashidi*, (trans.) N. Elias and Sir Edward Denison Ross, New York: Cosimo Inc., 2008. p. 696.

subservience.[4] There are clear indications of these circumstances: Babur had made promises and was a man of his word; Sunni animosity against him was escalating and not subsiding due to factors that nourished it; Babur was aware of his vulnerability against the Aūzbegs without foreign assistance and anticipated an impending attack; he would become aware of Muḥammad Jān's report and Najm Ṣānī's orders against him. Honesty, strategic considerations, and necessity all compelled him to fulfill his agreement. To determine the precise terms of that agreement, aside from the ones related to the khuṭba and the coins, requires a close examination of the sources to avoid interpreting metaphors as facts. Babur faced intense emotions, including ambition, religious fervor, sectarian bias, and fear. His challenge was greater than that faced by Henry of Navarre and Napoleon in Egypt; they only needed to appear as what secured their acceptance, while Babur had to adopt a persona that brought him hatred.

Khān-zāda was not the sole member of Babur's family to rejoin him after marrying an Aūzbeg. His half-sister Yādgār Sulṭān had been married to Ḥamza Sulṭān's son, 'Abdu'l-laṭīf, in AD 1502, when Shaybāni defeated the Khāns near Akhsī. Now that her half-brother had defeated her husband's family, she returned to her own people.*

19 March AD 1512 to 9 March of AD 1513

a) Return of the Aūzbegs

Encouraged by the departure of the Persian troops, the Aūzbegs, in the spring of the year, emerged from Turkistān, with their primary assault aimed at Tashkent, which was then under the control of Babur.[5] 'Ubaid Khān set out for Bukhārā. Before commencing his march, he had solemnly vowed that if successful, he would henceforth rigorously adhere to Musalmān Law. This vow was taken in Ḥazrat Turkistān at the shrine of Khwāja Aḥmad Yasawī, a saint revered in Central Asia for many centuries. He passed away around AD 1120. Tīmūr had undertaken a pilgrimage to his tomb in AD 1397, and subsequently, he founded the mosque that

* Refer Folio 9 in *Baburnama*.

still dominates the town, serving as a landmark for pilgrims to this day. 'Ubaid's vow, similar to Babur's in the AD 1526, represented a commitment to return to obedience. Both men made their oaths with the fervour of Ghāzīs, but with different targets in mind. Babur's oath was directed against the Hindus, whom he regarded as heathens, while 'Ubaid's oath was aimed at Babur, whom he saw as a heretic.

b) Bābur's defeat at Kul-i-malik

In Ṣafar (April–May of AD of 1512) 'Ubaid swiftly advanced and attacked the Bukhārā vicinity. Babur travelled from Samarkand to confront him. Several details of the ensuing events are not mentioned by Ḥaidar, and in one specific instance, it is mentioned by Khwānd-amīr but with contradiction to former. The point of contention between the two historians is Ḥaidar's claim that 'Ubaid had only 3000 men while Babur had 40,000. Analysing various factors one is safe to lend credibility to Khwānd-amīr's contrary assertion that Babur's force was relatively small. It's worth noting that Ḥaidar did not participate in this campaign; he was unwell in Samarkand and remained there for some time. Khwānd-amīr's details have the air of being well-informed, potentially acquired firsthand, perhaps from someone in Hindustan after AD 1527.

Several factors that weigh against the notion of Babur commanding a large, effective force at Kul-i-malik and favour Khwānd-amīr's account of the affair are as below:

1. 'Ubaid must have assessed the opposition he would face and brought 3,000 men. It's difficult to fathom where Babur could have mustered 40,000 men who were capable of fighting. In various times of crisis, Babur's immediate and consistently loyal troop is reported to be only 500.
2. As his cause was currently unpopular, there might have been few local additions to his force. Some Moghūls from Merv

and Kābul were in the vicinity of Samarkand, and most were with Sa'īd in Andijān.*

3. However, regardless of how many Moghūls were in the vicinity, none could be counted on to steadfastly support Babur's success. Moreover, if he had possessed a significant effective force, wouldn't he have attempted to hold Samarkand with the remnants of his defeated army until Persian assistance arrived?

All things considered, there are valid reasons to accept Khwānd-amīr's account that Babur confronted 'Ubaid with a relatively small force.

Following his account therefore we are informed as below:

> Babur in his excess of daring, marched to put the Aūzbeg down with a small force only, against the advice of the prudent, of whom Muḥammad Mazīd Tarkhān was one, who all said it was wrong to go out unprepared and without reinforcement. Paying them no attention, Babur marched for Bukhārā, was rendered still more daring by news had when he neared it, that the enemy had retired some stages, and followed him up almost to his camp. 'Ubaid was in great force; many Aūzbegs perished but, in the end, they were victors and Bābur was compelled to take refuge in Bukhārā. The encounter took place near Kul-i-malik (King's-lake) in Ṣafar 918 AH (April–May of AD 1512).

c) Babur Leaves Samarkand

Maintaining a foothold in Samarkand was not possible, so Babur gathered his family and entourage[6] and headed to Ḥiṣār. Accompanying him on this journey were Māhīm and her children, including Humāyūn, Mihr-jahān, and Bārbūl, as well as the motherless Ma'ṣūma. Gul-rukh was also with her son Kāmrān.†

There is no detailed account of Babur's specific route during this journey, and Haidar, who did not travel with Babur due to

* Mirza Muhammad Haidar Dughlt, *A History of the Moghuls of Central Asia: The Tarikh-i-Rashidi*, (trans.) N. Elias and Sir Edward Denison Ross, New York: Cosimo Inc., 2008. pp. 263-5.

† Gulbadan, *The History of Humāyūn* (Humāyūn-nāma), (ed.) Annette Susannah Beveridge, (trans.) Annette Susannah Beveridge, London: Royal Asiatic Society, 1902, Folio 7.

his illness in Samarkand, provides no information about it. This absence of information could be an indication that the Aūzbegs had not yet appeared directly on the road to Ḥiṣār. However, local tradition suggests that Babur may have taken a detour through Ferghana. It's plausible that Babur ventured into Ferghana with the hope of cooperating with Sa'īd Khān, especially since Tashkent was still resisting under Aḥmad-i-qāsim Kohbur. It's clear that not all activity in Babur's force had been extinguished because, during the siege of Tashkent, Dost Beg managed to break through the enemy's lines and enter the town. Sairām held out longer than Tashkent. There is only a hint, possibly a legend, regarding any such movement by Babur into Andijān.[7]

d) Babur in Ḥiṣār
Despite the significant gains and losses, he had experienced, Babur was still under 30 years of age.

After Babur's departure, the Aūzbegs reoccupied Bukhārā and Samarkand without causing harm to the townspeople. A few weeks later, in Jumāda-I (July-August of AD 1512), they followed him to Ḥiṣār. In the meantime, with the help of Mīrzā Khān, Babur had fortified the town by constructing massive earthworks that effectively closed off the streets. This led the Aūzbeg sulṭāns to believe that the defenders were prepared to sacrifice their lives to hold Ḥiṣār, and as a result, they chose not to launch an attack.[8]

e) Some sources suggest that the reason for the Aūzbegs' retreat was that Babur had received reinforcements from Balkh. While it's true that Bairām Beg had sent a force, it consisted of only 300 men. This small number could not have been alarming by itself, but it might have been seen as a precursor to a larger reinforcement. A more precise timeline of events would reveal whether the Aūzbegs had received news of Najm Ṣānī's army advancing through Balkh.

Qarshī and Ghaj-davān

In the meantime, Najm Ṣānī, leading around 11,000 men, set out on his mission to confront Babur. When he reached the Khurāsān frontier, he received news of the defeat at Kul-i-malik and Babur's retreat to Ḥiṣār. He gathered additional troops from Harāt and other regions and advanced to Balkh. There, he stayed for 20 days with Bairām Beg, possibly engaged in communications with the Shāh and Babur. Babur is said to have repeatedly requested assistance, which was provided, some sources claim, without the Shāh's permission. A rendezvous was established, and Najm Ṡānī marched to Tīrmīẕ. After crossing the Amū River, they camped near the Darband-i-ahanīn in Rajab (September–October of AD 1512).

As Babur approached through the Chak-chaq pass, Najm Ṡānī extended the courtesy of traveling several miles from his camp to give him an honourable reception. The combined armies then advanced toward Bukhārā, capturing Khuzār and proceeding to Qarshī. Babur initially intended to bypass Qarshī, as he had done on a previous march to Bukhārā, possibly to spare the lives of its people, who had once been his subjects and who were predominantly his fellow Turks. However, Najm Ṡānī insisted on taking Qarshī, citing it as 'Ubaidu'l-lāh Khān's stronghold. During its capture, the Aūzbeg garrison was massacred, and against Babur's pleas, all the townspeople, estimated at 15,000 individuals, including infants and the elderly, were killed. Among the victims was Banā'ī, who happened to be in the town. This action provoked intense anger against Najm Ṡānī and left Babur not only appalled by the merciless slaughter but also dismayed by the evident lack of regard that his illustrious fellow general held for him.

After the fall of Qarshī, Najm Ṡānī's forces advanced toward Bukhārā. As they approached the city, they learned that an Aūzbeg force led by Tīmūr and Abū-sa'īd, presumably from Samarkand, was on the way. Najm Ṡānī sent Bairām Beg to engage them, and the Aūzbeg forces withdrew to the north, taking refuge in Ghajdavān, with the combined armies following them. This move positioned Najm Ṡānī on the border of the desert, well-known to the Aūzbegs, with 'Ubaid on his flank in Bukhārā.

As for what transpired next, the sources vary, offering brief and sometimes conflicting accounts. They diverge more in the choice of details to record than in the description of the same events. Their most significant difference is in terms of timing, with one account suggesting a few days and another four months.

However, these periods might not pertain to the same event, and it is mentioned that the siege lasted for four months, indicating a substantial duration.

Initially, there were minor engagements with varying outcomes, and supplies began to run low. Both Najm Ṣānī's officers and Babur himself urged a retreat. However, Najm Ṣānī remained resolute and refused to listen to their advice. Eventually, 'Ubaid Khān rode out from Bukhārā with a formidable force and joined the Ghaj-davān garrison. The united Aūzbegs took position in the suburbs of Bukhārā, where walled lanes and gardens restricted the battlefield and diminished Najm Ṣānī's numerical advantage. On Tuesday, Ramẓān 3rd (12 November of AD 1512),[9] a decisive battle was fought, resulting in the routing of Najm Ṣānī's army and his own death.

f) Babur and Yār-i-aḥmad Najm Sānī

Some writers suggest that Najm Ṣānī's soldiers did not fight well, but it's important to consider that they may have been weakened by deprivation, and their desire to retreat. Regarding Babur, it is said that he, as the reserve, did not participate in the battle at all. It's difficult to find a compelling reason why, given the circumstances, he should risk the loss of his men. It appears that Haidar's strong language about this defeat would align with Babur's disposition as well. He wrote, 'The victorious breezes of Islam overturned the banners of the schismatics . . . Most of them perished on the field; the rents made by the sword at Qarshī were sewn up at Ghaj-davān by the arrow-stitches of vengeance. Najm Ṣānī and all the Turkmān amīrs were sent to hell.'

The belief that Babur had failed Najm Ṣānī persisted at the Persian Court, and his inaction was later used as a reproach to his son Humāyūn in AD 1544 when latter sought refuge with Ismā'īl's son Ṭahmāsp. Badāyūnī shares a story, although with significant inaccuracies in names and places, which reflects the view held at that time. The relevant part of the anecdote suggests that on the eve of the battle at Ghaj-davān, Babur shot an arrow into the Aūzbeg camp, bearing a couplet that expressed his ill-will toward the Shāh and perhaps also his rejection of the Shī'a guise he had previously adopted. I made the Shāh's Najm road-stuff for the Aūzbegs.

If fault has been mine, I have now cleansed the road.[10]

g) The Moghūls attack Babur

On his second return to Ḥiṣār, Babur faced significant danger when a sudden attack was launched by the Moghūls on his camp outside the town, where he lay at night. Firishta mentions that Babur had reproached them for their misconduct, but the lack of specific details connecting this incident with the earlier defeat suggests that their wrongdoings may have been part of the oppressive rule over the local population, later punished by 'Ubaidu'l-lāh Khān.

Awakened from his sleep by the commotion caused by his guards' resistance to the Moghūl attack, Babur managed to escape with great difficulty and without a single attendant, seeking refuge within the fort.[11] The conspirators looted his camp and then retreated to Qarā-tīgīn. Babur was in no position to confront them, so he left a few men in Ḥiṣār and went to Mīrzā Khān in Qūndūz.

In Babur's absence, Ḥiṣār endured a devastating famine, an extraordinary snowfall, and the depredations of the Moghūls. 'Ubaid Khān took revenge on behalf of Babur against the horde. Upon learning of their excesses, he encamped outside their position in Wakhsh, which was defended by rivers, hills, and snow. He waited until a path had thawed, then attacked them, avenging the year of misery they had inflicted on the Ḥiṣārīs. Ḥaidar notes that it was the treacherous actions of these Moghūls that led to the loss of Ḥiṣār for Bābur and its recovery for the Aūzbeg.[12]

These Moghūls were led by individuals who, when Sa'īd went to Andijān, chose to remain with Babur. One of the three mentioned by Ḥaidar was Ayūb Begchīk. He later regretted his disloyalty and, while lying on his deathbed some two years later (AD 1514) in Yāngī-ḥiṣār, confessed to Sa'īd Khān that his faithlessness to Babur in Ḥiṣār and the oath he had broken at the instigation of the Moghūl chiefs were causing him unbearable remorse.*

During this year, but before the Moghūl treachery against Babur, Ḥaidar left him and began his journey to Sa'id in Andijān, marking the start of his nineteen years of service.

9 March of AD 1513 to 26 February of AD 1514

During this year, Babur might have spent some time in Khishm.† For two or three months of that period, he had one of the Shāh's retainers in his service, Khwāja Kamālu'd-dīn Maḥmūd. Khwāja Kamālu'd-dīn had fled from Ghaj-davān to Balkh, where he learned that the people of Balkh were favouring an Aūzbeg chief whose arrival was imminent. Therefore, he decided to join Babur. In Jumāda II (August of AD 1513), upon hearing that the Aūzbeg sulṭān had left Balkh, Khwāja Kamālu'd-dīn returned to Balkh. However, he was not admitted into the city because the people of Balkh feared retaliation for their support of the Aūzbeg. This fear might indicate that he had brought a significant reinforcement to Babur. Khwāja Kamālu'd-dīn then continued into Khurāsān, where he was killed. The recapture of Balkh for the Shāh by Deo Sulṭān was a reversal of Aūzbeg control in the region, and this development helps explain how Babur came to be in Balkh in AD 1517.

26 February of AD 1514 to 15 February of AD 1515

Haidar's writings depict Babur as if he were in Qūndūz‡ during this year. According to Haidar, Babur endured significant hardship and want, but he bore it with his characteristic courtesy and patience. Eventually, he gave up hope of successfully recovering Ḥiṣār and returned to Kābul. It appears that he made the stay in Khwāst, as

* Mirza Muhammad Haidar Dughlt, *A History of the Moghuls of Central Asia: The Tarikh-i-Rashidi*, (trans.) N. Elias and Sir Edward Denison Ross. New York: Cosimo Inc., 2008. p. 351.

† Ghiyās̱ al-Dīn ibn Humām al-Dīn Khvānd Mīr, *Habib Al-Siyar*, Volume 3, Qazwin, Iran, Safavid period, 1579–80. p. 372.

‡ Mirza Muhammad Haidar Dughlt, *A History of the Moghuls of Central Asia: The Tarikh-i-Rashidi*, (trans.) N. Elias and Sir Edward Denison Ross, New York: Cosimo Inc., 2008. p. 263.

referred to later,* during which his daughter Gul-rang was born, as corroborated by Gul-badan's chronicle.

At the end of the year, after enduring the hardships of winter, Babur reached Kābul. When he had retaken Samarkand in AD 1511, he had entrusted Kābul to his half-brother Nāṣir Mīrzā. Nāṣir Mīrzā warmly welcomed Babur and professed his devotion and respect. He spoke of guarding Kābul on Babur's behalf and requested permission to return to his former fief, Ghaznī. Nāṣir Mīrzā's conduct deeply affected Babur, and it would have been perceived as a humane gesture during a time of disappointment and failure.

15 February of AD 1515 to 5 February of AD 1516

Rebellion of chiefs in Ghaznī

Shortly after his return to Ghaznī, Nāṣir Mīrzā passed away. Following his death, disputes erupted among various commanders in Ghaznī. Sherīm Ṭaghāī was one of the key figures involved, and the main source of the turmoil was the Moghūls. However, many others were also caught up in the conflict, including long-serving individuals like Bābā of Pashāghar.† ‡

Haidar did not have precise information about the exact cause of the dispute or why it had turned against Babur. He attributed the conflict to Satan taking hold of the chiefs' minds, resulting in an increase in vanity and wickedness. It's possible that the dispute revolved around the question of succession after Nāṣir's death. During the ensuing battle, Dost Beg distinguished himself, and Qaṃbar-i-'alī, the son of Qāsim Beg, hurried down from Qūndūz to contribute to Babur's victory. Many of the rioters were killed in the conflict, and others fled to Kāshghar. Sherīm Ṭaghāī was among those who fled, and since he received no welcome from Sa'īd Khān, he could not stay in Kāshghar. He eventually sought refuge with Babur, who, as Haidar notes, displayed his customary benevolence. Babur chose

* Refer Folio 241b in *Baburnama*.

† Refer folio 24b in *Baburnama*.

‡ Mirza Muhammad Haidar Dughlt, *A History of the Moghuls of Central Asia: The Tarikh-i-Rashidi*, (trans.) N. Elias and Sir Edward Denison Ross, New York: Cosimo Inc., 2008, p. 356.

to overlook Sherīm Ṭaghāī's past offences and focused on his prior services. Sherīm Ṭaghāī, however, passed away shortly thereafter.* 13

5 February of AD 1516 to 24 January of AD 1517

During this year, Babur may have spent his time in and around Kābul, benefiting from the tranquillity that followed the dispersion of the Moghūls. In the same year, Babur's son Muḥammad, known as 'Askarī because of his birth in a camp, was born. He was the son of Gulrukh Begchīk and the full brother of Kāmrān.

24 January of AD 1517 to 13 January of AD 1518

a) Babur visits Balkh
Khwānd-amīr provides some insights into Babur's actions during this year, particularly related to the activities of Badī'u'z-zamān Bāī-qarā's son, Muḥammad-i-zamān. Muḥammad-i-zamān had experienced significant wanderings, during a portion of which Khwānd-amīr was in his company.† In AD 1514, he was in the service of Shāh Ismā'īl and stationed in Balkh, but he was unable to maintain control of the city.

Babur invited Muḥammad-i-zamān to come to Kābul, and this invitation likely occurred after Babur's return to Kābul at the end of AD 1514. However, while on his way to Kābul, Muḥammad-i-zamān was dissuaded from entering the city by Mahdī Khwāja. Instead, he redirected his journey to Ghurjistān. Babur, annoyed by Muḥammad-i-zamān's failure to arrive, pursued him with the intention of punishing him. However, Babur was unable to reach Ghurjistān and returned to Kābul via Fīrūz-koh and Ghūr.

Ultimately, Muḥammad-i-zamān was captured and brought to Kābul. Babur treated him kindly, and after a few months, he arranged a marriage between Muḥammad-i-zamān and his daughter Ma'ṣūma. Subsequently, he sent Muḥammad-i-zamān

* Ibid, p. 357

† Ghiyās̱ al-Dīn ibn Humām al-Dīn Khvānd Mīr, *Habib Al-Siyar*, Volume 3, Qazwin, Iran, Safavid period, 1579–80, p.367.

to rule in Balkh. According to Khwānd-amīr, the events related to Muḥammad-i-zamān occurred in AD 1523. The marriage likely took place either at the end of AD 1517 or the beginning of AD 1518 when Muḥammad-i-zamān was 21 and Ma'ṣūma was 9. It is highly unlikely that Ma'ṣūma went to Balkh at that time. At some point in AD 1517, Babur is said to have visited Balkh, as reported by Khwānd-amīr.[14]

b) Attempt on Qandahār

In this year, Babur set out on a march toward Qandahār. However, this particular move concluded peacefully due to an unexpected illness that befell him when he was near the town. The illness appears to have led to negotiations, gifts, and terms that prevented a military confrontation.

The Tārīkh-i-sind provides what is claimed to be Shāh Beg's explanation for Babur's repeated attempts to capture Qandahār. According to Shāh Beg, Babur's persistence in seeking Qandahār was motivated by his inability to forgive Muqīm for capturing Kābul from the Tīmūrid 'Abdu'r-razzāq fourteen years earlier. This event had brought Babur to Qandahār in AD 1507 and led to the removal of Māhchuchak, Muqīm's daughter. Furthermore, by AD 1517, there were many unemployed Mīrzās in Kābul for whom suitable positions could not be found in regions where the Persians and Aūzbegs held sway. Seeking an outlet for their ambitions and those of Babur, they looked toward a confrontation with a weaker adversary.

Babur's decision to launch an attack in this year was reportedly made while Shāh Beg was still a prisoner in the custody of Shāh Ismā'īl in the Herāt region. However, Shāh Beg must have been released by that time, possibly due to the patient efforts of his servant Saṃbhal.

13 January of 1518 to 3 January of AD 1519

During this year, Shāh Beg's son, Shāh Ḥasan, arrived at Bābur's court after a quarrel with his father. Shāh Ḥasan remained in Babur's service for approximately two years. During this period, he was married to

Gul-barg, the daughter of Khalīfa. His return to Qandahār likely occurred shortly before Babur's renewed campaign against the city in AD 1520, which ultimately led to Babur's capture of Qandahār on Shawwāl thirteenth (6 September of AD 1522).[15]

In this year, the campaign in the northeastern territories of Kābul commenced, and an account of these events is continued in the diary for AD 1519. It appears that during this year, Chaghān-sarāī and the fortress at the head of the Bābā-qarā valley, which belonged to Ḥaidar-i-'alī Bajaurī, were captured.*

* Refer folio 216b of *Baburnama*.

Notes

Introduction

1 No history books of N.C.E.R.T. (till matriculation) ever elaborated the lives of revolutionaries. It was my fortune to be a student of D.A.V. Public School where specifically the *Dharam Shiksha* books dealt with individual chapters on people like Ram Prasad Bismil, Lala Har Dayal Mathur, Rani Lakshmibai etc. Had those books not been by my side, I would have left the subject of history without knowing of such great men and women, who walked on our land of Bharat. Right now, I do not have the books I studied in schools, but I'm sure that any alumni of D.A.V. (who were schooled there in late 1990s to early 2000s) would agree to it. The students who took up science stream after matriculation would never need to deal with the subject of history again unless their interests pile up. Then it would depend primarily on what sources they pick. At times, there would be books which would designate the revolutionaries as 'terrorists'. For example, Bipan Chandra writes in his book, *India's Struggle for Independence*, 'It is not accidental that nearly all the major new leaders of the revolutionary terrorist politics, for example, Jogesh Chandra Chatterjea, Surya Sen, Jatin Das, Chandrashekhar Azad, Bhagat Singh, Sukhdev, Shiv Varma, Bhagwati Charan Vohra and Jaidev Kapur, had been enthusiastic participants in the non-violent Non-Cooperation Movement.' (Bipan Chandra, 1989) In contrast if one gets a hand on *History of The Freedom Movement in India* by R.C. Majumdar, he would end up giving a completely different view which actually is very close to reality. For heaven's sake, who in India will see Bhagat Singh and allies as terrorists? In whole book, Majumdar has not made opinions about Bhagat Singh and other revolutionaries, but he has just penned out instances which could promote people to make an opinion about revolutionaries (Majumdar, 1962).

2 Class-VI (6th) N.C.E.R.T. Book for History, Chapter 7 (N.C.E.R.T., 2021).

3 Romila Thapar in her book, *Ashoka and the Decline of Mauryas* talks of edicts and inscriptions (Thapar, 1961) while trying to discredit the claim that Ashoka was already a Buddhist when he attacked Kalinga. In contrast, Charles Allen uses them to build the case otherwise. Moreover, if one reads the inscription (e.g., 1st Minor Edict of Maski) then it becomes very clear that during the Kalinga War, Ashoka was already a Buddhist. It can be understood from the fact that Maski Edict is dated to 260 BC wherein Ashoka claims to have been a lay-Buddhist for almost two and a half years (Hultzsch, 1925), and the Kalinga War had occurred only one year back (in 261 BC). Moreover, Charles Allen has concluded that Ashoka converted to Buddhism in 265 BC (based on reading of other edicts of Ashoka).

4 A.B. Scott writes on effect of British Education, 'The rise of a class of young prigs for whom it became the done thing to denigrate everything Indian in an attempt at blind imitation of the customs and attitudes of western people.' (Scott, 1973)

5 The post-modernism has penetrated deep into the architecture school, and works around it along with modernism inspire students at best. Especially, the architecture of India in the era of post-Independence was pretty much dictated by the whims and fancies of Le-Corbusier. The case-studies needed for pursuing design projects often takes people to the literature of modernism, post-modernism and then to the root of movements, Marxism. For example, I began to read about post-modernism, and ended up with Cultural Marxism.

The faculties across the universities and schools of architecture have been observing same off late (Kemper, 2018).

6 There have been long discussions by the Marxist School of Historiography to paint (Truschke, 2020) the uncovering of indigenous stories of Bharat as project of errors coloured by some political ideologies (Mukherjee, et al., 2001).

7 These thoughts on how the very journey to the great Ajanta and Ellora began my transformation, leaving away the cloak of communism elaborated in *Modi Again: An Ex-Communist's Manifesto*.

8 Being illusioned towards the wisdom, and valour of people in India from ancient times. I lived with the view that ancient India was the place of superstition and had been invaded continually after Steppe Aryans. I could never find the tale, which told, if ever we won a battle against any invader? I had firmly begun to believe that the traditions my parents want me to practice are icons of superstitions, somewhere passed on by the Aryan inavders. Needless to say, as explained earlier (refer footnote [3]) the Marxist historiography did have an impact on how I thought about history.

9 Primary sources are the raw materials of history—original documents and objects that were created at the time under study. They are different from

secondary sources, accounts that retell, analyse, or interpret events, usually at a distance of time or place (Congress).

10 I read the works *Das Kapital* and *The Communist Manifesto,* but neither had any such views about British Imperialism in India.

11 One may claim that there were always History books written by scholars like Jadunath Sarkar and R.C. Majumdar. But then we must not forget the fact that for a youth like me, who had chosen to bid a goodbye to history post school, the inputs of the NCERT books were the only tool to draw an impression about our history. At the same time, we are also aware about how systematically historians who did not yield to the lines of Nehruvian ideology for Historiography were shown way out (Balakrishna).

12 Details of Jalal-ud-din Muhammad (Akbar) would be dealt with in details with successive books from the series dealing with him. Though as of now to get current context, it would be suggestive for the people to go through *Fatehnama-i-Chittor (an annotated translation, 1971).*

13 The recent work of Sanjeev Sanyal on Revolutionaries (Sanyal, 2023) along with Vikram Sampath's works on Savarkar (Sampath, 2021) brings forth the fact that Bharat didn't win its independence only by passive Gandhian Movement.

14 The attempts were continually made to whitewash the atrocities committed by the Islamic Invaders (Maldahiyar, 2022) and the other East India Companies (Portuguese and Dutch).

15 Babur recognized himself as Tīmūrid as his father's lineage was from the line of Timur. In earlier sections brief premise has been given in footnotes that how the history of atrocities was whitewashed even though American Historian, Will Durant observed, Mohammadian conquest of India to be bloodiest (Durant, 1954).

16 As an example, I quote Babur from *Baburnama* as he writes in relation to his conquest of Chandiri. He writes (Babur):

> *Chandiri I stormed in 934 A.H. (1528 A.D.) and, by God's pleasure, took it in a few hours; in it was Rana Sanga's great and trusted man Midni Rao, we made general massacre of the Pagans in it and, as will be narrated, converted what for many years had been a mansion of hostility, into a mansion of Islam.*

17 Firoz Shah Tuglaq says (Afif, 1871):

> *'The next matter which by God's help I accomplished, was the repetition of names and titles of former sovereigns which had been omitted from the prayers of Sabbaths and Feasts. The names of those sovereigns of Islam, under whose happy fortune and favour infidel countries had been*

conquered, whose banners had waved over many a land, under whom idol-temples had been demolished, and mosques and pulpits built and exalted, the fragrant creed had been extended, and the people of Islam had waxen strong and warlike, the names of these men had fallen into neglect and oblivion. So I decreed that according to established custom their names and titles should be rehearsed in the khutba and aspirations offered for the remission of their sins.

18 Ahmad Sirhindi writes as below in a letter (Sirhindi, 1988) criticising the steps taken by Akbar written to Shaikh Farid alias Nawab Murtaza Khan who was opposed to Akbar's religious policy, and who supported Jahangir's accession after taking from the latter a promise that Islam will be upheld in the new reign:

Islam and infidelity (kufr) contradict one another. To establish the one means eradicating the other, the coming together of these contradictories being impossible. Therefore, Allah has commanded his Prophet to wage war (jihad) against the infidels and be harsh with them. (. . .) The abolition of jizyah in Hindustan is a result of friendship which (Hindus) have acquired with the rulers of this land . . . What right have the rulers to stop exacting jizyah? (. . .)

19 Common sense might suggest that here was a striking example of a refutable hypothesis that had in fact been refuted. Indo-European scholars should have scrapped all their historical reconstructions and started again from scratch. But that is not what happened. Vested interests and academic posts were involved. Almost without exception the scholars in question managed to persuade themselves that despite appearances the theories of the philologists and the hard evidence of archeology could be made to fit together. The trick was to think of the horse-riding Aryans as conquerors of the cities of the Indus civilization in the same way that the Spanish conquistadores were conquerors of the cities of Mexico and Peru or the Israelites of the Exodus were conquerors of Jericho. The lowly Dasa of the Rig Veda, who had previously been thought of as primitive savages, were now reconstructed as members of a high civilization. (Leach, 1990)

20 This is highly problematic narrative because it pushes us to believe India was fragmented because of language in the past. But had that been the truth how could Aadi Shankaracharya, travel down from south of India up to Kashmir and preach *Vedanta*? We have records wherein people of past interacted with people of different regions with varied languages and people used to be multilingual.

21 To begin to tell these tales Sanjeev Sanyal came up with his book *Revolutionaries*and Vikram Sampath with *Bravehearts of Bharat*.

22 The normal projection of Indian History has been that India was a fragmented country and was never united. Any attempt of someone to demystify the truths around Islamic Invasion or related subjects, gets a strong backlash because the normally accepted narrative is not in favour of those demystifications. Often that gets taglines like, '*saffronization*' and more with bulk of attacks flowing through the media pieces.

23 First wave had come through Tīmūr himself in AD 1398. In words of his biographer, Yazdi, 'Tīmūr's only aim till his death was to excite the Mussalmans to make war on enemy of their religion, (. . .) and Al-Quran praises above all others, those who risk their fortunes and lives in such a war'. (Yazdī, 1723)

24 Translated by author based on the Persian manuscript available in National Museum, New Delhi. This is copy of the MS of translated version of one commissioned under Akbar in 1589.

25 *Baburnama* was translated in English from Turkic by British Orientalist Annette Susannah Beveridge in 1922 (Beveridge, 1922). She used the Turkic version called the Haidarabad Codex (1915). Akbar had got it translated in Persian in AD 1589.

26 Interestingly, though the area of Akbar's extent was only 0.85 million sq. miles (Habib, 1982), way lesser than Maratha Empire at its peak academicians haven't hesitated to call his empire as 'Hindustan' while neglecting to address 'Haindavi Swarajya' of latter as empire of Bharat.

27 Timur's Biographer Yazdi writes, 'God hath recommended to Mahomet to excite the Muslamans to make war on the enemies of their religion, because it is the most excellent of all actions, and Alcoran praises above all others, those who risk their fortunes and lives in such a war.

'This was Timur's only aim, from the beginning of his life to his death, but he particularly executed at this time by beginning a war which he had a long while projected.' (Yazdī, 1723)

Part 1: Ferghana

Chapter 1: Babur's Home

1 In AD 1220, nearly all Central Asia and the territory of modern Kazakhstan were invaded by Mongols. There were no written documents about Taraz's growth under the Mongols after they razed it to the ground. Remnants of fire found during the excavation show that the city was burnt. Probably the town was renamed as Yany (new); while mentioning it, European and Arabic sources write, 'The city Yany, named Taraz before the conquest.' Archaeological finds show that the once-lively city under the Mongolian yoke lost its previous significance and independence. Settled life in Taraz ended and the decline began. Under the Chagatayids (descendants of Chagatai

Khān), coins were minted in Taraz until AD 1334. The Tsareviches, who, as Vasa of fourteenth century states, 'Burnt the Golden Horde, destroyed Taraz and other cities, and killed the population. They took everything they could take and burnt the rest. There was a mention of the city again in AD 1345 in the road guidebook as a city laid on the trade route from Transoxiana to Almalyk.' Steady internecine war in Central Asia interfered with the trade with distant countries, and the opening of the sea route from the Western European countries to India stopped the trade on the ancient silk road and led to the decline of the cities on this road.

2 The Syr Darya is a river located in Central Asia. The name has Persian origin which literally means Syr Sea or Syr River. A few people often referred to in this way. It originates in the Tian Shan Mountains of Kyrgyzstan and eastern Uzbekistan. Flowing 1,401.97 miles west it enters north-west through Uzbekistan and southern Kazakhstan. It finally ends in the northern remnants of the Aral Sea. It is among the two main rivers in the endorheic basin of the Aral Sea. The other important river is Amu Darya (Jayhun). During the Soviet era a tragedy was crafted. The extensive irrigation project of the Soviets came around both rivers, thereby diverting water into the farmlands. The effect did not show up immediately but in post-Soviet era, world's fourth largest lake; Aral Sea virtually disappeared.

3 Fanākat was also known as Banākaṯ, Benākaṯ (not to be confused with another town of Benkaṯ, another town of Šāš, later to become Tashkent). It was the main town of the medieval Transoxiana province of Šāš or ā .

4 Although Banākaṯ flourished in early Islamic times, but it almost certainly had a pre-Islamic history as a center of the Sogdians. According to Markwart, Wehrot und Arang, (Leiden, 1938, pp. 162-63), the name derives from Middle Persian bon 'base, foundation' plus kaṯ 'town', hence 'chief town, capital'. The town lays at the confluence of the Syr Darya or Jaxartes (which Jovaynī apparently calls 'the River of Fanākat') with its right-bank tributary the Āhangarān or Angren (medieval Nahr Īlāq) and at the mouth of the Gijigen valley, hence to the southwest of modern Tashkent; both the ruins of old Banākaṯ and of its replacement Šāhro īya have been noted by Russian archaeologists from AD 1896 onwards (Vasilii Vladimirovich Bartol'd, 1977).

Although there is not much information about the coming of Islam to Banākaṯ but local Iranian princes seem to have persisted there into Samanid times, and we have a detailed description in Moqaddesī, of the town in the second half of the 10th century. He calls it the capital of Šāš, with an orthodox Sunni but quarrelsome and turbulent population. There was a citadel (qohandez) with gates opening on to the inner town (madīna) and on to the inner one of the two outer towns (raba), where the majority of bāzārs lay; the Friday Mosque was up against the city wall. The town had extensive gardens and orchards and produced "Turkestan" cloth and bows.

Four stages to the north lay Asfījāb and the beginning of the Turkish steppes. It was apparently a place of some importance under the Qarakhānids, and coins were minted there under these princes (Jaeckel).

When Genghis Khān's hordes appeared in Transoxiana, the Qanḡlï Turkish garrison under the Ḵᵛārazmšāh's commander Iletgü Malek defended Banākaṯ for four days against five thousand Mongol troops under Alaq Noyon, Sögetü, and Taqāy. On its surrender, there was a general massacre of the garrison, whilst the male population was impressed into the Mongol forces (ala Ad-din ata Malik Juvaini, 1958). Barthold doubted that it was this event specifically which caused the town's destruction but opined that it probably fell into ruin in the later 7th /13th century. At any rate, in AD 1392 (year of the monkey), it was rebuilt by Tīmūr and named Šāhroḵīya after his son and successor Šāhroḵ (Yazdī, 1723).

5 'Ali-Shir Nava'i was a 15th century politican and polymath with expertise in poetry, politics, linguistics. He was a Hanafi Maturidi and was also known as a fine painter. He was celebrated as being one of the greatest representative of Chagatai literature. He considered that for literary pursuits Chagatai and other Turkic languages were superior to Persian. It was indeed a radical opinion in that era. He posited a view that Turkic vocabulary as being more rich, precise and malleable in comparission to Persian. He brought a work titled 'Muhakamat al-Lughatayn' (The Comparison of the Two Languages) with purpose to substantiate his claim of Turkic superiority over the Persian.

Because of his distinguished Chagatai language poetry, Nava'i is considered by many throughout the Turkic-speaking world to be the founder of early Turkic literature. Many places and institutions in Central Asia are named after him.

6 Osh is the second largest city in Kyrgyzstan, located in the Fergana Valley in the south of the country and often referred to as the 'capital of the south'. It is estimated to be the oldest city in the country with the history of more than three millenniums. The city has an ethnically mixed population of about 2,81,900 in 2017, comprising Uzbeks, Kyrgyz, Russians, Tajiks, and other smaller ethnic groups. It is about 5 km from the Uzbekistan border.

7 Historically Bara-Kuh has several names like, The Sulaiman-Too, The Sulaiman Tagh, and The Takhti-Suleimen. In the time when Babur lived, it was commonly known by its Persian name The Bara-Kukh. The name literally meant separately standing or a beautiful mountain. By around the ending years of thirteenth century, the name had received some distortions and was called, The Barak. According to the Chinese narratives 'a town at a highly respected mountain' existed in the first half of 1st millennium AD. It was known as Guishan-chane and has been identified by some researchers to be located exactly in the Osh city. According to Arabic sources of seventeenth century, Prophet Sulaiman (Biblical Solomon) stayed on this mountain.

8 Margilan is a city in Fergana Region of eastern Uzbekistan. It is elevated at 487 meters, located at the crossing of trade caravans from China to the west and vice versa (in a picturesque square). Margilan's root is in close association with the Silk Road opening. While it is not considered to be the birthplace of the city, but the Silk Road was the head keeper of its secrets for Margilan. Margilan was renowned for their silk goods from far west to far east as far back as the tenth century—the largest city in the Ferghana Valley.

According to European legend, Margilan was founded by Alexander. On a lunch stop, he was given chicken (murgh; in Persian) and bread (nan; in Persian), from which the town took its name. More reliable records indicate that Margilan was an important stop on the Silk Road by the ninth century AD, along the route going across the Alay Mountains to Kashgar.

9 Located on the alluvial fan of the Golrubar Creek in central Iran, Semnan happens to be the the capital city of the Semnan Province.It lies 216 km east of Tehran and 640 km west of Mashhad. It is habitat of a population of around 185, 129 people, and is considered the populous most city in the province. On an interesting note, the city is hub of the Samnani language, a sub-branch of the Caspian languages spoken to the north, and home to the Samnani ethnic group.

How the place got its name also has various theories. A few are mentioned below:

a) The place existed before Zoroastrianism and the tradition of idol-worship called samīna was prevalent. This led to the name Semnan.
b) Scythians had established a settlement in ancient times which went on to be called Sạkanān by Iranians.
c) According to the Islamic narratives of locality, the two sons of Prophet Noah, Sim An-Nabi and Lam An-Nabi were the first settlers of Semnan. They say that it is from these two names that Simlan came that over time the turned into Semnan.
d) Some say that Semnan was established by the mythical character Tahmuras (in Ferdowsi's epic poem, the Shahnameh), who had named his city Saminā.
e) We have a narrative that there existed an ancient language called *Sa ma nān*, and people named their city after it.
f) We hear of a Sermani tradition wherein women cooked breads amounting to three months in a day. The phrase *sa ma nān* meant 'three months of bread.' Hence a few postulate that name comes from this Sermani tradition.

10 Al-Hidayah fi Sharh Bidayat al-Mubtadi (593 AH/AD 1197) commonly referred to as al-Hidayah (lit. 'the guidance', also spelled Hedaya), is a twelfth century legal manual by Burhan al-Din al-Margilali, which is one

of the most influential compendia of Hanafi jurisprudence (fiqh). It has been subject of numerous commentaries. The book played a key role in the development and amalgamation of Islamic and British law known as Anglo-Muhammadan law.

11 Esfara, is a district in the Fergana valley to the south of the Jaxartes extending to the foothills of the Turkistan (Bottamān) range. The city of the same name in Tajikistanstands 107 km east of Ḵojand on the Esfara River, which is used extensively for irrigation.

Esfara (also Espara, Esfarah, Esbara, Asbara) should not be mistaken with Asfara/Asbara of southern Kazakhstan, reconstructed as Ašpara following A shi bu lai in the Chinese sources (Minorsky, 1937) (Chavannes, 1903). 'Asfara'is also noted as the name of a local Sogdian prince, the heir apparent to the king of Fergana, who controlled the rural district of Esfara, where he resettled the Sogdians in AD 721–22 who had emigrated eastward to avoid conversion to Islam. The district was known then as the Pass of 'EsÂām after 'Eṣām, born as 'Abd-Allāh al-Bāhelī, who had been appointed as governor there by Qotayba b. Moslem (Gibb, 1923) (Spuler, 2015).

When the era of Islam began, the name Esfara was applied to the district located south of what has been the main road connecting Ūš to Ḵojand; its towns ṬÂamāḵoš and Bāmkāḵoš, one mile apart, were probably located slightly to the north of the present town (Vasilii Vladimirovich Bartol'd, 1977). Ebn Ḥawqal mentions about the parti-coloured mountains with coal mines in the locality (Ḥawqal, 1967). Coal was mined there then (as now), sold at the low price of three donkey loads for one *derham*, and burnt for heat; the ashes were used for bleaching cloth (Spuler, 2015).

12 Muhammad Shaybāni Khān was (Y.Karasoy, 1998) one of the most formidable enemies of Babur and was also known as Abul-Fath Shaybāni Khān or Shayabak Khān or Shahi Beg Khān. He was originally named as 'Shibägh', which means wormwood or obsidian. He was born in the year AD 1451 to Sheikh Haidar, son of Abu'l-Khayr Khān and died on 2 December of AD 1510. As a powerful Uzbek leader, he consolidated various Uzbek tribes thereby laying the foundations for their dominance in Transoxiana and establishing the Khānate of Bukhara. He got the name Shaybāni for being descendant of Shiban (or Shaybān), the fifth son of Jochi (the eldest son of Genghis Khān).

13 This is summarized form of translated version of the *Baburnama* by Annette Susannah Beveridge,

14 Dervish or darvesh or darwīsh (from Persian: darvīsh) is an Islamic term. It broadly refers to the members of a Sufi fraternity (tariqah). (Britannica, 2009) But narrowly speaking it refers to a religious mendicant choosing to live with material poverty. (MacDonald, 2012) (Mansour Shaki, 2011) The latter usage is found particularly in Persian and Turkish (Dervi), corresponding to the Arabic term *faqir* (MacDonald, 2012). Their most common practice

is Sama, which is associated with the thirteenth century mystic Rumi. The folklores speak of dervishes having ability to perform miracles and described with supernatural power. One more essential point that can't be ignored is that the Sufis have played instrumental role in bringing Islamic conversions.

15 This ancient, fortified residence of Ferghana rulers, known as Aksikent or Akhsi as it was called at that time, was built on the hill at the junction of two rivers—the Kasansai and the Syr Darya. In the times of Babur, Akhsi was the second largest city in the Ferghana Valley. Time and natural disasters had no mercy on it and today the ruins of Aksikent are buried under the huge mud hill in twenty kilometres south-west of Namangan.

The archaeologists discovered that fortified settlement with a citadel, called Ahshi or Ahsi existed on the territory of Ferghana Valley already in the third century BC as part of the Dayuan state. In the environs of Ahsi, just as in the whole Ferghana valley, people bred 'blood-sweating' war-horses whom Chinese emperors craved for. Time and again war broke out for the possession of these heavenly fast horses. Historian Sima Qian in his chronicles Shiji (Records of the Historian) reports that in BC 103 commander Li Guanli with his army numbering 60,000 warriors sieged Aksikent for forty days blocking the access to the city of drinking water. But there were wells in the fortress and its defenders managed to hold out until the army of a friendly state of Kangju came to the aid of the city.

At the beginning of the first millennium the cities of the Ferghana Valley were conquered first by Kushan rulers, then by Turks. But it was at this time that Aksikent was turned into the economic centre of the state. Numerous trade caravans came here from Kashgar and China, Asia Minor and Byzantium. Locally made fabrics, pottery and metalware were in great demand in the international markets. Aksikent increased its significance after the Ferghana Valley was conquered by the Arabs and the town became the capital city of the area. Antique Aksikent was only two kilometres in perimeter. In the 8th-9th centuries, according to the medieval chronicler and geographer Maqsidi, the town grew into a large township encircled by the 18- kilometer-long outer wall with five gates. The archaeological excavation proved that there was in Aksikent a citadel with a splendid palace and a jail, whereas in shakhristan (inner city) there was a city mosque and bathhouses. On the bank of Syr Darya river there was a big square for Friday praying. In rabat—the trade suburbs of the city which were protected by outer walls and watching towers, there were bazaars and craftsmen workshops. Archeologists found coins minted in Aksikent in the ninth and eleventh centuries.

For five years since 2002 the ruins of antique and pre-Mongol Aksikent were researched by the scientists of the British-Uzbek archaeological expedition led by Professor of College London Institute of archaeology Tilo Rehren. In the urban quarters of craftsmen, the scientists discovered fire-resistant crucibles made of kaolin. Such crucibles could resist the temperature of 1300 degrees. For the smelting furnaces the local metallurgists used natural fuel—the wood of juniper tree which being burnt can provide high temperature. It was a necessary criterion for smelting steel from carboniferous iron ore which the nearby spurs of the Tien Shan mountains are rich in. After masterly hammering such steel became exclusively strong, bendable and had a specific pattern, that is, it became the steel known as 'Damask steel'. No wonder that in the Arabic chronicles of the 10th century it was mentioned that 'cold steel from Ferghana was used everywhere from Khorasan to Baghdad'. A British archaeologist suggested that not only ready-made cold steel weapons were imported from Aksikent, but the steel itself was delivered to Damascus by the merchants travelling along the routes of the Great Silk Road. In Damaskus, local smiths hammered swords and sabers which gained popularity both in the Orient and in Europe.

At the beginning of the thirteenth century Aksikent suffered the plundering raid of Kara-Khitan tribes, and later, in AD 1228, the Ferghana valley was conquered by one of Genghiz-khan's commanders—Jebe Noyan. The ruler of Aksikent, Ismoil, surrendered to the conquerors and even agreed to guide the Mongols in their raid against Samarkand. However, plundered and ruined by the Mongols Aksikent fell into decay. Only under Amir Timur the town was built up anew in several kilometers down the Syr Darya river to the west from ancient, pre-Mongol Aksikent. This new town on the steep riverbank occupied the area of one hundred hectares. And even though it lost its status of a capital city of the Ferghana Valley, it continued to be one of the most important trade and crafts centres. This is evidenced by numerous findings of glassware, metalware, and ceramics. The new entrenched citadel and the palace soon became the favourite residence of the Ferghana rulers.

Aksikent was razed to the ground in AD 1620 by a severe earthquake. The citizens who managed to survive this natural disaster moved to the north-east, to Namakkon settlement next to the salt-mines. Today this settlement is known as Namangan—a big regional center.

The ruins of Aksikent citadel look like the creation of nature, not the product of man's activity. Hardly visible are the remains of brickwork of once majestic buildings. From the mud walls, just as a thousand years ago, one can see the Syr Darya banks buried in verdure of gardens and groves.

Chapter 2: His Family and early life

1 Yunus Khān (AD 1416–1487 AD), was the Khān of Mughalistan. He reigned from AD 1462 until his death in AD 1487. Many historians claim him to be Ḥājjī `Ali of the contemporary Chinese records (Association for Asian Studies. Ming Biographical History Project Committee, 1976) (Rossabi,

2014). He was the maternal grandfather of Babur. Yunus Khān was a direct male-line descendant of Genghis Khān, through his son Chagatai Khān.

He was the eldest son of Vais Khān of Mughalistan who was assassinated in AD 1428. The issue of his succession had left Mughals split. Going against the tradition, majority of court favoured Yunus' younger brother, Esen Buqa to succeed (Association for Asian Studies. Ming Biographical History Project Committee, 1976 pp. 479-81). Looking at the prevailing situation, Yunus along with his supporters fled to Ulugh Beg, the Timurid ruler of Transoxiana. Against their hopes, they were imprisoned by Beg. But Beg's father, Shah Rukh appeared to be sympathetic to the young Yunus. Yunus received warm treatment. Shah Rukh sent Yunus to Yazd in Iran to get educated under Maulana Sharaf ad-Din Ali Yazdi. Yunus Khān spent studied under the Maulana in Yazd for quite a long time. He ends up becoming one of the most educated Mughals of his time. With the death of Maulana, Yunus felt dejected. He wandered around for some time but finally choses to settle down in the city of Shiraz in Iran.

According to a religious dignitary to Muḥammad-Haydar Mīrzā Dughlat:

> *I had heard that Yunus Khān was a Mughal, and I concluded that he was a beardless man, with the ways and manners of any other Turk of the desert. But when I saw him, I found he was a person of elegant deportment, with a full beard and a Tajik face, and such refined speech and manner, as is seldom to be found even in a Tajik.*

Time was passing quite smoothly for Yunus. He was already forty by then and things seemed to be changing its flow. In AD 1456, Abu Sa'id, the Timurid ruler of Transoxiana, sent for Yunus Khān. Yunus' brother Esen Buqa was frequently raiding Sa'id's territory, and this left him badly annoyed. Esen's raid had become a nuisance. Perhaps Abu Sa'id was aware about the friction amid Yunus and Esen. He was certain that Yunus would look at this as a comeback opportunity. Yunus had both a claim on his brother's throne and kinship ties within the community. Abu Sa'id therefore raised Yunus to *Khānship* by placing him at the head of an army. He was sent to Mughalistan with that army to take care of his brother Esen. As perceived by Abu Sa'id, Yunus Khān's ties of kinship and claim to tribal leadership proved great advantages. It wasn't too late before he gained the support of several emirs. He got in matrimonial tie with an Emir, Mir Pir Haji Kunji's family. He married his daughter, Isan Daulat Begum. She is believed to be his first wife although he was already above forty by then. She becomes mother to Yunus' three daughters:

1. Mihr Nigar Khānim (born, 1457), wife of Sultan Ahmed Mīrzā. He was the eldest son of Abu Sa'id.

2. Qutlugh Nigar Khānum (born, 1459), wife of Umar Shaikh Mīrzā II. He was fourth son of Abu Sa'id.
3. Khub Nigar Khānum (born, AD 1463), after Yunus died, her half-brother married her to Muhammad Hussain Mīrzā Kurkan. She was Mother of Mīrzā Muhammad Haidar Dughlat, a future ruler of Kashmir.

Esen had an ally named Emir Sayyid Ali of Kashgar. He died in the year Yunus' first daughter was born. Following which Ali's son Saniz Mīrzā looked to get help of Yunus in gaining power at Kashgar. Yunus Khān gracefully accepted the invitation and arrived in Kashgar. Shortly, he sent one of the most respectable Sayyids of Kashgar, Amir Zia-ud-Din, to Badakhshan to meet Shah Sultan Muhammad Badakhshi and seek one of his six daughters in marriage. Shah Sultan Muhammad Badakhshi was deemed to be a direct descendant of Iskandar Zulkarnain (Alexander the Great), son of Filikus Rumi (Phillip II of Macedon), who according to (dubious) legend left one of his sons in the isolated mountain country out of reach of rivals in hope that his progeny would continue his dynasty in the East. Shah Sultan Muhammad Badakhshi agreed to marry one of his daughters to Yunus Khān. After a year to this marriage, Yunus married fourth daughter of Badakhshi, Shah Begum. With the relevant practice in region of that time, Yunus beginning to marry post forty years of his age indicates of unsettledness. His consciousness of royal birth would have prevented him from accepting wives from commoner's family. Yunus Khān fathered two sons and two daughters by Shah Begum:

1. Sultan Mahmud Khān, eldest child by Shah Begum, born in AD 1462.
2. Sultan Ahmad Khān, second son, known later as Alacha (Slayer) Khān for his brutal attempts to bring down absolute power in the steppe by slaughtering the Kalmaks.
3. Sultan Nigar Khānim, wife of Sultan Mahmud Mīrzā, third son of Abu Sa'id.
4. Daulat Sultan Khānim, youngest sibling.

Yunus' brother Esen Buqa died in the same year when his first son was born. The Mughals were divided with the opinion of choosing Mughalistan's new Khān. Few looked forward at Esen's son, Dost Muhammad, while other lot supported Yunus. The Dughlat Amir of Kashgar, Muhammad Haidar Mīrzā, supported Esen's Son, but his brother Saniz Mīrzā, the Amir of Yarkand (He had taken Yunus Khān's help and invited him into Kashgar in AD 1457) supported Yunus Khān, and expelled Dost Mohammad from Kashgar. Dost Mohammad was not going to let it go at ease. He consolidated his hold in Eastern Mughalistan. It was known as Uyghurstan in that period. He became the ruler of that region taking up habitation in the town of Aksu, thereby giving away the ongoing nomadic lifestyle. In AD 1464, Saniz Mīrzā died, and as expected Dost Muhammad didn't let the opportunity go away. Dost goes on to plunder Kashgar thereby avenging his expulsion. But shortly, somewhere in the last days of 1460s Dost died and Yunus Khān was able to seize Aksu. The only child of Dost Muhammad, Kebek Sultan, was whisked away by his supporters to Uyghurstan, the old refuge of his father. He was only a purported ruler for few years till being killed by the same people who had whisked him away.

Yunus Khān kept ruling as the Khān from Aksu. He had also maintained good relations with the Timurids, and the founders of the Khazak Horde (in AD 1465–AD 66); Janybek Khān and Karai Khān. His alliance with Khazaks costed him rivalry with the Uzbeks. In 1468 AD, the Uzbek leader Shaikh Haidar came into confrontation with the Mughals. This conflict did not end up being a pleasing one for the Uzbeks. They end up being defeated. Shaikh Haidar was killed. This brought almost three decades pause among them until the rise of Muhammad Shaybāni by the end of the fifteenth century.

On the other hand, Yunus dealt with the Timurids far more differently. The Timurid ruler Abu Sa'id had been Yunus Khān'smentor. He was responsible for Yunus' rise from rags to riches. Abu Sa'id Mīrzā was killed by the White Sheep Turkmen in AD 1468 AD. Because of which his realm was split among his sons. Sultan Ahmad Mīrzā, the eldest son, governed Samarkand and Bukhara. Sultan Mahmud Mīrzā, the third son, assumed authority over Balkh and Badakhshan, while the fourth son, Umar Shaikh Mīrzā II, ascended as the ruler of Ferghana. Notably, all three of these princes would eventually marry Yunus Khan's three daughters, despite their initially contentious interactions with him.

With the passing of Abu Sa'id Mīrzā, Yunus Khān had held sway over the Mughals for approximately six years. However, during this time, his standing among his key Amirs had significantly declined. The source of their dissatisfaction was rather peculiar. They grew disenchanted with Yunus because he had embraced urban living, forsaking the traditional nomadic lifestyle of the Mughals. Having spent a considerable portion of his life in the towns of Yazd and Shiraz as a student, Yunus had acquired a taste for settled urban life, which seemed more comfortable to him. Due to this unusual point of contention, the Amirs extended an invitation to Shaikh Jamal Khān, Governor of Tashkent under Sultan Ahmad, to replace Yunus Khān and seize power.

The Mughals acquiesced to Shaikh Jamal Khān, who assumed authority and incarcerated Yunus Khān for a year. However, the outcome was far from what the Amirs had anticipated, and a period of regret commenced for them regarding their decision. Shaikh Jamal Khān proved to be an imprudent and inconsiderate ruler. He even offered Yunus's first wife, Isan Daulat Begum, who was the maternal grandmother of Babur, as a war prize to his officer, Khoja Kalan. Tragically, Khoja met his demise at the hands of Isan's female attendants when he attempted to remove her from her residence. This incident marred Shaikh Jamal Khān's reputation in the eyes of the Amirs, as he had demonstrated himself to be a reckless and insensitive administrator.

In AD 1472, the Amirs took action, having Shaikh Jamal Khān killed, and power was reinstated to Yunus Khān. However, they extracted a promise from Yunus to renounce urban living and return to the conservative Mughal nomadic lifestyle.

Subsequently, Yunus Khān received news of the demise of Kebek Sultan, Dost Mohammad's young son, who had been killed by his own followers. Encouraged by these developments, Yunus Khān extended his influence to Eastern Mughalistan (Uyghurstan).

Yunus Khān also began to actively involve himself in the affairs of the Timurids. He established kinship ties with many prominent Timurids, marrying three of his daughters to three sons of his former mentor, Abu Sa'id. Mihr Nigar Khānim wed Sultan Ahmad Mīrzā, Qutlugh Nigar Khānum married Umar Shaikh Mīrzā II in AD 1475, and their son was Babur. Finally, Sultan Nigar Khānum was wed to Sultan Mahmud Mīrzā, and their son, Sultan Vais Mīrzā (Mīrzā Khān), ascended to the throne of Badakhshan. Yunus Khān maintained a special connection with his second son-in-law, Umar Shaikh Mīrzā II, who was the father of Babur.

2 Umar Shaikh had allocated winter territories to Yunus Khān, as the Timurids were predominantly settled in urban areas, governing the adjoining provinces. Yunus Khān remained true to his promise to the Amirs by maintaining this arrangement. Umar, possessing a poetic disposition, occasionally found it challenging to manage highly volatile situations. At times, he sought the assistance of his father-in-law, Yunus Khān, to mediate conflicts with his elder brother, Ahmad Mīrzā. The source of their strained relationship since childhood was relatively unknown, yet Yunus Khān frequently stepped in to reconcile the issues between his two sons-in-law.

Despite his advancing age, Yunus Khān remained remarkably ambitious and astute. In AD 1484, during a period of ongoing conflict between Ahmad and Umar, Yunus Khān seized control of Tashkent. At the age of seventy, he once again yearned to transition from the nomadic lifestyle to settled urban living. This desire for city life persisted throughout his existence, except for a particular phase. Tashkent, a significant city along the Silk Route, boasted a cosmopolitan atmosphere akin to Persian cities and represented the epitome of Central Asian urban living. Observing the city's advantages and alluring amenities, Yunus decided to reside there for an extended period. However, this decision left the Mughals disgruntled. Yunus's son, Ahmad Alaq, led a faction of Mughals to Mughalistan in response.

Meanwhile, Yunus Khān was unable to quell the rise of Dughlat Mīrzā Abu Bakr, who had previously captured Yarkand, Khotan, and Kashgar from other members of his family. During the Ming Turpan Border Wars, he had annexed Hami in AD 1473, but the Chinese subsequently expelled him to Turfan.

In the late 1480s, Yunus Khān fell ill and remained ailing until his passing in AD 1487, which occurred in Tashkent. His eldest son, Sultan Mahmud Khān, succeeded him in Tashkent, while in the eastern regions, the Mughals followed Ahmad Alaq's leadership.

3 Nassiruddin Ubaidullah Ahrar, popularly known as Khwaja Ahrar was a Hanafi Maturidi member of the Golden Chain of the Naqshbandi Sufi order of Central Asia (Nishapuri, 2002). He was born in Samarkand, Uzbekistan in AD 1404to a religious and devout Muslim family (Ṣafī, 2001). Khwaja Mehmood Shashi bin Khwaja Shahabuddin was his father. The traditions say that Ahrar's forefathers had migrated from Baghdad and his lineage connected to Abu Bakr Siddique from his paternal side and Umar Farooq from the maternal side (Mawlānā Šayẖ., 2004).

Khwaja's father was a farmer by profession and a Hajji following footsteps of his father Shahabuddin Shahsi. Shahabuddin had good agricultural trade. His maternal grandfather Khwaja Daud was the son of a well-known Sufi Mystic Khwaja Khawand. Khawand was the son of Umar Baghistani, a famous shaikh who was honoured by Bahauddin Naqshband (Ṣafī, 2001 p. 250).

As per the local folklore of Tashkent, various miracles occurred in the life of Ahrar right from his birth. Ahrar's initial studies happened in Tashkent itself under the guidance of his uncle Ibrahim Shashi (Forming a Faction: The Ḥimāyat System of Khwaja Ahrar, 2009). AD 1425, when he had turned twenty-one years of age, Ibrahim took him to Samarkand for further studies. Somehow his health wasn't supporting the things and falling ill had become continual phenomenon. He had to quit and while brawling with the illness he dreamt of Jesus Christ. The tradition say that Jesus said, 'I'll teach you.'

He gained mystic training returned home at the age of twenty-nine. Returning home, he began to farm after having bought a piece of fertile land. Soon land began to give him a great yield. It was not more than a decade more that he ends up getting more fertile lands, establishing businesses, popular Turkish baths, and Khānqahs. He had also begun to send his trading caravans into China (Hamid Algar, 1992). Many historians claim that he had become one of the richest men of the central Asia (The economic status of a Timurid Sufi Shaykh: a matter of conflict or perception?, 1998). It is said that most of his wealth was invested in religious endowments. Claims run that he had done abundant charity in this phase. He once owned more than 3500 acres of cultivable land at one time.

Khwaja Ahrar had extreme involvement in socio-economic and socio-economic activities of Transaxonia. Though he was born in a poor family, by the age of touching maturity he turned into the richest person in the kingdom ("Review: The Letters of Khwaja 'Ubayd Allah Ahrar and his Associates * Jo-Ann Gross, Asom Urunbaev: The Letters of Khwaja 'Ubayd Allah Ahrar and his Associates"., 2004). All dervishes of the time saw him in high regard. Among the famous disciples, Maulana Abdur Rahman Jami was one of the important ones (Aḥrār, ʿUbaydallāh, 2015). He learned most of the things under the guidance of his father though was well guided by Khwaja Yaqub Charkhi in later phase (Ṣafī, 2001 p. 250).

As the story goes, Ahrar had very strong signs of being a socialist. He went to the Timurid Prince ruling at Samarkand to discuss troubling conditions of the people of land. Sultan's chief aid showed no interest and disallowed his entry into the court. Agitated Ahrar bragged, 'I have been commanded by God and His messenger to come here.' Still Sultan's aid showed no concern. Dejected Ahrar then wrote the name of the Sultan on the wall and having erased it with his saliva said, 'God will replace you with a King who is concerned for his people' and left. Some days later, another Timurid Sultan Abu Sa'id Mīrzā, gathered his forces and attacked Samarkand and won it for himself. Sultan Abu Sa'id Mīrzā later became the grandfather of Babur, the founder of the Moghul Sultanate. This appeared like an opportunity to Khwaja Ahrar. This union of the Abu Sa'id Mīrzā and Khwaja Ahrar was to prove decades long and fruitful for the whole kingdom. Khwaja had strong influence on Abu Sa'id's family. He had given name to Babur in his infancy as Zahiruddin Muhammad literally 'Defender of Religion'.

4 The Shahnameh or Shahnama 'The Book of Kings' is a long epic poem written by the Persian poet Ferdowsi between AD 977 and 1010. It is the national epic of Iran, Afghanistan, and Tajikistan. Consisting of some 50,000 *distichs*/couplets (two-line verses), it is one of the world's longest epic poems. It tells the historical past of the Persian Empire from the creation of the world until the Muslim conquest in the seventh century basing the mythical telling of the tale. Iran, Azerbaijan, Afghanistan, Tajikistan, being countries highly influenced by Persian culture apart from countries of proximity such as Armenia, Dagestan, Georgia, Turkey, Turkmenistan, and Uzbekistan celebrate this national epic (Bekhrad, 2018).

The work is of central importance in Persian culture and Persian language, regarded as a literary masterpiece. It is also important to the contemporary adherents of Zoroastrianism, in that it traces the historical links between the beginnings of the religion and the death of the last Sasanian emperor, which brought an end to the Zoroastrian influence in Iran.

5 Babur mentions his father as Turk here. It means that apart from Timurid identity of house ethically he considered himself a Turk.

6 The river Aras (Araxes or Araks) rises near Erzurum in Turkey and meets with the Akhurian River southeast of Digor. From Digor it flows along the

Armenia–Turkey border, and then runs close to the corridor that connects Turkey to Azerbaijan's Nakhchivan exclave. It then continues along the Iranian-Armenian and the Iranian-Azerbaijan border (Iranica). Its total length is around 660 miles and its watershed cover an area of around 39,000 sq miles. The Aras is one of the largest rivers in the Caucasus.

Long ago, the Greeks called it Araxes (Greek: Ἀράξης). Its modern Armenian name is Arax or Araks.Historically it was also known as Yeraskh in old Armenian, and its Old Georgian name is Rakhsi. In Azerbaijani, the river name is Araz. In Persian and Kurdish its name is Aras and in Turkish it is Aras.

The Armenian tradition has named the river after Arast. He was the great-grandson of the celebrated Armenian patriarch Haik (Bauer-Manndorff, 1981). The name was later Hellenized to Araxes and was applied to the Kura-Araxes culture, a prehistoric people who flourished in the valleys of the Kura and Aras. The river is also mentioned in the last chapter of the Aeneid VIII by Virgil, as "angry at the bridge," since the Romans built a bridge over it, so that it is thereby conquered. The river Aras has been associated with the biblical rivers Gihon and Pishon (The Birthplace of Man, 1929).

Interestingly, we get to hear from sources that Aras had status of mother for the Armenian folks. Robert H. Hewsen described Aras as the only "true river" of Armenia and as "Mother Araxes," a symbol of pride to the Armenian people (Robert H. Hewsen, 1997). According to Strabo, Araxes River in Armenia had no outflow to the Caspian Sea, and it spread out in plains creating a lake without outflow (Strabo).

The modern times saw Aras gaining a significant political boundary. As per the Treaty of Gulistan, and the Treaty of Turkmenchay, the river Aras was chosen as the border extent amid Russian Empire and Qajar Iran. Qajar Iran was forced to give away it's Caucasian Territories to Russia.

Aras gained significance as a geographic political boundary. Under the terms of the Treaty of Gulistan (24 October of AD 1813) and the Treaty of Turkmenchay (21 February of AD1858), the river was chosen as the border limit between the Russian Empire and Qajar Iran, as the latter was forced to cede its Caucasian territories to Russia (Dowling, 2014). This nineteenth century change made Aras River as the line of continental demarcation between Europe and Asia. In the twentieth century USSR and Iran built the Aras Dam in the Poldasht area creating the Aras Reservoir.

7 Tumen, or tümen ('unit of ten thousand' (web.archive.org); Old Turkic: tümän; Mongolian: Тумэн, tumen (Hans-Peter Vietze, 1998); Turkish: tümen; Hungarian: tömény), was a part of the decimal system used by the Turkic and Mongol people to organize their tribal life and armies. Tumen is a social and military unit of 10,000 households and soldiers.

8 It was assumed that the same type of military organization was used by the Magyars during the conquest of Hungary. According to the Persian explorer

and geographer, Ahmad ibn Rustah (AD 930), "Magyars are a race of Turks and their king rides out with horsemen to the number of 10,000 and this king is called Kanda" (Laszlo, 1996). He relied on the secondary sources and hence same cannot be confirmed with authority using this source. The reliable sources state that Magyars were linguistically Finno-Ugric-speaking peoples and did not speak Turkic. Modern scholarship finds that the Magyar/Hungarian cavalry units were called Bandeira and Dündar and not organized in units of 10,000 (Heath, 1984).

In Genghis Khān followed a military system wherein a tumen was recursively built from units of 10 (aravt), 100 (zuut) and 1,000 (mingghan), each with a leader reporting to the next higher level. Tumens were considered a practical size, neither too small for an effective campaign nor too big for efficient transport and supply. The military strategy was based on the use of tumens as a useful building block causing reasonable shock and attack (Corvisier, 1994). The commander of a tumen was a tümen-ü noyan, a term sometimes translated 'myriarch', meaning commander of 10,000 (Hsiao, 1978).

9 The Kipchaks were a Turkic Nomad group. They thrived in the Middle Ages living in the parts of the Eurasian Steppe. The first mention of them is found in the eighth century as part of the Second Turkic Khaganate. It appears that they had settled in the Altai region from where they expanded elsewhere in centuries to come. Their first phase of expansion happened being the part of Kimek Khānate. The next phase of expansion was as a part of a confederation with the Cumans. They finally settled downin the Pontic–Caspian steppe, Syr Darya and Siberia. The Cuman–Kipchak confederation was conquered by the Mongols in the early thirteenth century.

10 The story behind etymology of their name is quite interesting. The Kipchaks interpreted their name as meaning 'hollow tree' (Middle Turkic: kuv a aç) (Clauson, 1972). According to them, their original human ancestors gave birth to first progeny in inside a hollow tree (Baldick, 2012). Late Gyula Németh, was a Hungarian linguist and turkologist and a member of the Hungarian Academy of Sciences. He points the origin to be Siberian qıp aq 'angry, quick-tempered'. The same is attested only in the Siberian Sa ay dialect (a dialect of Khakas language) (Golden, 1992). Klyashtorny links Kipchak to qovı, qovuq 'unfortunate, unlucky'; yet Golden sees a better match in qıv 'good fortune' and adjectival suffix - āq. Regardless, Golden notes that the ethnonym's original form and etymology 'remain a matter of contention and speculation' (Golden, 1992).

Their name appears occasionally transliterated in other languages, such as Arabic: قفجاق, romanized: Qifjāq; Persian: قبچاق, romanized: Qabčāq/Qabcâq; Georgian: ყივჩაღები, romanized: Qivçaghebi; Turkish: Kıpçak; Crimean Tatar: Kıpçaq, Karachay-Balkar: Къыпчакъ, romanized: Qıpçaq; Uzbek: Qipchoq, Қипчоқ/قىپچاق; Uighur: قىپچاق, romanized: Qipchaq/Қипчақ; Kazakh: Қыпшақ, romanized: Qypşaq; Kumyk: Къыпчакъ, romanized: Qıpçaq; Kyrgyz: Кыпчак, romanized: Qıpçaq; Nogai: Кыпчак; Romanian: Copceac; and Chinese: 欽察 ~ 欽叉 ~ 可弗叉 ~ 克鼻稍 Qīnchá ~ Qīnchā ~ Kěfúchā ~ Kèbíshāo. Other English transliteration include Kypchaks and Qipchaks.

The Russian 'Polovtsy' was the name given to the Kipchaks and Cumans by the Rus' people - hence the Polovtsian Dances at the end of act 2 of Alexander Borodin's opera Prince Igor.

11 Youngest son of Timur, born in AD 1377.

12 Shah Rukh or Shahrukh was the ruler of the Timurid Empire between AD 1405 and 1447. He was youngest son of the Timur, who founded the Timurid dynasty in AD 1370. Shahrukh ruled only over the eastern portion of the empire established by his father that comprised most of Persia and Transoxiana. The western territories were lost to the invaders in the aftermath of Timur's death. Despite this, Shahrukh's empire remained a cohesive dominion of considerable extent throughout his reign, as well as a dominant power in Asia.

He had an absolute control of the main trade routes between Asia and Europe, including the great Silk Road, which in turn made him immensely wealthy. Unlike his father he chose Herat as his capital, though Timur's capital was in Samarkand. This was to become the political centre of the Timurid empire and residence of his principal successors, though both cities benefited from the wealth and privilege of Shahrukh's court.

He is said to be a great patron of the arts and sciences, and it flourished well under his rule. He spent his reign focusing on the stability of his lands, as well as maintaining political and economic relations with neighbouring kingdoms.

13 Yunus Khān had three daughters with Aisan Daulat Begum. They were:

1. Mihr Nigar Khānum
2. Qutlugh Nigar Khānum
3. Khub Nigar Khānum

Chapter 3: The Amirs of Mīrzās

1 The Bangash District is the traditional homeland of Bangash a tribe of ethnic Pashtuns. It stretches from Kohat to Tall and Spīn Ghar in Khyber Pakhtunkhwa, Pakistan, touching the smaller parts of Paktia, Afghanistan. The people from this tribe also live in Uttar Pradesh, India majorly in the city of Farrukhabad. The Bangash are also settled in large numbers in Uttar Pradesh, India, especially in the city of Farrukhabad (Iranica). If folk etymology is to be trusted, the name Bangash is derived from bon-kash, Persian for 'root destroyer', implying the fact that the brave Bangash during battles, won't stop until they had annihilated the enemy completely (Wylly, 2008).

Unlike other Pashtuns, the Bangash primarily follow Shia Islam (Iranica). They mostly speak a northern variety of Pashto like Afridi Pashto. Origin of tribe has multiple narratives. Of all the narratives, the most popular one goes this way:

> *The Bangash tribe descended from Ismail, a governor of Multan. It is said that Khalid ibn al-Walid was eleventh generation of Ismail. It is said that Khalid was the commander of Prophet Muhammad (Wylly, 2008). The legend states that Ismail moved from Multan to settle in Gardez, Paktia, and he married with a girl from Farmul in Urgun, Paktika. Ismail had two sons, Gār and Sāmil, who were the progenitors of the modern Gari and Samilzai clans of the Bangash, respectively (Iranica).*

Now, the reception of this legend is quite interesting. Although Historians reject this account stating it to be highly ambiguous, the Bangash are recognized as 'of Arab origin' in British records. It gets further interesting as the same Historians who see the legend as ambiguous piece of history accept that the Gar and Samel factions originated within the Bangash and slowly spread to the surrounding tribes of the Soleyman range. We also have Pashtun folklore which trace their origin back to Qais Abdur Rashid. Qais was a close confidant of Khalid.

2 Zamindawar is a region of great historical significance in Afghanistan. Zamindwar is quite large and extremely fertile with Helmand River being main source of irrigation. It is in the greater territory of the northern stretch of Helmand Province and covers the approximate area of modern-day Baghran, Musa Qala, Naw Zad, Kajaki and Sangin. It has been known as the district of hills very well populated. Musa Qala, standing on the banks of a river named Musa Qala itself & 60 kilometres north of the city of Grishk in eastern Helmand was the primary town (Griesbach, 1911).

3 Ghazi Mohammad Ayub Khan was born in 1857 and died in April 1914. He is also known as The Victor of Maiwand or The Afghan Prince Charlie. His was born to Amir of Afghanistan Sher Ali Khan, and his mother was the daughter of Saadat Khan, an influential Mohmand chief of Lalpura (Chisholm, 1911). He had a brother named Mohammad Yaqub Khan who too would become Amir of Afghanistan (Frank Clements, 2003).

He was the governor of Herat Province in the Emirate of Afghanistan for sometimes. He became Emir of Afghanistan from 12 October 1879, to May 31, 1880, (htt6) (htt7). He successfully led the Afghan troops at Maiwand during the Second Anglo-Afghan War crushing the British Army. But a defeat came to him at the Battle of Kandahar, and Ayub Khan was deposed and exiled to British India, but he didn't stich and escaped to Persia. A negotiation happened between Ayub and Sir Mortimer Durand, the ambassador at Tehran in 1988. Former became a pensioner of the British

Government and travelled to India until his death in Lahore, Punjab (Dupree, 2014) and he would be buried in Peshawar. He had eleven wives, fifteen sons, and ten daughters (htt8). Two of his grandsons, Sardar Hissam Mahmud el-Effendi and Sardar Muhammad Ismail Khan, served as brigadiers in the Pakistan Army (Rahi, 2021) (Effendi, 2007).

He is also remembered as the 'National Hero of Afghanistan', in Afghanistan.

During the second Anglo-Afghan war, Afghans under the command of Ayub Khan defeated the British troops at Maiwand on 27 July of AD 1880, emerging victorious. This victory was quite significant for Afghanistan as it rescued her from getting dismembered by Britain and saved Kandahar from a permanent British occupation.

Later Ayub Khan would unsuccessfully go on to besiege the better equipped British forces at Kandahar. 1 September of AD 1880, the British force led by General Fredrick Roberts defeated Afghan forces badly at the Battle of Kandahar, which shall be the end of the Second Anglo-Afghan War (Chisholm, 1911). In 1881, Ayub yet again tried to take Kandahar, this time from Amir Abdur Rahman Khan, but again failed.

4 The Battle of Ahmed Khel was fought on 19 April 1880, during the Second Anglo-Afghan War. It occurred on the road that connected Kandahar and Kābul in central Afghanistan. The command of Kābul was in hands of General Roberts and situation had begun to turn weaker at his end. To reinforce General, with a force of 7,200 Lieutenant General Donald Stewart began his march from Kandahar to Kābul on 27 March 1980. While they marched, Afghan Tribesmen shadowed them throughout making it one of the most uphill tasks.

On 19 April 1880, as the column led by Lieutenant General Donald had reached near the village of Ahmed Khel (about 23 miles from Ghazni) the road had turned quite narrow. An Afghan tribal force of about 12,000 to 15,000 placed along the hills began to shower all kinds of threat on the column's flank. Before Lieutenant General Stewart could reposition his men to respond appropriately, the mass of Afghan tribesmen began rushing over the hills and made lethal attacks. With a lot of difficulty, and a rigorous fight of around an hour, British force was successful in defeating the enemies. The casualties were higher on the Afghan side. Around 2000-3000 were killed on their side – compared with British Indian Armie's loss of 17 dead and 124 wounded. Stewart did not stop at this success and was able to take over Ghazni the next day. His march to Kābul continued without much resistance.

The news of victory reached General Roberts and ordered a Royal salute firing in Kābul proclaiming the much-needed victory, 'that it might have a quieting effect on the excitement which prevailed around Kābul.' When the column began to march back to Kandahar and they reached Ahmed Khel, it was found that graves of British soldiers had been desecrated. The bones remained scattered and exposed. (Roberts, 1897)

5 Zunbil, are also known as Zhunbil, or Rutbils of Zabulistan (htt10). They were a royal dynasty who resided to the south of Hindu Kush who ruled from AD 680until the Saffarid conquest in AD 870(htt11). The Zunbil dynasty was founded by Rutbil (Turkic: Iltäbär), the elder brother of the Turk Shahi ruler (either Barha Tegin or Tegin Shah), who ruled over a Khalaj, aHephthalite kingdom from his capital in Kābul (Wink, 2002) (Petrie, 2020) (Rehman, 2006). According to al-Tabari and Tarikh-i Sistan Zunbils had Turkish troops in their service.

According to the interpretation of Chinese sources by *Marquarts* and *de Groots* in 1915, the king of *Ts'ao* is said to have worn a crown with a golden fish head and was related to the Sogdians. The Temple of the *Zun* was recognizable by a large fish skeleton on display indicating a related merchantry deity. In addition to that Marquarts states the Zunbils to have worshipped a solar deity which might have been connected to *Aditya* (Surya). However, according to Shōshin Kuwayama puts a hypothesis that there was a clear difference between worshipers of the Hindu god *Surya* and followers of *Zhun*. His hypothesis derives from the existence of conflict between *Surya* and *Zhun* followers, which lead to the latter to migrate southwards towards Zabulistan from Kapisa (Historical Notes on Kāpiī and Kābul, 2000). But according to Professor André Wink the followers of this god were certainly Hindu despite parallel lines have been noted with pre-Buddhist religious and monarchy practices in Tibet coated with Zoroastrian influence in its ritual (Wink, 1991) (Bosworth, 1977). On the other hand, scholars like H. Schaeder and N. Sims-William have tried to show their connection with the Zoroastrian deity of that period (A Unique Alxon-Hunnic Horse-and-Rider Statuette, (Late Fifth Century C E) from Ancient Bactria / Modern Afghanistan in the Pritzker Family Collection, Chicago, 2019).

Coming to the territories of Zunbils, they had possession of region between what is now the city of Zaranj in southwestern Afghanistan and Kābulistan in the northeast. In the south their territory reached at times the cities of Rakhwad (al-Rukhkhaj) and Bost (near Kandahar). Zamindawar and Ghazni served as their capitals (Wink, 1991).

Etymologically, the title Zunbil can be traced back to the Middle-Persian *Zūn-dātbar* (*Zun the Justice-giver*). The geographical name of their capital *Zamindawar* also comes from Middle Persian '*Zamin-i dātbar*' (Land of the Justice-giver) (Bosworth, 2002).

For more than two centuries of their rule, the *Tokhara Yabghus*, followed by the *Turk Shahis* and the *Zunbils* were consistently an obstacle to the eastward expansion of Muslims Invaders. The Tokhara Yabghus were a dynasty of Western *Turk–Hephtalite* sub-kings with the title "Yabghus," who ruled from AD 625 in Tokharistan north and south of the Oxus River, with some smaller remnants surviving in the area of Badakhshan until AD 758. Their legacy extended to the southeast where it met the Turk Shahis and the Zunbils until the ninth century AD.

Came the year of AD 643and the catastrophe broke on the idolators, as the Arabian forces raided *Sistan* for the first time. The Turkic territory was under attack from the west of south (Kim, 2015).

A decade later, in AD 653, Abd al-Rahman ibn Samura of the Rashidun Caliphate led an army of around 6,000 Arabs reaching the pious shrine of *Zoon* in Zamindawar. The hate for idols reflected at its might and humiliation was the testimony they wished to lay on the idol they came across. The primary sources report that *Samura* broke one of the hands of the idol and plucked out the rubies that shined as the eyes of the god, to reflect in history about the worthlessness of the deity the Zunbils worshipped. Samura asserted to the marzbān (*a class of margraves, warden of the marches, and by extension military commanders*) that, "my intention was to show you that this idol can do neither any harm nor good." (Wink, 1990) (al-Baladhuri, 1924)

Almost two decades later in AD 665, the Arabs under Abd al-Rahman ibn Samura (now a general of the Umayyad Caliphate and caliphal governor of *Sijistan*), took over Kābul for the first time which weakened the *Nezak* Huns a big time (From the Sasanians to the Huns New Numismatic Evidence from the Hindu Kush, 2014) (htt13) (Kim, 2015). This power show of Samura won't last long, and the Turkic ruler Barha Tegin soon gave a bloody nose to the Arabs. He took back the areas of Kābul and Zabulistan (around Ghazni), as well as the region of Arachosia going as far as Kandahar. Thereby he found a new dynasty of the Turk Shahis in AD 665 (Kim, 2015) (Coinage of the Nezak).

We find the first mention of Rutbil in Arab sources dates to AD 666 (Rehman, 2006). It is postulated that he may be the brother or nephew of Barha Tegin, whom latter would have appointed as the governor in *Zabulistan* after conquering the region from *Ghar-ilchi* (Petrie, 2020) (Rehman, 2006). Rutbil along the king of Kābul got together in the campaign against the Arabs after Abdur Rahman ibn Samura was replaced as the governor of Sistan.

Rabi ibn Ziyad al-Harithi upon assuming governorship in AD 671 attacked Rutbil at Bost and drove him to al-Rukhkhaj (Petrie, 2020). His new successor Ubayd Allah ibn Abi Bakra continued the warring against Rutbil upon being appointed in AD 673. With no option left in given situation Rutbil had to negotiate a truce treaty for both Kābul and Zabul, in which the governor of Sistan acknowledged control of these territories by Rutbil and the King of Kābul (Petrie, 2020).

Came the death of first Turk Shahi ruler Barha Tegin and his dynasty split into two. In AD 680, Tegin Shah became the king of the Turk Shahis, and his realm ranged from Kābulistan to Gandhara and Zabulistan (Coinage of the Nezak). His lived with the title, "*Khorasan Tegin Shah*" (meaning Tegin, King of the East), and he was known as *Wusan teqin sa* in the Chinese sources. This grandeur of title which he earned was perhaps for the massive resistance he offered to the peril of Umayyad Caliph from the west (htt14).

It was somewhere in the range of AD 680-683 that Rutbil split from his brother the Shahi of Kābul, and established the Zunbil dynasty, paying temporary allegiance to Salm ibn Ziyad, the Arab governor of Sistan (Al-Tabari, 2015) (Rehman, 2006). And the area of Zabulistan came to be ruled by Rutbil, also spelled Zibil or Jibul (from Turkic: *Iltäbär* "Commander") (Ahmad Hasan Dani, 1996). Although the history hints that the two brothers were not at good terms but fought together against the Arabic Invasions (htt15).

Rubtil issued coins derived from Sassanian prototypes with very interesting look and feel. They had a Bactrian script legend on the obverse, a Pahlavi script legend on the reverse, and a short Brahmi script legend in the name of Śrī Vākhudevaḥ (Shri Vasudeva):

> Obverse: yypwlh. wtyp' / GDH / 'pzwt
> PWN ŠMY yzt' yypwl bgyh. wtyp' wh. m'n'n mlt'n MLK'
> King Jibul, [his] glory increased! In the name of god, Jibul, the Majestic Lord [is] King of brave men
> Reverse: Śrī Vākhudevaḥ / pncdh. z'wlst'n / 'pl plm'n yzd'n
> Shri Vasudeva / [minted in his] 15th [regnal year in] Zavulistan, by the order of the gods.
>
> —Coin legend of Rutbil (Ahmad Hasan Dani, 1996)

According to the analysis of Anthony McNicoll, the Zunbils ruled in the Kandahar area for nearly two and a half centuries until the late ninth century AD (Anthony McNicoll, 1996). His main capital Zamindawar was in the present-day *Helmand* Province of Afghanistan. The shrine of *Zoon (the one destroyed by the Samura)* was located about three miles south of Musa Qala in Helmand and the same can be traced even today. According to a few scholars the *Sunagir* temple mentioned by the Chinese traveller Xuan Zang in AD 640 is this very house of worship (Habibi).

The Umayyad governor of Sijistan and military commander, Ubayd Allah ibn Abi Bakra, led an *Army of Destruction* against the Zunbils in AD 698. But this campaign felt heavy on the Islamic Caliphate. He was defeated badly and was forced to bend offer a large tribute, give hostages including three of his sons, and take an oath not to invade the territory of the Zunbils ever. But the Muslim force was not ready to bend. It had been only two years to the big defeat of Ubayad Allah. In AD 700Al-Hajjaj ibn Yusuf appointed Ibn al-Ash'ath as commander of a huge Iraqi army which was also known as

"Peacock Army," to avenge from formidable Zabulistan. But here again the character of Caliph *Hajjaj* backfired. His overbearing made Ibn al-Ash'ath and the "Peacock Army" to rebel. Latter got an agreement with the Zunbils and the peacocks began to march back to Iraq. And it was during this retreat that mutiny against al-Hajjaj formally shaped into an anti-Umayyad rebellion (Kennedy, 2010).

But the Arab world was no less than tail of a dog, not ready to be straight. The Arabs continually kept claiming the nominal overlordship over the Zunbils. And eleven years after the retreat of al-Ash'ath, in AD 711 Qutayba ibn Muslim managed to force Zunbils to pay tribute. But the situation flipped back again. In AD 725-726, Yazid ibn al-Ghurayf, governor of Sistan failed to gain the tribute from Zunbils. The next time they would be able to extract tribute from the Zunbils only in AD 769, when Ma'n b. Za'ida al-Shaybanl shall defeat them near Ghazni (Bactrian Inscription from Yakawlang sheds new light on history of Buddhism in Afghanistan, 2003).

We have an interesting record from AD 726. The Korean Buddhist monk Hyecho had visited Zabulistan (Xiėyùguó) and had recorded that Kābul and Zabul were ruled by Buddhist Turkic kings. He also stated that the King of Zabul was nephew of the king of Kābul (Daryaee, 2021). Below is the text from his records:

> *From Kapisa I travelled further west and after seven days arrived at the country of Zabulistan which its people call She-hu-lo-sa-t'a-na. The native are Hu people; the king and cavalry are Turks. The king, a nephew of the king of Kapisa, himself controls his tribe and the cavalry stationed in this country. It is not subject to other countries, not even his own uncle. Though the king and the chiefs are Turks, they highly revere the Three Jewels. There are many monasteries and monks. Mahayana Buddhism is practiced. There is a great Turkish chief called Sha-tuo-kan, who once a year lays out his gold and silver, which is much more than the king possesses. The dress, customs, and products of this land are similar to those of Kapisa, but the languages are different.*

—Hyecho on Zabulistan in "An account of travel to the five Indian kingdoms." (Jain, 2011)

According to the Islamic Traditional account (written around a century after the incidence), after the Abbasids came to power in AD 750, the Zunbils submitted to the third Abbasid Caliph al-Mahdi (AD 775–785). But this account seems to be largely fictional in nature which was perhaps created to merely to show the power the caliphate. The contemporary incidences show that the people of the region continued to resist to be ruled by Muslims. The Muslim historian 'Abū l-'Abbās 'Aḥmad bin 'Abī Ya'qūb bin Ğa'far bin Wahb bin Waḍīḥ al-Ya'qūbī (died AD 897/8) recounts after a century of the alleged event that al-Mahdi asked for, and apparently obtained, the submission of various Central Asian rulers, including that of the Zunbils. The original account by Ya'qubi reads as below:

> *Al-Mahdī sent messengers to the kings, calling on them to submit, and most of them submitted to him. Among them were the king of Kābul Shāh, whose name was Ḥanḥal; the king of Ṭabaristān, the Iṣbahbadh; the king of Soghdia, the Ikhshīd; the king of Tukhāristān, Sharwin; the king of Bamiyan, the Shīr; the king of Farghana, ------ ; the king of Usrūshana, Afshīn; the king of the Kharlukhiyya, Jabghūya; the king of Sijistān, Zunbīl; the king of Turks, Tarkhan; the king of Tibet, Ḥ-h-w-r-n; the king of Sind, al-Rāy; the king of China, Baghbür; the king of India and Atrāḥ, Wahūfūr; and the king of the Tughuz-ghuz, Khāqān.*
>
> —Ya'qubi (died AD 897/8), Ta'rikh (Mathew S Gordon, 2018)

As per the contemporary records, the Arabs were able to obtain tribute from the Zunbils in AD 769, which shall happen after almost half a century when Ma'n b. Za'ida al-Shaybanl shall defeat them near Ghazni (Bactrian Inscription from Yakawlang sheds new light on history of Buddhism in Afghanistan, 2003).

Muslim writer Abu Abbas Al-Yaqoubi records in his book Kitāb al-buldān the destruction (AD 795) of a *Šāh Bahār* (Temple of the King). He mentions that the Arabs attacked the Šāh Bahār, "in which were idols worshipped by the people. They destroyed and burnt them." (al-Baladhuri, 1924)

In AD 815, the Abbasid caliph Al-Ma'mun defeated the Kābul branch of the Turk Shahis. As per the Islamic traditional records, with hope of taking advantage of the Great Abbasid Civil War (AD 811-819), the Turk Shahi ruler, Pati Dumi had invaded the parts of Khorasan. The defeat left a large cultural clot on them as they had to convert to Islam apart from ceding their key cities and regions. Soon a campaign was led against the Gandhara branch of Shahis too. With the Caliphate reaching Indus River, a critical defeat reach to their baggage too. But the land won't be Islamised yet and a new dynasty, the Hindu Shahi took over in Gandhara and Kābul in AD 822. The Zunbils would though remain unaffected by Al-Ma'mun's raids and shall continue ruling for about two more decades, before the final conflict which shall script their extinction from the land of Sun God worshippers (Rehman, 2006). The Zunbils would be finally defeated in AD 870 AD by the Muslim conqueror and founder of Saffarid dynasty Yaqub bin Laith al-Saffar (AD 861–879). He conquered the entire Zunbil territory from his base in Sistan (Other).

By setting his march against the Kharijites of Herat, and defeating them in AD 870-71, Yaqub bin Laith al-Saffar began his conquests of east.

Following which he marched towards Karukh and defeated Abd al-Rahman another *Khariji* leader (Bosworth, 1975). The campaign would intensify, and his army would then march to *Ghazna*, conquering the Zunbils, and further to Bamyan and Kābul, cornering the Hindu Shahis to the East. He kept conquering these territories in the name of Islam thereby appointing Muslim governors everywhere. After cornering the Hindu Shahis, the forces of Islam moved to north of the Hindu Kush and by 870 AD the whole of Khorasan was brought under Islamic Saffarid control. Having the Panjshir Valley under his control and here he would mint his Islamic silver coins (Bosworth, 1995).

According to C.E. Bosworth (author of Encyclopaedia of Islam), the Saffarids for the first time could bring Islamic expansion to the eastern Afghanistan after a bit more than two centuries of plundering raids done by the Muslim governors of Sistan that saw one of the fiercest resistances from the rulers of the region (Bosworth, 1975). This resistance was one of the most laudable in the Islamic experience.

On the other hand, Hindu Shahis still did not give up the fight and they kept defending through Gandhara against the eastern expansion of Islam till AD 1026.

The belt of Afghanistan what we see today had been resisting Islamic expansion till the early centuries and the *Dharmik* traditions flourished there in different forms for quite longer than we tend to think.

The Chinese monk *Xuan Zang* reported in his travel diary that during the early 700s that Zabul was full of numerous Buddhist stupas which he postulated to have been built by Ashoka in the third century BC. He also reported about hundreds of Buddhist monasteries, and dozens of Hindu temples. He also speaks about the temple of Hindu god *Zun* (one destroyed by Samura) that drew many pilgrims. In the earlier section we also read about the Korean Buddhist monk Hyecho visited Zabulistan in AD 726 and recorded that Kābul and Zabul were ruled by Buddhist Turkic kings, who followed Buddhism. The last phase of the Tapa Sardar Buddhist monastery in Ghazni, dates to the time of the Zunbils (Afghanistan).

The resemblance with Hinduism and the tradition of Zunbils has already been discussed in the earlier sections but here again some points are added to corelate with the earlier reading. The Zunbils worshiped a deity called *Zhūn* (or *Zūn*), from whom they derived their name (Wink, 2002). He is represented with flames radiating from his head on coins. Statues were adorned with gold and used rubies for eyes which Huen Tsang had addressed as "*sunagir*" (Habibi).

Scholars have varied opinion about the origin and nature of Zhun yet all of them hint for it to be of Pagan nature. A study concludes that Zhun was possibly connected to the deity of the river Oxus, the modern river *Amudarya* and holds it most likely that Zhun was the greatest deity worshiped in Zabulistan. According to F. Grenet the Zhun might be related to the Iranian solar deity *Mithra* (A Unique Alxon-Hunnic Horse-and-Rider Statuette, (Late Fifth Century C E) from Ancient Bactria / Modern Afghanistan in the Pritzker Family Collection, Chicago, 2019). Zhun has been linked with the Hindu god *Aditya* at Multan, along with connection to pre-Buddhist religious and kingship practices of Tibet and Shaivism (Bosworth, 1977). Some scholars have proven with empirical evidence and epistemology that the cult of *Zhun* was primarily Hindu and can't be seen as either Buddhist or Zoroastrian. Scholars have also deliberated connections between the *Zhun/Zun* and the Hindu god *Shiva*, suggesting a syncretic mixture of the Iranian and Indian gods in the Indo-Iranian borderlands of ancient Bactria (Etymology of Zhunbil and Identity of the Rulers of Kabul and Zabul in Seventh -Ninth Centuries C.E, 2016). This gives furthermore empirical evidence for the Out of India Migration Theory.

As far as the origin of this deity is concerned a few scholars also have *Zurvan hypothesis* according to which this deity *Zun* relates to the Sassanid Zoroastrian deity Zurvān, the deity of time.

Gulman S writes as below in his paper (Etymology of Zhunbil and Identity of the Rulers of Kabul and Zabul in Seventh -Ninth Centuries C.E, 2016):

> *Regarding origin of Žuna, Xuanzang had only mentioned that it was initially brought to Kapisa, later Begram from "far" and later moved to Zabul. There is no consensus as to who brought it and when. By identifying Žun with Sassanian Zurvān, the cult of Žun or *Zruvān can be viewed in a much wider context of Iranian history and religious developments. Žun, Like Zurvān, most likely represented the "god of time", a heresy in Zoroastrianism, which originated in response to the religious reforms introduced during second half of Achaemenid Empire. The cosmopolitan nature of the god is consistent with the variety of religions practiced in the region prior to the Islamization of Afghanistan.*

He holds a thesis that the Afghan followers of *Zun* were initially Zoroastrians in all probability. Mention of Zun and its devotees began to vanish with the end of Zunbil dynasty of Zabulistan in AD 870. According to Ibn Athir the followers of *Zun* accepted Islam in later phase (Etymology of Zhunbil and Identity of the Rulers of Kabul and Zabul in Seventh -Ninth Centuries C.E, 2016).

Scholar Ulf Jager states in his paper that, 'we should interpret "*Zhun*" as the name of the ancient Iranian deity of time, "Zurwan."' (A Unique Alxon-Hunnic Horse-and-Rider Statuette, (Late Fifth Century C E) from Ancient Bactria / Modern Afghanistan in the Pritzker Family Collection, Chicago, 2019)

Chapter 4: Umar Shaikh Dies

1 Murrain is an antique term for various infectious diseases that affected cattle and sheep (Scott).

2 Murrain was frequently used word in the mediaeval era for "death". It was never used to refer a specific disease. Rather it as used as an umbrella term for what are now recognized as several different diseases. The list includes rinderpest, erysipelas, foot-and-mouth disease, anthrax, and streptococcus infections. The researchers suggest that it could also some of the diseases from the list could also affect the humans. Whenever such disease turned into epidemic, the term murrain came into play. The records speak about major sheep and cattle murrains in Europe during the fourteenth century. It combined with the Little Ice Age, resulting in the Great Famine of AD 1315-1317. It had left population of Europe thinned badly just before the onset of another calamity of the Black Death in AD 1348.

We also have references of Murrain in Biblical translations relating to the fifth plague brought upon Egypt. The book of Exodus (9:3) says: 'Behold, the hand of the LORD is upon thy cattle which is in the field, upon the horses, upon the asses, upon the camels, upon the oxen, and upon the sheep: there shall be a very grievous murrain.'

'Pestilence' mentioned forty-seven times in forty-six verses of the Bible, is translated as 'murrain' by Christian apologists. One may check Psalms 91:3 KJV for confirmation.

A lot of superstitious stories too talk of the term. In few parts of Scotland, it was believed that force-fire cured it. In the current time, Murrain is used as a term for curse upon land and livestock, in various remote parts of Cumbria, England, and the Isle of Man. We also have a theory that during the medieval era the term became synonymous with witchcraft by a process of syncretism. A television show was inspired by this idea in AD 1975. The play was telecasted on ATV and was written by Manxman Nigel Kneal on 27 July of AD 1975. This was a part of the channel's Against the Crowd drama strand.

We have a famous work of Gustave Doré called 'The Murrain of Beasts' (or 'The Fifth Plague: Livestock Disease'), that appeared as one of his many illustrations for La Grande Bible de Tours AD 1866.

3 Kasan is an ancient town of Uzbekistan also known as Kosonsoy (Uzbek pronunciation) and Kasansay (Russian). It was called Kathan in ancient times. Kosonsoy in Namangan Region is different from the town of Koson of the Qashqadaryo Region of Uzbekistan and people often confuse the two to be same. Kosonsoy got its name after the river Koson which flows from high mountains of Kyrgyzstan to Turakurgan District of Namangan Region of Uzbekistan. The word 'soy'in Tajik and means a 'brook', a small stream.

As per the recorded history so far, the first settlement happened here during the reign of Kushan Empire (first century AD). Few local traditions also tell us that the word 'Koson' perhaps came from the word Kushan itself. Kosonsoy enjoyed being an essential part of Kushan Empire along with ancient city Akhsikent near Namangan city. We find the remains of ancient Mug Castle of Kushanids in the northern part of the city. We are also given a different theory for the name of city. Few folklores say that 'Koson'means 'big town'or 'strong castle'.

4 Nasir Mīrzā was third son of Umar Shaikh Mīrzā and half-brother of Babur. He was four years younger to Babur. His mother, Umid; a mistress of Umar Shaikh was an Andijāni.

Chapter 5: Sulṭān Husayn Mīrzā Khusrau Shah and Other Mīrzās

1 The Guk Sarai is one of Timur Beg's great buildings in the citadel of Samarkand. It has this singular and special characteristic: if a Timurid is to be seated on the throne, here he takes his seat ; if one lose his head, coveting the throne, here he loses it ; therefore the name Guk Sarai has a metaphorical sense and to say of any ruler's son, 'They have taken him to the Guk Sarai,' means, to death.(Pétis de La Croix)

2 Khwaja-i-kalan was one of seven brothers, six including Khwajaki Mulla-i-sadr died in Babur's service, while he himself served till Babur's death.

Chapter 10: The First Marriage

1 Aisha Sultan Begum was born a Timurid princess as the third daughter of Sultan Ahmed Mīrzā (the King of Samarkand and Bukhara, Babur's uncle) and his wife Qutaq Begum. She was probably named 'Aisha' after Prophet Muhammad's (pbuh) wife, 'Ā'ishah bint Abī Bakr (2008).

2 There is no primary source to talk about details of how Qambar escaped from the captivity of Tambal.

Chapter 13: Babur Becomes father

1 He was a Timurid poet, writer, statesman, linguist, Hanafi Maturidi mystic and a painter who was the greatest representative of Chagatai literature (Feldherr, 2012).

2 Babur has taken it from Būstān al-jāmi' li-jamī' tawārīkh al-zamān which is an Arabic chronicle from Ayyubid Syria written by someone anonymous. Most likely, it was written in Aleppo, in the years AD 1196–1197. As of now two manuscripts survive. One of them is dated to AD 14th century and is kept at Istanbul, Saray (2959) while the other one is at Oxford, Huntington (172). Although the text is corrupted in the Istanbul manuscript, the calligraphy is

quite neat, and the scribe is attributed to a qāḍī named 'Imād al-Dīn al-Iṣfahānī.

3 Mentioned as note 557 in translated version of Annette Susannah Beveridge.

Chapter 15: Samarkand Is Lost to Shaybāni (AD 1501)

1 Not much details about what he did next is available in *Baburnama*.

2 Given the contradiction in accounts, it is tough to conclude if she fell in hands of Shaybāni or marriage was a deal well consented to by Babur's mother.

Chapter 17: Babur in Tashkent (July AD 1502 AD–June AD 1503)

1 Passwords were of two kinds—in each tribe there is one for use in the tribe, such as Darwāna or Tūqqāī or Lūlū; (Darwāna [a trapdoor in a roof] has the variant dur-dāna, a single pearl; tūqqāī perhaps implies relationship; lūlū is a pearl, a wild cow etc.) and there is one for the use of the whole army. For a battle, two words are settled on as passwords so that of two men meeting in the fight, one may give the one, the other give back the second, to distinguish friends from foes, own men from strangers.

2 The gosha-gīr is an implement for remedying the warp of a bow-tip and string-notch.

Part 2: Kābul

Chapter 18: First Year of Kābul

1 In the Turkī tribes, applying razor to the face for the first time is celebrated with a great fervour. Babur's miserable circumstances would not admit of this. (John Leyden, 1886)

The text is ambiguous here, reading either that Sūkh was left or that Aīlāq-yīlāq was reached in Muḥarram. As the birthday was on the 8th, the journey very arduous and, for a party mostly on foot, slow, it seems safest to suppose that the start was made from Sūkh at the end of AH 909. and not in Muḥarram, AH 910. (Beveridge, 1922)

2 The ālāchūq, a tent of flexible poles, covered with felt, may be the *khargāh* (kibitka); Persian chādar seems to represent *Turkī āq awī*, white house.

3 Qur'an 3.26 (Sale, 1734)

4 Canopus is known as Suhail in Afghānistān and is one of the most clearly seen star in Afghānistān. The south gets its name from it, as it is never called Janūb but Suhail. The rising of Suhail marks one of their seasons (John Leyden, 1886). The honour attached to this star is due to its seeming to rise out of Arabia Felix.

5 Bodies (*būlāks*) were probably a group of a thousand fighter Turki Mīng.
6 This part of Persian manuscript could not be translated and hence the excerpt has been put directly from Annette Susannah Beveridge (Ghāzī, 1922).
7 Kāfirwash; they were Kāfirs converted to Muḥammadanism.
8 West might be more exact, since some of the group are a little north, others a little south of the latitude of Kābul.
9 i.e. the year now in writing. The account of the expedition, Bābur's first into Hindustan, begins on f. 145.
10 i.e. the countries groupable as Khurāsān

Chapter 19: Hindustan Project Fails for the Second Time

1 Mihmān-beglār, was an expression first used by Babur in *Baburnama,* explaining this instance, which perhaps happened due, presumably, to accessions from Khusrau Shāh's following. A very similar case has been addressed in in Max Müller's *Science of Language*, Vol-1" (Müller, 1891) where he says, 'Turkman tribes are under the command of Aūzbeg Khans of Khiva, Ferghana & Bukhara. They call themselves, however, not subjects, but guests of these Khāns.' (Referred the note of Annette Susannah Beveridge for understanding of the translation) (Ghāzī, 1922)
2 Also known as Takht pass. This pass has been known from times immemorial.
3 This speaks of Babur's tyranny against anyone who in his eyes would offend Islam and great people of Islam.
4 Narrated in section 'Nāṣīr Mīrzā's Misconduct' that how they were thus driven on from the Bārān-water.
5 Discussed in section 'Walī, brother of Khusrau Shāh dies & Kābul is gained'.
6 Babur addresses him as 'your honour' in *Baburnama*, which means even this time he had great honorific regards for Khusrau Shāh irrespective of whatever both did to each other.
7 Explained in 'Qaṃbar-'alī dismissed' of the chapter 18.
8 Author's opinion: This incidence gives us an idea that the Timurid society too firmly believed in superiority by birth.
9 In AD 1504, Baqi had persuaded Babur to come to Kābul & not Khurāsān. The same year he had also dictated the march to Kohāt, and the rest of that disastrous travel.
10 As per the notes of Annette Susannah Beveridge, probably this word is an equivalent of Persian goshī which was a tax on cattle and beasts of burden.
11 He uses the number 'nine' perhaps for the mystic value attached to it. For example, the Tarkhans had 'nine' privileges.
12 Nothing much is found about Bārān. As per the note 973 of Annette Susannah Beveridge it can be identified as the village marked Baian on the French Map.
13 Note 975 of Annette Susannah Beveridge gives a clarification as below:

For the Hazāra (Turkī, Mīng) on the Mīrzā's road see Raverty's routes from Ghaznī to the north. An account given by the Tārīkh-i-rashīdī (p. 196) of Jahāngīr's doings is confused; its parenthetical '(at the same time)' can hardly be correct. Jahāngīr left Ghaznī now, (911 ah.), as Bābur left Kābul in 912 ah. without knowledge of Ḥusain's death (911 ah.). Bābur had heard it (f. 183b) before Jahāngīr joined him (912 ah.); after their meeting they went on together to Herī. The petition of which the T. R. speaks as made by Jahāngīr to Bābur, that he might go into Khurāsān and help the Bāī-qarā Mīrzās must have been made after the meeting of the two at Ṣaf-hill (f. 184b).

14 Chīn Ṣūfī was loyal to Ḥusayn Mīrzā.

15 As per the note 981 of Annette Susannah Beveridge, Bābā Ilāhī may be the "Baboulei" of the French Map of 1904, on the Herī-Kushk-Marūchāq road.

16 The news of Sultan Husayn's death had yet not reached to Babur.

17 According to the note 1179 of Annette Susannah Beveridge, 'Murgh-āb is supposed to be the fortified place at the crossing of the river by the main North-Eastern Road. Khwānd-amīr had recorded that the information of his approach was hailed in the Mīrzās' camp as good news.'

18 According to the note 1183 of Annette Susannah Beveridge, it was perhaps it a recess, resembling a gateway. According to her, the impression conveyed by Bābur's words here would be to the artist who in B.M. Or. 3714, has depicted the scene, is that there was a vestibule opening into the tent by a door and that the Mīrzā sat near that door. It must be said however that the illustration does not closely follow the text, in some known details.

19 Balkh is a town in the Balkh Province of Afghanistan. It is situated around twelve miles north-west of the provincial capital Mazar-e Sharif. Amu Darya and the Uzbekistan border lies forty-six miles from Balkh.

Historically, the ancient land of Balkh had Hindu, Buddhist and Parsi inhabitants. It was one of the wealthiest and largest cities of Khorasan. The Persians (the Parsus of Rigveda) called the city s Zariaspa. The ancient Greeks (Dhruyus of Rigveda are their ancestors) called the city of Balkh as Bactra, giving its name to Bactria (Greeks called the city also Zariaspa).

20 According to the note 1187 of Annette Susannah Beveridge, following is mentioned with respect to the reason of Babur not kneeling:

Unless all copies I have seen reproduce a primary clerical mistake of Bābur's, the change of salutation indicated by there being no kneeling with Apāq Begīm, points to a nuance of etiquette. Of the verb yūkūnmāk it may be noted that it both describes the ceremonious attitude of intercourse, i.e., kneeling and sitting back on both heels (Shaw), and the kneeling on meeting. From Bābur's phrase Begīm bīla yūkūnūb [having kneeled with], it appears that each of those meeting made the genuflection; I have not found the phrase used of other meetings; it is not the one used when a junior or a man of less degree meets a senior or superior in rank (e.g. Khusrau and Bābur f. 123, or Bābur and Badī'u'z-zamān f. 186).

21 These are windows or balconies from which a ruler appears to the common people.

22 Annette Susannah Beveridge mentioned in her note 1195, for it probably being a gold embroidered garment.

23 As per the note 1217 of Annette Susannah Beveridge, it is the almshouse or convent founded during the Tīmūr's reign.

24 Gharchistan or Gharjistan is also known as Gharj Al-Shar. It was a medieval region on the north bank of the Murghab River, lying to the east of Herat and north of Hari River. It corresponds roughly to the modern Badghis Province of Afghanistan.

25 According to the note 1219 of Annette Susannah Beveridge, this name may be due to the splashing of water. A Langar which may be that of Mīr Ghiyāṣ, is shown in maps in the Bām valley; from it into the Herī-rūd valley Babur's route may well have been the track from that Langar which, passing the villages on the southern border of Gharjistān, goes to Ahangarān.

26 The right and wrong roads are shown by the maps of British India Survey and the French Military. The right road turns off from the wrong one, at Daulat-yār, to the right, and mounts diagonally along the south rampart of the Herī-rūd valley, to the Zirrīn-pass, which lies above the Bakkak-pass and carries the regular road for Yaka-aūlāng. It must be said, however, that we are not told whether Yaka-aūlāng was Qāsim Beg's objective; the direct road for Kābul from the Herī-rūd valley is not over the Zirrīn-pass but goes from Daulat-yār by "Āq-zarat", and the southern flank of Koh-i-bābā (bābār) to the Unai-pass (Holdich, 1910 p. 262).

27 According to the note 1223 of Annette Susannah Beveridge, the Hazāras appeared to have been wintering outside their own valley, on the Ghūr-bund road, in wait for travellers. They had been perennial highwaymen on the only pass to the north not closed entirely in winter.

28 According to the note 1233 of Annette Susannah Beveridge, this prayer is composed of extracts from the Qurān. She has represented as it stands in Mr. Erskine's wording (p. 216)

29 Babur always seems to have soft corner for the people who he held as own in some part of life.

30 As per the note 1236 of Annette Susannah Beveridge, they were ashamed for now putting a Tīmūrid in Babur's place in Kābul; viz. that he was believed captive in Herī and that Mīrzā Khān was an effective locum tenens against the Arghūns. Haidar sets down what in his eyes pleaded excuse for his father Muhammad Ḥusain.

31 Sons of Sultan Aḥmad Khān Chaghatāī.

32 As per the note 1243 of Annette Susannah Beveridge, Bārān seems likely to be the Baian of some maps. Gul-i-bahār is higher up on the Panjhīr road. Chāsh-tūpa will have been near-by; its name might mean Hill of the heap of winnowed-corn.

33 Following up the whole journey of Babur and finally reaching by this node, I could assume that he displayed bipolar traits.

34 At the ruler's disposition was manifestly taken the Fifth. It is observed that at least in two places dependents send gifts to Babur and the word used is *tassaduq,* which might be rendered as 'gifts for the poor'. This perhaps means that the *Padishah* did receive these in the place of the Imām of the Qurān's law (8.41) which asks one-fifth of spoil to be given to the Imām for the poor, orphans, and travellers.

35 According to the Islamic Law, a term is fixed after widowhood or divorce within which re-marriage becomes illicit. According to the note 1272 of Annette Susannah Beveridge, on coming into Herī on Moharram 11th, Shaybāni at once set about gathering in the property of the Tīmūrids. He had the wives and daughters of the former rulers brought before him. The great lady Khānzāda Begum who was daughter of Aḥmad Khān, niece of Sultan Ḥussayn Mīrzā, and wife of Muẓaffar Mīrzā, showed herself pleased in his presence. Desiring to marry him, she said Muẓaffar Mīrzā had divorced her two years before. Trustworthy persons gave evidence to the same effect, so she was united to Shaybāni in accordance with the glorious Law. Mihr-angez Begum, Muẓaffar Mirza's daughter, was married to 'Ubaidu'llāh Sultan (Aūzbeg); the rest of the chaste ladies having been sent back into the city, Shaybāni resumed his search for property.' Manifestly, Babur did not believe in the divorce Khwānd-amīr thus records.

36 As per the note 1280 of Annette Susannah Beveridge, Jahāngīr's son, thus brought by his mother, will have been an infant; his father had gone back last year with Babur by the mountain road and had been left, sick and travelling in a litter, with the baggage when Bābur hurried on to Kābul at the news of the mutiny against him (*Baburnama*, folio 197); he must have died shortly afterwards, seemingly between the departure of the two rebels from Kābul (*Baburnama*, folio 201b-202) and the march out for Kandahār. Doubtless his widow now brought her child to claim his uncle Babur's protection.

37 As per the note 1281 of Annette Susannah Beveridge, Persians pay great attention in their correspondence not only to the style but to the kind of paper on which a letter is written, the place of signature, the place of the seal, and the situation of the address. Chardin gives some curious information on the subject (Erskine). Babur marks the distinction of rank he drew between the Arghūn chiefs and himself when he calls their letter to him, 'arẓ-dāsht, his to them khaṯṯ. His claim to suzerainty over those chiefs is shewn by Ḥaidar Mīrzā to be based on his accession to Tīmūrid headship through the

downfall of the Bāī-qarās, who had been the acknowledged suzerains of the Arghūns now repudiating Babur's claim.

38 According to the note 1283 of Annette Susannah Beveridge, var. Kūr or Kawar. If the word mean ford, this might well be the one across the Tarnak carrying the road to Qarā (maps). Here Babur seems to have left the main road along the Tarnak, by which the British approach was made in AD 1880, for one crossing west into the valley of the Argand-āb.

39 Annette Susannah Beveridge has given below note on the terminologies:

> *Although barānghār, aūng qūl, aūng yān and aūng (right wing, right hand, right side and right) all have the same meaning, I have applied them in different senses in order to vary terms and mark distinctions. As, in the battle-array, the (Ar.) maimana and maisara i.e., what people call (Turkī) barānghār and jawānghār (r. and l. wings) are not included in the (Ar.) qalb, i.e., what people call (T.) ghūl (centre), so it is in arraying the centre itself. Taking the array of the centre only, its (Ar.) yamīn and yasār (r. and l.) are called (by me) aūng qūl and sūl qūl (r. and l. hands). Again, —the (Ar.) khāṣa tābīn (royal troop) in the centre has its yamīn and yasār which are called (by me) aūng yān and sūl yān (r. and l. sides, T. yān). Again, —in the khāṣa tābīn there is the (T.) būī (nīng) tīkīnī (close circle); its yamīn and yasār are called sūng and sūl. In the Turkī tongue they call one single thing a būī, but that is not the būī meant here; what is meant here is close (yāqīn).*

40 Annette Susannah Beveridge's note on Pīrī Beg: This Pīrī Beg was one of those Turkmāns who came (into Herī) with the Turkmān Begs led by 'Abdu'l-bāqī Mīrzā and Murād Beg, after Shāh Ismā'īl vanquished the Bāyandar sulṯāns and seized the 'Irāq countries (As per the note 1296 of Beveridge it was in AD 1502).

41 The name of whose house it was is missing in the manuscript of *Baburnama*.

42 Reason is not mentioned in the manuscript.

43 According to the note 1305 of Annette Susannah Beveridge, Shaybāni had most probably taken the route of Sabzār, Daulatābād, and Washīr.

44 Note of Annette Susannah Beveridge in this context:

> *Those holding their heads up in Badakhshān at this crisis were, of Badakhshīs, Mubārak Shāh and Zubair, Jahāngīr Turkmān and Muhammad the armorer. They had driven Nāṣir Mīrzā out but had not joined the Aūzbeg.*

45 Mirza Muhammad Haidar Dughlat writes, 'Shāh Begīm laid claim to Badakhshān, saying, "it has been our hereditary kingdom for 3000 years; though I, being a woman, cannot myself attain sovereignty, yet my grandson Mīrzā Khān can hold it".' (Dughlat, 1551 p. 203)

46 Non-Muslims/ idol worshippers
47 William Erskine gives an alternative name 'Kaliūn'to the fort and locates it in the Bādghīs district east of Herī. He and quotes from Abū'l-ghāzī in explaining of its strong position (Erskine, 1854 p. 282).
48 As per the note 1318 of Annette Susannah Beveridge, Abū'l-faẓl mentions of seeing this inscription during his period.
49 We find a lots of sources with varied opinion for Babur's supremacist assertion of this period. According to opinion of Annette Susannah Beveridge (note 1320), Babur was the only Tīmūrid ruler and a man of achievement. He filled the vacuum post the death of Ḥusayn Bāī-qarā's for Tīmūrid headship. If one observes Babur's actions carefully, it would be found that he was trying hard from long to replicate footsteps of Tīmūr Beg. But there were few who did not admit of his suzerainty. She writes in note 1320, 'Tīmūrids who had rebelled, Moghūls who had helped them, and who would also have helped Sa'īd Khān Chaghatāī, if he had not refused to be treacherous to a benefactor; there were also the Arghūns, Chīngīz-khānids of high pretensions.' In the gone by times, the Moghūl Khāqāns were known as the Pādshāh (supreme). The term Pādshāh has been recorded historically as the style of at least Sātūq-būghra Khān Pādshāh Ghāzī; but no Tīmūrid had been raised by his style above all Mīrzās. But when the Tīmūrids had the upper hand, Babur's Tīmūrid grandfather Abū-sa'īd asserted his de facto supremacy over Babur's Chaghatāī grandfather Yūnas (Haidar, 1895 pp. 82-83). It seems that for Babur, this assuming of the Khāqān style was a step to re-assert the Timurid Supremacy. This declaration of supremacy was very much synonymous to declaring over-lordship above Chaghatāī, Moghūl, and even over all the Mīrzās. Now that the Mīrzā Khān's rebellion was put to an end, the Arghūns were beaten & lost all possessions, his old Aūzbeg foe was now sitting at a way lesser fearing distance, and Kābul was once more his own, the sky for Babur had no dark clouds.
50 It appears that 'Khān' in Humāyūn's name may been sprouted from his mother's family. I have failed to find any strong record to establish from whose family did Māhīm (his mother) came from. This hasn't been addressed in primary sources written by Babur, Gulbadan and Abū'l-faẓl. Neither of them talks of her father's name.
51 Babur has not given any record of his death.
52 According to the note 1326 of Annette Susannah Beveridge, most of these soldiers had fought on the side of Babur in Kandahār.
53 In the note 1327, Annette Susannah Beveridge has summarized the position of 'Abdu'r-razzāq Mīrzā as below:

> *In the previous year he had been left in charge of Kābul when Babur went eastward in dread of Shaybāni, and, so left, occupied his hereditary place. He cannot have hoped to hold Kābul if the Aūzbeg attacked it; for its safety*

and his own he may have relied, and Babur also in appointing him, upon influence his Arghūn connections could use. For these, one was Muqim his brother-in-law, had accepted Shaybānī's suzerainty after being defeated in Qandahār by Babur. It suited them better no doubt to have the younger Mīrzā rather than Babur in Kābul; the latter's return thither will have disappointed them and the Mīrzā; they, as will be instanced later, stood ready to invade his lands when he moved East; they seem likely to have promoted the present Moghūl uprising. In the battle which put this down, the Mīrzā was captured; Babur pardoned him; but he having rebelled again, was then put to death.

54 According to the analysis put in note 1329 of Annette Susannah Beveridge, He seems to have been a brother or uncle of Humāyūn's mother Māhīm.

Epilogue: Three Invaders from Tramontana and Jihad

1 According to note 2056 of Annette Susannah Beveridge:

This alludes to the defeat of (an Abyssinian Christian) Abraha the prince of Yemen who (in the year of Muhammad's birth) marched his army and some elephants to destroy the ka'ba of Makka. 'The Meccans,' says Sale, 'at the appearance of so considerable a host, retired to the neighbouring mountains, being unable to defend their city or temple. But God himself undertook the defence of both. For when Abraha drew near to Mecca, and would have entered it, the elephant on which he rode, which was a very large one and named Maḥmūd, refused to advance any nigher to the town, but knelt down whenever they endeavoured to force him that way, though he would rise and march briskly enough if they turned him towards any other quarter; and while matters were in this posture, on a sudden a large flock of birds, like swallows, came flying from the sea-coast, every-one of which carried three stones, one in each foot and one in its bill; and these stones they threw down upon the heads of Abraha's men, certainly killing every one they struck.' The rest were swept away by a flood or perished by a plague, Abraha alone reaching Senaa, where he also died (Erskine). The above is taken from Sale's note to the 105 chapter of the Qorān, entitled 'the Elephant'.

Appendix B: Excerpts from *Baburnama* translation by Annette Susannah Beveridge (Events of Unchronicled Years)

1 The Tarikh-i-Rashidi gives the names of two only of the champions but Firishta, writing much later gives all five; we surmise that he found his five in the book of which copies are not now known, the Tārīkh-i Muḥ. 'Ārif

Qandahārī. Firishta's five are 'Ali shab-kūr (night-blind), 'Alī Sīstānī, Naẓar Bahādur Aūzbeg, Ya'qūb tez-jang (swift in fight), and Aūzbeg Bahādur. Ḥaidar's two names vary in the MSS. of the Tarikh-i-Rashidi but represent the first two of Firishta's list.

2 There are curious differences of statement about the date of Shaybānī's death, possibly through confusion between this and the day on which preliminary fighting began near Merv. Ḥaidar's way of expressing the date carries weight by its precision, he giving roz-i-shakk of Ramẓān, i.e. a day of which there was doubt whether it was the last of Sha'bān or the first of Ramẓān (Lane, yauma'u'l-shakk). As the sources support Friday for the day of the week and on a Friday in the year AH 915 fell the 29th of Sha'bān, the date of Shaybānī's death seems to be Friday Sha'bān 29th AH 915 AH (Friday, 2 December of AD 1510).

3 According to Annette Susannah Beveridge, the Turkī passage concerning wines drunk by Babur which I have noted on Folio 49 was during this occupation of Kābul. This is for the first time when Babur broke the Law against stimulants.

4 R.S. Poole found a coin which he took to be one struck in obedience to Babur's compact with the Shāh (B.M.Cat. of the coins of Persian Shāhs 1887, pp. xxiv et seq.; (Dughlat, 1551 p. 246)).

5 It was held by Aḥmad-i-qāsim Kohbur and is referred to on Folio 234b of *Baburnama*, as one occasion of those in which Dost Beg distinguished himself.

6 *aūrūq*. Bābur refers to this exodus on Folio 12b of *Baburnama* when writing of Daulat-sulṭān Khānīm.

7 It is one recorded with some variation, in Niyāz Muḥammad Khukandī's Tārīkh-i-shāhrukhī ('Ashūr, 1885) and Nalivkine's Khānate of Khokand (p. 63). It says that when Bābur in 918 AH (1512 AD) left Samarkand after defeat by the Aūzbegs, one of his wives, Sayyida Āfāq who accompanied him in his flight, gave birth to a son in the desert which lies between Khujand and Kand-i-badām; that Babur, not daring to tarry and the infant being too young to make the impending journey, left it under some bushes with his own girdle round it in which were things of price; that the child was found by local people and in allusion to the valuables amongst which it lay, called Altūn bīshik (golden cradle); that it received other names and was best known in later life as Kḥudāyān Sulṭān. He is said to have spent most of his life in Akhsī; to have had a son Tīngrī-yār; and to have died in 952 AH (1545 AD). His grandson Yār-i-muḥammad is said to have gone to India to relations who was descendants of Babur (JASB 1905 p. 137 H. Beveridge's art. The emperor Babur). What is against the truth of this tradition is that Gul-badan mentions no such wife as Sayyida Āfāq. Māhīm however seems to have belonged to a religious family, might therefore be styled Sayyida, and, as Bābur mentions (*Baburnama*, folio 220), had several children who did not

live (a child left as this infant was, might if not heard of, be supposed dead). There is this opening allowed for considering the tradition.

8 Bābur refers to this on folio 265.

9 The *Lubbu't-tawārīkh* would fix Ramẓān 7th.

10 Mr. Erskine's quotation of the Persian original of the couplet differs from that Annette Susannah Beveridge translations (Erskine, 1854 p. 326) (Badā'ūnī, 1898 p. 543).

11 Some translators make Babur go 'naked' into the fort but, on his own authority (Folio 106b), it seems safer to understand what others say, that he went stripped of attendance, because it was always his habit even in times of peace to lie down in his tunic; much more would he have done so at such a crisis of his affairs as this of his flight to Ḥiṣār.

12 Haidar gives a graphic account of the misconduct of the horde and of their punishment (Dughlat, 1551 pp. 261-63).

13 One of the mutineers named as in this affair (Dughlat, 1551 p. 257) was Sl. Qulī chūnāq, a circumstance attracting attention by its bearing on the cause of the lacuna in the Bābur-nāma, in as much as Babur, writing at the end of his life, expresses (Baburnaama, folio 65) his intention to tell of this man's future misdeeds. These misdeeds may have been also at Ḥiṣār and in the attack there made on Babur; they are known from Haidar to have been done at Ghaznī; both times fall within this present gap. Hence it is clear that Babur meant to write of the events falling in the gap of AH 914 onwards.

14 In AH 925 (Mīr pp. 227, 238), mention is made of courtesies exchanged between Babur and Muḥammad-i-zamān in Balkh. The Mīrzā was with Babur later on in Hindustan.

15 Mīr Ma'ṣūm's Tārīkh-i-sind is the chief authority for Babur's action after AH 913 against Shāh Beg in Qandahār; its translation, made in 1846 by Major Malet, shows some manifestly wrong dates; they appear also in the B. M. MS. of the work.

Bibliography

Afghanistan, Italian Archaeological Mission in, 'The Buddhist site of Tapa Sardar', https://ghazni.bdus.cloud/.

Afghanistan Tourism, https://web.archive.org/web/20120327153153/http://www.afghanistantourism.net/215/afghanistan-history/afghanistan-monarchs/.

Afghan Land, https://web.archive.org/web/20110709141554/http://www.afghanland.com/history/leaders/leaders.html.

Afif, Shams Siraj, Tarikh-i-Firuz Shahi, *History of India as Told by its Own Historians,* London: Trübner & Co, 1871, Vol. 3, p. 328.

Afridi, Gulman sher, *Etymology of Zhunbil and Identity of the Rulers of Kābul and Zabul in Seventh-Ninth Centuries C.E.*, 2016, *Journal of Asian civilisation, Vol. 39*, pp. 25–47.

Ahmed, Ishtiaq, *Fathnama—i chitor, March 1568 an Annotated Translation*, New Delhi: Indian History Congress, 1971, The Proceedings of the Indian History Congress. Vol. 33, pp. 350–361.

Ahmed, Khaled, *The Lucknow connection,* s.l.: *Indian Express.*

Aḥmad, K̲h̲wājah Niẓamuddīn, *The Ṭabaqāt-i-Akbarī: A History of India from the Early Musalmān Invasions to the Thirty-Sixth Year of the Reign of Akbar*. s.l.: Low Price Publications, 1992.

Aḥrār, ʿUbaydallāh, Gross, Jo-Ann, *Encyclopaedia of Islam, THREE*, edited by: Kate Fleet, Gudrun Krämer, Denis Matringe, John Nawas, Everett Rowson.

Aigle, Denise, *The Mongol Empire between Myth and Reality: Studies in Anthropological History*. Leiden: BRILL, 2014. p. 132.

Akbar, *Tuzk-e Babri,* (trans.) Abdul Rahim Khan-I-Khanan, illuminated, Delhi: Akbar, 1589. p. Folio 184b. This manuscript is available in National Museum, New Delhi. The Persian translation was done from the original Turkic manuscript of Babur. This was translated by author from the copy kept at National Museum, New Delhi.

ala Ad-din ata Malik Juvaini, 'Alā al-Dīn 'Aṭā Malek Joveynī, 'Alā' al-Dīn 'Aṭā Malik Juvaynī, *The History of the World-Conqueror, UNESCO collection of representative works: Persian series.* (ed.)John Andrew Boyle. (trans.) John Andrew Boyle. Reprint. Cambridge: Harvard University Press, 1958. pp. 91-92. Vol. 1. 0674404009, 9780674404007.

al-Baladhuri, Ahmad Ibn Yahya, *The Origins Of The Islamic State Vol -2: Translation of Kitab Futuh Al-buldan,* (trans.) Francis Clark Murgotten, New York: Columbia University, 1924, p. 232, Vol. 2.

—. 1924. *The Origins of the Islamic State, Translation of Kitab Futuh Al-buldan,* (trans.) Francis Clark Murgotten, New York: Columbia University, 1924. p. 144. Vol. 2.

Algar, Hamid, Muriel Atkin, Walter Feldman, Dru C. Gladney, Edward J. Lazzerini, Beatrice Forbes Manz, Christopher Murphy, Oliver Roy, Isenbike Togan, *Muslims in Central Asia: Expressions of Identity and Change,* (ed.) Jo-Ann Gross, Durham: Duke University Press, 1992.

Allen, Charles, *Ashoka: The Search for India's Lost Emperor.* s.l.: Hachette UK, 2012.

Alram, Michael, 'From the Sasanians to the Huns New Numismatic Evidence from the Hindu Kush', 2014, *The Numismatic Chronicle*, Vol. 174, pp. 261–291.

Al-Tabari, 2015, *The History of al-Tabari (Ta'rīkh al-rusul wa-al-mulūk): The Conquest of Iran A.D. 641-643/A.H. 21-23,* (trans.) G. Rex Smith, illustrated, New York: State University of New York Press, 2015. p. 76 (folio 2706). Vol. 14. 1438420390, 9781438420394.

Arnold, Guy, *World Strategic Highways.* s.l.: Routledge, 2014.

Asher, Catherine Blanshard, *Architecture of Mughal India, Volume 4, Part-1,* (ed.) Gordon Johnson, Cambridge: Cambridge University Press, 1992. p. 368. Vol. 4.

'Ashūr, Nīyāz Muḥammad ibn Mullā, *Tārīkh-i Shāhrukhī,* s.l.: Columbia University, 1885.

Babur, *Baburnama,* Folio 272.

—,Interpolated account of Bābur's mother's family. (ed.) Annette Susannah Beveridge, (trans.) Annette Susannah Beveridge, *The Bābur-nāma in English (Memoirs of Bābur).* London: Luzac and Co, 1922, p. 19.

—,*The Bābur-nāma in English (Memoirs of Bābur), Translated from the original Turki Text of Ẓahiru'd-dīn Muḥammad Bābur Pādshāh Ghāzī,* (ed.) Annette Susannah Beveridge, (trans.) Annette Susannah Beveridge. London: Luzac and Co, 1922. pp. 182–185.

—,*The Bābur-nāma in English (Memoirs of Bābur), Translated from the original Turki Text of Ẓahiru'd-dīn Muḥammad Bābur Pādshāh Ghāzī,* (ed.) Annette Susannah Beveridge, (trans.) Annette Susannah Beveridge. London: Luzac and Co, 1922. p. 13.

—,*The Baburnama: Memoirs of Babur, Prince and Emperor.* (ed.) Wheeler M. Thackston. (trans.) Wheeler M. Thackston. New York: The Modern Library, 2002. p. XVIII.

—,*Tukz-e Babri.* (trans.) Abdul Rahim Khan-I-Khanan, illuminated, Delhi: Akbar, 1589, p. Folio 214b. This manuscript is available in National Museum, New Delhi. The Persian translation was done from the original Turkic manuscript of Babur. This was translated by author from the copy kept at National Museum, New Delhi.

—,*Tukz-e Babri.* (trans.) Abdul Rahim Khan-I-Khanan, illuminated, Delhi: Akbar, 1589, p. Folio 161b. This manuscript is available in National Museum, New Delhi. The Persian translation was done from the original Turkic manuscript of Babur. This was translated by author from the copy kept at National Museum, New Delhi.

—,*Tukz-e Babri.* (trans.) Abdul Rahim Khan-I-Khanan, illuminated, Delhi: Akbar, 1589, p. Folio 7. This manuscript is available in National Museum, New Delhi. The Persian translation was done from the original Turkic manuscript of Babur. This was translated by author from the copy kept at National Museum, New Delhi.

—,*Tukz-e Babri.* (trans.) Abdul Rahim Khan-I-Khanan, illuminated, Delhi: Akbar, 1589, p. Folio 11. This manuscript is available in National Museum, New Delhi. The Persian translation was done from the original Turkic manuscript of Babur. This was translated by author from the copy kept at National Museum, New Delhi.

—,*Tukz-e Babri.* (trans.) Abdul Rahim Khan-I-Khanan, illuminated, Delhi: Akbar, 1589. This manuscript is available in National Museum, New Delhi. The Persian translation was done from the original Turkic manuscript of Babur. This was translated by author from the copy kept at National Museum, New Delhi.

—,*Tukz-e Babri.* (trans.) Abdul Rahim Khan-I-Khanan, illuminated, Delhi: Akbar, 1589, p. Folio 13b. This manuscript is available in National Museum, New Delhi. The Persian translation was done from the original Turkic manuscript of Babur. This was translated by author from the copy kept at National Museum, New Delhi.

—,*Tukz-e Babri.* (trans.) Abdul Rahim Khan-I-Khanan, illuminated, Delhi: Akbar, 1589, This manuscript is available in National Museum, New Delhi. The Persian translation was done from the original Turkic manuscript of Babur. This was translated by author from the copy kept at National Museum, New Delhi.

—,*Tukz-e Babri.* (trans.) Abdul Rahim Khan-I-Khanan, illuminated, Delhi: Akbar, 1589, p. Folio 24. This manuscript is available in National Museum, New Delhi. The Persian translation was done from the original Turkic manuscript of Babur. This was translated by author from the copy kept at National Museum, New Delhi.

—,*Tukz-e Babri.* (trans.) Abdul Rahim Khan-I-Khanan, illuminated, Delhi: Akbar, 1589, p. Folio 24. This manuscript is available in National Museum, New Delhi. The Persian translation was done from the original Turkic manuscript of Babur. This was translated by author from the copy kept at National Museum, New Delhi.

—,*Tukz-e Babri.* (trans.) Abdul Rahim Khan-I-Khanan, illuminated, Delhi: Akbar, 1589, p. Folio 56b. This manuscript is available in National Museum, New Delhi. The Persian translation was done from the original Turkic manuscript of Babur. This was translated by author from the copy kept at National Museum, New Delhi.

—,*Tukz-e Babri.* (trans.) Abdul Rahim Khan-I-Khanan, illuminated, Delhi: Akbar, 1589, p. Folio 53. This manuscript is available in National Museum, New Delhi. The Persian translation was done from the original Turkic manuscript of Babur. This was translated by author from the copy kept at National Museum, New Delhi.

—,*Tukz-e Babri.* (trans.) Abdul Rahim Khan-I-Khanan, illuminated, Delhi: Akbar, 1589, p. Folio 60b. This manuscript is available in National Museum, New Delhi. The Persian translation was done from the original Turkic manuscript of Babur. This was translated by author from the copy kept at National Museum, New Delhi.

—,*Tukz-e Babri.* (trans.) Abdul Rahim Khan-I-Khanan, illuminated, Delhi: Akbar, 1589, p. Folio 64. This manuscript is available in National Museum, New Delhi. The Persian translation was done from the original Turkic manuscript of Babur. This was translated by author from the copy kept at National Museum, New Delhi.

—,*Tukz-e Babri.* (trans.) Abdul Rahim Khan-I-Khanan, illuminated, Delhi: Akbar, 1589, p. 64b. This manuscript is available in National Museum, New Delhi. The Persian translation was done from the original Turkic manuscript of Babur. This was translated by author from the copy kept at National Museum, New Delhi.

—,*Tukz-e Babri.* (trans.) Abdul Rahim Khan-I-Khanan, illuminated, Delhi: Akbar, 1589. This manuscript is available in National Museum, New Delhi. The Persian translation was done from the original Turkic manuscript of Babur. This was translated by author from the copy kept at National Museum, New Delhi.

Ibid.

—,*Tukz-e Babri.* (trans.) Abdul Rahim Khan-I-Khanan, illuminated, Delhi: Akbar, 1589, p. Folio 73. This manuscript is available in National Museum, New Delhi. The Persian translation was done from the original Turkic manuscript of Babur. This was translated by author from the copy kept at National Museum, New Delhi.

—,*Tukz-e Babri.* (trans.) Abdul Rahim Khan-I-Khanan, illuminated, Delhi: Akbar, 1589, p. Folio 75b. This manuscript is available in National

Museum, New Delhi. The Persian translation was done from the original Turkic manuscript of Babur. This was translated by author from the copy kept at National Museum, New Delhi.

—,*Tukz-e Babri.* (trans.) Abdul Rahim Khan-I-Khanan, illuminated, Delhi: Akbar, 1589, p. Folio 76. This manuscript is available in National Museum, New Delhi. The Persian translation was done from the original Turkic manuscript of Babur. This was translated by author from the copy kept at National Museum, New Delhi.

—,*Tukz-e Babri.* (trans.) Abdul Rahim Khan-I-Khanan, illuminated, Delhi: Akbar, 1589, pp. Folio 77b-78. This manuscript is available in National Museum, New Delhi. The Persian translation was done from the original Turkic manuscript of Babur. This was translated by author from the copy kept at National Museum, New Delhi.

—,*Tukz-e Babri.* (trans.) Abdul Rahim Khan-I-Khanan, illuminated, Delhi: Akbar, 1589, p. Folio 79. This manuscript is available in National Museum, New Delhi. The Persian translation was done from the original Turkic manuscript of Babur. This was translated by author from the copy kept at National Museum, New Delhi.

—,*Tukz-e Babri.* (trans.) Abdul Rahim Khan-I-Khanan, illuminated, Delhi: Akbar, 1589, p. Folio 82. This manuscript is available in National Museum, New Delhi. The Persian translation was done from the original Turkic manuscript of Babur. This was translated by author from the copy kept at National Museum, New Delhi.

—,*Tukz-e Babri.* (trans.) Abdul Rahim Khan-I-Khanan, illuminated, Delhi: Akbar, 1589, p. Folio 85. This manuscript is available in National Museum, New Delhi. The Persian translation was done from the original Turkic manuscript of Babur. This was translated by author from the copy kept at National Museum, New Delhi.

—,*Tukz-e Babri.* (trans.) Abdul Rahim Khan-I-Khanan, illuminated, Delhi: Akbar, 1589, p. Folio 86. This manuscript is available in National Museum, New Delhi. The Persian translation was done from the original Turkic manuscript of Babur. This was translated by author from the copy kept at National Museum, New Delhi.

—,*Tukz-e Babri.* (trans.) Abdul Rahim Khan-I-Khanan, illuminated, Delhi: Akbar, 1589, p. Folio 87. This manuscript is available in National Museum, New Delhi. The Persian translation was done from the original Turkic manuscript of Babur. This was translated by author from the copy kept at National Museum, New Delhi.

—,*Tukz-e Babri.* (trans.) Abdul Rahim Khan-I-Khanan, illuminated, Delhi: Akbar, 1589, p. Folio 89. This manuscript is available in National Museum, New Delhi. The Persian translation was done from the original Turkic manuscript of Babur. This was translated by author from the copy kept at National Museum, New Delhi.

—,*Tukz-e Babri.* (trans.) Abdul Rahim Khan-I-Khanan, illuminated, Delhi: Akbar, 1589, p. Folio 94. This manuscript is available in National Museum, New Delhi. The Persian translation was done from the original Turkic manuscript of Babur. This was translated by author from the copy kept at National Museum, New Delhi.

—,*Tukz-e Babri.* (trans.) Abdul Rahim Khan-I-Khanan, illuminated, Delhi: Akbar, 1589, pp. Folio 95b-96. This manuscript is available in National Museum, New Delhi. The Persian translation was done from the original Turkic manuscript of Babur. This was translated by author from the copy kept at National Museum, New Delhi.

—,*Tukz-e Babri.* (trans.) Abdul Rahim Khan-I-Khanan, illuminated, Delhi: Akbar, 1589, p. Folio 97b. This manuscript is available in National Museum, New Delhi. The Persian translation was done from the original Turkic manuscript of Babur. This was translated by author from the copy kept at National Museum, New Delhi.

—,*Tukz-e Babri.* (trans.) Abdul Rahim Khan-I-Khanan, illuminated, Delhi: Akbar, 1589, p. Folio 99. This manuscript is available in National Museum, New Delhi. The Persian translation was done from the original Turkic manuscript of Babur. This was translated by author from the copy kept at National Museum, New Delhi.

—,*Tukz-e Babri.* (trans.) Abdul Rahim Khan-I-Khanan, illuminated, Delhi: Akbar, 1589, p. Folio 100. This manuscript is available in National Museum, New Delhi. The Persian translation was done from the original Turkic manuscript of Babur. This was translated by author from the copy kept at National Museum, New Delhi.

—,*Tukz-e Babri.* (trans.) Abdul Rahim Khan-I-Khanan, illuminated, Delhi: Akbar, 1589, p. Folio 100. This manuscript is available in National Museum, New Delhi. The Persian translation was done from the original Turkic manuscript of Babur. This was translated by author from the copy kept at National Museum, New Delhi.

—,*Tukz-e Babri.* (trans.) Abdul Rahim Khan-I-Khanan, illuminated, Delhi: Akbar, 1589, p. Folio 101b. This manuscript is available in National Museum, New Delhi. The Persian translation was done from the original Turkic manuscript of Babur. This was translated by author from the copy kept at National Museum, New Delhi.

—,*Tukz-e Babri.* (trans.) Abdul Rahim Khan-I-Khanan, illuminated, Delhi: Akbar, 1589, p. Folio 108b. This manuscript is available in National Museum, New Delhi. The Persian translation was done from the original Turkic manuscript of Babur. This was translated by author from the copy kept at National Museum, New Delhi.

—,*Tukz-e Babri.* (trans.) Abdul Rahim Khan-I-Khanan, illuminated, Delhi: Akbar, 1589, p. Folio 109. This manuscript is available in National Museum, New Delhi. The Persian translation was done from the original

Turkic manuscript of Babur. This was translated by author from the copy kept at National Museum, New Delhi.

—,*Tukz-e Babri.* (trans.) Abdul Rahim Khan-I-Khanan, illuminated, Delhi: Akbar, 1589, p. Folio 110b. This manuscript is available in National Museum, New Delhi. The Persian translation was done from the original Turkic manuscript of Babur. This was translated by author from the copy kept at National Museum, New Delhi.

—,*Tukz-e Babri.* (trans.) Abdul Rahim Khan-I-Khanan, illuminated, Delhi: Akbar, 1589, p. Folio 112b. This manuscript is available in National Museum, New Delhi. The Persian translation was done from the original Turkic manuscript of Babur. This was translated by author from the copy kept at National Museum, New Delhi.

—,*Tukz-e Babri.* (trans.) Abdul Rahim Khan-I-Khanan, illuminated, Delhi: Akbar, 1589, p. Folio 11. This manuscript is available in National Museum, New Delhi. The Persian translation was done from the original Turkic manuscript of Babur. This was translated by author from the copy kept at National Museum, New Delhi.

—,*Tukz-e Babri.* (trans.) Abdul Rahim Khan-I-Khanan, illuminated, Delhi: Akbar, 1589, pp. Folio 114b-115. This manuscript is available in National Museum, New Delhi. The Persian translation was done from the original Turkic manuscript of Babur. This was translated by author from the copy kept at National Museum, New Delhi.

—,*Tukz-e Babri.* (trans.) Abdul Rahim Khan-I-Khanan, illuminated, Delhi: Akbar, 1589, p. Folio 116. This manuscript is available in National Museum, New Delhi. The Persian translation was done from the original Turkic manuscript of Babur. This was translated by author from the copy kept at National Museum, New Delhi.

—,*Tukz-e Babri.* (trans.) Abdul Rahim Khan-I-Khanan, illuminated, Delhi: Akbar, 1589, p. Folio 117b. This manuscript is available in National Museum, New Delhi. The Persian translation was done from the original Turkic manuscript of Babur. This was translated by author from the copy kept at National Museum, New Delhi.

—,*Tukz-e Babri.* (trans.) Abdul Rahim Khan-I-Khanan, illuminated, Delhi: Akbar, 1589, p. Folio 121. This manuscript is available in National Museum, New Delhi. The Persian translation was done from the original Turkic manuscript of Babur. This was translated by author from the copy kept at National Museum, New Delhi.

—,*Tukz-e Babri.* (trans.) Abdul Rahim Khan-I-Khanan, illuminated, Delhi: Akbar, 1589, p. Folio 125. This manuscript is available in National Museum, New Delhi. The Persian translation was done from the original Turkic manuscript of Babur. This was translated by author from the copy kept at National Museum, New Delhi.

—,*Tukz-e Babri.* (trans.) Abdul Rahim Khan-I-Khanan, illuminated, Delhi: Akbar, 1529, p. Folio 144b. This manuscript is available in National Museum, New Delhi. The Persian translation was done from the original Turkic manuscript of Babur. This was translated by author from the copy kept at National Museum, New Delhi.

—,*Tukz-e Babri.* (trans.) Abdul Rahim Khan-I-Khanan, illuminated, Delhi: Akbar, 1529, p. Folio 146. This manuscript is available in National Museum, New Delhi. The Persian translation was done from the original Turkic manuscript of Babur. This was translated by author from the copy kept at National Museum, New Delhi.

—,*Tuzk-e Babri,* (trans.) Abdul Rahim Khan-I-Khanan, Delhi: Akbar, 1529, p. Folio 150. This manuscript is available in National Museum, New Delhi. The Persian translation was done from the original Turkic manuscript of Babur. This was translated by author from the copy kept at National Museum, New Delhi.

—,*Tuzk-e Babri,* (trans.) Abdul Rahim Khan-I-Khanan, Delhi: Akbar, 1589, p. Folio 151b. This manuscript is available in National Museum, New Delhi. The Persian translation was done from the original Turkic manuscript of Babur. This was translated by author from the copy kept at National Museum, New Delhi.

—,*Tuzk-e Babri,* (trans.) Abdul Rahim Khan-I-Khanan. Delhi: Akbar, 1589, p. Folio 12. This manuscript is available in National Museum, New Delhi. The Persian translation was done from the original Turkic manuscript of Babur. This was translated by author from the copy kept at National Museum, New Delhi.

—,*Tukz-e Babri,* (trans.) Abdul Rahim Khan-I-Khanan, illuminated, Delhi: Akbar, 1589, p. Folio 152b. This manuscript is available in National Museum, New Delhi. The Persian translation was done from the original Turkic manuscript of Babur. This was translated by author from the copy kept at National Museum, New Delhi.

—,*Tukz-e Babri,* (trans.) Abdul Rahim Khan-I-Khanan, illuminated, Delhi: Akbar, 1589, p. Folio 153b. This manuscript is available in National Museum, New Delhi. The Persian translation was done from the original Turkic manuscript of Babur. This was translated by author from the copy kept at National Museum, New Delhi.

—,*Tukz-e Babri,* (trans.) Abdul Rahim Khan-I-Khanan, illuminated, Delhi: Akbar, 1589, p. Folio 154b. This manuscript is available in National Museum, New Delhi. The Persian translation was done from the original Turkic manuscript of Babur. This was translated by author from the copy kept at National Museum, New Delhi.

—,*Tukz-e Babri,* (trans.) Abdul Rahim Khan-I-Khanan, illuminated, Delhi: Akbar, 1589, p. Folio 155. This manuscript is available in National Museum, New Delhi. The Persian translation was done from the original

Turkic manuscript of Babur. This was translated by author from the copy kept at National Museum, New Delhi.

—,*Tukz-e Babri,* (trans.) Abdul Rahim Khan-I-Khanan, illuminated, Delhi: Akbar, 1589, p. Folio 157b. This manuscript is available in National Museum, New Delhi. The Persian translation was done from the original Turkic manuscript of Babur. This was translated by author from the copy kept at National Museum, New Delhi.

—,*Tukz-e Babri,* (trans.) Abdul Rahim Khan-I-Khanan, illuminated, Delhi: Akbar, 1589, p. Folio 158b. This manuscript is available in National Museum, New Delhi. The Persian translation was done from the original Turkic manuscript of Babur. This was translated by author from the copy kept at National Museum, New Delhi.

—,*Tukz-e Babri,* (trans.) Abdul Rahim Khan-I-Khanan, illuminated, Delhi: Akbar, 1589, p. Folio 159. This manuscript is available in National Museum, New Delhi. The Persian translation was done from the original Turkic manuscript of Babur. This was translated by author from the copy kept at National Museum, New Delhi.

—,*Tukz-e Babri,* (trans.) Abdul Rahim Khan-I-Khanan, illuminated, Delhi: Akbar, 1589, p. Folio 162b. This manuscript is available in National Museum, New Delhi. The Persian translation was done from the original Turkic manuscript of Babur. This was translated by author from the copy kept at National Museum, New Delhi.

—,*Tukz-e Babri,* (trans.) Abdul Rahim Khan-I-Khanan, illuminated, Delhi: Akbar, 1589, p. Folio 163. This manuscript is available in National Museum, New Delhi. The Persian translation was done from the original Turkic manuscript of Babur. This was translated by author from the copy kept at National Museum, New Delhi.

—,*Tukz-e Babri,* (trans.) Abdul Rahim Khan-I-Khanan, illuminated, Delhi: Akbar, 1589, p. Folio 183b. This manuscript is available in National Museum, New Delhi. The Persian translation was done from the original Turkic manuscript of Babur. This was translated by author from the copy kept at National Museum, New Delhi.

—,*Tukz-e Babri,* (trans.) Abdul Rahim Khan-I-Khanan, illuminated, Delhi: Akbar, 1589, p. Folio 185b. This manuscript is available in National Museum, New Delhi. The Persian translation was done from the original Turkic manuscript of Babur. This was translated by author from the copy kept at National Museum, New Delhi.

—,*Tukz-e Babri,* (trans.) Abdul Rahim Khan-I-Khanan, illuminated, Delhi: Akbar, 1589, p. Folio 186b. This manuscript is available in National Museum, New Delhi. The Persian translation was done from the original Turkic manuscript of Babur. This was translated by author from the copy kept at National Museum, New Delhi.

—,*Tukz-e Babri,* (trans.) Abdul Rahim Khan-I-Khanan, illuminated, Delhi: Akbar, 1589, p. Folio 187. This manuscript is available in National Museum, New Delhi. The Persian translation was done from the original Turkic manuscript of Babur. This was translated by author from the copy kept at National Museum, New Delhi.

—,*Tukz-e Babri,* (trans.) Abdul Rahim Khan-I-Khanan, illuminated, Delhi: Akbar, 1589, p. Folio 187b. This manuscript is available in National Museum, New Delhi. The Persian translation was done from the original Turkic manuscript of Babur. This was translated by author from the copy kept at National Museum, New Delhi.

—,*Tukz-e Babri,* (trans.) Abdul Rahim Khan-I-Khanan, illuminated, Delhi: Akbar, 1589, p. Folio 188. This manuscript is available in National Museum, New Delhi. The Persian translation was done from the original Turkic manuscript of Babur. This was translated by author from the copy kept at National Museum, New Delhi.

—,*Tukz-e Babri,* (trans.) Abdul Rahim Khan-I-Khanan, illuminated, Delhi: Akbar, 1589, p. Folio 189. This manuscript is available in National Museum, New Delhi. The Persian translation was done from the original Turkic manuscript of Babur. This was translated by author from the copy kept at National Museum, New Delhi.

—,*Tukz-e Babri,* (trans.) Abdul Rahim Khan-I-Khanan, illuminated, Delhi: Akbar, 1589, p. Folio 190. This manuscript is available in National Museum, New Delhi. The Persian translation was done from the original Turkic manuscript of Babur. This was translated by author from the copy kept at National Museum, New Delhi.

—,*Tukz-e Babri,* (trans.) Abdul Rahim Khan-I-Khanan, illuminated, Delhi: Akbar, 1589, p. Folio 192b. This manuscript is available in National Museum, New Delhi. The Persian translation was done from the original Turkic manuscript of Babur. This was translated by author from the copy kept at National Museum, New Delhi.

—,*Tukz-e Babri,* (trans.) Abdul Rahim Khan-I-Khanan, illuminated, Delhi: Akbar, 1589, p. Folio 193b. This manuscript is available in National Museum, New Delhi. The Persian translation was done from the original Turkic manuscript of Babur. This was translated by author from the copy kept at National Museum, New Delhi.

—,*Tukz-e Babri,* (trans.) Abdul Rahim Khan-I-Khanan, illuminated, Delhi: Akbar, 1589, p. Folio 194. This manuscript is available in National Museum, New Delhi. The Persian translation was done from the original Turkic manuscript of Babur. This was translated by author from the copy kept at National Museum, New Delhi.

—,*Tukz-e Babri,* (trans.) Abdul Rahim Khan-I-Khanan, illuminated, Delhi: Akbar, 1589, p. Folio 194b. This manuscript is available in National Museum, New Delhi. The Persian translation was done from the original

Turkic manuscript of Babur. This was translated by author from the copy kept at National Museum, New Delhi.

—,*Tukz-e Babri,* (trans.) Abdul Rahim Khan-I-Khanan, illuminated, Delhi: Akbar, 1589, p. Folio 196. This manuscript is available in National Museum, New Delhi. The Persian translation was done from the original Turkic manuscript of Babur. This was translated by author from the copy kept at National Museum, New Delhi.

—,*Tukz-e Babri,* (trans.) Abdul Rahim Khan-I-Khanan, illuminated, Delhi: Akbar, 1589, p. Folio 197b. This manuscript is available in National Museum, New Delhi. The Persian translation was done from the original Turkic manuscript of Babur. This was translated by author from the copy kept at National Museum, New Delhi.

—,*Tukz-e Babri,* (trans.) Abdul Rahim Khan-I-Khanan, illuminated, Delhi: Akbar, 1589, p. Folio 197b. This manuscript is available in National Museum, New Delhi. The Persian translation was done from the original Turkic manuscript of Babur. This was translated by author from the copy kept at National Museum, New Delhi.

—,*Tukz-e Babri,* (trans.) Abdul Rahim Khan-I-Khanan, illuminated, Delhi: Akbar, 1589, p. Folio 199. This manuscript is available in National Museum, New Delhi. The Persian translation was done from the original Turkic manuscript of Babur. This was translated by author from the copy kept at National Museum, New Delhi.

—,*Tukz-e Babri,* (trans.) Abdul Rahim Khan-I-Khanan, illuminated, Delhi: Akbar, 1589, p. Folio 199b. This manuscript is available in National Museum, New Delhi. The Persian translation was done from the original Turkic manuscript of Babur. This was translated by author from the copy kept at National Museum, New Delhi.

—,*Tukz-e Babri,* (trans.) Abdul Rahim Khan-I-Khanan, illuminated, Delhi: Akbar, 1589, p. Folio 200. This manuscript is available in National Museum, New Delhi. The Persian translation was done from the original Turkic manuscript of Babur. This was translated by author from the copy kept at National Museum, New Delhi.

—,*Tukz-e Babri,* (trans.) Abdul Rahim Khan-I-Khanan, illuminated, Delhi: Akbar, 1589, p. Folio 201b. This manuscript is available in National Museum, New Delhi. The Persian translation was done from the original Turkic manuscript of Babur. This was translated by author from the copy kept at National Museum, New Delhi.

—,*Tukz-e Babri,* (trans.) Abdul Rahim Khan-I-Khanan, illuminated, Delhi: Akbar, 1589, p. Folio 202b. This manuscript is available in National Museum, New Delhi. The Persian translation was done from the original Turkic manuscript of Babur. This was translated by author from the copy kept at National Museum, New Delhi.

—,*Tukz-e Babr,* (trans.) Abdul Rahim Khan-I-Khanan, illuminated, Delhi: Akbar, 1589, p. Folio 205b. This manuscript is available in National Museum, New Delhi. The Persian translation was done from the original Turkic manuscript of Babur. This was translated by author from the copy kept at National Museum, New Delhi.

—,*Tukz-e Babri,* (trans.) Abdul Rahim Khan-I-Khanan, illuminated, Delhi: Akbar, 1589, p. Folio 206. This manuscript is available in National Museum, New Delhi. The Persian translation was done from the original Turkic manuscript of Babur. This was translated by author from the copy kept at National Museum, New Delhi.

—,*Tukz-e Babri,* (trans.) Abdul Rahim Khan-I-Khanan, illuminated, Delhi: Akbar, 1589, p. Folio 215. This manuscript is available in National Museum, New Delhi. The Persian translation was done from the original Turkic manuscript of Babur. This was translated by author from the copy kept at National Museum, New Delhi.

—,*Tukz-e Babri,* (trans.) Abdul Rahim Khan-I-Khanan, illuminated, Delhi: Akbar, 1589, Folio 208. This manuscript is available in National Museum, New Delhi. The Persian translation was done from the original Turkic manuscript of Babur. This was translated by author from the copy kept at National Museum, New Delhi.

—,*Tukz-e Babri,* (trans.) Abdul Rahim Khan-I-Khanan, illuminated, Delhi: Akbar, 1589, Folio 211. This manuscript is available in National Museum, New Delhi. The Persian translation was done from the original Turkic manuscript of Babur. This was translated by author from the copy kept at National Museum, New Delhi.

—,*Tukz-e Babri,* (trans.) Abdul Rahim Khan-I-Khanan, illuminated, Delhi: Akbar, 1589, p. Folio 213. This manuscript is available in National Museum, New Delhi. The Persian translation was done from the original Turkic manuscript of Babur. This was translated by author from the copy kept at National Museum, New Delhi.

—,*Tukz-e Babri,* (trans.) Abdul Rahim Khan-I-Khanan, illuminated, Delhi: Akbar, 1589, p. Folio 215. This manuscript is available in National Museum, New Delhi. The Persian translation was done from the original Turkic manuscript of Babur. This was translated by author from the copy kept at National Museum, New Delhi.

—,*Tukz-e Babri,* (trans.) Abdul Rahim Khan-I-Khanan, illuminated, Delhi: Akbar, 1589, p. Folio 318b. This manuscript is available in National Museum, New Delhi. The Persian translation was done from the original Turkic manuscript of Babur. This was translated by author from the copy kept at National Museum, New Delhi.

—,*Tukz-e Babri,* (trans.) Abdul Rahim Khan-I-Khanan, illuminated, Delhi: Akbar, 1589, p. Folio 160. This manuscript is available in National Museum, New Delhi. The Persian translation was done from the original

Turkic manuscript of Babur. This was translated by author from the copy kept at National Museum, New Delhi.
—,*Tukz-e Babri,* (trans.) Abdul Rahim Khan-I-Khanan, illuminated, Delhi: Akbar, 1589, p. Folio 105b. This manuscript is available in National Museum, New Delhi. The Persian translation was done from the original Turkic manuscript of Babur. This was translated by author from the copy kept at National Museum, New Delhi.
—,*Tukz-e Babri,* (trans.) Abdul Rahim Khan-I-Khanan, illuminated, Delhi: Akbar, 1589, p. Folio 122. This manuscript is available in National Museum, New Delhi. The Persian translation was done from the original Turkic manuscript of Babur. This was translated by author from the copy kept at National Museum, New Delhi.
—,*Tukz-e Babri,* (trans.) Abdul Rahim Khan-I-Khanan, illuminated, Delhi: Akbar, 1589, pp. Folio 12B-124. This manuscript is available in National Museum, New Delhi. The Persian translation was done from the original Turkic manuscript of Babur. This was translated by author from the copy kept at National Museum, New Delhi.
Badā'ūnī, 'Abd al-Qādir ibn Mulūk Shāh, *Muntakhabu-t-tawārīkh,* (ed.) George Speirs Alexander Ranking, (trans.) William Henry Lowe George Speirs Alexander Ranking, Calcutta: Asiatic Society of Bengal, 1898. Vol. 1.
Badā'ūnī, Abd al-Qādir ibn Mulūk Shāh, *Muntakhabu't-tawārīkh Vol-3*. p. 273.
Bailey, H.W., *Indo-Scythian Studies: Being Khotanese Texts Volume VII*. s.l.: Cambridge University Press, 1985.
Balabanlilar, Lisa, *The Emperor Jahangir: Power and Kingship in Mughal India,* Noida: Bloomsbury Publishing, 2020.
Balaji, Murali, *Saving History from Historians,* New Delhi: Open, 2015.
Balakrishna, Sandeep, 'Indian Historiography at 75', Dharma Dispatch, https://www.dharmadispatch.in/commentary/indian-historiography-at-75.
Balabanlilar, Lisa, 'The Begims of the Mystic Feast: Turco-Mongol Tradition in the Mughal Harem', 2010, *The Journal of Asian Studies*, Vol. 69, p. 128.
Baldick, Julian, *Animal and Shaman: Ancient Religions of Central Asia,* London: IB Tauris, 2012. p. 55.
Ball, Warwick, Allchin, Norman Hammond Raymond Allchin, *The Archaeology of Afghanistan: From Earliest Times to the Timurid Period,* s.l.: Edinburgh University Press, 2019, p. 379.
Barthold, Vasilii Vladimirovitch, 'Mir Ali-Shir: A History of the Turkman People', *Four Studies on the History of Central Asia, Volume 3,* 1962, p. 21.
Bates, Thomas R., *Gramsci and the Theory of Hegemony*, 1975, *Journal of the History of Ideas, Vol. 36*, pp. 351–366, 2013.
Bauer-Manndorff, Elisabeth, *Armenia, Past and Present,* New York: The Armenian Prelacy, 1981. p. 49.
Becker, Carl L. *Declaration of Independence: A Study in the History of Political Ideas*. New York: Knopf Doubleday Publishing Group, 1970, p. 27.

Beckwith, Christopher I., *The Tibetan Empire in Central Asia: A History of the Struggle for Great Power Among Tibetans, Turks, Arabs, and Chinese During the Early Middle Ages.* s.l.: Princeton University Press, 1993, pp. 88–89.

Begum, Gulbadan, *Part-II, Gulabadan Begum's Book, Humayun-Nama.* (trans.) Annette Susannah Beveridge, *Humayun-Nama: The History of Humayun,* London: Royal Asiatic Society, 1902, p. 85.

Bekhrad, Joobin, BBC, 'The Book of Kings, the Book that Defies Iranians', 2018, BBC, https://www.bbc.com/culture/article/20180810-the-book-of-kings-the-book-that-defines-iranians.

Bellew, Henry Walter, *History Of Káshgharia.* Foreign Department Press, 1875, p. 62.

Bengal, Asiatic Society of, *Journal of the Asiatic Society of Bengal, Part 2,* Calcutta: Bishop's College Press, 1843. Vol. 12.

Bernier, François, *Travels in the Mogul Empire* AD *1656–68,* (ed.) Vincent A Smith, (trans.) Archibald Constable, London, Edinburgh, Glasgow, New York, Toronto, Melbourne, Bombay: Oxford University Press, 1916.

—*Travels in the Mogul Empire* AD *1656–68,* (ed.) Vincent A Smith, (trans.) Archibald Constable, London, Edinburgh, Glasgow, New York, Toronto, Melbourne, Bombay: Oxford University Press, 1916, pp. 136-139.

— Bernier, François, *Travels in the Mogul Empire* AD *1656–68,* (ed.) Vincent A Smith, (trans.) Archibald Constable, London, Edinburgh, Glasgow, New York, Toronto, Melbourne, Bombay: Oxford University Press, 1891, 1916. p. 223.

— Bernier, François, *Travels in the Mogul Empire* AD *1656–68,* (ed.) Vincent A Smith, (trans.) Archibald Constable, London, Edinburgh, Glasgow, New York, Toronto, Melbourne, Bombay: Oxford University Press, 1891, 1916. p. 205.

Belozerskaya, Marina, *Medusa's Gaze: The Extraordinary Journey of the Tazza Farnese.* s.l.: Oxford University Press, 2012, p. 88.

Beveridge, Annette Susannah, *The Bābur-nāma in English, (Memoirs of Bābur) Translated from the original Turki Text of Ẓahiru'd-dīn Muḥammad Bābur Pādshāh Ghāzī,* London: LUZAC & CO, 1922.

— *The Bābur-nāma in English, (Memoirs of Bābur) Translated from the original Turki Text of Ẓahiru'd-dīn Muḥammad Bābur Pādshāh Ghāzī,* London: LUZAC & CO, 1922. p. 189.

Bipan Chandra, Mridula Mukherjee, Aditya Mukherjee, K.N. Panikkar, Sucheta Mahajan, *India's Struggle for Independence, 1857–1947,* (ed.) Bipin Chandra, New Delhi: Penguin Books, 1989. p. 237.

Blankholm, Joseph. *The Secular Paradox: On the Religiosity of the Not Religious,* New York: NYU Press, 2022. p. 8.

Borjian, Habib, Esfara, Encyclopædia Iranica Foundation, Inc., 1998, https://www.iranicaonline.org/articles/esfara.

Bosworth, C.E., Banākat. *Encyclopædia Iranica,* Encyclopædia Iranica Foundation, 1988, https://iranicaonline.org/articles/banaka-benaka-in-jovayni-fanakat-the-main-town-of-the-medieval-transoxanian-province-of-sas-or-cac-to-be-dist. 2330-4804.

Bosworth, Clifford Edmund. 'Pandjhir', *Encyclopaedia of Islam,* Leiden: BRILL, 1995, Vol. 8, p. 258.

—,*The Medieval History of Iran, Afghanistan, and Central Asia,* Farnham: Variorum Reprints, 1977, p. 344.

—, *The Tahirids and Saffarids.* (ed.) William Bayne Fisher, Richard Nelson Frye, Peter Avery, Ilya Gershevitch, John Andrew Boyle, Ehsan Yarshater, Peter Jackson R. N. Frye. *The Cambridge History of Iran.* Cambridge: Cambridge University Press, 1975, Vol. IV, p. 110.

—, 'Zamindawar', *The Encyclopaedia of Islam.* s.l.: Leiden: Brill, 2002, p. 439.

Branko Soucek, Saint Soucek, 'Dynastic tables', *A History of Inner Asia.* s.l.: Cambridge University Press, 2000, p. 324.

Britannica, 'Dervish', Editors of Encyclopaedia, *Encyclopedia Britannica,* 2009.

Cacopardo, Alberto M., Augusto S. Cacopardo, *Gates of Peristan: History, Religion and Society in the Hindu Kush,* s.l.: University of Michigan, 2001.

Carrington Goodrich, Luther, Chaoying Fang, 'Association for Asian Studies: Ming Biographical History Project Committee', *Dictionary of Ming Biography, 1368–1644.* s.l.: Columbia University Press, 1976.

Chailand, Gerard, Blin, Arnaud, *The History of Terrorism: From Antiquity to Al Qaeda,* California: University of California Press, 2007, p. 87.

Chavannes, Édouard, *Documents sur les Tou-Kiue (Turcs) occidentaux,* St Petersbourg: Commissionnaires de l'Academie Imperiale des Sciences, 1903. p. 10.

Chisholm, Hugh, Ayub Khan, *Encyclopædia Britannica Eleventh Edition.* Eleventh. Cambridge: Cambridge University Press, 1911, p. NA.

Christian Answers, https://christiananswers.net/dictionary/murrain.html.

Ch'i-Ch'ing Hsiao, The Military Establishment of the Yuan Dynasty, *Harvard East Asian Monographs,* s.l.: Harvard University Asia Center, 1978, pp. 9–10.

Chua, Amy. *Day of Empire: How Hyperpowers Rise to Global Dominance - and why They Fall,* New York: Double Day.

CIA, *The KGB in Asia: Society of Subversion,* New York: CIA, 1999.

Clauson, Gerard, *An Etymological Dictionary of Pre-13th Century Turkish,* Oxford: Oxford University Press, 1972. p. 581.

Clements, Frank, Ludwig W. Adamec, *Conflict in Afghanistan: A Historical Encyclopedia,* Santa Barbara: ABC-CLIO, p. 35. 2003.

Cohen, Richard J., *An Early Attestation of the Toponym Ḍhillī,* s.l.: American Oriental Society, October–December 1989, Journal of the American Oriental Society, Vol. 109, pp. 513-9.

Congress, Library of, 'Getting Started with Primary Sources', https://www.loc.gov/programs/teachers/getting-started-with-primary-sources/#:~:text=What%20are%20primary%20sources%3F,distance%20of%20time%20or%20place.

Corvisier, André, *A Dictionary of Military History and the Art of War*. s.l.: Blackwell Publishing, 1994, p. 529.

Daily Times, dailytimes.com.pk/82850/china-to-finance-90-of-sukkur-multan-motorway/.

Dale, Stephen Fedric, *Babur: Timurid Prince and Mughal Emperor, 1483–1530*. Cambridge: Cambridge University Press, 2018. 9781107107267.

Dani, Ahmad Hasan Dani, Litvinsky, B.A., 'History of Civilizations of Central Asia: The Crossroads of Civilizations, A.D. 250 to 750', *Volume 3 of History of Civilizations of Central Asia: The Age of Achievement: A.D.750 to the End of the Fifteenth Century: Historical, Social and Economic Setting*. Paris: UNESCO, 1996, Vol. 3, pp. 379–380.

Daryaee, Touraj, *Sasanian Iran in the Context of Late Antiquity: The Bahari Lecture Series at the University of Oxford*, Leiden: BRILL, 2021. p. 16. 9004460667, 9789004460669.

Dasgupta, Surajit, *A History of 'Tolerance'*. Bengaluru, Coimbatore: Swarajya, 2015.

Dever, William G., *What Did the Biblical Writers Know and When Did They Know It?: What Archeology Can Tell Us About the Reality of Ancient Israel*. s.l.: Wm. B. Eerdmans Publishing, 2001, p. 98.

Die Münzprägungen des Islam. zeitlich und örtlich geordnet. I. Band (alles Erschienene): Der Westen und Osten bis zum Indus mit synoptischen Tabellen. Herausgegeben von Peter Jaeckel.

Dictionary.com, https://www.dictionary.com/browse/murrain.

Docherty, Paddy, *The Khyber Pass: A History of Empire and Invasion*, s.l.: Union Square Press, 2008.

Dowling, Timothy C., *Russia at War: From the Mongol Conquest to Afghanistan, Chechnya, and Beyond*, s.l.: ABC-CLIO, 2014.

Dughlat, Mirza Muhammad Haidar, *Tarikh-i-rashidi; a history of the Moghuls of central Asia*, 1551.

Dughlt, Mirza Muhammad Haidar, *A History of the Moghuls of Central Asia: The Tarikh-i-Rashidi*, (trans.) N. Elias and Sir Edward Denison Ross, New York: Cosimo Inc., 2008. p. 696.

Duncan, George S., *The Birthplace of Man*, 1929, *The Scientific Monthly*, Vol. 29, pp. 359–362.

Dupree, Louis, *Afghanistan: Volume 818 of Princeton Legacy Library*, Princeton: Princeton University Press, 2014. p. 418.

Durant, Will, *The Story of Civilization, Our Oreintal Heritage*, New York: Simon and Schuster, 1954. p. 459. Vol. 1.

Effendi, M.Y., *Punjab Cavalry Evolution, Role, Organisation, and Tactical Doctrine 11 Cavalry (Frontier Force) 1849–1974,* Karachi: OUP Pakistan, 2007. p. 66.

Eller, Jack David, 'What Is Atheism', (ed.)Phil Zuckerman, *Atheism and Secularity: Volume 1: Issues, Concepts, and Definitions (Praeger Perspectives),* Santa Barbara, California: Praeger, 2010, pp. 1–18.

Elliot, Henry Miers, *The History of India, As Told by Its Own Historians: The Muhammadan Period,* (ed.) John Dawson, London: Trübner & Co, 1873. Vol. 5.

Elliot, Sir H.M., 1867–1877, *The Hindu Kings of Kábul,* London: Packard Humanities Institute, 1867–1877, p. 3.

Encylopedia.com https://www.encyclopedia.com/places/asia/pakistan-and-bangladesh-political-geography/peshawar.

Encylopedia.com https://www.encyclopedia.com/places/asia/pakistan-and-bangladesh-political-geography/peshawar.

Encyclopædia Iranica, 'Araxex River', *https://iranicaonline.org/,* https://iranicaonline.org/articles/araxes-river.

Encyclopaedia Iranica, '*Pashtun Tribe*', https://iranicaonline.org/articles/bangas-pashtun-tribe.

Erskine, William, '*A History of India Under the Two First Sovereigns of the House of Taimur, Báber and Humáyun*', Harlaw: Longman, Brown, Green, and Longman, 1854.

—, *A History of India Under the Two First Sovereigns of the House of Taimur, Báber and Humáyun,* Harlow: Longman, Brown, Green, and Longmans, 1854. Vol. 2.

Feldherr, Andrew, *The Oxford History of Historical Writing, Volume 2: 400-1400,* Oxford: Oxford University Press, 2012. p. 275. Vol. 2.

Gandhi, Surjit Singh, *History of Sikh Gurus Retold: 1606-1708 C.E, Vol-*2. s.l.: Atlantic Publishers & Dist, 2007.

Ghāzī, Ẓahiru'd-dīn Muḥammad Bābur Pādshāh, *The Bābur-nāma in English (Memoirs of Bābur) Translated from the original Turki Text of Ẓahiru'd-dīn Muḥammad Bābur Pādshāh Ghāzī,* (ed.) Annette Susannah Beveridge, (trans.) Annette Susannah Beveridge, London: Luzac & Co, 1922, pp. 199–227.

—, *The Bābur-nāma in English (Memoirs of Bābur) Translated from the original Turki Text of Ẓahiru'd-dīn Muḥammad Bābur Pādshāh Ghāzī,* (ed.) Annette Susannah Beveridge, (trans.) Annette Susannah Beveridge, London: Luzac & Co, 1922, Footnote 3.

—, *The Bābur-nāma in English (Memoirs of Bābur) Translated from the original Turki Text of Ẓahiru'd-dīn Muḥammad Bābur Pādshāh Ghāzī,* (ed.) Annette Susannah Beveridge, (trans.) Annette Susannah Beveridge, London: Luzac & Co, 1922, pp. 527-528.

—, *The Bābur-nāma in English (Memoirs of Bābur) Translated from the original Turki Text of Ẓahiru'd-dīn Muḥammad Bābur Pādshāh Ghāzī,* (ed.) Annette

Susannah Beveridge, (trans.) Annette Susannah Beveridge, London: Luzac & Co, 1922, pp. 522-525.

Gibb, H.A.R, *The Arab Conquests in Central Asia,* London: The Royal Asiatic Society, 1923. pp. 49, 62.

Golden, Peter B., *An Introduction to the History of the Turkic Peoples: Ethnogenesis and State-formation in Medieval and Early Modern Eurasia and the Middle East (Turcologica),* Wiesbaden: Harrassowitz, 1992, p. 271.

Gordon, Matthew, Chase F. Robinson, Everett K. Rowson, Michael Fishbein, *The Works Of Ibn Wāḍiḥ Al Yaʿqūbī,* Leiden: BRILL, 2018. p. 1138. Vol. 3.

Grewal, Royena, *Babur: Conqueror of Hindustan,* New Delhi: Rupa Publications, 2015.

Gross Jo-Ann, *The Economic Status of a Timurid Sufi Shaykh: A Matter of Conflict or Perception?,* 1998, *Iranian Studies*, Vol. 21, p. 85.

Grousset, René, (trans.) Naomi Walford, *The Empire of the Steppes: A History of Central Asia,* First English Edition, New Brunswick: Rutgers University Press, 1939, p. 497.

Gulbadan, *The History of Humāyūn (Humāyūn-nāma),* (ed.) Annette Susannah Beveridge, (trans.) Annette Susannah Beveridge, London: Royal Asiatic Society, 1902.

Habib, Irfan, 'Agrarian Relations and Land Revenue'; Irfan Habib Tapan Raychaudhuri, *The Cambridge Economic History of India,* Cambridge: Cambridge University Press, 1982, p. 242.

—, *An Atlas of the Mughal Empire: Political and Economic Maps with Detailed Notes, Bibliography and Index,* New York: Oxford University Press, 1982. p. VII.

Habibi, Abdul Hai, 'The Temple of Zoor or Zoon in Zamindawar', Alamahabibi, http://alamahabibi.net/English_Articles/Zoor_or_zoon_temple.htm.

Ibid.

Haidar, Dughlát Muhammad, (ed.) N. Elias., (trans.) Sir Edward Denison Ross, *The Tarikh-i-rashidi: A History of the Moghuls of Central Asia; an English Version.* London: S. Low, Marston and Company, 1895, pp. 253–4.

Haider, Najaf, *Structure and Movement of Wages in the Mughal Empire,* 2008.

Haig, Lt Colonel Sir Wolseley, (ed.) Sir Richard Burn, *The Cambridge History of India,* Cambridge: Cambridge University Press, 1937. Vol. IV.

Hans-Peter Vietze, Klaus Koppe, Gabriele Nagy and Tumenbajaryn Daschzeden, *Wörterbuch Mongolisch-Deutsch.* 1998.

Ḥawqal, Muḥammad Ibn, *Kitāb ṣūrat al-arḍ,* (ed.) Johannes Hendrik Kramers, (trans.) Johannes Hendrik Kramers, Leiden: Maṭbaʻ Brīl, 1967.

Heath, Ian, *Armies of the Middle Ages - Volume 2 The Ottoman Empire, Eastern Europe and the Near East, 1300–1500,* Wargames Research Group, 1984, pp. 58-59.

Hebraeus, Bar, *The Chronography of Abu'l-Faraj*, Oxford: Oxford University Press, 1932, p. 444.

—, *The Chronography of Gregory Abû'l Faraj, the Son of Aaron, the Hebrew Physician, Commonly Known as Bar Hebraeus: Being the First Part of His Political History of the World,* (ed.) Sir Ernest Alfred Wallis Budge, (trans.) Sir Ernest Alfred Wallis Budge, Oxford: Oxford University Press, 1932. p. 507. Vol. 1.

Heinlein, Robert A., *Time Enough For Love.* New York: ACE, Penguin Random House LLC., 1987. p. 250.

Hewsen, Robert H., Richard G. Hovannisian, *The Armenian People From Ancient to Modern Times. Volume I: The Dynastic Periods: From Antiquity to the Fourteenth Century,* New York: St. Martin's Press, 1997. p. 7.

Houtsma, Martijn Theodoor Houtsma, *E.J. Brill's First Encyclopaedia of Islam, 1913-1936,* BRILL, 1993, Vol. 5, p. 788.

Holdich, Thomas, *The Gates of India,* London: Macmillan & Co Limited, 1910.

Hulsewé, Anthony François Paulus, *China in Central Asia: The Early Stage: 125* BC–AD *23; an Annotated Transl. of Chapters 61 and 96 of the History of the Former Han Dynasty,* s.l.: Brill Archive, 1979, p. 162.

Hultzsch, Eugen, *Inscriptions of Asoka,* Oxford: Claredon Press, 1925. p. 174.

'Ināyat Khān, Muḥammad Ṭāhir Āšnā ʿInāyat Ḫān, *The Shah Jahan Nama of 'Inayat Khan: An Abridged History of the Mughal Emperor Shah Jahan, Compiled by His Royal Librarian: The Nineteenth-century Manuscript Translation,* (ed.) Wayne Edison Begley Z. A. Desai, (trans.) Abraham Richard Fuller, London: Oxford University Press, 1990. pp. 251–52.

Insight Guides, *Insight Guides Silk Road,* s.l.: Apa Publications (UK) Limited, 2017.

Jackson P., Boyle, J.A., Fisher, W.B Fisher, *The Cambridge History of Iran, Vol 5.* p. 55.

Jäger, Ulf, (ed.)Paula Roberts, Mark Swofford Victor H. Mair., *A Unique Alxon-Hunnic Horse-and-Rider Statuette, (Late Fifth Century C E) from Ancient Bactria / Modern Afghanistan in the Pritzker Family Collection, Chicago.* 290, Philadelphia: Department of East Asian Languages and Civilizations, University of Pennsylvania, 2019, Sino-Platonic Papers, Vol. 1, pp. 2–72.

Jaffar, S. M., *The Mughal Empire from Bābar to Aurangzeb,* Michigan: University of Michigan, 2008.

Jahangir, *Tarikh-i Salim Shahi,* s.l.: Sushil Gupta, 1952.

Jahangir, Nuru-d-din, *Tuzuk-i-Jahangiri: or, Memoirs of Jahangir,* (ed.) Henry Beveridge, (trans.) Alexander Rogers, London: Royal Asiatic Society, 1914. pp. 60, 91–92, 161. Vol. 2.

Jain, Sandhya, *The India They Saw: Foreign Accounts,* New Delhi: Prabhat Prakshan, 2011. p. 333. Vol. 1.

'Jehangir', Mirza Nur-ud-Din Muhammad Salim, *The Tūzuk-i-Jahāngīrī, Or Memoirs of Jahāngīr,* (ed.)Henry Beveridge, (trans.) Alexander Rogers, London: London Royal Asiatic Society, 1909. p. 16.

Jo-Ann Gross, Asom, *Review: The Letters of Khwaja 'Ubayd Allah Ahrar and his Associates,* Algar, Hamid, *Urunbaev: The Letters of Khwaja 'Ubayd Allah Ahrar and his Associates*, Oxford: Oxford Centre for Islamic Studies, May 2004, Journal of Islamic Studies, Vol. 15, pp. 224–226.

Jordan, William Chester, *The Great Famine: Northern Europe in the Early Fourteenth Century*. s.l.: Princeton University Press, 1996.

Kāšifī, Ḥusain Wā'iẓ, *Anwār-i Suhailī*. s.l.: Asiatic Lithographic Company, 1834.

Kemper, Nicolas, 'The Postmodern Revival in Schools Has Architecture Deans Worried: Are Their Fears Well-Placed?', 2018, https://commonedge.org/the-postmodern-revival-in-schools-has-architecture-deans-worried-are-their-fears-well-placed/.

Kennedy, Hugh, *The Great Arab Conquests: How the Spread of Islam Changed the World We Live In,* London: Hachette UK, 2010. p. 128.

Kim, Hyun Jin, *The Huns,* London: Routledge, 2015. pp. 58–59.

Korab-Karpowicz, W. Julian, *A History of Political Philosophy: From Thucydides to Locke*. New York: Global Scholarly Publications, 2010. p. 291.

Kumar, Anant, 'Monument of Love or Symbol of Maternal Death: The Story Behind the Taj Mahal', June 2014, Case Reports in Women's Health, Vols. 1–2, pp. 4–7.

Kuwayama, Shoshin, *Historical Notes on Kāpiī and Kābul*, s.l.: Jinbun kagaku Kenkyusho, Kyoto University, March 2000, ZINBUN, Vol. 34, pp. 25–77.

Lahori, Abdul Hamid, *Badshahnama*; (ed.) Henry Miers Elliot, (trans.) Henry Miers Elliot, *Shah Jahan,* Lahore: Hafiz Press, 1875, pp. 39, 3–78.

Láhorí, Abdu-L Hamíd, *Bádsháh-Náma;* Henry Miers Elliot, (ed.) John Dowson, *The History of India, as Told by Its Own Historians,* London: Sh. Mubarak Ali, 1867–77, Vol. VII, p. 12.

Lane-Pool, Stanley, *Babar,* Oxford: Oxford, 1899.

Laszlo, Gyula, *The Magyars: Their Life and Civilisation,* s.l.: Corvina, 1996, pp. 41–42.

Leach, Sir Edmund, 'Aryan Invasions Over Four Millennia', Emiko Ohnuki-Tierney, (ed.) Emiko Ohnuki-Tierney, *Culture Through Time: Anthropological Approaches,* Stanford: Stanford University Press, 1990, pp. 227–245.

Lee, Jonathan L. Nicholas Sims Williams, 'Bactrian Inscription from Yakawlang sheds new light on history of Buddhism in Afghanistan', 2003, *Journal of the Institute of Silk Road Studies*, pp. 159–184.

Leyden, William Erskine John, *Memoirs of Zehir-Ed-Din Muhammed Baber: Emperor of Hindustan,* s.l.: Longman, Rees, Orme, Brown, and Green, 1886.

Lonely Planet, https://web.archive.org/web/20110607080116/http://www.lonelyplanet.com/pakistan/north-west-frontier-province/the-khyber-pass. Luther, Martin, 'On Secular Authority: How Far Does the Obedience Owed to it Extend?', s.l.: http://www.yorku.ca/comninel/courses/3020pdf/Luther.pdf, 1523.

MacDonald, D.B., *Darwīsh*, P. Bearman, et al, *Encyclopaedia of Islam,* s.l.: Brill, 2012.

Maddison, Angus, *Contours of the World Economy,* AD *1–2030,* New York: Oxford University Press, 2007.

—,*The World Economy, A Millenial Perspective.* s.l.: OECD, p. 109.

Majumdar, R.C., *History of the Freedom Movement in India,* Calcutta: Firma. K.L. Mukhopadhyay, 1962. p. 513. Vol. 3.

Maldahiyar, Aabhas, 'History-phobia of Audrey Truschke: Denial of Islamic invaders and the Hara-Kiri of credibility', Mumbai: Firstpost, 2022.

—, 'Tipu Sultan: When an Islamist Tyrant Is Turned into a Freedom Fighter, Missile Man and Dharma Saviour' Firstpost, 2022.

—, 'Whitewashing Genocides: Why KS Lal's Claims of 80 million Hindus Killed by Islamic Barbarism Hold Water', Firstpost, 2022.

—. 2022. *Whitewashing genocides: Why KS Lal's claims of 80 million Hindus killed by Islamic barbarism hold water.* Mumbai: Firstpost, 2022.

Malhotra, Rajiv, *Weaving India's MAHAKATHA (Grand Narrative) for the 21st Century,* Shimla: Indian Institute of Advanced Studies, Infinity Foundation, Radhakrishnan Memorial Lecture.

Mansour Shaki, Hamid Algar, *DARVĪŠ,* Encyclopædia Iranica, 2011.

Manz, Beatrice Forbes, *The Rise and Rule of Tamerlane,* Cambridge: Cambridge University Press, 1999. pp. 13–14.

Manz, Beatrice Forbes, *Tamerlane's Career and its Uses,* s.l.: University of Hawai'i Press, 2002, *Journal of World History,* Vol. 13, p. 25.

Marozzi, Justin. 2004. Tamerlane: Sword of Islam, Conqueror of the World. *Tamerlane: Sword of Islam, Conqueror of the World.* s.l.: HarperCollins, 2004, pp. 269–74.

Marx, Karl and Engels, Frederick, *The Buying and Selling of Labour-Power*; (ed.) Frederick Engels, (trans.) Samuel Moore and Edward Aveling, *Capital, A Critique of Political Economy, Book One: The Process of Production of Capital,* First English Edition, based on fourth German Edition, Moscow: Progress Publishers, Moscow, 1887, Vol. 1, 6, pp. 118–124.

Marx, Karl, 'The British Rule in India', *New York Daily Tribune,* 10 June 1853.

—, 'The Future Results of British Rule in India', *New-York Daily Tribune,* 23 June 1853.

Mawlānā Šayẖ., Masatomo Kawamoto, *Maqāmāt-i Ḫwāǧa Aḥrār: Taḏkira-i Ḫwāǧa Nāṣir ad-Dīn 'Ubaydallāh Aḥrār,* Tokyo: Mu'assasa-i Muṭāla'āt-i Zabānhā wa Farhanghā-i Āsiyā wa Āfrīqā, 2004. p. 21.

McNicoll, Anthony, Warwick Ball, 'Excavations at Kandahar 1974 and 1975: The First Two Seasons at Shahr-i Kohna (Old Kandahar) Conducted by the British Institute of Afghan Studies', *Issue 1 of Society for South Asian Studies Monograph,* s.l.: British Archaeological Reports Limited, 1996.

Minahan, James B., *Ethnic Groups of North, East, and Central Asia: An Encyclopedia,* Santa Barbara: ABC-CLIO, 2014.

Minorsky, V., *Hudud al-'Alam, The Regions of the World, A Persian Geography, 372 A.H.- 982 A.D.*, London: Oxford University Press, 1937. p. 289.

'Minute by the Hon'ble T.B. Macaulay', dated the 2nd February 1835, http://www.columbia.edu/itc/mealac/pritchett/00generallinks/macaulay/txt_minute_education_1835.html.

Mīr, Ghiyās̱ al-Dīn ibn Humām al-Dīn Khvānd, *Habib Al-Siyar, Volume 3, Qazwin, Iran, Safavid period, 1579-80.*

Moffett, Samuel Hugh, *A History of Christianity in Asia, Vol. I: Beginnings to 1500, Volume 1,* s.l.: Orbis Books, 2014, p. 276.

Moon, Farzana, *The Moghul Saint of Insanity,* s.l.: Cambridge Scholars Publishing, 2015.

Moosvi, Shireen, *The Economy of the Mughal Empire, C.1595: A Statistical Study,* Oxford: Oxford University Press, 2015. p. 301.

Morgan, David, *The Mongols,* Second, Illustrated, New York: Wiley, 2007. p. 272.

Multidimensional Poverty Peer Network, 'National Measures: New Afghan Multidimensional Poverty Report', 31 March 2019. https://mppn.org/new-afghan-multidimensional-poverty-report/.Mukerjee, Radhakamal, *The Economic History of India, 1600–1800,* s.l.: Kitab Mahal, 1967.

Mukherjee, Aditya, et al, *Communalisation of Education,* New Delhi: Delhi Historians' Group, 2001.

Müller, Friedrich Max, *Ural Altic Family*: *The Science of Language*. New York: Charles Scribner's Sons, 1891, p. 414.

Mundy, Peter, *The travels of Peter Mundy in Europe and Asia, 1608–1667.* (ed.) Lt Col. Sir Richard Carnac Temple, Cambridge: Cambridge University Press, 1907. pp. 40–48. Vol. II.

Myers, Bernard Samuel Myers, *Encyclopedia of World Art,* New York: McGraw-Hill, 1959, p. 445.

Nalwa, Vanit, *Hari Singh Nalwa, Champion of the Khalsaji (1791–1837),* New Delhi: Manohar, 2009.

NCERT, *Our Pasts-1, Textbook in History for Class VI,* New Delhi: NCERT, 9 December 2021.

Nishapuri, Mir Abd al-Avval, *Malfuzat Ahrar, Markaz-i Našr-i Dānišgāhī,* Tehran: Presses universitaires d'Iran, 2002, p. 208.

Noelle, Christine, *State and Tribe in Nineteenth-Century Afghanistan, The Reign of Amir Dost Muhammad Khan (1826–1863),* Abingdon-on-Thames, Taylor & Francis, 2012.

Noguès, Olivier, 'Wonders of the World', https://www.wonders-of-the-world.net/Taj-Mahal/Cost-of-the-Taj-Mahal.php.

Northern Earth, https://archive.is/20060925024416/http://www.northernearth.co.uk/86cure.htm.

[Online] https://web.archive.org/web/20160905090203/http://pro.geo.univie.ac.at/projects/khm/showcases/showcase15?language=en.

[Online] https://web.archive.org/web/20160316041852/http://pro.geo.univie.ac.at/projects/khm/showcases/showcase16?language=en.

[Online] https://web.archive.org/web/20160905094603/http://pro.geo.univie.ac.at/projects/khm/showcases/showcase14?language=en.

[Online] https://web.archive.org/web/20160828064427/http://pro.geo.univie.ac.at/projects/khm/showcases/showcase13?language=en.

[Online] https://web.archive.org/web/20160905094603/http://pro.geo.univie.ac.at/projects/khm/showcases/showcase14?language=en.

[Online] https://web.archive.org/web/20160905094603/http://pro.geo.univie.ac.at/projects/khm/showcases/showcase14?language=en.

Padshah, Nuru-d-din Jahangir, *The Tuzuk-i-Jahangiri: or, Memoirs of Jahangir,* (ed.) Henry Beveridge, (trans.) Alexander Roger, London: Royal Asiatic Society, 1909. p. 72. Vol. 1.

Paul, Jürgen, *Bādghīs*; Marc Gaborieau, et al. *The Encyclopaedia of Islam Three,* Leiden: BRILL, 2010, p. 200.

Paul, Jürgen, 'Forming a Faction: The Ḥimāyat System of Khwaja Ahrar', *International Journal of Middle East Studies*, Vol. 23, pp. 533–48, 2009.

Pétis de La Croix, François, *The History of Genghizcan the Great, First Emperor of the Antient Moguls and Tartars.*

Petrie, Cameron A., *Resistance at the Edge of Empires: The Archaeology and History of the Bannu basin from 1000 BC to AD 1200,* Oxford: Oxbow Books, 2020, p. 69.

Polo, Marco, *The Travels of Marco Polo,* (trans.) Henry Yule, Edinburgh: Oliver and Boyd, 1845.

Prasad, Ram Chandra, *Early English Travellers in India: A Study in the Travel Literature of the Elizabethan and Jacobean Periods with Particular Reference to India,* s.l.: Motilal Banarsidass, 1980.

PTI, 'DU Book Calls Bhagat Singh a "revolutionary terrorist", Courts Controversy', *The Hindu*, 27 April 2016, https://www.thehindu.com/news/national/du-book-calls-bhagat-singh-a-revolutionary-terrorist-courts-controversy/article8528456.ece.

Rahi, Arwin, Express Tribune, Express Tribune, 2021, https://tribune.com.pk/article/97429/the-legacy-of-sardar-mohammad-ayub-khan-the-victor-of-maiwand.

Rahim, Abdul (trans.), *Khan-i-Khanan*, s.l.: Akbar, p. Folio 83b. This manuscript is available in National Museum, New Delhi. The Persian translation was done from the original Turkic manuscript of Babur. This was translated by author from the copy kept at National Museum, New Delhi.

Rahim, Abdul (trans.), *Khan-i-Khanan*, s.l.: Akbar, p. Folio 198. This manuscript is available in National Museum, New Delhi. The Persian translation was done from the original Turkic manuscript of Babur. This was translated by author from the copy kept at National Museum, New Delhi.

Rathi, Akshat, *The lies Brits Tell Themselves About How They Left Behind a Better India,* New York: Quartz, 2017.

Raychaudhuri, Tapan, *The State and the Economy, The Mughal Empire,* (ed.) Irfan Habib Tapan Raychaudhuri, *The Cambridge Economic History of India,* Cambridge, New York, New Rochelle, Melbourne, Sydney: Cambridge University Press, 1987, Vol. 1, VII.1, p. 173.

Raychaudhuri, Tapan, Irfan Habib, *Cambridge Economic History of India,* s.l.: Cambridge University Press, 1987.

Rehman, Abdur, *The Last Two Dynasties of the Sahis: An Analysis of Their History, Archaeology, Coinage, and Palaeography,* Islamabad: Centre for the Study of the Civilizations of Central Asia, Quaid-i-Azam University, 2006. pp. 58–67.

Richards, J.F., 'Fiscal states in Mughal and British India'; (ed.) Francisco Comín Comín, Patrick K. O'Brien Bartolomé Yun-Casalilla, *The Rise of Fiscal States, A Global History, 1500–1914,* Cambridge, New York, Melbourne, Madrid, Cape Town, Singapore, Sao Paulo, Delhi, Mexico City: Cambridge University Press, 2012, 17, p. 410.

Roberts, Earl Frederick Sleigh Roberts. 1897. *Forty-one Years in India, Volume* 2. London: Richard Bentley and Son, 1897. pp. 362-380. Vol. 2. NA.

Roe, Sir Thomas, *The Embassy of Sir Thomas Roe to India, 1615–19: As Narrated in His Journal and Correspondence,* (ed.) William Foster, London: Hakluyt Society, 1899. Vol. I.

Roemer, Hans R., *Encyclopædia Iranica Foundation,* 2004, https://iranicaonline.org/articles/hosayn-bayqara.

Rossabi, Morris., *From Yuan to Modern China and Mongolia,* Columbia: BRILL, 2014. p. 48.

Ṣafī, 'Alī ibn Ḥusayn Kāshifī, *Beads of Dew from the Source of Life,* (trans.) Muhtar Holland, Oakland Park: Al-Baz Publishing, 2001. p. 245.

Sale, George, The Alcoran of MOHAMMED, *The Koran,* London, 1734, pp. 37–38.

Sampath, Vikram, *Savarkar: A Contested Legacy,* Gurgaon: Penguin Viking, 2021.

Sanyal, Sanjeev, *Revolutionaries: The Other Story of How India Won Its Freedom,* New Delhi: HarperCollins India, 2023.

—, *The Ocean of Churn,* s.l.: Penguin, 2017.

Saunders, John Joseph, *The History of the Mongol Conquests,* illustrated, reprint, Philadelphia: University of Pennsylvania Press, 2001. p. 173.

Scott, Adolphe Clarence, *The Theatre in Asia,* Michigan: University of Michigan, 1973. p. 51.

Scott, Gordon R., http://www.taa.org.uk/TAA/murrain.htm.

Section 20, 'The Kingdom of Suoche 莎車 (Yarkand)', *The Western Regions According to the Hou Hanshu: The Xiyu Juan 'Chapter on the Western Regions' from Hou Hanshu 88,* 2003.

Simha, Rakesh, 'Islamic Loot: How the Mughals Drained Wealth Out of India, IndiaFacts', 22 May 2022. https://www.indiafacts.org.in/islamic-loot-how-the-mughals-drained-wealth-out-of-india/#:~:text=%E2%80%9CThis%20is%20how%20the%20money,Muslim%20holy%20men%20throughout%20the.

Sirhindi, Ahmad, *Maktubat-i-Imam Rabbani,* (trans.) Maulana Muhammad Sa'id Ahmad Naqshbandi, Deoband: Darul Uloom Deoband, 1988. p. 388. Vol. 1.

Slight, John, *The British Empire and the Hajj.* s.l.: Harvard University Press, 2015.

Spuler, Bertold, *Iran in the Early Islamic Period: Politics, Culture, Administration and Public Life between the Arab and the Seljuk Conquests, 633-1055,* (ed.) Gwendolin Goldbloom, and Berenike Walburg Robert G. Hoyland, (trans.) Gwendolin Goldbloom, and Berenike Walburg Robert G. Hoyland, Leiden: BRILL, 2015. pp. 37, 254, 302.

Strabo, *Geography of Strabo, Book 11, Chapter 14.*

Subtelny, Maria, *Timurids in Transition: Turko-Persian Politics and Acculturation in Medieval Iran, Volume 7.* s.l.: Brill, 2007, pp. 43–44.

Tarn, William Woodthorpe, *The Greeks in Bactria and India.* s.l.: Cambridge University Press, 2010.

Thapar, Romila, *Asoka And The Decline Of The Mauryas,* Oxford: Oxford University Press, 1961. pp. 34, 259.

THE RUTBILS OF ZABULISTAN AND THE "EMPEROR OF ROME". [Online] https://web.archive.org/web/20160905090203/http://pro.geo.univie.ac.at/projects/khm/showcases/showcase15?language=en.

Thomas, David, Chesworth, John A., *Christian-Muslim Relations. A Bibliographical History, Volume 6 Western Europe (1500–1600),* 2015.

Thomas, Edward. 1871. *The Revenue Resources of the Mughal Empire in India, from A.D. 1593 to A.D. 1707: A Supplement to The Chronicles of the Pathàn Kings of Dehli.* Oxford: Trübner, 1871. p. 28.

Truschke, Audrey, *Hindutva's Dangerous Rewriting of History*; Jules Naudet and Nicolas Jaoul (dir.) Aminah Mohammad-Arif, *South Asia Multidisciplinary Academic, The Hindutva Turn: Authoritarianism and Resistance in India,* 2020, Vol. 24, 25, pp. 136–150.

Urubshurow, Victoria Kennick, *Introducing world religions,* Providence, Utah: Journal of Buddhist Ethics Online Books, 2008, p. 6.

Vasilii Vladimirovich Bartol'd, W. Barthold, *Turkestan Down to the Mongol Invasion.* Middlesex: E.J.W. Gibb Memorial Trust, pp. 169, 407, 116–18.

—, *Turkestan Down to the Mongol Invasion,* Cambridge: E.J.W. Gibb Memorial Trust, 1977. p. 160.

Vereshchagin, Vasili Vasilievich, *The Apotheosis of War, 1871,* Tretyakov Gallery, Moscow, s.l.: 1871.

Vogelsang, Willem, Afghanistan: *Afghanistan: mensen, politiek, economie, cultuur, milieu,* s.l.: Wiley-Blackwell, 2002, p. 188.

Vondrovec, Klaus, *Coinage of the Nezak:* Coins, Art and Chronology II—The First Millennium C.E. in the Indo-Iranian Borderlands, pp. 169–190.

Watts, Sheldon, *British Development Policies and Malaria in India 1897-c, 1929,* 1999, 1999, Past & Present, pp. 141–181.

West, Barbara A., *Encyclopedia of the Peoples of Asia and Oceania,* s.l.: Infobase Publishing, 2010.

Whiting, Marvin, *Imperial Chinese Military History,* s.l.: iUniverse, p. 277.

Wink, André., *Al-Hind: Early medieval India and the expansion of Islam, 7th-11th centuries,* s.l.:BRILL, 2002, pp. 112–114.

—, *Al-Hind: The Making of the Indo-Islamic World,* s.l.: BRILL, 1990, p. 118.

Wink, Andre, *Al-Hind the Making of the Indo-Islamic World: The Slave Kings and the Islamic Conquest: 11Th-13th Centurie,* Leiden, New York, Koln: BRILL, 1991, p. 321. Vol. 2.

Wink, André, *Al-hind: The Making of the Indo-islamic World,* Leiden: BRILL, 1991, pp. 118, 119. Vol. 1.

Winters, R., Hume, J.P., Leenstra, M., *A famine in Surat in 1631 and Dodos on Mauritius: a long lost manuscript rediscovered.*, s.l.: The Society for the History of Natural History, 2017, Archives of Natural History, Vol. 44, pp. 134–50.

Winters, R., Hume, J.P., Leenstra, M., *A famine in Surat in 1631 and Dodos on Mauritius: a long lost manuscript rediscovered.*, s.l.: The Society for the History of Natural History, 2017, Archives of Natural History, Vol. 1, pp. 134–50.

Witzel, Michael, Indocentrism; (ed.) Edwin Bryant and Laurie Patton, *Indo-Aryan Controversy Evidence And Inference In Indian History,* London, New York: Routledge, 2005, p. 348.

Wright, George Frederick Wright, *Asiatic Russia, Volume 1.* s.l.: BiblioBazaar, 2009, pp. 47–48.

Wylly, Harold Carmichael, *The Borderland*, s.l.: Macmillan, 2008, p. 15.

Karasoy, Y., *Shiban Han divani,* Ankara: s.n., 1998.

Yazdī, Sharaf al-Dīn ʻAlī, *The History of Timur-Bec, Known by the Name of Tamerlain the Great, Emperor of the Moguls and Tartars: Being an Historical Journal of His Conquests in Asia and Europe,* London: John Darby, 1723, Vol. 2.

—,*The History of Timur-Bec, Known by the Name of Tamerlain the Great, Emperor of the Moguls and Tartars: Being an Historical Journal of His Conquests in Asia and Europe,* London: John Darby, 1723, Vol. 1.

— *The History of Timur-Bec, Known by the Name of Tamerlain the Great, Emperor of the Moguls and Tartars: Being an Historical Journal of His Conquests in Asia and Europe,* London: John Darby, 1723, p. 267. Vol. 1.

'Zamindawar', *Encyclopædia Britannica, Vol 28.* s.l.: Cambridge University Press, 1911, p. 953.

Acknowledgements

In embarking on this captivating odyssey through the life and legacy of Babur, known as the 'chessboard king', I find myself humbly indebted to a constellation of individuals whose unwavering support, encouragement and influence have intricately woven the tapestry of this ambitious endeavour.

To the revered Bhagwan Ram, I attribute the true orchestration of this work, to feeling like a mere vessel through which this historical saga flows.

My heartfelt gratitude commences with Tejal Pardhy, my cherished life partner, whose steadfast encouragement and firm presence during life's ebbs and flows have been a steady source of inspiration. Her unyielding support has ignited the flames of my passion for writing, urging me to persistently pursue this literary voyage.

To my esteemed parents, Atish Maldahiyar and Ruby Sinha, I owe an immeasurable debt of gratitude for their enduring blessings and unwavering support, serving as the guiding beacon illuminating my aspirations. Their unflagging belief in my endeavours has fortified my journey at every step.

My sincere appreciation extends to my in-laws, Kalidas Pardhy and Pradnya Pardhy, whose unwavering faith and blessings have consistently fortified my resolve to embark on this ambitious undertaking.

Reflecting on my formative years, the enchanting storytelling sessions with my grandmother, Shanta Devi, planted the seeds of narrative artistry within me. Although brief, my time with my late grandfather, Nath Sahay, continues to inspire me profoundly.

The untiring interest and blessings of my grandmother-in-law, Meenakshi Pardhy, and the unwavering advocacy of my sister Apoorwa and her husband Aman, serve as constant reminders of the expectations vested in me, compelling me to perpetually strive for excellence.

During my schooling at D.A.V. Public School, Hazaribagh, mentors and educators like Kiran Mishra, Sampa Srivastava, Pushpa Tiwari and the late Manoj Verma played pivotal roles in nurturing my passion for writing. Heartfelt gratitude to the ever-encouraging principal, Ashok Srivastava, for fostering an environment conducive to nurturing young talents.

Special acknowledgement goes to my mentors, Sanjadhi Chatterjee and Nishant Manapure, from my architecture school days. Their guidance, especially during challenging times, emphasized the intrinsic link between storytelling and architecture, profoundly shaping my creative perspective.

I deeply appreciate the camaraderie I share with my colleagues at Colliers, especially Kaushik and Mayukh, whose friendship and steadfast support transcend mere workplace interactions. Our enduring discussions on historical concepts and designs, stemming from our architecture school days, have significantly influenced my ideas. Heartfelt thanks to Harshit Sastry for his fresh insights on the subject matter related to bygone eras, which have been invaluable.

Dr Vikram Sampath's mentorship and unwavering support have been invaluable in reinforcing my endeavours in historical writing. The insightful guidance and feedback from acclaimed authors Amish Tripathi and Ashwin Sanghi, alongside Dr Sampath, during the formative stages of *Babur: The Chessboard King*, have been instrumental in refining the manuscript.

The scholarly blessings of Bibek Debroy carry immense significance, adding a profound layer of credibility to this work and inspiring me to deliver my best.

I am deeply grateful to Mohandas Pai and Ratan Sarda for their unwavering encouragement, which fuelled the evolution of my thoughts on Twitter into the substantial project it has become. Their belief in the book's potential acted as the driving force behind its creation. Additionally, sincere thanks to Paresh Rawal and Swaroop Sampat, whose unwavering support since our first connection continues to motivate me. Heartfelt thanks to Dr Anand Ranganathan for pushing me to improve my research every passing day. Prof. Heeraman Tiwari's support in facilitating my access to the National Archives is deeply appreciated. Gratitude to everyone at the National Archives and National Museum for their assistance in accessing the manuscripts.

My heartfelt gratitude to Penguin Random House, particularly Premanka Goswami, for warmly embracing this project. Premanka's steadfast trust and astute guidance played a pivotal role in refining the initial draft into a polished manuscript. I extend my heartfelt gratitude to Yash Daiv for his meticulous editing, which significantly enhanced the book's readability. Yash's invaluable feedback and insightful suggestions substantially elevated the manuscript to a remarkable extent. Additionally, Neeraj Nath's captivating cover design added invaluable depth and allure to its overall appeal.

The RCS fellowship provided by Asha Jadeja ji and the Motwani Foundation was instrumental in facilitating extensive research, including my foray into Persian studies, enriching the depth and authenticity of this historical narrative.

Finally, to every individual who engaged with my columns, articles and Twitter threads, I extend profound gratitude. Your continuous support and encouragement have served as a constant motivator, urging me to evolve and deliver my best work.

This book stands as a testament to the collective efforts and unwavering support of these remarkable individuals. I am profoundly grateful for their invaluable contributions in shaping this narrative, and their influence will forever resonate within these pages.